THE FLYING]
The 1972 Builders' Strike &

Dave Ayre, Reuben Ba
Jimmy Graham and ᴅave ᴴarker

The Des Warren Trust Fund

To the families, friends, supporters and
members of the North Wales 32

Patrick Kevin Butcher
John Carpenter
Malcolm Clee
Glyn Davies
John Garry Davies
William Charles Leslie Hooson
William Hough
Derrick Hughes
Alfred James
John McKinsie Jones
Colin Kelly
John Elfyn Llywarch
Peter Richard Moroney
Dennis Morris
George Arthur Murray
Kenneth Desmond Francis O'Shea
William Michael Pierce
Terence Renshaw
Graham Roberts
Gwyn Edward Roberts
John Kenneth Seaburg
Peter Alfred Sear
Bryn Thomas
Kenneth Thomas
Eric Tomlinson
Samuel Warburton
Dennis Michael Warren
Peter Westwater
Edward Leonard Williams
Gwynfor Williams
Thomas Bernard Williams
Thomas Brian Williams

No justice, no peace

the Flying Pickets

THE 1972 BUILDERS' STRIKE
& THE SHREWSBURY TRIALS

Dave Ayre, Reuben Barker, Jim French
Jimmy Graham & Dave Harker

The Flying Pickets: The 1972 Builders' Strike and the Shrewsbury Trials
Dave Ayre, Reuben Barker, Jim French, Jimmy Graham and Dave Harker

First published in April 2008 by The Des Warren Trust Fund
Copyright © The Des Warren Trust Fund

ISBN 9781905192359

Maps © Philip's © Crown copyright. All rights reserved. Licence number 100011710
Back cover photograph: Bristol flying pickets, 1972. From *Socialist Worker* archive
Photographs on pages 193-200: David Bagnall, © *Shropshire Star*
Cover illustration by John Foker of Bearpark Artists Cooperative
Typeset by Bookmarks Publications
Printed by Cambridge Printing

Contents

Introduction

1972 was the highest point of class struggle in Britain since the 1926 General Strike. Early that year the miners used mobile groups of 'flying pickets' to win solidarity from workers in other industries and completely trounced the National Coal Board. In the summer, the dockers smashed the Industrial Relations Act by forcing the Tory government to free the jailed pickets known as the 'Pentonville 5'. By then tens of thousands of building workers, led by the unofficial Building Workers' Charter, had begun the industry's first national strike for almost fifty years. They used flying pickets to visit working sites and left the contractors reeling; yet union leaders settled for a pay rise that would soon be eaten away by inflation and failed to end the divisive piecework system called the 'lump', which continues to undermine site union organisation to this day.

The big contractors were determined to exact revenge and to undermine effective mass picketing, so they persuaded their Tory minister friends to send in the police. Eventually, 32 pickets from North Wales—one of the weakest areas of unionisation—were put on trial. The main Shrewsbury Crown Court trials of 24 pickets— the 'Shrewsbury 24'—began in October 1973. We show that the Crown case was based on coerced, falsified and even unsigned 'statements' from unwilling pickets, on fatally flawed evidence from serially *mistaken* 'lumpers' and policemen, on a common law 'conspiracy' charge that required no direct proof of guilt, on legal chicanery of the lowest kind, and on a seriously misled jury. The Court of Appeal later quashed the 'affray' convictions.

Trade union activists and socialists across the country supported the pickets financially, and there were protest strikes after the first three jailings in December, but there was no effective national leadership, so we failed to mount a campaign of immediate mass action like that which freed the Pentonville 5. The 'Shrewsbury 6'—as they became after the second trial in February 1974—stayed in jail. That spring, many voters expected that the incoming Labour government would free the 6, but the Cabinet and almost all the other 'Old Labour' MPs and union leaders let the men and their families suffer. This book analyses why the Communist-led defence campaign failed to prevent any of the 6 serving out their sentences and why Des Warren stayed in jail until August 1976.

Together with Labour's attacks on the unions in 1979, the Tory anti-union laws of the early 1980s and the legitimising of violent police attacks on mass pickets in 1982, the Shrewsbury jailings prepared the ideological groundwork for the miners' defeat of 1985. All that has undermined the trade union movement ever since and the criminalising of effective mass picketing, plus the Tories' anti-union laws, are safe in the hands of New Labour today.

We hope that today's socialists and union activists will learn from our successes, so that they don't have to reinvent the wheel, but also from our mistakes, so that they don't repeat them. We believe that the Shrewsbury trials were the third most significant defeat for the British labour movement in the 20th century, but were they an unnecessary defeat and, we ask, what is to be done about it today?

This book uses a mass of previously unpublished material, including veteran flying pickets' memories. Our main documentary source, the Working Class Movement Library's North Wales 32 Collection, is stored chronologically and has a searchable *Catalogue*, so there is no need for thousands of footnotes. This and our other documentary sources are detailed in the *Bibliography*. Trade union and other organisations get their full titles first time they appear, but are then referred to by initials and are listed that way in the *Index*.

For readers who would like to put the 1972 building workers' strike in a wider economic and political context, Ralph Darlington and Dave Lyddon's *Glorious Summer* is a good place to start.

Comradely thanks to Andy Ayre, Simon Basketter, Ian Birchall, Paul Brook, Geoff Brown, John Charlton, Andy Coles, Dave Cope, Chris Corrigan, Ralph Darlington, Sarah Davies, Emily Greenaway, John Flanagan, Keith Flett, Laurie Flynn, Steve Hope, Reg Johnson, Alain Kahan, Penny Kay, Matt Kelly, Charlie Kimber, Peter Liversidge, Paul Mackney, Annie Makepeace, Jean Murray, Sean O'Donoghue, George Paizis, Dave Peers, Lesley Phillips, Mary Phillips, Dave Renton, Peter Robinson, Dave Rogers, Colin Sparks, John Sturrock, Mark Thomas, Christine Vié, Patrick Ward, Sam Webb, Mike Weaver and Granville Williams for information, encouragement and criticism. We also acknowledge the help of individuals who prefer to remain anonymous. No faults in any of the analysis that follows are anyone's but ours.

CHAPTER I

Veterans

Dave Ayre

I knew only one grandparent—my mother's mother, Grandma Hugill. She and Granddad were from Muker in what was then the North Riding of Yorkshire, but they had eleven children and needed money, so they moved to Crook in County Durham. Granddad worked in the huge coke oven and coal by-product plant at Bankfoot Works. The polluted atmosphere must have been a dramatic contrast to a rural village. I remember Grandma as a large, dignified woman, dressed in black. Their daughter, Annie—'Nan'—worked in a shoe-shop in Crook before she married Norman Ayre. He had been apprenticed to 'Old Dodds', the cabinet-maker, but had to go to work in the pit for higher wages, because he was his family's breadwinner.

I was born in 1931. I was their first child, but that day my father got the sack from the pit, so I was a bad omen. The 'Depression' was underway and all the men got their notice. My parents never had any spare money, so they had a really tough time; but father loved the feel and texture of wood and he made, reshaped and restored furniture, sometimes for a few coppers.

My brother Ken was born in 1932. He loves nature and has inherited father's love of wood. He is a talented, self-taught artist and carves beautiful sculptures, mainly of birds, out of the natural shapes of branches. He worked for the National Coal Board as a statistician, so he saw how they massaged figures to help shut pits.

In 1932 we moved a couple of miles up the hill to Stanley Village and lived in a cottage in the 'pit opening', the middle one of four lanes off a long street of 102 houses called Wooley Terrace. I remember the tread of the pitmen's hob-nailed boots going to Wooley Pit every foreshift, backshift and nightshift. The only break was when there was an accident or when the men were on holiday. Our cottage was a one up and one down called a 'back-to-back', because it backed onto another. The only outside door and windows were at the front, though we had extensive views of the Pennines. We had one cold tap. The toilets were across the road and many were shared. The pits held ash from our coal fire and 'midden men' shovelled the contents on to horse-drawn carts and dumped it in 'shit tips'—landfill sites.

When I was very little I used to love to visit Old Dodds's workshop and see him in his white apron. He was a superb craftsman and used machines only to make mortices. On one wall was a World War One aircraft propeller that looked like a lovely piece of sculpture.

The headmaster at my school was a councillor. He had a reputation for being a bit of a radical—a socialist even—but his social conscience wasn't very tender. He had a 'dunces' section and discriminated against kids from large families and neglected homes. He used to pick them out, drag them in front of the class and humiliate them. It was appalling. Everything was regimented. When the whistle went you had to stand in long lines in the playground, wait for it to be blown again and then march in, line by line.

When I was about six I experienced the dramatic consequences of the fact that the cottages were 'tied'. They belonged to the coal owner. I came back from school one day and saw our neighbours, Mr and Mrs Morrison, sitting on their furniture outside their cottage. It was raining buckets, they were in tears and all the people were booing the 'candymen'—bailiffs—who were dragging out the furniture. Mr Morrison was in his late sixties and had stopped working at the pit, so the coal owner wanted him out. Mrs Morrison was a bit of a crabby old so-and-so—and no doubt we were pests—but for the most part she was a really likeable, upstanding, chapel-going sort. It really moved me to see this couple, and the furniture that they had struggled for all their lives, out in the rain. Tanny Bodiner took them in. It was a fine example of pit-village solidarity, but I knew there was something wrong with the world.

The chapels played a key role in village life and especially the Wesleyan Methodists. (The coal owners ran the Anglican Church.) My mother was a staunch Wesleyan, so going to chapel every Sunday was a must for us kids. I never really enthused about it, though we looked forward to the annual trips. My mother was a bit conservative in many ways, but she voted Labour.

Early every July, on a Friday, Wooley Pit Durham Miners' Association banner was paraded round the village, accompanied by a brass band. On the Saturday my father carried me to the pitmen's 'Big Meeting' in Durham, but when I was seven I went by myself.

In 1938 my father was a hewer at Hedleyhope Pit. He had to walk four miles there in all weathers, across some of the highest terrain in the county, and four miles back after he and his 'marrers'—mates—had put in a hard shift, just to earn enough to feed us. One night there was a terrific storm and he didn't get back at the usual time. I heard mother stirring and could tell she was really upset, so I said that I'd go out to find him, being the eldest—toughy! But when I opened the door the blizzard was so intense that it was impossible to breathe. After what seemed like hours the door burst open and father—a stout fellow and only in his forties—staggered in with his unshaven face covered in ice. He collapsed on the floor in front of the fire and lay for half an hour or so, but a hot bath revived him and he went to bed. Next day the snow was so deep that it was like walking through frozen trenches; but he had to go to the pit, just to scratch a living. Half the men in the village had to do the same. You can imagine the impact all this had on our consciousness as kids.

I failed the '11-plus' examination for Wolsingham Grammar School. Maybe I was an inverted snob—that was quite common in pit villages. Going to grammar school guaranteed you a good job, yet many of us believed that the elite few who went there didn't get in because of their abilities, but because they were the children of managers and business people. I didn't know there were subjects like economics, politics, sociology, geography and history. All we got were the three Rs. The girls were expected to get married and keep house or 'go to place'—become a servant for some rich family, which often meant moving away—not develop themselves and have a career. It was taken for granted that most lads would leave school at fourteen to go down the pits. Teachers would say: 'You will have to be good at adding and subtracting because when you start work you'll have to be able to calculate your wage packet.'

Before I left school I went down a pit, once. Some kids who were screening coal 'on bank'—at the surface—and whitewashing walls told me it was 'a piece of cake'. It was OK at the bottom of the shaft, because it was a Friday, so the coal-cutting machinery was switched off; but I could hear the groans of the pit props that much better in the silence and I was bloody frightened. I didn't see the coal face, but father told me that the roof was only eighteen inches high, at best. He was a six-footer, so you can imagine the struggle he had. I have a photograph of him taken underground by his marrer Ted Hildreth. Father said that the cutting-machines were installed without adequate safeguards, so there were maimings and fatalities. Chris Tenby, a big strong lad, was mangled by the blades and never worked in the pit again. It was the talk of the village. Father told me that the coal dust the machines threw out was so dense that you couldn't see your outstretched hand in front of your face. He had a ritual when he got back from the pit. He spat the jet-black phlegm that had built up in his throat onto the fire. He just had to do it. On warm, humid, airless nights he could hardly walk or breathe. It was terrible to see him. The Wooley Terrace houses had back doors and most families put up wooden fences to give themselves a bit of privacy; but it wasn't unusual to see white-faced men wracking their bodies, trying to breathe and disgorge coal dust at the same time. Even today you can easily recognise old miners.

Miners raised such issues at the 'Consultative Committee', but it wasn't negotiation. There was little tradition of union militancy in the pits, mainly, I suspect, because of the 'moderate'—right wing—leadership of Durham Miners' Association. The Secretary, Sammy Watson, was based at the magnificent Red Hill headquarters in Durham. He had an air of working class 'aristocracy' and was revered by some miners, but scorned by others. (He later stopped any opposition to pit closures and negotiated his members out of a job.)

The doctor's 'surgery' in Stanley Village was Mrs Moses' front room and her living room was the 'waiting room'. She had a large family and her husband had been killed in the pit, so she was graciously allowed to remain in her tied house at the cost of this almost permanent intrusion into family life. We had a particularly flamboyant and charismatic GP called Pearson, who drove fast cars and almost killed himself when he hit a horse; but when the pit buzzer signalled an accident, he was straight there. He would return from underground black with coal dust and maybe with tears in his smart suit. His care for 'his pitmen' was undisputable and it was appreciated. Many villagers said he was 'part of the family' and he was treated like one. 'Going to the dentist' meant sitting on Clara Gaskell's stout-legged table to have a tooth pulled out by the visiting dentist, 'Old Crawshaw'. There was no concept of fillings then!

I left school in 1945, a few days before my fourteenth birthday. We all got bad reports. I hated it. It made me an instinctive socialist.

I was apprenticed at Johnson & Sons, a small building company in Crook. The bosses were staunch Wesleyans and it was a good firm. They did new building, repairs and restorations, so my training was varied. My father was heartily in favour of life-long learning and insisted that I attend night-class three times a week. What a chore for a young lad, and, just like his father, a keen biker! I toured large parts of Britain and raced at weekends, mainly in time trials, but sometimes in the occasional mass start. I also rode in a few national championships and was sponsored for the Isle of Man International Road Race, where I finished fourth.

My father was pleased that I hadn't gone down the pit, but insisted that I join the union. 'Make sure you pay your union money and your rent—in that order—through life, because if you don't pay your union money you'll never be able to pay your rent.'

Crook branch of the Amalgamated Union of Building Trade Workers had been founded in November 1947 and the December minutes were written by Brother Palin, the Secretary, and signed by the branch President, Brother Harker. Brother King was a scrutineer for elections to union positions and delegate to the Labour Party Annual Conference and the North East Coast Friendly Conference, familiarly known as the 'Penny Conference', because of the penny a week collection. The branch felt that there was a need for us to have a more powerful voice in the union, so we were affiliated to this bricklayers' strike fund. It was a left wing organisation and our branch already had a reputation for taking industrial action.

In 1948 my father got Tommy Simpson, a bricklayer at the pit, to 'swear me in' as a member of Crook AUBTW. I stood outside the branch room while they discussed my 'qualifications' and then, after questioning me about my capabilities, they let me join. The branch met fortnightly, so members could pay their dues and discuss union business, and it was fairly active. Harry Palin was a very, very skilful brickie, and was building and repairing kilns at West Hunwick Brickworks, but that December he resigned as Secretary and Russell King was elected in his place.

There had always been divisions between craftsmen and labourers and there used to be many building unions until 1918, when most of them formed the National Federation of Building Trade Operatives (NFBTO), which negotiated pay and conditions with the National Federation of Building Trade Employees (NFBTE) at the National Joint Council for the Building Industry (NJC).

In 1949 Crook branch elected a delegate to the NFBTO, but there was no mention in the minutes of the New Builders Leader meeting in Sunderland, even though that Communist Party organisation had been in touch. The branch elected a delegate to Bishop Auckland Trades and Labour Council, but asked the Secretary to 'attempt to inaugurate a Trades Council in Crook'. There were no nominees for the TUC Congress or the AUBTW Conference. In 1950 Harry Palin became our delegate to the new Crook Trades Council. We supported Lambeth AUBTW 'in the attempt to stop interference' by the Executive Council 'with the General Rules' in the nomination of candidates for the general secretary. It was now the Cold War and Brother Lewis 'advised on the future status of Communists in the union'. Letters from the CP-led British Peace Committee were to 'be ignored'. We also discussed the question of 'Sub-contracting on a Labour only basis'—piecework. Harry Palin presented me with a spirit level as 'apprentice of the year'—'in recognition of his technical studies and his interest in Union work'. By 1951 the branch had 87 members. In 1952 we heard correspondence about the ENV engineers' strike in London. We found our recent NJC pay rise 'inadequate' and our EC should 'take further steps to secure a further increase'.

I was now 21 and had to do two years compulsory 'national service' in the armed forces. I hung on to the very last minute, hoping that conscription would end, but I was assigned to the Durham Light Infantry and was sent to train at nearby Brancepath Camp. Like many others I was not a model soldier. I hated using firearms and sought to avoid them by various methods, but that wasn't a good attitude for someone being trained to be a killer, because we were scheduled to go Korea where a war was going on. If I'd gone I doubt whether I'd be writing this now. Fortunately, we were sent to Wüppertal on the Ruhr in occupied West Germany. We weren't allowed to take our bikes, but my fitness put me in good stead. Cross-country running was part of our training and, to my surprise, I won, even though there were experienced runners in the field. I ended up running for the battalion and then for the British Army of the Rhine, so I avoided most day-to-day routine. I was designated as a 'batman', which meant looking after the officer class. They usually had a marquee to themselves—a far cry from what we squaddies had. I particularly remember one arrogant character. I had to go to the field cookhouse for my meal and his and I was often at the rear of the queue; but one day I was first. Something had infuriated me, so I took a bit of quiet revenge. I put his meal on a cold stone and ate mine. His was literally stone cold, but he had to eat it or do without. Another time a chaplain told me that he was 'just one of the lads'. I asked him if he was a captain, and he said he was, so I told him that the only way that 'the lads' could get into the officers' quarters was as a servant. They asked me to be a corporal twice, but I turned it down. That was the only time I've ever missed Durham Big Meeting.

While I was away, Crook AUBTW kept going. In 1953 a 'vote of censure was moved on Head Office' for not replying about a strike ballot. The branch now had a 'Craft Section' and a 'Labourer Section'. It approved the Secretary's actions regarding the Labour-controlled local authority's bonus scheme and instructed him to apply for affiliation to the Labour Party. In 1954 the branch agreed to loan a book on 'Direct labour' to members for a fortnight. The question of the hydrogen bomb was referred to the Trades Council.

During 1954 I completed my national service and returned to Johnson & Son's; but contracts were getting thin on the ground, so I was catapulted into the manic world of private contractors. I worked for local firms, including Lawson's and Waggett's, and for large national contractors like Tarmac, Wimpey and Laing, mainly building council houses at Crook and Willington. We had to chuck bricks down fast, but the houses were really well built compared to many today. Occasionally, the Clerk of Works was a union member, but the conditions on non-unionised sites could be shocking and running water was a rarity. Organising a union at site level has always been difficult, especially on private sector contracts that last a year or two at most, because activists usually have to start from scratch. I was often sacked. Sometimes I didn't last a week.

Doris Berry had been to Wolsingham Grammar School, but didn't like its segregated system. Her father was manager of Bankfoot Power Station and she was a tracer in the NCB drawing office at Beamish. We got married in 1956 and lived in East Lodge, the former home of the industrialist, Joseph Pease; but then we moved to a Wooley Terrace cottage. I built the first inside water closet in the street, but neighbours were very concerned that our lads might get diphtheria. We had three—David, Paul and Andy. My cycling diminished, but somehow my union activities increased.

Crook AUBTW tackled the long-standing problems in the industry—low wages, long hours, health and safety issues and the lack of apprentices. There was a constant chase for members and a struggle to keep them in, because we moved around so often; but we had a solid core, a sound branch structure and an active membership.

The pits had been taken out of private ownership in 1947, but, like all the other 'nationalised' industries, the NCB ran on capitalist lines and most of the former managers were kept on. When my father was in his fifties he was summoned to St Mary's consultancy in Newcastle and they reckoned he had 12 percent pneumoconiosis 'contamination'. He still had to work in high dust levels and when it rose to 25 percent we sued the NCB. The doctor persuaded him to have an operation on a hernia, but just as he was getting over that he had a fatal heart attack. It was just too much for his body. They did an autopsy and showed me part of his lungs. It was just like a lump of coal. We got some money, but he was dead, aged 62.

For as long as I can remember, the Labour Party has controlled Durham County Council. (That's not surprising. My father used to tell me how Churchill and the Tories sent troops against Welsh miners.) So I joined. Russ King worked for the 'Old Labour' Urban District Council, but it was reluctant to grant union recognition. When I spoke to them once I was told in no uncertain terms that if I didn't shut up and sit down they would call the police. Russ eventually got elected as a steward. He was by no means a leftwinger, but he was a committed trade unionist. He was our delegate to the AUBTW National Delegate Conference, active in the Labour Party and secretary of the embryonic Wear Valley and District Trades Union Council, to which our branch sent a large delegation. In 1957 we had to complain about the 'Old Labour' Urban District Council employing contractors who used non-union labour.

During World War Two the building unions had agreed to adult training schemes alongside traditional apprenticeships, but the 1945 Labour government didn't nationalise the industry. In 1947, during the post-war building boom, Aneurin Bevan, the Labour Minister of Health, put the unions under pressure and they allowed employers to negotiate bonus schemes. In 1951 the Tories got back in and during the 1950s the contractors didn't train enough apprentices; so in 1960, when there was another boom, there was a shortage of skilled men. More and more contractors offered 'labour only' deals. They would supply materials to a 'subbie'—sub-contractor—and he would negotiate a price for supplying them with labour. The subbie negotiated a lower price with workers and pocketed the difference. Tax and National Insurance stamps were negotiable. But 'labour only' didn't get much of a toehold in the North East.

In 1961 Harry Weaver was elected as NFBTO General Secretary, though other officials thought he was 'Marxist-sympathising'. He negotiated two hours off the 44-hour week. I was elected as a member of Crook Branch Committee and in 1962, with the support of Russ King and Harry Palin—who didn't talk about politics, but was almost certainly solid Labour, like most veterans—I was elected as our delegate to the Bishop Auckland meetings of the NFBTO. The experience widened my political horizons.

There's only me left now to tell this tale, out of a gang of three brickies and two labourers. Williamsons, a regional firm, won the contract to build Durham County Council's last brick-built comprehensive school at Staindrop. Lord Barnard owned the nearby Raby Castle and his estate was dotted with white-painted cottages. That colour seemed appropriate, because there was no trade union tradition in that area. We started the 'footings'—the first courses, up to the damp-proof course—in October, when the weather could be volatile, to say the least. Getting to work was a problem, because public transport didn't run regularly, but I had an old Triumph 650 Twin motorbike with a sidecar. It was a half-hour trip, so me and our hod-carrier, Billy Chipchase (a Crook branch stalwart who would take on the steward's job when others wouldn't) were often cold and wet when we arrived. There was no toilet, no cabin, no canteen and no drying facilities, so we used a hawthorn hedge. Eventually, we discovered that Williamsons had a bus in a nice dry garage and we pressured them into using it to get us to and from work. More pressure resulted in a 'cabin'—a primitive shed with a corrugated iron roof and an ash floor. Later, they gave us the additional luxury of a small stove, fuelled with scrap wood and coke, because by this time the weather was really foul. A week or so before Christmas, when it was snowing heavily, our gang was given our cards and told that we couldn't use the firm's transport to get home, so we began hoofing it the six miles to Bishop Auckland to get a bus. We must have been a sorry sight with our 'bait'—lunchboxes—and tool-bags on our backs and huddled up in our army greatcoats in the teeth of a blizzard. After four miles a wagon driver I knew stopped and took us home. We were grateful for this working class solidarity, because we were frozen stiff. We learned afterwards that Williamsons stopped running the bus for the other men.

After driving about 250 miles, looking for a 'kick in' at numerous sites, we got a start at a huge Tarmac housing site at Redcar on the North Yorkshire coast. Transport was provided, but it left Bishop Auckland—eight miles from Stanley Village—at 6.45am, so I had to leave home at 6.00am. Still, it was mid-winter and it was a job. We were put in larger gangs. Three of our hod-carriers were Pakistani lads and they were fantastic workers. Only one could speak English, but we soon gained their confidence and became friends. They told us that there were open Nazis on Teesside, so they had kept themselves very much to themselves on site. We showed them how to work out their wage slips. They were being underpaid and bonus payments were 'light'. We told management that anyone working with us would have to get the union rate and an equal share of the bonus. They agreed. In fact, they made up for what had been withheld from the three lads, who joined the union. Brilliant! Then we were sacked.

We chased wagons carrying bricks and got a start at Washington New Town with Shepherd Construction, a York firm. They didn't pay that high a wage, but they went 'by the book' when it came to nationally negotiated NFBTO-NFBTE working rules. We built up a strong organisation. I was elected as the brickies' steward and then as 'convenor'—the leading steward.

Early in 1963 Russ King and I were nominated for an AUBTW weekend school. That summer, after the NFBTE refused to meet the NFBTO claim, Harry Weaver led the first national strike in the industry for forty years. Around 500 sites were absolutely solid for five days, but just as the action was beginning to bite he settled for less than half the pay claim and no progress whatever towards a forty-hour week. Some NFBTO union conferences threw the deal out, but the rank and file hadn't prepared and the officials got their way. Crook AUBTW had paid a supplement to lads on strike and we raised the Local Levy Fund by two shillings a quarter. I became our delegate to the 'Penny Conference'.

Bill Kerriss had been a Crook AUBTW member in the 1950s but later joined the National Union of General & Municipal Workers. He worked at the 'Pipeworks'—North Bitchburn Fireclay Company—where he and other brickies lined and repaired the kilns that were used for making glazed pipes. Stewards from the NUGMW, the Electrical Trade Union, the Plumbing Trade Union and the Transport and General Workers'

Union were on the Joint Shop Stewards' Committee. Bill was a staunch Communist Party member and became convenor. He ran a tight ship. In 1963 he joined our branch.

Reuben Barker, who also worked at the Pipeworks, transferred from the NUGMW to Crook AUBTW in 1964. He was a leftwinger and a committed trade unionist and was always ready to take on the steward's job. Like me, he had been sacked time and time again.

Reuben Barker

Witton Park village is about three miles south of Crook. In its day it was a hive of industry with pits, ironworks, brickyards, railways and farming, and there were Welsh, Irish, Scots, Italian and Belgian families, all with their own colourful history.

My father had been in World War One, but he never spoke about it. I was born in 1929. The 1930s were the days of the means test and my father was blacklisted. The twenty shops were full of goods, but my parents had very little money. However, they had an allotment and kept hens and goats, so they made ends meet. I had three brothers and three sisters. We all went to Witton Park Council School and I left in 1943, aged fourteen, during World War Two.

My first job was in a fruiterer's warehouse, but my ambition was to be a blacksmith. After applying at various forges and being told that I was far too light, I heard that there was a job coming up in a firm that owned three brickyards, two pits and farms near North Bitchburn. I got a start, but no blacksmith vacancy opened up, so I made the best of it. I was the only one with a bike and was expected to run around with messages. In winter 1944 (presumably on the government's say-so) our managers gave us a ration of sugar and tea, but then asked for it back, because it had to be used in a canteen and we didn't have one. We'd already used ours at home.

They asked me if I wanted to be a bricklayer, working with three men. I didn't get on with the father very well, though he was very good at his job and was about to retire; but his two sons were great to work with and were good bricklayers. On a long wall they'd put me in the middle to lay bricks towards one of them, but the best job was building 'beehive' kilns, with 200 bricks at the bottom of the dome and building up to sixteen at the top, leaving a circular hole. There was lots of work at the brickyard, the pits and the farms, so we were never idle. One brickie laid bricks with one hand. The bosses asked why. He said that they weren't paying him enough for two.

When the father retired, the sons moved away. I'd just been married, so we moved to Shildon to live with my parents-in-law. I started working for Shaw & Knight Enamelstone as a repair bricklayer. One spring my wife and I got one of four little old miners' cottages down in Escomb. It was in the middle of a field. There was no tarmac road and no street lights, so when it was dark there was only the moon. There were foxes and hedgehogs in the orchard only ten yards away. The big farm horse, Sam, was a regular visitor, as were harvest mice. There was no water—just a spring—and my first weekend job was rebuilding the outside toilet.

Two years later we bought a house at Victoria Street in Howden-le-Wear. I was travelling eight miles to and from work, so when a man from North Bitchburn Pipeworks told me that the management wanted to see me, I went along and got a start along with four other brickies.

One day the management got another firm to do our work. I was elected to go to the office with the NUGMW steward, Bill Kerriss, who told me that we couldn't get the extra sixpence (2.5p) an hour that we were after. Nobody was in the office, so I sat in the boss's chair. The foreman told the boss about that and when he arrived he kept looking at me while he demanded of Bill what was going on. When I stood up there was a look of satisfaction on the boss's face, but before Bill spoke I said we wanted two shillings (10p). They were both surprised, but they had a debate and we got one shilling (5p). After we left Bill asked me why I hadn't left the negotiating to him and said he wasn't going to ask me to go with him again, but I let him take the credit.

Jim French

My father's parents died when he was quite young and his uncle brought him up in Byker in east Newcastle. James Ernest French was the first 'boy', as they were called, to ride on the new steam wagon from Newcastle to Morpeth. (Prior to that horses did the trip.) He started work at Newcastle Breweries and stayed there for thirty years. He did most jobs and eventually became a 'cellarman', looking after the beer. I don't think he joined a union.

My mother's mother was originally called Mary Morgan. She and her sister Helen were born in Hartlepool, the younger girls in a Catholic family of 22. Mary married Edward Child and they lived in Gosforth, just north of Newcastle. Grandma was very domineering and owned eight fish and chip shops, while Grandpa ran a decorating business. Ruth was their only child—though they took in an orphan called Ted—and she later became a tailoress and sometimes worked for Mr Cohen in Newcastle. She married James French and they lived with her parents.

I was born at home in Gosforth, weighing 4.5 pounds, on a cold November day in 1937. My older sister, Theresa—Grandma's favourite—went to a private school and became a State Registered Nurse in Newcastle Royal Victoria Infirmary, but I was much closer to my younger sister, Mary, who worked at Wills' tobacco factory. We later went to the Youth Hostel Association and dances together. Looking back, I think we were middle class, because at one time we had two cars—a Singer Bantam and a Morris 8.

When I was little I used to go to the Catholic Church twice on Sundays. From time to time the priest came for Sunday tea and blessed the house, but even though I was quite shy I tended to question the reasons for things. I went to St Charles' Roman Catholic School and on Mondays I had to say what colour cassock the priest had been wearing at Sunday Mass. I always tried to skip Mass, so I often didn't know. The nuns caned me regularly. I hated it. When I was eleven my parents tried to get me into the Catholic College at Durham, but that didn't work out. Then they sent me to Eastcliffe, a private school, but that was a disaster, too. So I went back to St Charles' to be ridiculed by the other children.

In 1953 I became an apprentice at Walker Naval Yard, east of Newcastle. Grandpa had worked there during World War Two and got me in. I met all kinds of men who preached trades unionism and socialism. They talked about the hardships they had faced, the struggles they had endured and the appallingly unsafe working practices they put up with. The Yard management would help some men get safety boots, but only those in certain trades. When the buzzer went at the end of the day the gates would open and we faced large numbers of children begging for any bait you had left over.

In 1958, after I'd completed my apprenticeship, I left the Yard, partly because of the noise that the pneumatic caulking machines made when they were making ships watertight, but also because I wanted more varied work. I got a job as a painter for Shield

Brothers, a building firm across the Tyne at Swalwell, west of Gateshead. The work was quite varied and in some ways it was a good outfit, though I was occasionally viewed with suspicion because I came from the Yard and questioned everything.

There were a large number of union members—though not 100 percent—but the steward got the job because nobody else would do it. He'd worked there all his life and some things got swept under the carpet. For example, the men relied on getting their wages on Fridays, but one Friday we had to wait until Saturday. I asked for extra pay, as set out in the Working Rule, but Mr Shield told the steward: 'tell them if they don't like it, go somewhere else.' Most lads were in the Blaydon branch of the Amalgamated Society of Painters and Decorators, so I joined. It was quite an active branch and I enjoyed the meetings, though I'd hear tales of employers doing worse things than I'd ever heard about at the Yard. One chap who had worked for a small firm for over forty years fell off a ladder. His boss never visited him or paid his wages. After he'd been on the sick for a month the boss sacked him. He wasn't in a union. Some men talked about whether the Labour Party would get back in. Most branch officers were Labour and some were Methodist lay preachers.

In 1959 I was called up to do my national service. I could do three years in the Army and Navy or two in the Royal Air Force, so I joined the RAF. I worked as an assistant cook—a great job!— and was stationed in Hull, Henlow, Cardigan and Catterick. In 1961, after I'd finished 'square bashing'—drill—at the passing out parade, I made my way back to the billet in high spirits. I saluted a mate of mine. Unfortunately, there were two officers behind me and they gave me a right lecture about 'Queen and country'.

I met Gwen Horner when I was at Catterick. She was from a good working class family in Darlington. Her dad had been in the Canadian Mounties—a bit of a black sheep, like me, I suppose— and he'd done all kinds of jobs to earn a crust for his family. In 1961 Gwen and I got married and she kept me on the right road.

I worked in Newcastle for uncle Ted, who ran Grandpa's decorating business; but it's not always a good move, working for relations. The money was poor—about £11 a week (worth about £170 today). We had our son Michael by then; so after eighteen months we moved to Darlington and we've lived there ever since. I worked for a Catterick firm, JD & S Tighe, but when they asked me to paint in the rain I walked off site. I soon got a job at the North of England School Furnishing Company. It was a good firm and I learned how to spray paint. Management and unions had agreed that everyone had to be in a union, either before they started or immediately afterwards—a 'closed shop'. The convenor, Cecil Spence, was a Labour councillor in Darlington and a bit of a firebrand. At first I thought he was good, but he made the most basic mistake. The management offered him a Director's job and he took it. A year later, they sacked him. He got no shop floor support.

CHAPTER 2

The lump

Great Britain Limited

1964 was a boom year for British employers, under a Tory government; but that October Labour scraped into office with a majority of four. They tried to maintain the National Health Service and other parts of the welfare state by cutting the armed forces east of Suez and allowing colonies to govern themselves. There were socialist MPs, but hardly any were in powerful positions, and most at the top were firmly wedded (or resigned) to a capitalist future—'Great Britain Limited'. So the Cabinet encouraged union leaders, most of whom were Labour Party members, to go for 'moderate'—low—wage claims, in the 'national interest'—shareholders' profits. In 1965 the building unions accepted a pitiful offer 'in accordance with the desires' of George Brown, Secretary of State for Economic Affairs, and James Callaghan, the Chancellor of the Exchequer. Within a month the Cabinet introduced a 'wage freeze' and the builders' pittance was deferred for a year.

Some big contractors now sub-contracted all their work. A 'self-employed' worker lost the right to unemployment benefit, compensation for work-related accidents or illness and any hope of a secure job or promotion. Sub-contractors added holiday pay and National Insurance contributions onto the nationally negotiated basic rate to form a tempting 'lump' sum for those who worked on a 'labour only' piecework basis, but paying National Insurance stamps and Income Tax was now the responsibility of each individual. (Some subbies gave employees Friday morning off so that they could pretend to be unemployed and claim the 'dole'—social security benefits.) Big contractors didn't need so many supervisors or office staff and 'lumpers' didn't appear on their books, so they paid less to the government's apprentice-training scheme. Lumpers often bodged the work, but did it quickly, so contract deadlines were less of a problem. Direct Works—local authority—repair gangs could be left to tackle lump work on council houses at the ratepayers' expense. Big contractors made huge profits on government contracts. In 1965 to 1966 Wimpeys made £11,000,000 from its 31,000 employees—around £90 a week at today's values—and paid shareholders a dividend of 15 percent. Other firms paid 20 percent.

The lump undermined union recruitment, organisation and finances, and the AUBTW was 'bleeding to death'. Officials achieved nothing by negotiations, but in September, when nine carpenters on a Turriff contract in London didn't produce Amalgamated Society of Woodworkers' cards, 51 others stopped work. Management sacked them, but 300 other men came out in sympathy. They were sacked, too, but the TGWU made the dispute official and after three weeks management agreed to a closed shop.

In March 1966 Labour won a working majority of 97. Eric Heffer, a former Merseyside joiner and ASW steward, was re-elected as a Labour MP. He felt that parliament should be 'a platform for socialist ideas', but wasn't confident that the Cabinet could bring about a 'fundamental change in society', since, 'with the noticeable exception of Barbara Castle', it was 'from the centre and right of the party'. In May the Phelps-Brown Committee acknowledged that there were up to 200,000 lumpers, but the government shouldn't interfere in the labour market. A minority looked for an alternative.

The Communist Party

The Communist Party was founded in 1920, in imitation of the Bolsheviks. It recruited engineers, miners, dockers and transport workers, especially in the East End of London, South Wales, the West Riding of Yorkshire, the North East and Lowland Scotland; but in 1921 alone the Russian-led Comintern gave it £24,000 (worth over £500,000 today). In the 1930s CP leaders accepted Stalin's anti-Marxist ideas about 'socialism in one country' and his 1939 pact with Hitler, but in 1941, after Hitler invaded Russia, the CP backed the 'war effort'. By 1942 the CP claimed 56,000 members. General secretary Harry Pollitt praised a docker comrade who broke a strike. By 1945 the CP claimed 45,000 members and sales of 100,000 for the *Daily Worker*. In the general election, 21 CP candidates got 102,000 votes, and two were elected; but Labour won by a landslide. Up to 1947, according to Eaden and Renton, the CP acted as the Labour government's 'most loyal prop', but then the US president committed himself to intervene against any revolution that he believed was 'communist'. Labour's acceptance of Marshall Aid in 1948 made the British economy and foreign policy dependent on the USA, just as the Cold War got underway. CP membership began to slide. In 1949 the TUC banned CP delegates to trades councils and the TGWU banned them from holding union positions. Labour kept wage rises below inflation, yet in 1950 the 100 CP candidates got 91,000 votes and lost the MPs. In 1951 ten CPers got 21,000 votes. Labour won most votes and got 295 seats, but the Tories got 321.

The CP cultivated 'left' Labour MPs, because they saw the state not as something to be smashed, as the Bolsheviks had done, but as a machine that could be steered leftwards if the driver (Labour) listened to the passenger (the CP). In 1956, after Russia invaded Hungary, 10,000 CPers left. In 1961, CPers in the ETU were found guilty of ballot rigging. (Rightwingers took over and banned CPers from holding positions.) Even so, the CP claimed 34,000 members in 1963 and was strong in Sheffield, Manchester and London engineering, Clyde shipyards, the Scottish and Welsh coalfields and the Birmingham and the London building industry—where they had 200 members.

Lou Lewis started work as a joiner in the Liverpool shipyards and joined the CP during his national service. By 1963 he was the 'Federation Steward'—the senior NFBTO steward—on the vast Paternoster site in London.

In 1963 Myton's, a Taylor Woodrow subsidiary, lost £35,000 a week (worth £500,000 today) on their Barbican contract for the Tory Kensington and Chelsea Council, because of their absurdly low tender. Such large contracts employed a lot of workers over a longer period than was usual in the private sector, so the stewards negotiated good bonuses with only one strike. The real cost of the entire Barbican project was set to double to £40,000,000, but contractors could recoup it at the ratepayers' expense, once the jobs were completed, because of the character of the contract.

In 1966 Lewis got a job at Myton's. He had a reputation for negotiating good bonuses and was elected as Federation Steward and Chairman of the Works Committee. In September the NFBTE tried to stop the rise in bonuses in London. Myton's Works Committee improved some of theirs, but negotiations broke down on others, and there was a work to rule. In October the NFBTO-NFBTE Disputes Panel confirmed some Myton bonuses, but left others unresolved. The stewards wanted union leaders to make the dispute 'official'.

George Smith had been a CPer up to 1954 and in 1958 he was elected as ASW General Secretary, partly thanks to CP votes; but late in 1966, under a Labour government, he refused to back the 'little

Caesars' at Myton's. That same day the site managers sacked three steel-fixers for working to rule. The workforce voted to strike. The district secretaries of six unions and the NFBTO regional secretary called on their ECs to make the dispute official and the TGWU and AUBTW did so; but Smith, officials of the smaller unions and Harry Weaver organised an NFBTO meeting that let Smith decide whether to declare any strike official. The TGWU and AUBTW withdrew official support from the Myton stewards and Smith negotiated a deal. If the workers accepted cuts in negotiated bonuses and the removal of almost all of their stewards' negotiating rights, Myton's would concede a closed shop, but the stewards' future would be decided 'through procedure', which Smith controlled. The picket continued. Then other managers went on the offensive.

In 1963 Sunley's had begun work on their £5,000,000 contract for the Ministry of Public Building and Works at Horseferry Road. Their managers had a record of victimising militant stewards and if any got past the blacklist they could sack them as 'unsuitable' at two hours' notice within the first six days, in accordance with the Working Rule. In 1964 the CP joiner Jack Henry got a start but was sacked after three days. There was a strike, and the unions made it official, so he was eventually reinstated. In 1965 the management sacked the federation steward, CPer Pete Kavanagh, so the men elected Henry. Sunley's profits quadrupled, but penalty clauses of £900 a day kicked in if the contract wasn't completed by October 1966. Time lost through strikes didn't incur contractual penalties, so managers demanded unacceptable clocking-in arrangements and a gang bonus. A mass meeting rejected these proposals. A Sunley's director later claimed that James Mills, the ASW Vice-President, advised him to sack the Works Committee. Mills denied it, but four days after imposing the new arrangements the site managers did just that. The TGWU and AUBTW made the dispute official, but the ASW stopped strike pay, sacked the district secretary, the CPer Jack Rusca, for giving £10 to each picket at Christmas and ousted the management committee that told him to do so. CP union militants looked for allies at site level, but their leaders focused on union bureaucrats.

A tightly knit group of politically motivated men

Baruch Mendelson was born in the Ukraine in 1910, the son of a Jewish religious teacher. His two older sisters joined the Bolsheviks, but the rest of the family emigrated to Canada after 1917. Mendelson won a scholarship to the University of Alberta and became a barrister, but in the mid-1930s he joined the International Brigade, fought in Spain and was wounded twice. After the Spanish revolution was defeated he settled in Britain. He was a tank commander in World War Two and was captured at Tobruk in 1941. Helped by Italian partisans, he organised a breakout and got to Britain. By 1953, as 'Bert Ramelson', he was the CP Yorkshire district secretary. Then came Hungary in 1956. In the late 1950s he wrote about Trotskyism for the Political Committee. In 1959 a new organisation, the Socialist Labour League, recruited several disgruntled CPers, but was controlled by the Trotskyist Revolutionary Communist Party, which operated clandestinely in the Labour Party. In 1960 the CP Central Education Department's 'Notes on Trotskyism' was concerned with SLL attempts to 'turn the workers away from the task of winning the official trade union organisation for a fighting policy'.

In 1964 the CP Organisation Department warned members that the SLL was attempting to 'penetrate the party'. 'We have to make clear that all these groupings without exception are out to destroy the party and to weaken and confuse the British Labour Movement.' The party 'will not tolerate association with these people, or failure to fight for our policy when they appear'. CP membership had begun to decline. The 'Trotskyist Study Group' was led by Betty Reid and in the September *Marxism Today* she focused on the SLL, but noted that *International Socialism* had 'influence in one or two universities'. After Labour scraped into office that October, the CP veteran John Campbell was confident that 'Dedicated Disrupters' could be stopped from penetrating workers' organisations 'under false colours'. The CP began building 'Broad Lefts' with left wing Labour Party members in the National Union of Mineworkers and the Draughtsman's & Allied Technicians' Association. In 1965 several CP veteran leaders retired and Ramelson was appointed as national industrial organiser. The industrial and economic departments were merged and he exercised considerable power over policy through the Economic Committee. By 1966 CP membership had fallen by 3,600 in four years, its general election performance was the worst for decades and rebranding the *Daily Worker* as the *Morning Star* had not increased sales. Its power lay in the unions.

Industrial Research & Information Services helped employers to operate blacklists and during the 1962 elections for general secretary of the National Union of Seamen, IRIS publicised CP support for Jim Slater. In 1964 he and Joe Kenny, a left wing Labour Party member, were elected to the NUS Executive Committee. Merchant seamen's pay—under £11 for a 44-hour week—was lower than any European country except Spain and ship's masters could issue fines without appeal. The big shipping firms made huge profits—P & O raked in £23,000,000 in 1965—and paid dividends of over 10 percent. The NUS had a closed shop agreement, but there were no stewards on board ships. Union elections tended to take place when oppositionists were at sea and NUS headquarters was home to IRIS.

In February 1966 the NUS put in a claim for a forty-hour week and a rise of 12/6d a month (62.5p). In April the employers offered a gradual reduction to a forty-hour week by 1968, a cut of fifteen days' paid leave a year, no pay rise and no new pay claim until 1969, unless there was a substantial rise in the cost of living. The NUS called a strike for 16 May. On the 23rd, as the strike began to bite, the Labour government declared a State of Emergency, which empowered them to deploy troops in a civilian dispute. On the 26th they set up a Committee of Inquiry, led by Lord Pearson, which reported on 8 June and proposed minor improvements in the employers' offer. The NUS rejected the proposals. On the 20th, paraphrasing an MI5 report, Labour Prime Minister Harold Wilson told the House of Commons that the NUS strike was the work of a 'tightly knit group of politically motivated men who, as the last general election showed, utterly failed to get their views accepted by the majority of the British electorate'. They were 'determined to exercise back-stage pressures, forcing great hardship on the members of the union and their families, and endangering the security of the industry and the economic welfare of the nation'. On the 29th Wilson told the Commons that 'the whole formidable power of the Communist Party's industrial apparatus has for some time been directed' towards taking over the NUS 'and the seamen's strike with all its background of justification for industrial action, has provided the ground'. His 'evidence' was that Slater and Kenny had stayed in a CPer's flat in London and Bert Ramelson had paid them a visit. (Ironically, Ramelson had advocated a return to work.) The Ministry of Labour exerted pressure on the employers and extracted a slightly less bad offer. The NUS was in danger of bankruptcy and its EC—which didn't contain one CPer—recommended the deal. Thousands of members catcalled speakers—including CPers—who argued for a return to work; but the strike was over by July.

In July the Labour Cabinet announced another 'wage freeze'. Eric Heffer and a few other leftwingers abstained, but the TUC and the Labour Party Conference went along with it. In September the Cabinet introduced Selective Employment Tax, which taxed firms according to the number of their employees. It was intended to eliminate 'over manning' and many employers used it as an excuse to sack workers, cut overtime pay, bonuses, severance pay, holidays, holiday pay and accident insurance, and then offered a contract to survivors or new recruits on a self-employed basis. They also picked off militants—especially CPers. Labour had made trade union activity a political issue and the CP had outlawed work with the SLL, but Communist militants needed allies.

The International Socialists

In 1946 the 29-year-old Jewish Marxist Ygael Gluckstein was expelled from Palestine. He and Chanie Rosenberg went to London and joined the 400 mainly working class members of the Revolutionary Communist Party. In autumn 1947 the Labour Home Secretary gave him 24 hours to leave the country. He went to Dublin, while Rosenberg worked as a teacher and remained politically active.

Gluckstein had begun to question why the ending of World War Two had not resulted in the revolutions that Trotsky had predicted back in 1939, just before Stalin had him assassinated. In the summer of 1948 Gluckstein's 'The Class Nature of Stalinist Russia' argued that Russia was not a workers' state, but a 'state capitalist' formation that couldn't be reformed by a political revolution at the top and required a social revolution from below. The former RCP leaders in 'The Club' didn't like this departure from 'orthodox Trotskyism' and Gluckstein and his supporters either left or were expelled. Gluckstein, Duncan Hallas and Geoff Carlsson (both engineers), and others, began building a new organisation.

In September 1950, as 'Tony Cliff', Gluckstein and others published 350 copies of a duplicated *Socialist Review*. In 1951 they became the Socialist Review Group and, under a Tory government, Cliff was allowed back to London. In 1954 Syd Bidwell, a former railway worker and now a tutor for the National Council of Labour Colleges, joined the SRG. In the late 1950s Eric Heffer attended NCLC courses and became associated with SRG members and by 1960 he was President of Liverpool Trades Council and a Labour councillor. That year about sixty SRG members published a quarterly, *International Socialism*, and in 1961 they published a monthly *Industrial Worker* and a fortnightly *Socialist Review*. Recruitment was slow, but the quality was high.

Paul Foot was born in Palestine in 1937. His father was a diplomat and his uncle Michael was a Labour MP. Paul went to

Shrewsbury School and, after his national service in Jamaica, he went to University College, Oxford, where he was an active Liberal. In 1961 he worked as a cub reporter for the *Scottish Daily Record* in Glasgow and joined the Labour Party's Young Socialists, but in 1962 Cliff recruited him to the SRG. That year they became the International Socialism Group and in 1963 Foot edited what was now *Labour Worker*. In 1964 he went to London to work on the *Sun* (then a Labour paper) and the *Sunday Telegraph*, but also wrote for *Private Eye*. Thanks to recruitment in the Campaign for Nuclear Disarmament and the Labour Party, IS had over 200 members and *Labour Worker* had a circulation of 2,000.

In 1960, after his national service, Roger Protz joined the Young Socialists. He was appointed as editor of *New Advance*, but at the Easter 1961 Conference he distributed a pamphlet criticising the Labour Party leadership and was sacked. He joined the SLL and edited *Keep Left*; but in 1964 he joined the tiny Revolutionary Socialist League and reportedly helped to edit *Militant*. He broke with the SLL that Easter. In 1965 he joined IS and by 1966 he had replaced Foot as editor of *Labour Worker*.

In January 1966 IS members led the shop stewards' committee at the London engineering firm, ENV. They and other IS union militants and dissident CPers including Jim Hiles, a carpenter, established the London Industrial Shop Stewards Defence Committee. They had been involved in engineering and building disputes and wanted to generalise opposition to the Labour government's wage restraint policy and counter its hostile attitude to shop stewards. They had contacts in Manchester, Teesside, Newcastle and Glasgow, and a conference attracted 200 delegates. Tony Cliff and Colin Barker (an Oxford graduate) produced *Incomes Policy, Legislation and Shop Stewards*, with an introduction criticising CP policy by the Maoist Reg Birch. It reportedly sold 15,000 copies, mainly to militants. In March the SLL, the ENV shop stewards and the CP-led London Docks and Exhibition Workers stewards lobbied MPs against Labour's prices and incomes policy.

Syd Bidwell was elected as a Labour MP, but IS expelled him.

The Liaison Committee for the Defence of Trade Unions

In spring 1966 the CP leaders endorsed Ramelson's policy to 'broaden... considerably our contact with other trade unionists' via Broad Left organisations. By summer Jim Hiles was secretary and

Lou Lewis was chairman of the London 'lobby committee'. Delegations from CP strongholds in London, Manchester, Sheffield, Glasgow and elsewhere lobbied MPs. According to McIlroy and Campbell, the lobby committee distanced itself from the LISSDC and Ramelson suggested that it broaden its campaign to other issues. By September the 'lobby committee' was the Liaison Committee for the Defence of Trade Unions. Hiles canvassed selected union bodies and at least fifteen of the 21 sponsors were shop stewards' committees in factories with a workplace CP branch. Most were in London, though some were in Birmingham, Sheffield and Manchester. The LCDTU included a few non-CPers, but meetings weren't publicised and Hiles issued invitations. In December the LCDTU Conference 'against the wage freeze, unemployment and in defence of our trade unions' attracted 671 delegates from 201 shop stewards' committees, 130 union branches, fifteen district committees, sixteen trades councils and nine union defence committees. No LCDTU minutes were circulated. Soon after, Hiles had his ASW card removed for activity 'detrimental' to the union.

In January 1967 an internal CP document, 'Ultra-Left Groupings', noted 'this curious organisation', IS. 'Many people are confused by its denunciation of both Trotskyists and Communists', its refusal to make 'a distinction between the capitalist and socialist states' and its being against 'all bombs and all bosses everywhere'. Paul Foot's pamphlets on race relations and 'anti-capitalist questions' were 'useful', but *Labour Worker* was a puzzle, because it was 'for workers' control and nationalisation to be fought for by developing a national shop stewards and rank and file militant movement *against* the weight of the organised trade union movement'. Betty Reid acknowledged that IS had 'some young and committed and extremely active socialists' and produced 'often useful and well prepared material', so 'it may well be possible to find common ground with individual members'.

Sunley's got injunctions restraining pickets from 'watching or besetting' their Horseferry Road site in London and wanted damages for 'unlawful conspiracy'. Building workers from all over the city volunteered to picket if any were charged with contempt of court, but Mr Justice James allowed six men to picket peacefully. By February eighty were picketing Myton's Barbican site. IS had 400 mainly student members, but eight were arrested at the Barbican picket, where their comrade Frank Campbell was a steward.

In February Jim Hiles issued 651 credentials for the LCDTU Conference and delegates arrived from 133 union branches and 103 shop stewards' committees.

In March the NFBTO and NFBTE agreed that the Myton's Works Committee shouldn't be re-employed. An ASW official failed to convince all except five men to go back, so he threatened to turn a blind eye to scabs. Workers at Turriffs' and Laing's sites voted to support the Myton pickets and set up a Joint Sites Committee.

In April, 450 pickets stopped a scab coach, but the ASW expelled Lou Lewis for disobeying instructions to lift the picket. (He was later reinstated, but banned from holding union credentials for three years. The big contractors blacklisted him for six.) His comrade, the ASW London District Secretary, Jack Rusca got his job back in August.

Ray Gunter, the Minister of Labour, was the Cabinet's key link to union officials. He was a fierce opponent of militants and hated CPers, so the NFBTE rushed to him for support in the Barbican and Horseferry Road disputes. In May he set up a Court of Inquiry under 67-year-old Scottish Appeal Court judge, Lord Cameron, with Pat Lowry, Personnel Director of British Leyland, and Danny McGarvey of the Amalgamated Society of Boilermakers. They had completed their work by August. Paul Foot's *The Anti Cameron Report* noted that Sunley's managers accepted responsibility for provoking a strike. But while the report accepted their need for 'private' meetings with the NFBTO President and a senior civil servant, it attacked the stewards for 'secret and subversive' meetings, called the Joint Sites Committee 'unnecessary', noted that Henry and Lewis had recruited for the CP on site and recommended that the NFBTO define and restrict stewards' powers and discipline those who failed to comply.

In September the LCDTU lobbied Parliament. Hugh Scanlon— who had left the CP in 1954, but was a firm supporter of the Broad Left—became President of the Amalgamated Engineering Union, thanks to strong CP support, even though the dissident CPer Reg Birch was also a candidate. Birch was expelled from the CP.

In October there was another 'balance of payments' crisis and 'run on the pound'. The Chancellor of the Exchequer, Roy Jenkins, persuaded the Cabinet to devalue the pound, which hurt workers' living standards far more than shareholders' dividends.

In November Sunley's management and senior union officials secretly met a senior civil servant and then put an advertisement in the papers, demanding a return to work at Horseferry Road. Next morning 2,000 police—some on horses—attacked pickets and allowed scabs to reopen the site. The strikers went back on the divisive bonus scheme and with no limit on overtime, while the Works Committee were not allowed bonus or overtime and were spied on continuously. Henry was sacked for refusing to work on an unsafe scaffold, but was reinstated through procedure. Site managers changed, but the Works Committee demanded union cards from lorry drivers, persuaded lumpers to leave and negotiated an orderly run-down, with the stewards being the last to leave.

By the end of 1967 over 300,000 building workers were unorganised and many were lumpers. The NFBTO unions had 417,000 members. The TGWU had 56,000 of them, the ASPD 60,000 and the AUBTW 81,000; but the ASW had 120,000 and wielded great influence at national negotiations.

In Place of Strife

In 1965 Harold Wilson had set up a Royal Commission on Trade Unions and Employers' Associations, under Lord Donovan. In June 1968 its report had 'no hesitation in saying that the prevalence of unofficial strikes, and their tendency... to increase, have such serious economic implications that measures to deal with them are urgently necessary'. The growing gap between basic pay and earnings was cutting profits and dividends.

The Tories used the Donovan report to bolster their *Fair Deal at Work* and encouraged 'responsible trade unionism' by insisting on compulsory secret ballots on an employer's 'last offer' and criminalising sympathy strikes and blacking to win closed shops.

Roy Jenkins reintroduced prescription charges and put off raising the school leaving age. Twenty Eight Labour MPs abstained on the key vote. Paul Foot now worked full-time for *Private Eye* and his *The Politics of Harold Wilson* tore apart the Labour government's record. After the collapse of the partly prefabricated—'systems built'—Ronan Point tower block in East London, Foot investigated corruption in the building industry. A weekly *Socialist Worker* was launched in September, edited by Protz, with a print order of 5,000.

The CP condemned the Russian invasion of Czechoslovakia in August, but claimed only 30,000 members, of whom 49 percent did not pay the 5p weekly dues, while the income of as much as £100,000 a year from the Soviet Union declined sharply. The new programme, *The British Road to Socialism*, aimed for a socialist majority in Parliament through mass struggle and unity between the CP and the Labour Left, especially in the union bureaucracies.

Kevin Halpin was born in 1927. He became AEU convenor at Briggs Bodies and at Fords, but was victimised in 1962. In 1968 he supported the Russian invasion of Czechoslovakia. In November, together with Lou Lewis and Jim Hiles, he argued that the LCDTU aimed 'to activate the official machinery of the unions and TUC, not to replace it'. Many CP militants were not in geographical branches and industrial branches declined, while a few of them won union positions and delegacies to union conferences and the TUC.

The NFBTO conceded the first wage cut accepted by any union since the General Strike; but there was an acute shortage of skilled labour and big contractors in London and Birmingham paid 'plus rates' that could double the nationally negotiated basic wage.

Wilson's 'Kitchen Cabinet' wanted to act as 'referee' between capital and labour, but the TUC and the Labour Party Conference opposed a Prices and Incomes Bill; so Wilson asked Barbara Castle to draft a White Paper. In January 1969 *In Place of Strife* sought to end unofficial strikes with compulsory secret ballots and a 'cooling-off period' and fine union officials who failed to police stewards.

The CP published demands from union bodies where it remained influential and wanted a recall of the TUC and a 24-hour strike. By late that month the LCDTU felt confident enough to call for a one-day stoppage. In the event, somewhere between 65,000 and 150,000 came out on 27 February, but outside Scotland and Merseyside the response was sporadic. Militant shop stewards' committees had attended a 2,500 to 3,000-strong lobby of a union conference and Hiles drew up a list of those that would broaden the LCDTU's base while retaining CP control. He invited some non-CPers, but the CP members caucused beforehand. In April the LCDTU Conference attracted 1,700 delegates. The LCDTU had drawn up the resolutions and no amendments were taken from the floor. Delegates urged the TUC to call a national one-day strike on May Day. Kevin Halpin, now the LCDTU chairman, claimed that 50,000 struck in Liverpool and 20,000 in Sheffield on May Day, but various estimates put the national total between 90,000 and 250,000. In June, 56 Labour MPs voted against *In Place of Strife* and the TUC gave a 'solemn and binding undertaking' to try to control strikes; so the Cabinet dropped the Bill.

Before World War Two the CP had followed John Maclean's perspective on full-time trade union officials: 'We will support the officials just as long as they rightly represent the workers, but we will act independently immediately they misrepresent them.' But in 1969 Ramelson argued that 'it's no good having militants at the bottom and not at the top' when there was 'a very important minority of leftwingers at the TUC'. CP militants should go for officials' jobs, align themselves with reformist socialists in the unions and the TUC

General Council and pressurise Labour MPs. That summer the new TGWU General Secretary, Jack Jones, a former International Brigader and a member of the Labour Party's National Executive Committee, was elected with CP support. The TGWU lifted its 20-year-old ban on Communists holding official positions. The CP now had allies at the top of two large unions.

CHAPTER 3

The Building Workers' Charter

A shortage of key cadres

Jim Arnison was born in Salford in 1925. His father worked in a foundry, but by the early 1930s he was on the dole. He acted as Labour Party election agent and brought in CPers to help canvass his ward, but then the Labour Party expelled him. Jim's mother, who brought up four children, was in the CP. She left the Labour Party soon after and was later a Party Congress delegate.

In 1939 Jim left school, became an apprentice plumber and joined the Plumbers', Glaziers, Heating & Domestic Engineering Union. In summer 1942 he joined the YCL and the CP, studied political economy, 'dialectical materialism' and 'anti-Communist propaganda', and believed that the Hitler-Stalin pact was Russia's way of seeking 'respite', after Britain and France refused an alliance.

In 1943, aged eighteen, Arnison was called up for the navy. He trained as a radar operator and in 1944 he joined the crew of a light cruiser. That summer the ship was involved in the Normandy landings. In 1946 he visited Hiroshima. He was demobbed that October, but didn't rejoin the YCL until 1947. By 1953 he was President of his branch of what was now the Plumbers' Trade Union and a delegate to the District Committee. He got a job with Salford Direct Works and was elected as shop steward and then as federation steward. In 1956 he 'welcomed Khruschev's revelations' about Stalin's 'violation of Socialist democracy', but he was troubled by the Hungarian 'uprising'. He left the YCL—aged 31—for the CP and knocked about with an electrician called Dennis Dugen.

In 1961 Arnison was appointed as the full time organiser for the Manchester Area CP. He and his wife stuck the long days and low pay until 1964 when he got a start on a site where lumpers worked, but insisted on being directly employed. In 1965 he was appointed as the northern correspondent of the *Daily Worker*. In

1966 the Eccles CP parliamentary candidate got 1,239 votes. Labour got 25,000.

In 1966, when up to 200,000 building workers were on the lump, several young CP shop stewards from large organised sites built the unofficial Manchester Building Workers' Forum and the Merseyside Shop Stewards' Building Operatives' Committee, on the model of the London Joint Sites Committee. Arnison now worked for the rebranded *Morning Star*. In 1968 the younger, often graduate comrades' response to the Russian tanks that invaded Czechoslovakia convinced him that there was 'a shortage of key cadres of working class stock in the leading positions', but in 1969 the 'Tankies' were politically defeated at Party Congress. Arnison recalled 'particular resentment at site level' over the 'infamous productivity-flexibility' national agreement of February 1970. The CP had a broad base in the industry, but the initiative for a national 'rank and file' organisation came from left wing site militants, and they had to overcome some internal CP opposition.

In April 1970 the unofficial London, Manchester and Merseyside organisations held a conference in Manchester. Many of the 288 delegates, including 159 from 54 sites, were CPers. Alan Abrahams was in the chair. (He had joined the CP aged 26 in 1957, and was a member of Ellesmere Port ASW and responsible to the party's Merseyside Area Committee for its 'Building Group'.)

The Building Workers' Charter 'became the property of the meeting':

* £1 per hour basic rate of pay for a five-day, 35-hour week.
* Three weeks holiday with full pay plus the retention of Christmas Day and Boxing Day as statutory holidays, and the introduction of New Year's Day and May Day as additional paid holidays.
* A full comprehensive pension scheme...
* De-casualisation of the building industry...
* Adequate safety and welfare regulations...
* Democratise the trade unions by making:
  A) Delegate Conferences policy making bodies.
  B) All TU officials submit themselves for election every three years and branch officials every year.
  C) The disbanding of Selection Boards.
* Full recognition of elected stewards and regular area meetings.
* Establishing 100 percent compulsory TU membership.
* Total opposition to the 'lump'.

* Full protection of shop stewards.
* The establishing of one fully democratic union for the building industry.
* Full nationalisation and public ownership of the building industry.

Dennis Dugen of the Salford branch of the recently merged EEPTU became national secretary and a collection was taken to finance a paper.

Between 1958 and 1969 the ASW and ASPD had lost 40,000 members and in June 1970 they agreed to merge. Lump contracts had doubled in five years, one worker died and twenty were injured on average each weekday, and most union officials were a serious threat to stewards' ability to negotiate decent wages and conditions at site level. Speakers at the AUBTW Conference insisted on a merger with the new ASWPD that guaranteed 'full democracy'.

The turnout at the June 1970 General Election was the lowest for 35 years. Labour's vote was nearly 2,000,000 lower than in 1951 and the government fell, as did the anti-lump Construction Industry (Contracts) Bill. CP candidates averaged 654 votes and won no seats.

Bill Jones chaired an unofficial Merseyside Committee meeting. (He was a member of Kirkby ASWPD, Chairman of Huyton and Kirkby Trades Council and a delegate to Liverpool Trades Council, the CP's Merseyside Area Committee and its North West District Committee.) 300 building workers made a 'huge collection' and ordered 1,000 copies of the new Charter paper.

The Building Workers' Charter: Organ of the Rank and File Building Workers, appeared early in August. It was produced by the London Joint Sites Committee and cost sixpence (about 27p today). It noted that various union claims included £1 an hour, three weeks' continuous annual holiday, withdrawal of the productivity and penal clauses, a National Building Corporation, more Direct Labour schemes, an end to labour only, the amalgamation of building unions with the fullest democracy, and in the AUBTW's case, all the *Charter* demands. Craftsmen's basic pay was around £17.50, yet some exhibition workers got £29. Lou Lewis stressed that the *Charter* would report struggles, learn from failures, generalise successes and publicise meetings—especially union elections. Charter area secretaries were in place in London (Lou Lewis), Liverpool (Frank Marsh, a CP ASWPD steward) and Manchester (Kevin Greene).

SW Litho had printed 10,000 copies. In spite of party discipline, CP militants had used the International Socialists' press.

The Industrial Relations Act

In August 1970 the Tories' Industrial Relations Bill aimed to empower an Industrial Relations Court to fine unions that indulged in an 'unfair industrial practice', sought to outlaw 'secondary picketing'—asking for solidarity—and was very similar to *In Place of Strife*. The TUC opposed it. Castle called it a 'Blacklegs' Charter'.

In September the *Charter* reported that police had told 2,000 Ellesmere Port strikers to move onto the pavement, but there wasn't enough room. Police immediately made arrests, kept them until 10.00pm and refused any calls to solicitors. 5,000 picketed the court, where 44 were fined and bound over to keep the peace for two years. The *Charter* now had orders from Northern Ireland, Perth, Dundee, Glasgow, Edinburgh, Workington, Barnsley and Corby.

In October the AUBTW leaders transferred members and assets to the ASWPD. If the members voted for it in a ballot, the two unions would hold separate conferences in 1971, but officials would operate under the direction of appointed regional secretaries.

The *Charter* reported that Dennis Dugen, Alan Abrahams and Bert Smith had addressed a Stoke meeting. (Smith was convenor at a small site in St Helen's, Chairman of Manchester Building Workers' Forum and a leading CPer.) They called a meeting to establish a 'Charter Group', ninety people turned up and CPer Tommy Walker became North Staffs Area Secretary. Members of the unofficial Merseyside Committee told a Wigan meeting that the paper's 'editorial committee' would provide speakers and cash. At Widnes Abrahams 'condemned the inadequacy' of union leaders.

The November *Charter* reported that the AUTBW Manchester Divisional Council had passed three *Charter* demands. Lou Lewis had addressed McAlpine workers in Runcorn about the LCDTU strike call for 8 December. The paper needed cash to be 'viable'.

The LCDTU issued 1,800 Conference credentials to 300 branches and districts, 155 stewards' committees, 55 trades councils and four union ECs. Labour MP Syd Bidwell spoke. The Conference Declaration committed delegates to 'all forms of activity including industrial action' to stop the Industrial Relations Bill becoming law.

The *Charter* reported that '1,700 delegates from all over Britain' had shown 'a determination, supported by many TU officials, to fight NOW'. *Charter* sales had topped 10,000 and it had 'strong contacts' in Widnes, Stevenage and South-East Essex. 25 stewards from eight Glasgow sites heard Sonny McGowan stress the need to organise to strike on 8 December. In London Myton management had locked the gates and called the police, but the workers went off site and voted to come out. The ASWPD West of Scotland Committee had called a mass meeting on the 6th, but the national leaders instructed members not to attend or strike on the 8th.

The LCDTU claimed that 600,000 came out on 8 December, including some Clydeside sites, plus 20,000 in Liverpool and 100,000 in Manchester. Other estimates were that between 350,000 and 750,000 came out nationally, including 100,000 in London and Scotland, as well as Manchester. It was the biggest political strike since 1926 and it was 'unofficial'. In one year trade union membership had increased by 15 percent.

In spite of rapid inflation, the NFBTE refused to bring negotiations forward and to delete a Working Rule that legitimised the lump. The NFBTO wanted £30 for 35 hours and threatened to withdraw from negotiations. The battle lines were drawn.

SW later reported that site managers at Laing's, the main contractors at the £13,000,000 St Thomas's Hospital site in London, had sacked 21 directly employed carpenters early in 1970 and hired lumpers from the subbies, Whelan and Grant. The ASWPD supported the dispute that followed, but then withdrew recognition and disciplined two officials. George Smith and two EC members negotiated a Working Rule that allowed 'bona fide' subbies to operate, so long as their employees' union subs were paid. Two Laing's directors admitted that they paid block subs because union officials helped to keep out 'disruptives'. Whelan and Grant joined the NFBTE and paid tax-free handouts of up to £30 a week to selected joiners. One landlord reportedly cashed £11,000's worth of cheques a few days before Christmas.

Laurie Flynn was born in 1946 into a working class Edinburgh family. His father was an activist in the National Union of Printing, Bookbinding & Paper Workers and both parents were members of the Independent Labour Party. Laurie went to Edinburgh High School and then to the London School of Economics. He left in 1968 with a degree in Sociology, worked in an ink factory for a few months and then as a clerk at *The Times* for about a year. In 1969 he joined IS. He helped to produce the rank and file paper, *The Dockworker*, and wrote for *Socialist Worker*. 880 IS members now sold 8,000 copies a week. The IS teachers' paper, *Rank and File*, was supported by dissident CP members of the National Union of Teachers.

By 1970 Flynn worked at *Construction News*, which sold 50,000 copies a week and made more money for the Thomson Organisation than the *Sunday Times*, because the advertising revenue was pure profit. But it became 'contaminated with honest journalism', thanks to the editor, a liberal Jewish refugee from Nazi Germany, and Flynn, who had contacts with the *Sunday Times* 'Insight' team and investigated building workers' problems. *Construction News* confirmed that 'sweeteners' were paid on some London sites 'to keep the carpenter gangs working quickly and stop union attempts to organise proper bonus targets'. The McAlpine's Christmas party at the Dorchester (which they owned) included enough Tory ministers to 'make it virtually impossible to get a cabinet quorum', Lord Citrine (a former TUC General Secretary), Lord Soskice (a former Labour Home Secretary), Ray Gunter (a former Labour minister of labour, but now a director of Securicor) and Lord Thompson, the owner of *Construction News*.

By late 1970 nationally up to half of the 1,250,000 building workers were on the lump. The AUTBW had lost around 30,000 members since 1958 (8,000 since 1969) and the ASWPD had lost 18,000 in its first year. Falling subs incomes couldn't support national officials in the manner to which they had become accustomed, so the leaders of seven NFBTO unions with a total of 280,000 members agreed to merge and they appointed George Smith as general secretary. The union would inherit over 100 officials, yet they agreed to appoint twelve regional secretaries and regional organisers. Several Communists had been elected as district secretary. None were successful, but after Ivor Jordan resigned from the CP he was appointed as Regional Secretary for East Anglia.

Early in 1971 the *Charter* Editorial Board consisted of delegates from London, Glasgow and the North West. They hoped that the new union would ban lumpers and supported the LCDTU call for a strike against the Industrial Relations Bill.

On 12 January an estimated 180,000 came out on strike and there was a TUC demonstration against the Bill. In February the AUEW National Committee decided to call for strikes on 1 and 18 March, the day of the Special TUC Congress to discuss the Bill. On 18 March around 1,250,000 came out on strike. An estimated 3,000,000 days had been 'lost' to strikes in engineering, but the Special TUC Congress voted against industrial action by 21 votes to four. They advised unions not to register under the Industrial Relations Act when it became law and to boycott the Industrial Relations Court. On 24 April 700 delegates attended the LCDTU Conference. Bill Jones was chairman. The Conference Resolution called for a campaign to get the Labour Party committed to repealing the Act and making the TUC insist on non-registration and establish 'local campaigning and action committees' based on trade union branches and shop stewards' committees 'to initiate and coordinate local solidarity action with workers who have come into conflict with the law'. The *Morning Star* characterised Trotskyist LCDTU delegates as 'political teddy boys, comics who tell workers how to organise', but 'take care how you criticise Scanlon and Jones'.

Bill Jones also chaired the Charter Conference. The Conference resolution called for a one-day strike and local demonstrations on 8 June to support the demand for £35 for 35 hours. Dennis Dugen acknowledged that the *Charter* hadn't a 'national base' and had 'a weak position' in Yorkshire, the North East and the Midlands. The May *Charter* reported that union regional conferences had passed *Charter* demands and called for industrial action to defeat the lump. In June the LCDTU reiterated the LC conference resolution, but did nothing for the next six months.

In June the new Union of Construction Allied Trades & Technicians had 262,000 members and a deficit of over £380,000, yet all officials' pay was levelled up. The twelve elected Regional Councils would meet every six months and an elected Regional Committee of five would meet monthly. UCATT withdrew from the NFBTO—leading to its demise—and dominated national negotiations. Under this coordinated pressure, the NFBTE agreed in principle to delete the rule that legitimised the lump.

In August, when the Industrial Relations Act became law, the TUC told unions to de-register. The political battle lines were drawn.

Chucked in at the deep end

Dave Ayre's disillusionment with Labour had begun in 1964.

> They shut many pits and subsidised new factories and when people heard about the much better working conditions, many went there. Yet employment was often part-time and once the grants stopped they usually closed. In 1965, as part of its drive for industrial 'efficiency'—making British capitalism more competitive at the workers' expense—the Redundancy Payments Act encouraged workers to sell their jobs.
>
> In September 1965 Reuben Barker and Bill Kerriss were elected to Crook Branch Committee. In November, after Russ King was elected as a Northern Divisonal Organiser, I was chucked in the deep end as branch secretary, 'pro tem'.

In 1966 I was a delegate to Trades Council meetings and the AUBTW National Delegate Conference. Crook branch complained about the local council's use of subbies and reminded the Executive Council of our strong opposition to the government's prices and incomes policy. In June I was elected as branch secretary and Bill Kerriss was elected as chairman. We supported the National Union of Seamen's strike and the Trades Council organised for seamen to speak at workplace meetings. We also got to know about the Myton dispute and tried to pressurise the Northern Divisional Council and the EC to give support. Our success was minimal, but members got regular updates.

The NFBTO-NFBTE pay deals had been sacrosanct in the North East, but in February 1967, following a TV programme called *The Lump*, Crook AUBTW discussed 'the present jungle like state of affairs in the industry'. The Divisional Council organised picketing of 'labour only' sites—especially those working weekends—and made sure that members understood that they could get a better deal through collectivism; but union membership figures declined. In May we mandated Bill Kerriss to propose a motion at the Divisional Labour Party, demanding the abolition of Selective Employment Tax, which encouraged employers to avoid National Insurance and Income Tax and encouraged 'labour only'. The Labour Party told us that delegates must be members. Bill was a Communist and nobody else was keen to go.

Labour-controlled Durham County Council didn't employ brickies on most council house contracts, because they used prefabrication, and a major employer, Consett Iron Company, was threatened with closure. Falling union membership, the lump, SET, unemployment, redundancy pay and Labour's pro-employer policies made it harder still. Reuben Barker was sacked and Bill Kerriss was suspended, but with members' support and Russ King's negotiating we got them reinstated.

Bill, Reuben and I used the TUC distance-learning scheme, based at Tillicoultry. We also attended the excellent AUBTW weekend schools, courses and seminars, where one influential teacher was Owen Parsons, a Marxist lawyer whose firm represented our union. We had many memorable arguments and developed a broader, more political frame of reference for our trade unionism. In 1968 Crook branch discussed the US involvement in Vietnam, condemned Enoch Powell's racist

The Flying Pickets

speech, demanded the freeing of Greek political prisoners and nominated me as a delegate to the next Labour Party Conference.

In January 1969 Crook AUBTW supported the amalgamation with the ASWPD, but was split on *In Place of Strife* until May, when we held an informed debate and condemned the 'Penal Clauses'. In June I reported back on the TUC Special Conference that backed the Labour Cabinet. Regional AUBTW officials like Barney McIntyre supported *In Place of Strife* and, given their ready access to sites, this was a warning to those of us in opposition. However, Reuben was on the Branch Committee and Bill was nominated as a delegate to the National Delegate Conference and the Trades Council, where several other members didn't belong to the Labour Party. The Trades Council took a leading role in organising the thousands who went to the LCDTU London demonstration from County Durham and sent a delegate to the Teesside Federation of Trades Councils. After Labour lost the General Election, Jim Harper of the NFBTO told us that *In Place of Strife* would have been 'a tremendous asset to the building industry', while the Tories' *Fair Deal at Work* promised 'a tough time'.

Laurie Pringle, a CPer who was Secretary of Newburn ASWPD, and a man from Durham City ASWPD were delegates to the Charter Conference that April and I may have heard about it from them. The Charter's concerns chimed in with ours and it looked like a way of changing our union's culture. We invited Dennis Dugen. The members expected some kind of firebrand, full of rhetoric, but Denis was a quietly spoken man and he patiently explained the Charter's aims and strategy. We thought he was a good lad. At the next branch meeting we affiliated, but we weren't aware of other branches in our region doing so.

That autumn I found my first TUC Congress stimulating, mainly for the discussions in the AUBTW caucus. In the plenary sessions I would have liked more vigorous support on the labour only issue and wondered if our union's motions were ill drafted. I felt that too much time was spent on Czechoslovakia; but the Inland Revenue Staff Federation delegate's report on tax fiddles by the self-employed was very useful. My abiding impression was of the vast field of trade union, social and political affairs that the TUC deals with. It got me away from the rather parochial attitude of the branch and our union.

Dave met Jim French at regional AUBTW meetings.

In the mid-1960s Jim had gone to work at William Brown's Sawmills in Darlington for more money.

It was an old-established firm owned by paternalistic Tories. The boss knew all the men by their first names, but nearly everyone was on a different rate of pay. I was elected as steward, got interested in Darlington ASPD branch and became its treasurer. The two ASW branches in the town were quite active and the secretary of one, Charlie Lowther, was in the CP. When I became ASPD Branch Secretary I attended Charlie's branch for guidance. I was always interested in what he had to say. Our ASPD branch wasn't affiliated to the North East Coast Friendly Conference, but Charlie's ASW and Albert Lund's AUBTW branches were.

In June 1970 Darlington ASW and ASPD became the ASWPD. In December Jim and Charlie went to the LCDTU Conference.

Darlington ASWPD affiliated to the Charter. Charlie got hold of copies of the *Charter* and I sold them. Yuills allowed me onto their site near Darlington, but when they found out what the paper was advocating I was escorted off again. Ideal Decorators in Darlington adopted a more heavy-handed approach. I was grabbed by the arm, had it pushed up my back, was thrown into the back lane and told not to return, '*or else*'.

Charlie Lowther was connected with Lou Lewis and Pete Carter.

Birmingham Building Workers' Joint Shop Stewards Committee

Pete Carter was born in 1939. He joined the Young Communist League in 1960 and by the mid-1960s he was its national organiser. In 1968 he and other YCL leaders had to explain themselves to the general secretary, John Gollan, for calling a meeting about legalising drugs, but in spite of a threat of disciplinary action, the meeting went ahead. Carter became a plasterer in Birmingham. In 1969 he joined the AUBTW and was elected as a steward and then as convenor, but by 1970 he was blacklisted. He got a job on a Bryant site under an assumed name. Bryant's annual profits were over £1,000,000 and its dividend was 14 percent. Birmingham was a 'lump town' and Carter was the only city activist at the first Charter conference.

Ken Barlow had been an apprentice joiner in North Staffordshire. After serving in the forces in World War Two he became an ASW official. He was a left wing member of the Labour Party. In January 1971 he was appointed as UCATT Midland Regional Secretary. When he took over in June he found two organised sites in Birmingham. He won the support of the Regional Council and a 'core of shop stewards and activists' and the situation rapidly improved. National leaders 'left, right and centre for different reasons *hated* the *Charter*' and 'on three occasions I came very close to being dismissed because of my admitted association'.

By summer a company called Labour Force had set up an office in Birmingham. Nationally, they claimed to represent 150,000 workers who wouldn't strike, go-slow, ask for overtime, holiday pay, several days' notice and severance pay, and would pay their own Income Tax and National Insurance. They had screened out 'troublemakers' and their Security Department could plant agents to provide employers with 'a complete appraisal of unauthorised happenings' and reports on those 'suspected of causing dissension or inciting employees to defection'. They could also supply guards, mobile patrols, dogs and armoured vans. Contractors could have men ready to work 'all the hours you like'.

In August UCATT Midland Regional Council began a campaign to 'Kill the Lump' and win £1 an hour. Carter became Secretary of the Birmingham Building Workers Joint Shop Stewards Committee. They organised a 150-strong picket of Labour Force's offices, where the manager claimed to be against the lump, but was adamant about 'the right of an ordinary working man to be self-employed'. Applications to join UCATT flooded in and ten sites were organised. Carter wrote the front-page story for the August *Charter*, whose paid sale of under 5,000 didn't cover its costs.

In September workers at Bryant's huge Woodgate Valley site claimed parity with the firm's other sites. Site managers sacked two stewards for being a minute late. Delegates from organised sites visited 77 others; a loudspeaker van toured the city centre and Barlow did two television interviews. Posters and thousands of leaflets argued for an official half-day strike and a demonstration against the City Council's contracts with firms that used lumpers. Bryant decasualised Woodgate Valley, but managers imposed a totally unacceptable bonus scheme. The BJSSC and union officials asked the men to elect stewards, and when managers tried to sack the brickies and labourers' stewards, they went on strike.

The October *Charter* noted that the BJSSC had put big city contractors on notice to end the lump and the TGWU had promised to stop lorries crossing picket lines. Bryant were reportedly blacklisting union members. The NFBTE had refused to discuss the national claim, so pressure should go on union negotiators by preparing 'to go into battle to win our rights'.

Woodgate Vale managers refused to negotiate, so all 180 men came out and UCATT Midland Regional Council made it official. Twenty sites stopped for a day. Carter led a march and 1,200 lobbied the City Council, including a delegation from the unofficial Merseyside Committee and stewards from Upper Clyde Shipbuilders, which had been occupied against closure. A Labour MP 'made it clear' that a Labour government would 'outlaw' the lump.

Next day Woodgate Vale management sacked the strikers. A Regional Disputes Panel found in the men's favour, but Bryant called for a National Disputes Panel. Men from four other Bryant's sites went on official strike and Woodgate Vale workers went back to a lump-free site. Six more Bryant sites were being organised.

In November the NFBTE offered craftsmen £1.20 a week. Industrial action became a distinct possibility, but UCATT was geared up for 500,000 members and administrative costs kept rising and benefits shrank. The EC looked for 'savings' and threatened to close the Liverpool office. A staff member's job was on the line, but her sisters in the Manchester office came out in solidarity. Eric Hughes, the appointed North West Regional Secretary, crossed their picket line, but the CPer Bert Smith—now the elected Regional Council Chairman—joined the pickets. The Liverpool woman did a 'work-in', the District Committee paid her wages, the Manchester women refused overtime and the EC backed down.

The Tories introduced the Tax Exemption Certificate. Anyone could now become 'self-employed', call their home their 'office' and their partners their 'staff', and add in electricity, gas, transport, and telephone costs and the fees of an accountant to deduct these 'business expenses' from Income Tax. There were now 150,000 unemployed building workers and 300,000 lumpers.

Hired, fired and hired again

Dave Ayre recalls: 'I read the *Star* occasionally, got on well with Communists and went to CP meetings with other members of Crook AUBTW. I particularly recall a talk on Ireland by Desmond Greaves.'

Early in 1971 Crook Trades Council supported the post workers' strike. In February Dave, Reuben Barker and Bill Kerris went to the TUC demonstration against the Industrial Relations Bill. The Trades Council gave £2 to UCS, and Bill Kerriss was the delegate to the Teesside Federation of Trades Councils.

Reuben recalls:

After the Hepworth Group bought the pipeworks, all they wanted were the orders, so they made us redundant. I went for a job at Lax & Sons.

'Come in. Just a minute till I answer this phone. Is there something we can do for you?' This was the senior boss.

'Have you anything for a single bricklayer?'

'Yes. Can you read drawing specifications? We have this job starting in a few weeks, but we can fix you up on other sites. We pay guaranteed wage, holiday stamps, bonus, and sick pay. Can you start tomorrow?'

I gave that a lot of thought, but then I asked the wrong question: 'Do you recognise the union?'

'Better come back next week till we think about it.'

I walked to the door, because I'd been told that they didn't care for unions, but then the senior boss's son, who was also a director, said: 'We employ thirty men and you are the only one to tell us about being in a union. I want you to start tomorrow.' His father disagreed strongly, but he stood his ground and wrote down my phone number.

'If you change your mind, give me a ring.'

'Start tomorrow, eight o'clock. A van in the yard will take you to the site.'

In ten minutes I'd been hired, fired and hired again. I could have told them how many men were in the union, yet even though they had kept quiet, the firm was abiding by Working Rules and had a private pension scheme. Being honest was the best thing to have done.

Three weeks later I was elected as steward. When some of the men started to tell me what was wrong with the union, I replied: 'Let me tell you what's wrong: you aren't in it.' I decided to keep good relations with the bosses because I'd learned at union schools about the need for good communications, so when members came with complaints I always made sure that they came into the office with me to talk about it and if I wanted anything for myself, I'd offer to pay for it.

It was the best firm I ever worked for. The work was varied—housing estates, a police station, churches, farm offices, renovations, factories and steelworks. If you did a good job in a reasonable time there was no harassment.

Dave Ayre was working with two brickies and a hod-carrier from Willington, and Dave, being the youngest, sometimes had to take the hod. They got a 'kick in' with Edgar Lawson, a Darlington firm, on the extensions to the Technical College. It was lump work—they were paid according to the number of bricks they laid—but they were desperate, the price seemed fair, the weather was good and it was either that or the dole. The job was 'dead walling'—building between steel stanchions—but the glazed bricks had to be soaked, so they became heavy and took the skin off their fingers, because there was no protective gear. Dave had to leave home at 6.00am, walk a couple or so miles to Crook to catch the first train to Darlington and then get a bus to the site. He got home after 6.30pm.

That summer Dave was Crook branch delegate to the Labour Party Conference. As secretary, he informed the union EC about the branch's 'strong views' about not registering under the Industrial Relations Act. He was also a delegate to the Northern Regional Conference and he and Bill Kerriss went to the Teesside Federation of Trades Councils' meeting on unemployment as Trades Council delegates. The branch sent £2.50 (worth about £25 today) to the UCS 'fighting fund' and asked the Regional Committee to follow suit. (They sent £20.) In autumn the branch sent a letter of solidarity to Aston branch for 'their struggle against the lump'.

Late that year Reuben began going to Crook Trades Council and Crook branch paid for seats on its bus to the TUC demonstration against unemployment in Newcastle. The branch's nominee, Gerry Cassidy, was elected to the incoming UCATT General Council. The branch expressed 'alarm' at 'the apparent unfair representation' for the first conference, but Dave was subsequently nominated as a delegate. Charlie Lowther, the elected Regional Council Chairman, suggested they should 'campaign vigorously' for £30 for 35 hours. Dave's gang had no guaranteed minimum pay for bad weather.

About a week before Christmas, our labourer was ill, and we were working on the 'top lift' of a scaffold, building a tricky double chimney-flue in a blizzard. Being 'self-employed' we could get no dole, so we got soaked through and frozen solid. It was a hard lesson. I knew nothing about Adam Smith and

Karl Marx's theories, but I learned that shortage of work and an abundance of labour power equalled excessive exploitation. I'd been sacked so many times at Christmas that my kids thought it was part of the Father Christmas story, except that the 'sack' was empty. It was then that I truly learned where my politics lay.

Early in 1972 Crook UCATT BB [Bricklayers' Branch] 145 elected Bill Kerriss, the convenor of the council's Direct Labour Department, as chairman, Dave Ayre as secretary, and Reuben Barker as treasurer and Trades Council delegate. After the NFBTE rejected the union claim, Crook UCATT suggested to the EC 'that national and regional campaigns be implemented'. The motion to the National Delegate Conference called for a 'strong stand' to achieve at least £30 for 35 hours and an extra week's holiday. A solidarity letter went to the National Union of Mineworkers.

The Brum breakthrough

The NUM General Secretary, Joe Gormley, was a Labour Party rightwinger, but by late 1971 the Broad Left activists had a strong organisation at pit and district level. A conference voted unanimously for an overtime ban and a ballot on strike action produced a 58.8 percent majority on an 85 percent turnout. Attitudes hardened when the Tories refused to fund an acceptable offer. On 9 January 1972 the NUM went on its first all-out national strike since 1926. All 289 pits were closed and 'flying pickets'—groups of strikers in cars or buses—asked for solidarity at power stations.

In January management at Bryant's Woodgate Vale site in Birmingham sacked two directly employed men who refused to work with non-union labour. Pete Carter used an assumed name to get a job at a Bryant's site, but he was soon sacked, and when he returned managers accused him of trespass. Activists campaigned to get him reinstated, but then John Shortland got the same treatment.

On 8 February the Tories declared a state of emergency. On the 10th, as NUM members picketed Saltley Coke Depot, they were joined by hundreds of engineers and also by building workers from a demonstration outside the court in support of Carter and Shortland. The police closed the gates. It was a famous strategic victory.

The February *Charter* welcomed the 'well known militant leftwingers' elected to the UCATT General Council. Midland

Regional Council supported the Building Workers' National Delegate Conference—'Charter' was dropped—which was to be in Birmingham, where CP brickie Phil Beyer was Area Secretary.

Delegations from UCATT London Regional Council and London, Liverpool, Birmingham and Stoke Charter groups lobbied the national negotiations and demanded an end to the lump. Union negotiators rejected an extra £1.40 a week for craftsmen. George Smith addressed the lobby. Lou Lewis announced that Pete Carter and Kevin Halpin would speak at a meeting about wages, the lump, blacklisting and the Industrial Relations Act.

The Birmingham Joint Shop Stewards Committee organised a strike of 800 men from sixteen of Bryant's sites and a demonstration outside their head office. Carter gave Bryant one week to comply with their demands. Soon after, Phil Beyer went to a site that needed bricklayers and tried to get a job, but was turned away. Carter addressed the angry workforce outside the gate and within days the legal proceedings against him and Shortland had been dropped as 'an act of good faith'. They were both to get jobs on sites where they'd been told they would never work again and Bryant would encourage employees to join UCATT. 2,000 men got a 50 percent rise—almost seven times the NFBTE offer. Craftsmen got £30 for a forty-hour week and labourers got £26. A Gilbert Ash site—a Bovis subsidiary—struck for parity.

Because of the NUM strike there were massive lay-offs in industry and a Tory-appointed Court of Inquiry decided that miners were a 'special case'. They accepted a 22 percent rise and went back to work on 28 February. That day the Tory government announced a £35,000,000 grant to keep UCS afloat. Soon afterwards a minister argued that the Industrial Relations Court should penalise strikers for breach of contract when 'due notice' wasn't given and use criminal law against the 'unfair industrial practice' of mass picketing.

On 7 March the NFBTE negotiators asked for a nine-day adjournment. Soon after, forty lumpers at a Cubitt site in Birmingham joined UCATT, went on strike and were joined on the picket line by twenty directly employed men. Carter organised a 5p weekly levy across the city for them and the Gilbert Ash strikers. He told managers that if they tried to break the picket he would 'march 1,000 building workers to the site and do a "Saltley gate" on them'. He also called on the government to amnesty unpaid Income Tax and National Insurance, so that employers couldn't threaten to expose evaders. Within days Cubitt's men won their case through procedure and began fighting for parity with Bryant workers.

Subbies sacked five men at a London site. The TGWU's Hugh Cassidy and UCATT's Alan Tattam addressed 400 workers. They voted to strike if the men were not reinstated in a week.

UCATT North West Regional Council backed a 5,000-strong Liverpool demonstration in favour of the national claim. Liverpool Teaching Hospital delegates, the London Charter Group and several major sites lobbied the negotiations in London. 10,000 Manchester building workers stopped for a day and 1,000 demonstrated.

On the 30th union negotiators rejected an extra £2 a week for craftsmen. That would mean that those with economic dependents would still be £3 below the Family Income Supplement threshold.

The *Star* reported that sixty stewards at a Glasgow Charter meeting heard Pete Carter call for better pay and conditions and raised £100 for the May Day demonstration. Eighty delegates 'representing' 4,000 Birmingham workers were authorised to vote for a strike. UCATT North West and Northern Regional Councils congratulated the Midland Regional Council for supporting the Charter Conference. (This isn't in the Northern Region minutes.)

In the April *Charter* Pete Carter reported on the 'Brum breakthrough'. Ken Barlow was 'out with the lads on the picket every day'. They had recruited 2,000 members and 100 stewards had been elected in a year. Whatever was won nationally would be added to the local agreement and they were negotiating for dartboards, dominoes and cards in site cabins. The *Star* reported that Carter was convinced that the NFBTE had pressured Bryant into reneging on the agreement. Barlow had 'some differences' with the EC, and Bryant wanted to 'resort to previous anti-union practices', yet two 'unsuitable' brickies were 'fitted into gangs' by the lads on site.

At the CP Merseyside Area Committee, Tony McClelland argued that the party manifesto should be distributed on sites and there should be a 'builders public meeting'. The minutes noted: 'In all struggles [there] must be [a] conscious effort to build the Party'.

I was a fighter on the job

Des Warren was born in Broughton near Chester in 1937. During the war his father was in the army and his mother drove a horse and cart on a milk round. After the war his father worked in the steel industry. Des went to a Chester secondary modern school and left at fifteen. Reportedly, he trained as a chef in the posh Grosvenor Hotel and then worked in the kitchen of the De Havilland factory for nine months, but got bored. He got a job as a bricklayer's mate, but packed it in after three days—'It was mid-winter, and I didn't fancy that lark one bit'—so he went to Crewe as an apprentice painter and decorator. In 1955, before his apprenticeship ended, he began his national service in the Royal Horse Artillery.

From 1957 Warren worked as a painter near Chester and in Essex and London. In 1961 he qualified as a steel-fixer and by 1963 he was working at McAlpine's Vauxhall factory site at Ellesmere Port. He was left out of the discussions on wages and conditions and CPer Alan Abrahams told him it was because he was a foreman. 'To get over this I became a shop steward, but then the management said I couldn't be a steward and a foreman, so I stopped being a foreman.' CPers were 'doing most of the fighting' and in 1964 he joined the party in Liverpool, but he was 'never encouraged to take up any political work or given any political instruction'. Party leaders were 'handling the political questions'. 'I was a fighter on the job.'

Warren worked for Myton's at the Barbican in London and fought against the lump. In 1966 he and his comrades attended rank and file seamen's meetings and invited them to theirs. He believed that right wing union leaders connived with contractors to get rid of leading stewards and especially CPers. He got blacklisted and went north, but his partner left and he couldn't find work, so the kids had to live with relations or foster-parents or go into care. In 1969, as a taxi driver in Liverpool, he met Elsa. They married and in 1970 they and the kids moved to Prestatyn. Warren used a false name to get a job on the sea wall, but he was sacked in days.

In June 1971 four members of the unofficial Merseyside Committee spoke at Prestatyn. Local building workers wanted to know how 'to stop the years of frustration and feeling of let down' by the Chester-based UCATT official, Albert Prest. They elected a committee of thirteen. Billy Regan—a UCATT steward at Cubitt's site in Colwyn Bay, who had been to the Charter Conference—became North Wales Area Secretary.

Warren got a job on Taylor Woodrow's Telephone Exchange contract in Chester and in November there was a strike over lumpers. In December a union-employer National Disputes Panel upheld the Regional Disputes Panel's decision in favour of the strikers and UCATT made the dispute official. Taylor Woodrow management hired scabs, who were escorted onto the site by police, and private investigators to enquire about the stewards. The UCATT regional secretary, Eric Hughes, negotiated a return to work for most men, but the joiners' stewards wouldn't go back at first and two steel-fixers,

The Flying Pickets

including a steward, wouldn't go back at all. The men rejected the deal, put on a picket and drove the lumpers away. In January 1972 Prest told one steward that a manager had told him that the strike was unofficial. The steward contacted the Regional Council. Two days later Hughes told the stewards that he had just heard that strike pay had been stopped to the one member qualified to receive it in December. He negotiated another deal. Scab steel-fixers arrived, but a picket including men from Liverpool, Runcorn, St Helens and Shotton kept them out. Next day management claimed that the steel-fixers' steward had been sacked for hitting a foreman. The National Disputes Panel decided that the he was 'properly discharged in accordance with rule' and was 'not covered by the re-engagement recommendation'. The men demanded that he be reinstated. Another steward, Tony Ledgerton, got a sworn statement that the steel-fixers' steward didn't hit the foreman. The February *Charter* carried a photograph of a picket under a sign for 'Lumpie Woodrow'. Warren was in the middle. The UCATT EC refused to make the dispute official and next day management told the men that anyone on unofficial strike would be sacked. They went back. Warren couldn't find work and a family of seven lived on £23 a week social security.

According to the *Guardian*, Taylor Woodrow pulled out of the contract two years later. Two years after that a building that cost £1,500,000—twice the agreed price—was pulled down as unsafe.

We want £30 now, shorter hours and longer holidays

On 28 April 1972 Pete Carter's full-page *Star* article invited readers to join the CP. According to the *Charter*, 865 delegates were accredited at the Charter Conference on the 30th, including 647 from UCATT and 207 from the TGWU. Ken Barlow sent apologies, because the EC had threatened to discipline him. At least 260 delegates were from Merseyside and 200 were from Birmingham. Alan Abrahams was in the chair. Pete Carter pointed out that the wage element in house building had gone down from 55 percent to 35 percent between 1938 and 1968, while 177,000 building workers were now on the dole and two thirds of the 1,000,000 or so in work were lumpers. Dennis Dugen stressed that unity was 'of paramount importance'. The Charter was 'supporting union officials in fighting the lump and getting the campaign for £30 for 35 hours under way,' not 'hindering them'. The *Charter* Editorial Board called for a lobby of the UCATT Conference in June to argue for 'immediate action to achieve the claim in full'. Delegates voted to increase the print run to 15,000. Credentials, donations and a collection raised £1,000, plus £650 in IOUs (equivalent to about £15,000 today).

At the LCDTU Conference in April Jimmy Reid from UCS, Jack Dunn of Kent NUM, Eddie Marsden of the AUEW and Alan Sapper of the Association of Cinematograph, Television & Allied Technicians were on the platform, but only eighty shop stewards' committees were represented. The Conference Resolution called for a national stoppage on May Day.

The *Star* reported that delegates 'representing some 200,000 building workers' had 'demanded' the 'recall of the TUC', were in 'total opposition to the Industrial Relations Act', wanted 'a national strike to force a General Election' and backed the TGWU refusal to pay a £55,000 Industrial Relations Court fine. Bert Smith had argued 'in his personal capacity' that union leaders should 'lead from the front and not from behind'.

The *Star* reported that Glasgow sites stopped on May Day and 2,000 marched. Most of the 2,000-strong LCDTU London demonstration were building workers. Jack Henry stressed the need to get rid of the lump. At Westminster Hall, with George Smith on the platform, Lou Lewis demanded 'no wavering on our demands'.

Dave Ayre and Bill Kerriss had been Crook UCATT delegates to the Charter conference and reported back on the 'possible impact on our leadership in their current wage negotiations'. The employers' 'apparently final offer' was 'unequivocally rejected' and the Regional Committee and EC were to be told that, 'should no further offer be forthcoming', a 'planned programme of direct industrial action' should 'be implemented' and 'supported by regional demonstrations'. Reuben Barker agreed to be 'distribution agent' for the *Charter*, which was to be financed from branch funds.

On 17 May the UCATT, TGWU, NUGMW and Furniture Timber & Allied Trade Union ECs set up a National Action Committee to coordinate the work of Regional and Area Action Committees in the event of a strike. Next day union negotiators rejected a final offer of an extra £2.40 a week for craftsmen. One week later the unions gave a month's notice of a strike.

Pete Kavanagh staged a sit-in on a crane on a Lovell site in London to protest at his and others' victimisation and against the lump. He stayed there for nine days in spite of a court order. His action inspired sit-ins at one Bryant site in Birmingham and two in Manchester. By 5 June the Manchester workers had won £35 for forty hours. That day every Edinburgh site was stopped and 2,000 marched through the city. A separate agreement for Northern Ireland came into force and contractors—especially in Birmingham, Liverpool and Dundee—were reportedly 'wavering'.

Back in February thirteen NUM pickets had been arrested at Langannet Power Station, but the Scottish Area EC had declared that all pits would be idle until they were out of prison. The Lord Advocate for Scotland flew up and released them on bail. On 6 June the thirteen went on trial. The Secretary of Glenrothes Trades Council noted that 'policeman after policeman paraded in front of the court giving evidence which varied from the confused and contradictory to the downright untruthful'. There were four miners and three miners' wives in the jury and they acquitted all the men.

Crook UCATT was flourishing. Dave Ayre recalls: 'We had over 200 members, which wasn't bad for a small town, especially since most of us worked in the private sector. In spite of check-off arrangements for collecting subs we continued with fortnightly meetings and that soon showed its strengths.' On 3 June Dave and Bill Kerriss were delegates to the Teesside Federation of Trades Councils. On the 7th Crook UCATT heard that the EC wanted a levy of £1 per member and had 'proposals for industrial action'. Members voted 44 to 1 in favour.

On the 12th, the first day of the UCATT conference, Hugh D'Arcy of the EC, the Scottish TUC and the CP, pointed out in the *Star* that employees' earnings were often £20 a week and the average (with bonus) was £28. Despite opposition from officials, the delegates—including Jim French—voted by 100 to 77 for every member to have the right to be a delegate to the Labour Party Conference. Alan Abrahams insisted: 'We want £30 now, shorter hours and longer holidays.' Delegates voted to go for £35 a week for 35 hours, with double time for overtime; but the union had lost 21,000 members in 1971 and had a deficit of £360,000, so they agreed to the EC plan for selective strikes. Ten Regional Action Committees, based on English, Scottish and Welsh Regional Joint Councils of the building unions, plus co-opted lay members, were empowered to select the sites to strike. Sixty of the 39 largest contractors' most profitable sites would be pulled out on 26 June, sixty more the following week, and so on. There would be a complete ban on overtime over forty hours, a £1 weekly levy on members at work, and strike pay would be £6 a week (worth £60 today). The *Charter* supported this strategy.

CHAPTER 4

The selective strike

Rally the troops, disrupt the employer and inform the public

A subbie at Cubitt's £56,000,000 World's End site in Chelsea had
victimised Lou Lewis and others and 300 were out before Monday 26 June 1972, when the first national building workers' strike
since 1923 began. Several London sites and two big joinery firms
struck for the day and lobbied the NFBTE headquarters. Within
days 400 pickets had closed two more sites. 600 Covent Garden
site workers voted to come out. The *Star* noted that a 'co-ordinating committee' of 'representatives of the jobs which have been
called out and stewards from sites which have helped picketing'
would give a lead.

In lump-ridden Bristol, 1,000 men voted for a national strike.

The Midland Regional Action Committee's 'Strike news[s]heet',
'DECLARATION OF WAR!', explained the strategy. UCATT stewards
had the National Action Committee 'Guide to Pickets' and badges.
Stewards and 'interested members' had met in Birmingham, Leicester, Nottingham and Stoke. They should make regular collections,
ban overtime and 'find out what is happening in your area and offer
your help'. £800 was raised in a week.

300 Merseyside stewards had organised for all major sites to stop
at lunchtime on the 26th. In Runcorn, 500 men at a Monks contract
blocked the roads and outnumbered police. Next day eighty police
arrived, but 200 engineers and boilermakers heard the strikers' case
and put in their own pay claim. Merseyside Action Committee policed
the overtime ban and levied 50p a week. The North West Regional
Action Committee set up Action Committees in Barrow, Preston and
Chester. Unselected sites in St Helens, Wigan and Skelmersdale took
industrial action and planned regular half-day strikes. So did some in
Manchester, where they raised £800.

A three-site Leeds 'co-ordinating committee', chaired by CPer
Arthur Dale, levied £1 from men at work, encouraged non-members
to strike and targeted Doncaster, Barnsley, York and Hull.

Three Glasgow sites came out. The Charter built a 5,000-strong demonstration, but the Action Committee and the Scottish Regional Action Committee vetoed further action during the annual holiday. By 3 July 10,000 were out across the country. CPer Jack Henry was Chairman of the London Co-ordinating Committee of UCATT and TGWU delegates from twelve sites. They closed a site that allowed overtime and lobbied a council about lumpers. UCATT official Alan Tattam organised a meeting for stewards not on strike to discuss the next steps. A Beckton site raised £290 for the strike fund and sent £10 to the *Star*. Lou Lewis later acknowledged that the London Charter group 'went to sleep' because 'key' members were 'so involved in running the dispute', though they had 'a couple of meetings' to 'discuss tactics'.

In the South West, 400 more came out and formed an unofficial committee. Officials said that an all-out strike wasn't possible.

Ninety sites were out in Birmingham. 4,000 demonstrated outside the NFBTE office and Barlow, Carter and Mike Shilvock—the Regional Action Committee Chairman—argued for an all-out strike. (The *Star* noted that ten people joined the CP, making fifty recruits in four weeks.) Nearly £2,000 had been collected from the 24,000 at work, but 260 branches had contributed nothing and were exhorted to change their rules or 'forget them for the duration'. 250 more men would be called out. Regional Action Committees were 'empowered to make COMPANY DEALS', but 'none are taking place in *this* region'. Over 900 were out at eleven sites in the region and there were Derby, Nottingham, Leicester and Stoke Action Committees.

Stoke CP member Tommy Walker had 'three little notebooks'.

One contained the jobs that needed stopping, the second carried a day to day report of jobs stopped, and the third contained the names and addresses of all stewards being elected. I also presented each steward with a notebook so that he could get the names of his men and put them on a rota for pickets. Also I wrote my own name and address with phone number so that I could be contacted… [W]e now have an army of 300 or 400 lads waiting for any action that the employers may want.

125 Midlands sites struck for a day. 1,000 marched through Stoke.

There were clashes with electricians at Runcorn, because EETPU officials had told them to cross picket lines. One picket was arrested, but nobody crossed. Sixty pickets stopped overtime at five

Manchester sites in an hour and policed the eleven sites at work. The Regional Action Committee announced that big contractors wanted a local deal. Fifteen more sites would be out on the 10th, making 24 in all. Seven more sites were out in Leeds and the strike was 'escalating so fast' that the leaders 'cannot keep pace'.

In Glasgow, 250 strikers and others picketed EETPU members. Three Scottish contractors agreed to £30 for 35 hours and four days' holiday in two years' time. The NFBTE condemned this 'irresponsible unilateral action'.

By the 17th over 12,000 men were out from 180 sites, including fifteen more on Merseyside. London pickets recruited hundreds of lumpers and threatened to picket Fleet Street over the news blackout. In Southampton 'approximately 44' sites were out and it was 'escalating fast'. The *Charter* hadn't been seen in Bristol before, but old copies sold out fast. Thirteen South West sites were out. Strikers were angry that officials refused to call an all-out national strike. The Midlands overtime ban was broadening and demonstrations helped to 'rally the troops', 'disrupt the employer' and 'inform the public'. Demonstrations were planned in Leicester, Nottingham, Stoke and Birmingham. The Regional Action Committee would consider a 'DRAMATIC ESCALATION' on the 19th.

We picketed from where we were strong

By early 1972 Dave Ayre was convenor at Shepherd's multi-million pound North Tees General Hospital contract in Stockton.

> We had negotiated a 'post-entry' closed shop—you had to join once you started—on-site dues collections and face-to-face meetings with site managers, but it still wasn't easy being a union activist and we had many sackings, blacklistings and problems with union officials. I decided to do an Open University course. My mother commented that I was 'leaving my station', but Jennie Lee's brainchild was one of the most progressive moves any government has undertaken, because people with no formal academic qualifications could hope to get a degree through six years' part-time study. The Foundation Course in Social Sciences covered economics, philosophy, psychology and sociology. It took me fifteen hours a week, but I loved it. I read on the bus to and from work and during tea and lunch breaks. Most students were apolitical local government

workers, civil servants and teachers. Apart from a lad who worked on the railways, I was the only manual worker.

I was a severely disillusioned member of the Labour Party's Northern Regional Executive, but the final straw came early in 1972 when they sidelined discussion about the NUM strike to discuss an MP's garden party. I felt that the CP was too rigid and 'disciplined'. In February I was waiting for an OU tutorial in Durham and reading Michael Barratt Brown's *From Labourism to Socialism*, when a voice said: 'You'll never achieve fundamental change towards socialism and break the hold of capitalism through parliamentary politics. It would always take a revolution of the working class to achieve socialism.' That was Jean Murray of the International Socialists. My experience had already taught me that fundamental change wouldn't come through parliament, so I bought a copy of *International Socialism* and was attracted by its policies. I knew very little about IS, but when I went home I got in touch through OU contacts and signed up, as I recall, at the Durham branch. I remember meeting Martin Shaw, Bob Clay from Teesside and John Cowley from Tyneside.

Jean and Dave went to IS meetings regularly.

On 26 June a housing estate in south Middlesbrough and a big hotel in the town centre were pulled out on strike. The UCATT Northern Regional Committee Chairman was Charlie Lowther, the Vice-Chairman was Jack Spowart and Harry Mitchell and Bobby Chisholm were members. So the CP held four of the five elected positions and the regional secretary, Jim Harper, was an ex-CPer.

On the 28th the Northern Regional Council heard that 194 stewards had collected £70 for the 'Hardship Fund'. They and the other 309 stewards were urged to 'collect everywhere', write to the press, local radio and MPs and 'pester' the NFBTE office in Durham with telegrams. 'Go out and have a word with the lads on the picket lines, stand with them and have a chat—give them encouragement'—'you don't need to be a building trade worker to do this'. An 'Appendix' to minutes was a 'Strike Bulletin'. A forty-hour week was the maximum. 'Report violations—please be accurate—try to interfere yourselves to have violations stopped—we support you. Many firms have yielded to pressure.' Strike pay was being distributed but 'no details are given here for obvious reasons.' As for the £1 levy, 'the sooner you pay this to London or Ourselves the quicker the lads who are on strike get it and we hope a little extra.' Morale had 'Never Been Higher'. Pickets were to be appointed and supplied with armbands and the Regional

Action Committee (chaired by Lowther) would 'look after fares, etc'. A few small firms had signed a 'specimen interim agreement', but 'the big fellows hesitate to bite so pressure must be increased.' 'Of course, people would like ALL OUT—but where do we get the cash. Obviously, we can't tell you the sites in advance, Employers have ears. TWENTY-TWO JOBS OUT to date.'

Jimmy Graham was still at work. He recalls:

My father's father was a cobbler for the well-known Bishop Auckland firm of McIntyre's and my father was a steam engine fireman at the London & North Eastern Railway's Tindale shed. I was born in November 1945. We lived at my grandparents' house, but when I was two my father left my mother and went back to Scotland. When I was about five I used to wander up our back street to a scrap yard at the top and watch the horses and carts bringing in scrap and rags. I went there more and more often and when I was seven I started to go with a van driver to Stockton to collect rabbit skins that were dried in the yard. What an adventure for a young lad! In 1960 I left school, aged fifteen, and started work at the scrap yard.

In 1965 I went to work as a labourer on the Durham motorway site for more money—up to £11 a week! Then I worked in a Shildon factory, mixing paint and filling tins. It was a filthy job. I joined the TGWU, but I wasn't a steward. Then I went to Patons and Baldwins factory in Darlington as a cone-winder and machine minder. That was the cleanest job I've had and I got £22 a week for three shifts. I joined the National Union of Bleachers, Dyers & Textile Workers, but there were no activists there, either. When the factory was put on short time the cut in wages meant that travelling to Darlington wasn't an option.

In summer 1972 I was working for Durham County Council, building a school at the back of my house, but the first I heard of the building workers' strike was when officials came on site in June and asked if the six of us wanted to join UCATT. We all did. I became a member of the Bishop Auckland branch, but local authority workers weren't involved with the strike and there was no steward on site, so the question of supporting strikers financially was never discussed.

Later he worked for Durham Water Board. 'There was no union and no steward. We agreed with the lads on strike, and watched it unfold across the country, but there was no organised support.'

The Flying Pickets

Dave Ayre recalls: 'Ours wasn't one of the sites selected in the first week, but we had held large meetings on Friday lunchtimes and local dockers launched a major campaign in support.' Brown's at Darlington wasn't selected but Jim French recalls meetings to organise support and he took days off to picket and collect the levy. 'Some who stayed at work gave a £1 per week. Sometimes it was hard to collect, but we were all in the same boat.'

In July Crook UCATT was concerned about 'the lack of urgency and apparent ambiguity' over strike pay and asked the Regional Action Committee to take 'urgent and forthright action' and provide a list of strikers. Some local authority and ancillary workers 'felt they ought to play a greater part in the concerted action'. Local authority workers raised £7 for the strike fund. The Trades Council gave £10. Dave and Bill Kerriss reported on the NFBTE demonstration and argued for a one-day regional strike and demonstration. The strike bulletin was discussed. Dave and Bill reported on stewards' meetings and site visits 'to maintain the overtime ban'. A Billy Row site would be 'picketed until compliance'. Sites outside the area would be 'reported to organiser'.

Reuben Barker had been fairly happy at Lax & Sons.

At Christmas, bricklayers, joiners and plasterers got turkeys and the labourers got chicken or pork. The pork always looked better than the turkeys, but it was the only firm I've ever worked for that gave me anything. Lax's had never had a dispute, but in July 1972 pickets stopped some of their sites. Men who wouldn't even talk about unions when I started were telling me that they were withdrawing their labour. We agreed to tell management, but only me and my labourer—a man with 26 years' service and a company pension—arrived in the yard. I told the senior boss: 'We've all decided to support the strike.' He looked round, saw us two and said: 'Who's we?' I looked like a fool, but his son would arrange a meeting in the joiners' shop in two days' time. The senior boss wouldn't allow a union official to attend, to avoid 'provocation', but I could speak. Given the backup we'd had, I agreed.

On the day the joiners' shop had a platform for the senior boss, his two sons and the works manager, so they could look down on everyone and talk down to them, too. The senior boss got up, wagged his finger and said he knew 'his men' well. 'You are fools. There'll be no strike pay, no social security and no holiday stamps, but there will be loss of earnings. The union hasn't called you out and you should leave it to management and the union to sort it out.' One of the sons said that he wouldn't work for what was currently on offer and we were worth more than that, but 'there will be no vote: it's all in or all out'. He got a very nasty look from his father, who said: 'We will now let Reuben speak on behalf of the union.' They offered me the platform, but I said: 'I'll just stand here and speak.' I refused to accept the hint about a local deal and reported the latest news from UCATT. When they opened the doors all but four ragged trousered philanthropists walked out. 'The bosses made better speeches than you.' 'That's why they're all on strike but you.'

At the gate next morning, strike-breakers came flying out, but when we complained one of the senior boss's sons locked the gate, so I was able to picket Lax's gates and those of the woodworking firm next door. A driver bringing timber turned his lorry round and Norvites' manager called the police. Two arrived on big horses and demanded to know where the pickets were. There was only me and my little dog, but somehow they didn't believe me. They looked around, called at the office and then off they went.

After three days picketing on my own I went to a Billy Row site with a busload of Bishop Auckland pickets. The site agent told me that only one man was working there, but only one picket could go down to talk to him, so I volunteered. When he saw me coming he picked up his shovel, started to threaten me and ranted on that he had just come out of jail, this was his first job and he had his old mother to keep. But he didn't tell me to go away and his temper began to cool. I asked him who looked after his mother while he was in jail. He was depressed. He was working in a trench with three inches of water and the agent didn't want him there. I invited him to talk to the pickets on the gate and he jumped out of his trench and followed me. I never saw him again after that.

We visited a bridge site at Meadowfield. The agent was the best-dressed building worker I've ever seen, with polished brown shoes, white shirt, grey suit and a pink bow tie. We asked him if it was all right to speak to the workers and then wandered around. We knew some of the men from clubs, pubs, betting shops and football, and we left them to make the site safe before they went home. A factory was being built at Belmont. The agent gave us permission, but then the boss came

The Flying Pickets

storming into the site in his Aston Martin and laid down the law about trespassing and stopping work. We told him that we got permission, and after some discussion we left. No doubt the poor agent got a rollicking.

As Reuben puts it, 'We picketed from where we were strong.'

Flying pickets

Late in 1971 *Construction News* had published stories about how McAlpine won a huge contract, though theirs was not the lowest tender, and how they treated workers at the Barbican as 'political footballs' to get payments above the tender price. They had hired private eyes to follow the paper's journalists and enquire into their private lives and political beliefs. They accused them of 'left wing bias' and demanded action. The Thomson Organisation told the editor to vet cartoons, keep industrial relations stories off the front page, stop criticising advertisers and get rid of Laurie Flynn. The editor and his deputy resigned. The new editor insisted that articles that were mildly critical had to be cleared by the firms concerned. The journalists went on unofficial strike for four days and continued the fight through the National Union of Journalists. When the new editor refused to print an article showing a clear breach of the law they refused to supply copy. Flynn went to work full-time for *SW*.

In January 1972 Gerry Kelly, a UCATT steward at Bryant's Woodgate Valley site in Birmingham, reported briefly in *SW* on the fight for a closed shop. In February he reported on the Birmingham struggle. He noted that Phil Beyer had been blacklisted and reported the campaign to have Pete Carter and John Shortland reinstated.

In the year to March 1972 the number of IS branches had risen from 77 to 113 and the membership from 1,300 to 2,351, of whom 725 were white-collar workers and 613 were manual workers. *SW*'s print order had risen from 13,000 to 28,000 and its readership was over 50,000. Four 'rank and file' papers had a total print-run of almost 12,000. IS Conference aimed to build ten factory branches. There were insufficient comrades to form a building workers' 'fraction', but 'a key part of penetrating the advanced layer of militants' was 'joint activity with those militants who are in the CP or who still look to it for guidance' but didn't like the CP's policy of working with vacillating and unreliable 'left trade union bureaucrats'. (The CP's Betty Reid was concerned that IS had 'made a conscious turn to try and recruit from the factories' to add to an 'almost entirely student membership' of 'about 1,000'.)

Early in April Flynn's two-page feature in *SW*, 'On the Lump', revealed that after the Labour government introduced Selective Employment Tax the big contractors had sent a man round the country to explain that the lump was legal. He was now the boss of Labour Force. Flynn held up the Birmingham victories as a model for other activists, quoted Carter and advertised the Charter Conference. Employers had told Mr Bryant that 'he should have used the police, the courts, anything' to prevent a unilateral deal. *SW* noted that Glasgow Charter had organised 700 men to march to the union office. All sites would send delegates to the Charter Conference on 30 April and 100 would build a May Day strike.

In June *SW*'s 'Militants Set Pace on Building Sites' noted the union claim and the leaderships' collaboration with employers. The Charter was 'a serious force in the industry' and the CP militants' 'enormous contribution' included 'the first serious attempt to stamp out the cancer of labour only sub-contracting' in Birmingham. *SW* quoted George Kelly, an IS member and EETPU steward from Glasgow Corporation Workshops, on the CP-controlled Liaison Committee for the Defence of Trade Unions.

I think what is happening today is a tremendous show of verbal militancy. But unless this is carried back into the areas it is of no worth at all and will be mere shadow boxing. LCDTUs in the areas should be built and structured so that they can refer back to the centre.

We have to have a situation where contrary points of view can be put at conference, so that we can come out with a principled programme that can lead to this [Industrial Relations] Act being smashed.

It would be criminal if we went back to the areas and the power of the delegates here were lost. The lesson has to be learnt from the Minority Movement. We can build a rank and file movement.

SW noted that the LCDTU leadership seemed unwilling to learn from the 1930s experience of CP rank and file organisation and offered 'No Real Lead in the Fight to Kill the Tories' Law'.

Early in July *SW* reported on the builders' strike and appealed for solidarity. Roger Rosewell, the IS Industrial Organiser, reported to the EC on a discussion with 'GK' and others 're strategy and action'.

By the 10th an unofficial Bristol Strike Committee, chaired by Dennis Johnson, had called a meeting of 300 scaffolders who voted unanimously to come out. The next *SW* stressed that the dispute looked set to be 'a long and bitter fight'. As the number of strikers rose, levies would fall, so collections had to be made more widely. Gerry Kelly of UCATT argued for an all-out strike on big contractors' sites, mass picketing of sites and suppliers, a rigid overtime ban, regular levies, 'guerrilla sympathy strikes' elsewhere and winning support from TGWU lorry drivers, EETPU members and the TUC. 'Round the Sites' argued that Pete Carter was correct: 'If we are not careful we could lose this strike with the tactics of the selective strike.' 'We need to stop all sites for a speedy settlement.'

The Pentonville 5

By 1972 about 20,000 registered dockers' jobs had been lost in six years and UCATT conference had pledged support to those in London who were threatened with prison under the Industrial Relations Act for picketing 'unregistered labour'—lumpers.

On Friday 21 July four dockers were sent to Pentonville Prison for picketing Midlands Cold Storage after an Industrial Relations Court order. CPer Vic Turner picketed the prison and soon joined the four inside. They refused to purge their contempt.

On Saturday the London Port Shop Stewards' Committee wanted a poster. Laurie Flynn introduced the only IS docker, Bob Light, plus CPer Michael Fenn and others, to Ross Pritchard and Jim Nichol at the IS printshop. 'One docker in the dock, all dockers out of the dock', was widely flyposted. IS also printed Fenn's leaflet, which had five prison bars with the men's names and a caption: 'Five Trade Unionists Are Inside—Why Aren't You Out?'

On Sunday Bert Ramelson ordered sixty leading CP trade unionists to put pressure on the TUC by closing down Fleet Street and building a general strike by Friday. On Monday London CP branches contacted industrial members. LCDTU affiliates were asked to build on the 'considerable response' to calls for industrial action and make it into a general strike. There would be an 'emergency' LCDTU meting on Friday.

SW was out by Wednesday. 'Strike Now: Free 5'. The giant Vestey Corporation secretly owned Midlands Cold Storage.

By Wednesday around 40,000 dockers were out across the country. London and Liverpool CP dockers were in touch with each other and the successful unofficial strikes and the Industrial Relations Court's fine on the TGWU had widened the unofficial network to 50,000 other workers, including those at Shotton BSC, Liverpool Teaching Hospital, Merseyside factories and even Midlands Cold Storage. Other factory workers promised support. CP and IS networks pulled out Fleet Street EETPU members.

Bob Light went to see his IS comrade Frank Campbell at the World's End site in London. 'Frank went inside and shouted: "There's a dockers' picket line, everybody out". And they all came out.' Light went to Heathrow Airport with an IS engineer and pulled out the ground staff. In two hours there were no flights. Several London sites stopped work in addition to the twenty already out.

The TUC called for a one-day strike, the Tories beamed in 'The Official Solicitor' and the Law Lords released the five men. The Industrial Relations Act was in tatters.

On Friday TGWU dockers voted to go on strike the next day.

IS support for the NUM and the Pentonville 5 had sharply improved its standing in the movement and during July weekly sales of *SW* reached 21,000. Early in August Tony Merrick, Con Clancy and Derek Watkins of the Pentonville 5 were on the platform at an IS victory meeting in East London. Michael Fenn and Eddie Prevost, a TGWU member at London's Royal Docks, joined IS.

Dissatisfied with the official tactics

In the *SW* printed on 25 July 1972, Gerry Kelly reported that flying pickets pulled out non-members and lumpers at seven Bristol sites. When 300 arrived at one site, lumpers who had voted not to come out 'walked off and joined the strike'. Workers at another site 'got fed up waiting for the flying pickets, and walked out before they got there'. The TGWU promised strike pay to new recruits and one branch signed up 300 in a fortnight. The local 'No Action Committee' soon 'dropped right out of things'. Kelly later reported that the Bristol Strike Committee controlled mass meetings.

> Every morning 300-400 workers would assemble outside the union hall. They were divided into two groups, and given a list of sites... Pickets would arrive outside a site with loudhailers, and shout at the workers through them until they stopped work. Not one single site rejected the call to strike. Some firms, particularly those with subbies, tried shifting them from site to

site. The flying pickets literally chased them across Bristol. One crane driver started at the Broad Plain site. The flying picket closed that. So he was moved to Baldwin Street. They closed that the next day. When they found him again on the third day at Blackboy Hill, he yelled: 'Oh no, not you again! You're picking on me!'

Flying pickets had been central to the miners' victory.

The NFBTE had rearranged their offer to give craftsmen £25 a week from August and £29 from the following May, plus one day's extra holiday. National officials insisted that it be put to the members and George Smith announced that he would be recommending the offer to UCATT before the holidays ended.

UCATT Northern Regional Council met on 26th. None of the three EC members turned up and none had addressed a mass meeting. 'Sub committees' of strikers were to be encouraged to make site collections, though strike pay couldn't be given out during the annual holiday between 31 July and 14 August. The EC had reached an agreement with the British Woodwork Manufacturers' Association, but the only improvement was an 'additional holiday', so the Council supported members—including Browns of Darlington, where Jim French worked—opposing it. They also agreed to 'an expression deploring' the general secretary's recommendation of the NFBTE offer. Three firms who were prepared to sign agreements were referred to the Regional Action Committee. The Council would sponsor a piece in the *Star* during the TUC Congress urging 'all possible action to secure release of trade union members jailed by the Industrial Relations Court'. UCATT should argue for the TUC to call a one-day national strike to release the Pentonville 5. If that failed the TUC should call a general strike.

Birmingham Action Committee declared an all-out strike and began spreading it with flying pickets. On 1 August the Midland Region Action Committee newssheet, headed 'TOTAL ESCALATION', reported that fifty city sites were on all-out strike, Staffordshire sites were 'pulled out daily', Nottingham sites were 'clamouring to be pulled out' and the situation in Leicester was 'satisfactory'. Local authority workers should stay at work, ban overtime and make weekly collections. The Committee would vote against an offer short of the full claim.

In *SW* Gerry Kelly reported that Birmingham and London officials wanted an all-out strike. Most big Birmingham sites were out. In London, 500 men had joined the union at one site, and levies were going well. Kent NUM and other unions had promised donations. The National Action Committee had given no lead on pickets' pay, but seventy Ipswich pickets had chartered a bus and pulled out 100. Norwich stewards would 'halt all contracts'. The Eastern Regional Action Committee had shut 27 sites.

Dave Ayre recalls:

> I read Laurie Flynn's fantastic article about the Vestey Corporation and about the victory of the Pentonville Five. From then on, along with other comrades, I sold the paper on Saturday mornings in Durham. I sometimes thought it was a bit obsessed with the strike weapon, which could have been intimidating for some potential recruits, but the information, ideas and arguments stimulate self-confidence. SW was a breath of fresh air and I took political ideas into my trade union work.

Crook UCATT unanimously rejected the offer. Dave reported that 'about 60 percent' of members paid the strike levy and after the Billy Row picket 'over half of the operatives left the site'. 'Further preparations for continuing this operation' were postponed.

Merseyside Action Committee, chaired by Bill Jones, called for mass meetings in Liverpool and Chester on 15 August.

The *Star* reported that some national officials would accept next year's offer immediately, but Alan Tattam predicted an escalation if the full claim wasn't met. A Bristol mass meeting and seventy Sheffield stewards had demanded the full claim. No UCATT regional representative had accepted the offer. Midland, North West, Yorkshire and Eastern Region representatives had called on the EC to escalate the strike. UCATT, FTAT and NUGMW negotiators were empowered to accept a better offer, but the TGWU wanted to consult members, so further negotiations were adjourned.

Len Eaton of UCATT and Bob Johnson of the TGWU put their names to 25,000 leaflets advertising the London Regional Action Committee's call for a half-day strike and demonstration against the offer on 8 August. An all-out strike was going to be proposed and it was fully supported by the Charter and the Joint Sites Committee. UCATT Southern Region opposed the deal. A 600-strong meeting in Bristol also rejected it and would send coaches to the London demonstration, as would Cambridge and Stevenage. 100 sites were out in the Birmingham area and three-quarters of those in and around Stoke. Meetings in Stoke and Liverpool voiced strong opposition to the offer and Manchester and Chester Action Committees and the North West Regional Action Committee rejected it. Hundreds of Leeds UCATT and TGWU members wanted an all-out strike. The TGWU Building Group's lay members rejected the offer and called for a co-ordinated union response. By 8 August 120 Birmingham sites were stopped. 4,000 marched, including groups from Bristol, Cardiff, Wolverhampton and the Isle of Man. Large contingents from Leeds, Bradford, Rotherham, York, Bristol and Norwich were on the 8,000-strong London demonstration. Jack Henry reported that the agreement 'will not be ratified by UCATT' and the EC had agreed to a 'most rapid intensification', without strike pay.

Motivated by electoral considerations

In the August 1972 IS *Internal Bulletin* Roger Rosewell acknowledged that the CP were 'better organised in the building industry than elsewhere'. 'Their leading militants are very good' because they have 'to prove themselves as fighters over and over again', but they were 'uncritically supporting the current official union policy', because they were 'motivated by electoral considerations'. He urged all IS branches to work around this dispute and hold public meetings where 'some prospects of success exist'. He would call meetings of IS building workers and 'if these are successful then a fraction can be built'. (According to an EC 'perspectives' document, this would be 'in the next few weeks'.)

Early in August *SW* reported that 4,000 Glasgow men had ignored the UCATT Scottish Regional Secretary. Hundreds of McAlpine's workers had marched to the Edinburgh UCATT offices, bringing out the giant St James's Square site and two others on the way. Stoppages had been organised in every major Scottish city and most workers voted for all-out strikes and flying pickets. The Yorkshire Regional Action Committee hoped to close every site in a few days and a Liverpool meeting was to hear a proposal for an all-out strike. In Wolverhampton, Stoke and other Midland towns there was already an all-out strike. In Southampton, 700 men gave overwhelming support to the Southern Regional Action Committee call to continue the struggle. *SW* concluded: 'Massive unofficial action alone has stopped the union leaders from ending the strike.'

Laurie Flynn's 'The Rot on The Sites' noted that big contractors were 'unrivalled as pitiless exploiters'.

Construction in Britain is dominated by two large outfits, the McAlpines and Laings. Both are family firms of obscure origin but now of immense economic and political power in our society, and set the style for all types and sizes of construction firms. Between them they have the two employers' associations carved up, with Laing's orchestrating the National Federation of Building Trades Employers and McAlpine's fronting the Federation of Civil Engineering Contractors...

When the British Steel Corporation got ready to build its new basic oxygen steel-making plant in Scunthorpe, the biggest civil engineering contract ever awarded in Britain, McAlpine came second on the bid prices, after a small civil engineering outfit called Mitchell Construction. But all sorts of extras were added to the Mitchell tender by the BSC's consulting engineers and magically the contract was awarded to... you know who.

Every major redevelopment job on London's south bank has been handled by McAlpines, who just seem to have a way of obtaining all the juicy contracts...

They are also building the last part of the Barbican, that famed scene of alleged communist subversion 'exposed' by a witch-hunting Labour government committee of inquiry, which was in fact an employers' ploy to raise their contract payments by stalling the job.

There had been a 'conspiracy' between Laing's, the subbies Whelan and Jones and the union about lumper carpenters at St Thomas's Hospital, and Laing's were also involved in a systems building scandal. At Milford Haven bridge had collapsed during construction, killing five workers. After a media blackout, more died when it collapsed again. Union leaders were the problem: 'Never again can construction workers afford some spurious unity with those who look militant and then sell the pass.'

On the 10th Lou Lewis put the Joint Sites Committee's all-out strategy to the London Regional Action Committee. 'We want every striker active, a strike centre which can send 50 or 100 pickets to a site if need be' and 'the maximum number of cars available' to 'halt all sources of supply to the building industry'.

Next day UCATT regional officials and the EC voted for an all-out strike and would propose that to other unions on the 13th.

That weekend 100 Eastern Region stewards launched an 'all-out campaign' to close all sites. Half the sites in Bradford, most of those in Leeds and Halifax and all of those in Barnsley were out. After a

700-strong meeting in Leeds, flying pickets brought out lumpers on three housing estates. Many Sheffield sites decided to come out on the 14th. 22 sites in Preston and 36 in Leicester were out. Dundee, Aberdeen and West of Scotland stewards voted for all-out strike.

By the 14th up to 100,000 were on strike. Salford, Wythenshawe and Altrincham sites were stopped. A Bolton meeting called by employers backfired into a total shutdown. In Wigan, Skelmersdale and most of Warrington an all-out strike was underway. About four-fifths of Liverpool sites were stopped. A 2,500-strong North Wales meeting voted to come out. Strikes were snowballing in Scotland, Nottingham and Ipswich. A sixty-strong London Co-ordinating Committee meeting agreed to Lou Lewis's proposal that a motion to close every site should be put to a mass meeting on the 17th. The militant pickets and union officials were starting to take control.

CHAPTER 5

The escalation

This is a backs-to-the-wall fight

On 15 August 1972 George Smith announced that all union strike pay was stopped forthwith and that UCATT was willing to reach 'company agreements' on the basis of the full claim.

Those agreements would break union unity, take the best-organised sites and branches out of the struggle and leave weak ones exposed and financially unsupported by their unions.

Lou Lewis recalled: 'From that moment' the EC 'lost any grip of it, because strike pay had been the only weapon they had'. He had 'a map with six grids on it, and teams in each grid to close the jobs down and others to make sure they stayed closed. It was like a military operation.'

The NFBTE bleated about 'extremists' 'forcing' men to stop work, but the TGWU put the blame for any violence on lumpers and agreed to 'the most rapid intensification'.

35,000 were out on Merseyside, all sites were stopped and 10,000 marched through Liverpool. 3,000 of them couldn't fit into the stadium to hear union officials and Bill Jones. Pete Carter organised a 200-strong 'mobile picket' to close Midland builders' suppliers.

SW called for mass picketing of suppliers and power companies and rank and file control of the strike. 'No settlement without reference back. No local retreats on the claim. All negotiations to include elected strike committee representatives.' 'Immediate campaign for collections, donations and solidarity action from other unions and from the TUC.' Eighty shop stewards had toured Glasgow sites and called for a strike against the 'sell-out'. 300 stewards voted for an all-out strike for the full claim. The UCATT regional secretary claimed that the action had ended, but 2,000 workers demonstrated in the pouring rain. They unanimously decided to use flying pickets to stop sites, 'whatever the officials thought', and split up into four groups to do so. 4,000 lobbied the UCATT office for an all-out strike. The regional secretary claimed this was local policy, but next day the Regional Action Committee denied it. Pickets remained at sites while others went further afield. *SW* argued for a 'regional rank and file committee' to be set up to cover Aberdeen, Dundee, Edinburgh and Glasgow, to prevent officials signing a separate Scottish deal.

In *SW* Don Quinn, convenor of the World's End site in London, called the lump a 'cancer'. 'A few months back you could look for a job in the papers and not see more than one in a week that wasn't on the lump. On the lump you couldn't straighten your back from one end of the day to the other!' It was 'pure slavery' and 'they can sack you on the spot'. If you have an accident 'you get nothing'. John Fontaine, the brickies' steward, added: 'You have a pace-maker in front of you who gets £4 more than you, and you have to keep up with him.' Subbies advertised for 'greyhounds only', 'meaning speed merchants'. 'But we're not dogs; we're human beings'. The lump 'increases unemployment fantastically. Four men do 20 men's work. And when you're over 45 you're finished completely.' 'If we don't fight it, there's no hope for trade unionism in the industry'. But there was 'a wind of change'. 'You can go to a site, stop it and give out union forms. They elect their stewards on the spot and the site is organised in a single day.' On the non-union site next door there were 'no proper eating facilities, no washing facilities' and men had to 'keep a change of clothes in cardboard boxes in the middle of the site, where the rain can't get at them'. Yet they had stopped that site 'with a wink'. Every site had to be pulled out and every supplier picketed. 'This is a backs-to-the-wall fight.'

Over 3,000 men were now out in the Southern Region, plus 3,000 in Bristol and 1,200 in Nottingham. Most sites in Stoke, Leicester and York were stopped. There were Co-ordinating Committees in Liverpool, St Helens, Birkenhead, Skelmersdale, Kirkby and Warrington. Merseyside Action Committee was spreading the strike to Liverpool Corporation building depots to force councillors to concede the private sector claim. Bert Smith noted that 'the lads' were 'in advance' of the National Action Committee.

On 17 August the *Star* quoted Jack Henry: 'We are determined to win not only a decisive victory on the wages question', but also 'finishing once and for all the lump merchants and doing away with victimisation and blacklisting'. At the London Co-ordinating Committee mass meeting Lou Lewis called for 'effective picketing'. 'Next week you won't be travelling two or three miles—you will be travelling ten, 20 or 25 miles.' Pete Carter reported that Midlands flying pickets would target builders' suppliers.

The National Action Committee estimated that up to 5,000 sites were affected and the strike was getting 'solid support' in the South West, Eastern, Yorkshire, Northern and North West Regions. 45 sites were stopped in Southampton and 25 more were about to come out. In Scotland, over sixty officials had decided to escalate the action, but called on 5,000 Glasgow Corporation building workers who had come out in solidarity to go back. A major national contractor was reportedly on the brink of signing an agreement and national officials anticipated other 'go-it-alone' moves.

Alan Abrahams and Lou Armour (a UCATT official and fellow CPer) visited a Cheshire site. A foreman swung a shovel at Abrahams, injuring his arm. He saw a second blow coming and thought he was going to be killed, so he used a spirit level in self-defence and broke five of the man's ribs and caused a lung to collapse. He was later charged with causing 'grievous bodily harm'.

On 18 August Beatrix Campbell's interview with George Smith appeared in the *Star*. There was likely to a total stoppage by the end of the following week. Employers were 'bound to believe that it's intimidatory for busloads of pickets to descend on the job, but they have guilty consciences'. The only violence he knew about were two scabs attacking peaceful pickets. National officials would now sign company agreements that were 'reasonably related to the claim'. The *Star* noted that over 15,000 West of Scotland men wanted an all-out strike. 'Right wing union officials' were 'howled down and jeered every time the crowd felt they were diluting the full claim'. The UCATT regional secretary overcame 'initial heckling' to report eight company agreements 'conceding the union's demand'. He 'hoped this would be multiplied within the next few weeks'.

On the 21st the *Star* reported an 'enthusiastic meeting' in Leeds. There had been 'incidents of police harassment', but the Leeds, Bradford and Harrogate Co-ordinating Committee had pulled out 150 men at a Harrogate hospital and stopped a Bradford site. Most York sites were idle. 400 London sites were stopped and the Co-ordinating Committee was targeting Bovis managers who had sent telegrams to strikers, claiming that their sites had 'resumed normal working'. They planned to picket the Stock Exchange site, though after 'incidents' involving electricians, EETPU members would also be present. Some strikers were not getting social security payments. Sir Keith Joseph, the Tory Secretary of State for Social Services, came from the family who owned the big contractors, Bovis.

The National Action Committee pointed out that most complaints of violence came from the Yorkshire NFBTE. Many papers didn't report that police had 'no complaint', or lumpers' attacks on pickets. An *SW* 'Builders' Strike Leaflet' noted that officials were stopping sites coming out. National negotiators were believed to be ready to settle for £25 a week for craftsmen in a two-year deal.

On the 22nd the *Star* reported that officials and 'strike leaders' would address a march in Manchester. A UCATT official was appealing for pickets to co-ordinate their work from Hulme Labour Club. 50,000 men from 2,000 North West sites were out. 400 Liverpool pickets had moved along the site of the M62 and met Warrington pickets coming the other way. Pickets had shut down all major sites in the Bolton and Burnley areas. The eight Scottish firms who signed the 'model agreement' had been 'roundly condemned' by the NFBTE. GMWU officials had sent Dundee Corporation workers back to work, but Glasgow Corporation workers stayed out.

On the 23rd the *Star* reported the UCATT Scottish Regional Secretary's claim that 36 firms had signed company agreements. Police had broken a 50-strong Glasgow picket to let EETPU members through. 53 Blackburn sites were stopped, but the UCATT official needed 'more rank and file support'. Thirty Swansea flying pickets had shut the last Merthyr sites. Five Birmingham pickets arrested at a cement depot were charged with 'disorderly conduct'.

SW reported that Bristol UCATT officials had hidden in the back room of their offices until strikers winkled them out, but they still refused to call out men on the M5 contract. 500 were out in Lowestoft and Cambridge and pickets expected to close about half the Peterborough sites in two or three days. All big Huddersfield sites were stopped and pickets were moving out to smaller towns. Scottish UCATT officials were crowing about a company agreement that allegedly included a minimum of £30 a week, yet many men would get only £25.50, bonus would be calculated on £20 and they had accepted a forty-hour week. In Edinburgh, Charlie McManus, the CP chairman of a 2,400-strong meeting, had refused to allow amendments to motions that supported an all-out strike and agreed to company agreements short of the full claim. *SW* was sardonic about the George Smith interview in the *Star*, given that the CP had borne the brunt of his witch-hunts when he was ASW General Secretary and when the UCATT EC appointed no CP officials. All this showed 'the desperate need for rank and file organisations' to 'take the initiative locally and nationally, independently of the union leaders'.

On the 24th the *Star* reported Smith's estimate that 200,000 men were on strike on 7,000 sites: 60,000 in the North West, 50,000 in Scotland, 30,000 in London, 16,000 in Yorkshire, 14,000 in Northern,

12,000 in the Midlands and over 10,000 in the Eastern region. (So 8,000 were out in the Southern, South West and Wales Regions.) He predicted that 300,000 would be out by the 25th. Fifty firms had signed company agreements, but they couldn't be named for fear of disciplinary action by the NFBTE. Fifty more were negotiating.

Midland flying pickets normally used up to a dozen men, but that evening 26 left Birmingham. At 5.00am next day they were joined by thirty Stoke pickets at a cement works near Leek. As the loaded tankers came out, eighty police laid into the pickets. Ken Barlow was present. The local MP complained to the Chief Constable about a Chief Inspector. (One picket was later fined £50 for 'assault' on a policeman who suffered no injury.) When the drivers came back they decided to stop deliveries and the cement workers came out.

Police outnumbered 100 pickets at a Birmingham cement depot and stopped Pete Carter speaking to drivers. (Six pickets were charged with obstruction and were later given a nominal fine.) Barlow believed the police were 'under instruction to "toughen up"'.

By the 25th 270,000 were out. Nottingham strikers had given Carter an enthusiastic hearing. Glasgow Corporation workers ignored GMWU officials and stayed out. Pickets shut twelve major sites around Scunthorpe. West Middlesex Action Committee's Hugh Cassidy needed 'pickets and other helpers'. Burnley and Rossendale sites were out, but there were social security problems.

An *SW* 'Builders' Strike Special' stressed that 'Rank and File Action Can Win the Full Claim' by 'militant all-out national action, as Birmingham and Bristol have insisted from early on', but not by selective strikes and company agreements. Hundreds had lobbied a Glasgow stewards' meeting, which voted 289 to 10 to stay out:

> A thorough going victory on wages and conditions will smash the lump for all time. It will smash reliance on massive amounts of overtime to gain an approximation to a living wage. It will vastly reduce accidents because the vast majority are actually due to overlong hours of work. And it will mean jobs for unemployed construction workers.

The next step was to 'put the pressure on cement and brick works'. Pat Mooney of the TGWU and Martin Barker reported that non-members had joined the Bristol flying pickets. They booked buses to picket the M5 site, but the officials told them not to go, allegedly because of a company agreement. Next day a mass meeting decided to picket and found the money for the buses. Dave Lister and

Andrew McGiveer reported that 100 London city centre sites were stopped. Birmingham officials had been prevented from signing a company agreement that was well short of the full claim. A mass meeting in Edinburgh booed UCATT official Jimmy Stocks when he argued for selective strikes. The Scottish Regional Action Committee had been told to consider ways of 'extending' the strike, but the vote for all-out strike was lost. Steve Jefferys reported: 'Glasgow Solid', but there was no network linking activists.

On the 26th the *Star* celebrated the fact that 'some 20,000' strikers were going back after employers 'conceded the claim'.

SW reported that 300,000 workers were involved in the biggest and longest strike in any industry for years, yet some officials were discouraging solidarity from local authority workers, seeking to curb effective picketing and signing secret company agreements. The *Charter* still hadn't appeared. A Charter meeting in Manchester on the 27th had begun to plan a national strategy that involved closing cement works, but couldn't agree about company agreements, even though those that were known were short of the national claim, would soon be eaten into by inflation, contained nothing solid about cutting the working week, didn't end the lump and demoralised those striking for the full claim. A member of the Lowestoft strike committee found a UCATT official who lived in the town and was on the Labour Party's Management Committee, but was happy for non-members to work on the roof of the Labour headquarters. Pickets stopped Yarmouth sites in two days and Lowestoft sites in a week. Camden Council workers were out in solidarity and the London Regional Action Committee planned events that 'workers from other industries will be invited to join'. The Department of Social Security made difficulties and the Inland Revenue let lumpers avoid tax.

CP Scottish UCATT officials recommended offers short of the full claim, but 4,000 Edinburgh workers voted down a proposal from a CP Regional Organiser to accept 'model agreements'.

On the 31st, according to an *SW* 'Special', the Edinburgh Action Committee, which was dominated by officials and CP members, decided not to allow votes at the weekly mass meetings.

Without major hostilities

Every major Teesside site had come out over the Pentonville 5. By 7 August North Tees General Hospital workers were straining at the bit and voted to come out. The stewards arranged for local men to picket and drove around in cars, pulling out less well-organised sites. Managers on a Stockton site were hostile but the men came out 'with no bother' and others did so 'without major hostilities'. Dave Ayre believes that the *Charter* persuaded most men to go on strike.

Browns of Darlington were out by the 14th. Jim French recalls:

> At some sites it was difficult, to say the least, to persuade men on low incomes to join the union and then go straight out on strike and do without wages or strike pay. There were queues of men trying to get social security for food, bills and mortgages. The lads used to say that the staff were trained to say that they would talk to their supervisors and then go out of the room, pick their nose, come back and say 'Sorry'. I believed them. But such was the strength of feeling about rubbish wages and conditions that the strike snowballed and stewards at big local authority Housing Department sites made collections.

By the 16th craftsmen had struck at 110 sites in the Northern Region. All but two major Newcastle city sites were idle and 500 men demonstrated. UCATT regional secretary Jim Harper told the *Star* that though many men had been reluctant to come out, it would take a lot to get them back. Andy Affleck, another official, added: 'We aim for a complete stoppage.'

Crook UCATT heard that 'all construction operations' were likely to be 'stopped by the end of the week'. 'Due to the speedy escalation' there would be weekly meetings in the Mill House Inn 'for the duration'. The Crook woodworkers' branch would be invited and the local fund would pay pickets' expenses.

On the 19th the *Star* reported that 'flying squads of building workers in five busloads' had shut Cramlington, Morpeth, Washington, Sunderland, Consett and Stanley sites. Eddie Philipson, a UCATT official, insisted: 'All they did was ask the men to down tools and join the strike, and they did just that. At not one site was the call rejected.' Over 12,000 were out. (Dave Ayre knew that the key activist north of the Tyne was George Stephenson.)

That day, one day after George Smith's comments about company agreements in the *Star*, UCATT's Northern Regional Council held a 'special meeting'. At least five of the ten elected members present were in the CP. Ex-CPer Jim Harper reported 'about six agreements' and 'others were nibbling', but members were reluctant to go back. Local authorities were to offer a separate national agreement. The council called for them to 'come to terms with our claim' or be put 'in dispute'. The Regional Chairman, Charlie Lowther, wanted to 'keep the pot boiling re finance', a 'strike headquarters' at Darlington and a 'march through the town'. Gerry Cassidy noted there was 'not much success' in the Stanley and Consett area 'until the pickets went in'.

On the 23rd the *Star* quoted Jim Harper that 20,000 men were out in the Northern Region. A Newcastle firm that belonged the Federation of Master Builders had signed a company agreement giving 1,200 employees a basic wage of £30. The NFBTE had 'bitterly attacked' them for 'pure self-interest', but other firms were 'settling the claim independently'. Andy Affleck reported that there would be a mass meeting in Middlesbrough that day and another in Newcastle on the 25th. Pickets were 'mopping up smaller sites who pretend they have not yet heard there is a strike on'.

Dave Ayre knew that Crook UCATT was straining at the bit, but:

> I was staggered when 93 members turned up for the first
> meeting in the market place along with over fifty lads from
> other unions and some who weren't members of any union at
> all. They couldn't all get into the room at the Mill House Inn, so
> we went outside and sat on the green in front of the church.
> Neither the police nor the locals knew what was going on.

Gerry Cassidy and Laurie Pringle from the Regional Council and Russ King spoke about 'pressure from local authority workers to become involved', but recommended the current policy 'until a positive total involvement line was undertaken'. King detailed the Newcastle agreement, but the meeting voted unanimously for 'all out strike action'. Dave recalls:

> After that we hired the Elite Hall—a large dancehall—and it
> was packed out every week for report-back meetings. Crook
> was geographically isolated, so we decided the branch would
> become an Action Committee in its own right and activists
> from other construction unions would be welcome to join us
> on Crook market place at 6.00am every day except Sundays.
> We did most organisational work at branch meetings and other
> decisions were taken on the hoof. I didn't have a car, but
> Reuben's old Saab was the lead vehicle when we went out
> picketing in larger numbers, though sometimes we split up. Jim
> Harper and Regional Committee members Jack Spowart and
> Charlie Lowther were great about what we were doing, but

one official said we were a 'law unto yourselves'. If we'd listened to him the lads would have crucified us, because they wanted to picket in their own way. Bill Kerriss's members at the council weren't officially involved, but in spite of the officials' efforts they supported our pickets and made financial contributions. You couldn't wish for better mates than Bill and Reuben on a picket line.

They focused on the area around Crook and Bishop Auckland: 'On most occasions our picketing was successful and we got every assistance from site workers. A Spennymoor crane operator said: "I'll make sure no one works on this site" and promptly coupled the concrete mixer and hauled it into mid-air. It hung there for weeks.'

When picketing is effective it is illegal

On 1 September the *Star* reported that flying pickets were bringing out sites in Oxford. 40,000 were out in South Wales and a UCATT official acknowledged that 'mobile squads of pickets have played a major part'. A 350-strong Pontypridd meeting had launched a Charter group and two people joined the CP. Eleven NFBTE members had agreed to meet the union claim. Andy Affleck knew of 24 signed company agreements in the Northern Region and buses had been laid on for a mass meeting in Newcastle next day. 2,000 were expected in Newcastle on the 2nd, but in the event 'about 1,500' turned up. Jim Harper announced over thirty company agreements conceding £30 for 35 hours and 'cost-of-living clauses' and there would be a meeting every Wednesday to 'organise picket squads'.

On the 4th the *Star* reported that the police had brutally evicted thirteen strikers sitting-in at Warrington DSS office and a woman from the Claimants Union had been taken to hospital.

Next day national union officials released the names of 91 firms that had signed company agreements and claimed that about 20,000 men had gone back on a guaranteed £30 a week or better. In Scotland, 46 firms had agreed to two days' extra holiday, twenty had conceded 35 hours and 26 were prepared for 'steps to be taken' in 1973 to reach 35 hours 'over a period'. 4,000 Birmingham strikers had applauded Pete Carter's announcement that Charter policy was to close cement works and Ken Barlow had led a march to a nearby cement depot. 900 London sites were shut. The CP Merseyside Area

Committee noted the 'magnificent stands' that 'forced over 100 firms to sign a pay deal'.

An *SW* 'Building Workers' Special' demanded the full claim. It argued against 'company deals' and for mass pickets at cement works. Because of inflation and VAT, £25 a week plus £5 guaranteed bonus would be worth £27.50 in summer 1973 and £25 in summer 1974. In London 850 sites were out and no company agreements had been signed. In Birmingham, Gerry Kelly noted that the local strike committee, 'led by Charter militants', called fortnightly mass meetings of up to 4,000, pressured reluctant UCATT officials into supporting action and decided 'all strategy and some policy'. No company agreements had been signed, even those that conceded the full claim. TGWU officials had been 'very poor'. The strike was solid in Wigan. The Action Committee called daily meetings and aimed to link up with other parts of the North West regularly. Chorley, Blackburn, Bolton and Birkenhead Action Committees were determined to stay out for the full claim, but there had been company agreements on Merseyside. A Bradford mass meeting had voted for the full claim and against company agreements. None of the rank and file members at an Edinburgh mass meeting had been allowed to speak, so an 'ad hoc committee' of convenors, stewards and activists drew up a plan.

1 Organise a total stoppage of all building work in Edinburgh.
2 Organise a mass picketing of any site that fails to respond to the strike call.
3 Mass meetings to be policy making bodies...
4 Demand the national executive organise a total stoppage.
5 Demand immediate strike pay for single strikers.
6 A national campaign for collections, donations and solidarity action from other trade unions.
7 No retreat on the original demand of £30 for £35. No to the model agreement.

The strike was solid in the West of Scotland and especially in Glasgow, where local authority workers were still out, but officials and 'many' CPers supported company agreements.

On the 7th the *Star* reported that William Hilton—a former UCATT research worker, but now a director of the Federation of Master Builders and a Labour MP—had called for 'a settlement that is universally applied', but Harry Ewing, Labour MP for Stirling, had given 200 strikers his full support. Many Glasgow Corporation workers were still out, but single men were being denied social security. A UCATT official had been arrested on a picket line and remanded on £50 bail. Four pickets at a Basildon lump site were charged with 'obstruction' and one with a 'breach of the peace'.

On the 9th the *Star* reported that the Basildon employer used a helicopter to fly lumpers over a picket. The London Regional Action Committee was appealing for money and support on pickets. Every North West major site, except the Stockport motorway, was out.

By the 11th 25 Glasgow strikers were sitting-in at a DSS office that refused to pay single strikers. Next day, after rumours of a 'compromise', 12,000 Merseyside strikers braved the rain and voted to tell the national negotiators to stand firm.

SW held up Wigan Action Committee as a model. Major sites had been stopped, including several that employed lumpers. Local authority and demolition workers had come out, members of the National Union of Railwaymen had struck for a day to prevent supplies reaching lump sites and AUEW members, NUM members and the Trades Council had raised £3,000. The Action Committee Chairman observed: 'When picketing is effective it is illegal', but police were 'not going to beat us back to work'.

SW noted that sixty delegates from thirteen North West Action Committees had voted by forty votes to nil for a resolution criticising the national union leaders' support for local and company deals. 'The only open dissension from this line came from three Liverpool delegates, led by Billy James' [ie Jones], the CP Chairman of the Merseyside Action Committee. UCATT officials had persuaded an Aberdeen workforce that the employer had met the full claim, but after they went back he changed his mind. The 'model agreement' made no concessions on the working week and the £28 offered for October 1973 would be worth £26, because of inflation. Parts of the known company agreements were worse than the current national agreement and officials had signed one behind the Lowestoft Action Committee's back. There was the danger of 'enormous confusion', so militants should demand that 'before any settlement is made, it be put to mass meetings of those who have borne the brunt of the struggle, the rank and file'. Sites that were organised before the dispute began 'must take the initiative in ensuring that non-unionised and previously lump sites do not return to work until union cards have been issued and stewards recognised'. There should be no retreat on a national deal. Officials were happy 'to allow rank and file militants and some local officials to spread the strike and organise the industry properly', while 'they wait for the rank and file to tire of the struggle so that they can then carve out a deal and resume cosy relations with the big building bosses'.

A mass meeting in York had voted to stay out and then 200 men went across the road to a hospital site and closed it down. Hull dockers had loaned their bus to flying pickets. Most Coventry sites were shut and Oxford was receiving attention. However, 'informal talks' had begun at the TUC Congress, where George Smith 'managed to pass the week without making any public reference to the strike, still less any appeal for solidarity and financial support'. What was required was mass picketing of building suppliers, an appeal to the movement for sympathy action and funds and a nationally co-ordinated rank-and-file strategy.

Roger Rosewell reported on an IS Building Workers Meeting of over forty. Most were UCATT members from London, Cambridge, Lowestoft, Birmingham, Wolverhampton, Kirkby and Edinburgh. UCATT leaders' policy was to sign 'sweetheart company agreements' with big contractors in return for policing the rank and file. The EC contained 'a number of awful CPers', who also controlled the General Council and used it as 'a justification for foot-dragging'. However, there were 'very deep splits' in the CP about the *Charter*. The Editorial Board's failure to publish the *Charter* showed that they were 'trapped between a genuinely revolutionary strategy' and 'control over this or that union post or body'. One UCATT branch secretary—presumably Dave Ayre—was an IS member and had lists of branch meeting places, so while all comrades should make contacts, building workers should have 'frank off-the-record discussions' with dissident CP activists, because CP leaders 'will support some sort of settlement that falls very far short of the claim'. The meeting decided to argue for a TUC levy and workplace collections. Union officials should waive their pay. The TGWU should release funds to all strikers and establish a national hardship fund. Local DSS claims committees should be set up, joint site committees and rank and file strike committees established, cement works and other suppliers picketed and UCATT members in other industries called out on an all-out national strike. No company agreements should be signed. After the strike there should be campaigns for 100 percent trade unionism to 'smash the lump'. A special *SW* article should be written on flying pickets. All IS building workers should be active in the Charter and set up groups where none exist. There should be a call for a Charter Conference and a new Editorial Board. The IS Building Workers' Fraction would meet twice a year—John Fontaine was elected unopposed as secretary—with a National Fraction Committee of elected delegates meeting in between to co-ordinate activity. They should produce an 'SW Special' immediately and then every two months. (This report did not appear in the IS *Internal Bulletin* until October.)

He gave us a UCATT tie and instructed us to cool our militancy

On 30 August Crook UCATT members were concerned about 'divisive' company agreements. Some local firms were still working and 'a Mobile Picket' would be organised. 22 volunteered. Dave Ayre feels that the branch did well:

> We had very little money, but Reuben did a fantastic job. Pickets got sandwiches every day they went out, petrol money was always there and so was hardship money. It got harder to keep members interested when mothers and wives weren't getting pay packets and branch funds didn't last long, but our flying pickets intensified because we received hints that sites might be drifting back. In the early stages the police presence had been negligible, but as days turned to weeks their interest increased. Our intelligence gathering was very loose, but 'scouts' informed us that a site near Shildon was showing an element of stubbornness, so we decided to pay a visit. A few of us drove into the village with Reuben, myself and a couple of other lads in the front car. Reuben said: 'We have company. The boys in blue are joining our convoy.' Not saying another word, he headed for the beautiful village green. 'What's thoo deein'?' 'Just watch.' The convoy was ploughing a deep furrow. We were asked for our credentials at the site office. Only union officials were authorised to go onto sites, but my site authorisation letter worked wonders. The lads came out, but half-heartedly, so further visits would be needed.

They decided to picket cement works. Reuben recalls:

> Fifteen miles up the dale at Eastgate near Stanhope, the Blue Circle cement works was still operating. When three cars full of pickets arrived we found that there was only one entrance at the top of a steep incline. Most drivers were in the TGWU, but they had a good social club with a football field and I'd visited there with teams in the past. They also had a big canteen, so I was volunteered to go for twelve bacon 'sams'—sandwiches. The

women in the canteen wondered who wanted that many. Once I'd got the sams in my bag I told them that they were for the pickets. They didn't know whether they'd done the right thing or not. It wasn't long before a manager came to move us. He had a Hitler moustache, but we were on a public footpath and there wasn't much he could do, so he called the police. Just before they arrived a tanker driver stopped and asked if he could help. He locked his tanker's door, left it blocking the gate and walked down the hill, so nobody could get in or out. The police arrived—an inspector in one car, four policemen in another and two on motorcycles. The inspector demanded to know who stopped the lorry and started getting annoyed and threatening us, but we weren't breaking any law because we were standing in groups of three. There was a queue waiting to get in and out and he wanted to know who was stopping them. Someone shouted: 'The driver stopped the bloody wagon.' There were smiles all round. The inspector had to walk down the hill. He came back with the manager and then disappeared, looking for the driver, but failed to find him. A police motorcyclist asked us why we were on strike. I told him we wanted the same wages and conditions that he had. He reminded me that the police had once gone on strike. Then a TV crew arrived. How they found out about it we don't rightly know, but their first words were: 'Will there be trouble?' Few of the workers on that site joined the strike, but we left pickets on the gate.

Dave adds:

We had no problems with the stewards. In fact they were supportive. Billy Wilthew, the convenor, worked in the quarry up on the fell and he was great. He used to 'put' coal tubs for my dad and knew what it was all about. The TV crew filmed Reuben and I as we spoke with lorry drivers. Some lads—big lads, too—said 'this is getting too big for us' and stayed in the background, but we were on TV that night. Next day Reuben and I were summoned by Jim Harper and Jack Spowart. Harper got on his high horse, angrily spelling out to us that picketing suppliers was not part of UCATT strategy. The TV coverage had given a 'militant dimension' to the strike and such activity must cease forthwith. He gave us a UCATT tie and instructed us to cool our militancy.

Reuben recalls:

We didn't get a lot of sympathy from one UCATT official. I'd had a better welcome from employers. He was against the strike and believed it should have been settled by national negotiations, yet employers could have reached an agreement if they'd wanted to. Anyway, we got some money for the hardship fund, which was what we'd gone for. Money was getting short. Some single men who lived in lodgings couldn't pay their rent and were asked to leave. I owed back rent for my council house and got notice to quit. But we carried on with the strike and the good weather was in our favour.

Two days later we went to a concrete plant at St Helen Auckland and stood at the gate as buses, cars and vans came flying out. The drivers had been told that anyone who stopped would be sacked. Next morning we came earlier and caught the men walking in. Someone once told me: 'To move a mountain, just keep chipping away at it.' We managed to talk three or four into joining us and left them picketing the gate. Other pickets worked for that firm, but most of its sites were working. Their batching plant was in a big field and there were railway engine sheds. It was all fenced off with only one big entrance gate and that was locked, so we waited until the Shawnee Poole tractors came out. There were four of them, each carrying ten tons of concrete. I asked the first driver if they had a steward and the other three thought we'd refused to let them out. The police arrived and complained about us stopping men working. They hadn't been told the truth. We couldn't have stopped such huge machines if they'd wanted to get out. Then the police complained that we'd stopped them getting their breakfasts in the canteen.

On 6 September 100 turned up at the Elite Hall in Crook. Dave reported that sites were being picketed with 'considerable success'.

In the second half of August the NFBTE had written to members, claiming that 'moderate elements' amongst the strikers were 'being forced into intemperate action' by 'groups of militants'. They wanted contributions to an 'intimidation dossier' which would 'be passed to the government with a view to trying to stop similar kinds of pressure being exerted in the future'.

Dave recalls:

We decided to picket the NFBTE meeting at the County Hotel in Durham, one of the poshest in the county. When we arrived the hotel was undergoing refurbishment, so we thought we'd try to kill two birds with one stone. Reuben and I climbed through an open widow on the ground floor and surprised everyone. We had limited success in persuading lads to pull out, but some did. The local NFBTE Chairman spoke to us at length about a 'dossier'. It would include our names, amongst others, and would document our activities. Action could be taken against us. This was our first hint about the dodgy dossier, but we treated it rather cavalierly and reminded him that we were fortunate to live in the North East, which had a rich trade union culture inherited from the long history of miners' struggles, and repercussions could occur if anyone fell foul of this dossier.

Reuben recalls they heard that work was going on at Durham Prison.

We decided to pay a visit. We asked the agent for permission to go up to the cells to talk to the men who were working there and then Dave and I and a few more climbed up a ladder propped near an open window. Some workers were hiding, but others came out and some were union members. It looked like something out of an old film, with them in the cells and us outside, talking through the bars. Then we were accused of trespassing on Crown property, so we left.

Dave recalls that 'the scabs were pretty mild'. Whether they were entirely sympathetic was doubtful, but they 'got the treatment'.

On the 13th eighty turned up at the Elite Hall. Russ King reported on 'the progress of the strike throughout Teesside'. 'Interim Agreements relative to Health Services and Local Authorities were read and discussed.' The meeting sent a telegram to the national negotiators 'urging that there be no "Sell Out" and that a strong stand be maintained for original claim'. Dave recalls: 'We never did any damage, issued threats or said one wrong word, and there'd been no serious assaults on pickets. The strike had stayed solid and drift back stayed minimal, due to our vigilance, though some lads were tired. So was Reuben's Saab. Its engine packed in not long afterwards.'

Victory or sell-out?

On 14 September the *Star* reported that Labour-controlled Birmingham City Council would not evict strikers who couldn't pay their rent. Wandsworth Borough Council building workers supported the strike and the biggest local contractor and other employers would pay the full claim if no settlement was reached at the national negotiations. The London Regional Action Committee had called for a lobby. The TGWU would need to consult members, so 'speculation about an end to the dispute today is groundless'.

Big civil engineering contractors' lucrative government contracts had been badly affected, so they pressed the NFBTE to settle. They offered craftsmen £28, rising to £29.60 in 1973 and £32 in 1974. (London and Liverpool rates would be 20p higher and labourers would get 85 percent of these figures.) However, inflation had to rise over 8.5 percent before a cost of living increase kicked in. There would be one day's extra holiday from winter 1972-1973 and two days more from winter 1973-1974, but no reduction in the forty-hour week before October 1973 and no national negotiations before November 1974. Workers would be 'in direct employment of a builder, contractor or sub-contractor'. The lump would stay.

Next day's *Star* headline was 'Building Workers Condemn Deal'. 300 men from Edinburgh, Sheffield, St Helens, Wigan, Liverpool, Kent and London had lobbied the negotiations. The UCATT EC had ratified the deal and wanted members back on the 18th. TGWU negotiators had voted against. The Chairman of Sheffield Action Committee announced: 'The whole of the Yorkshire area will stay out', and the lobbiers planned 'future action'.

The Times reported that 'several union leaders left the employers' quarters by a side door to avoid the 400 demonstrators chanting in the street outside. When the details were made known, cries of '"We've been sold down the river" echoed across the road.' One negotiator told demonstrators that the deal was a 'washout', though it would cost the employers £100,000,000 a year.

On the 16th the *Star* headline was 'Angry Reaction in Building Industry'. The TGWU now expected its members to go back on the 18th. A 300-strong Leeds meeting had rejected the deal with one vote against and called for flying pickets. UCATT North West Regional Council had demanded full consultation before a return to work. Birmingham stewards had rejected the deal and 100 occupied the NFBTE offices for an hour. Pete Carter announced: 'There will be no return to work here on Monday, and we are organising a mass rally for Tuesday to decide on our next moves.' The London Regional Action Committee had recommended 'an organised return to work', though any site that was not 100 percent unionised and lump-free would remain in dispute. Bristol men had voted to go back, but Merthyr, Pontypridd and Swansea Action Committees

The Flying Pickets

were to recommend striking for the full claim. A mass meeting in Stoke decided to picket for a further week. Most of the 2,000 Dundee strikers rejected the deal, Edinburgh men accepted and 4,000 in Glasgow shouted down an EC member and he walked out. The Glasgow Action Committee Chairman noted that the deal was worse than the known company agreements. He called for a vote and claimed that a 'substantial majority' rejected the deal.

In *SW* John Fontaine stressed that there were no mass meetings to discuss the return to work in London, where Regional Action Committee members were appointed, not elected; but there had been a 'Wave of Protest' and another three weeks would have seen the NFBTE concede the full claim and 'translated the slogan "Kill the lump" into a reality'. George Smith had admitted that if employers persisted in using the lump, they would be rejecting the agreement: 'On this basis we will be back in dispute.' At World's End they had had a struggle to stop a steward from being victimised and the bonus from being cut. UCATT and TGWU officials and the Regional Action Committee refused to honour pledges to organise joint site action against such attacks and had issued hundreds of overtime permits. When a site delegation put their case they refused to act. Fontaine argued for maintaining the Co-ordinating Committees and stewards' 'Combine Committees' to link major contractors' sites in order to struggle for 100 percent union membership, the election of officials and delegate conferences with policy-making powers. *SW* reported that Tommy McTurk, the CP Glasgow UCATT official, had allowed no discussion and the vote was split down the middle.

Arthur Dale told the *Star* that Leeds men were going back to fight for 100 percent trade union membership and an end to the lump. Mass meetings at Merthyr and Pontypridd had voted to go back. Four Manchester sites stayed closed, as did nearly all Birmingham sites, but men returned elsewhere in the Midlands.

Mixed feelings

The strike had been solid in Darlington. Jim French recalls:

> We achieved the biggest rise that any union had won at that time, but that was down to the activity of the rank and file, not the negotiators. A lot of disillusioned men blamed the national officials and said we should have stuck out longer to win the full claim, but others were glad to be back. The overall view was

that we had achieved a lot, but we hadn't conducted the strike well because UCATT was brand new. Brown's management fell into line and all the enhanced rates for their 'blue-eyed' favourites were stopped. We got a great deal and older members still talk about it. It's something that we should be proud of and a story that should be told in all stewards' courses in every union. Of course, some employers tried to fiddle the lads and the NFBTE didn't stop there.

Reuben Barker recalls:

Some of Lax's men still claim that I took them out of the gate, but I couldn't have taken 40 out if they hadn't wanted to go. One scaffolder reckoned that the strike was the best thing ever because he'd spent all his time fishing; but a joiner who never got to work before 8.30am complained that I got him out of bed at 6.00am to go picketing. None of them acknowledge that nobody was disciplined. The union was out in the open and production went up after six weeks' rest, but old traditions die hard. A labourer missed the van one morning and decided to walk the four miles, even though it was raining. The senior boss drove past him and then told the site foreman to send him home for being late. On another occasion some of us were putting in a new fireplace in Crook. We gave it all a good clean and the woman was very pleased, so she gave us money for a drink. When the senior boss arrived she told him that his men had done a good job and that she'd given us money. He said: 'That money belongs to me. I pay their wages.' Another time the manager arranged for a joiner to start on my site, but he never arrived. I asked the manager where he was and he said that he'd sent him home for a week. I told him he was out of order and asked him to arrange a meeting with the bosses. The senior boss, both of his sons and the manager met me and the joiner, who was a bag of nerves. The senior boss told us that he had to support his manager. I told him that he shouldn't send a joiner home who was needed on site and had a wife and child to support. He didn't seem to care too much, but the sons asked us what we wanted. We wanted his pay reinstated and a procedure whereby men got two verbal warnings and a written warning. One of the sons said that the joiner had refused to work Saturdays, Sundays and overtime. I reminded him that overtime wasn't compulsory and he left. The other son—who went cycling with Dave Ayre—agreed to what we wanted.

The Flying Pickets

Dave Ayre had mixed feelings:

> We got the biggest percentage increase we have ever had and
> nobody in Crook UCATT was victimised; but we didn't get all
> were after—35 hours, £10 more a week and an end to the lump.
> Some of us were of the opinion that local deals ought to have
> been officially opposed and that with a bit longer on strike we
> could have wrung more from the employers. Most lads at
> North Tees General Hospital felt happy about the outcome and
> there was no claw-back from bonus. Those who had picketed
> the site told us about a few scabs—joiners from the
> Northallerton area, which was not renowned for its trade union
> culture—so on the 22nd the stewards decided to down tools
> until they were removed. The joiners' steward and I went to
> negotiate with the site manager. He wasn't going to be dictated
> to by us and was under the impression that we had had our fill
> after weeks on strike, but higher management were horrified
> and implored us to start work. We explained why we couldn't
> and I think that, deep down, they must have had some respect
> for us, because instructions were given to remove the scabs.
> There's no doubt that the strike achieved an overwhelming
> feeling of self-confidence and made the stewards' work much
> easier. The activists had learned about the role of officials, but
> not defeating the lump was a strategic defeat.

A list of 26 'Members on Picket Duty During Dispute'—mostly
'Mobile Pickets'—was appended to the Crook UCATT minutes.

On 19 September 12,000 marched to Liverpool Pierhead to join
7,000 others. They slow-handclapped the UCATT Regional Secretary and barracked CPer Bill Jones, who appealed for a return to
work and a fight to change the national leadership. 100 supported
him on the first vote and none on the second. They voted to stay out.

Thousands demonstrated in Birmingham. Pete Carter denounced
the deal as a 'sell-out'. A majority accepted the UCATT Midland
Regional Council and Action Committee recommendation and voted
to strike for another week. Late that night the Action Committee
Chairman, Mike Shilvock, opened his door and saw four masked
men. A knife slashed at him and someone broke the safety chain.

> There was a running punch-up, back up the hall to the bedroom
> of my flat, with me doing most of the running, obviously,
> whereupon they threw me bodily into the bedroom and thereby

set about giving me a systematic working over on the floor, with their fists and their boots, ending up with pulling my arm out of my socket, breaking it at the elbow with an Irish whip, and breaking my toes by stamping on my foot.

...I gave an almight[y] shout of pain from this, whereupon the leader gave the command to the other three: 'That's it.'

The *Daily Express* reported a top policeman's suggestion that angry building workers had done it. The *Daily Mirror* blamed a 'militant heavy gang', angry at Shilvock's 'sell-out'. Shilvock described it as a 'paramilitary style attack'. Ken Barlow believed it was a 'professional beating-up', but the police were useless.

On the 21st a majority of the 7,000 at Liverpool Stadium voted to go back on the 25th. UCATT North West Regional Council wanted the full 1972 claim met in 1973. In Birmingham, Bryant refused to honour the pre-strike agreement and 1,500 stayed out.

On the 28th the *Star* quoted Lou Lewis. It was the 'general opinion', including 'the average lad who doesn't take an active part in union affairs', that 'another couple of weeks and they could have wrested that much more from the employers that would have made a settlement look reasonable', but the full claim could be won in 1973.

According to Ken Barlow, 'Brum lads were the last to go back', a week after everybody else. Three major firms didn't start for another week because the men were being short-changed.

On 6 October the *Star* reported that a Southend firm had refused to take back the EETPU steward and deputy steward and 46 men went on strike. Electricians from Watford and Thurrock sites joined their picket line, but when twelve of them returned a few minutes late they were not allowed to start. 200 went on a half-day strike.

SW reported that a sub-contractor at the World's End site had refused to pay the wage rise. Workers staged a short sit-in at the UCATT offices and demanded that an official call out other Cubitt sites, but he didn't. 353,000 Tax Exemption Certificates had been issued in a year, but photocopies could be bought in pubs and big contractors and the Inland Revenue accepted them.

Crook UCATT heard that George Smith had written, 'expressing thanks to members involved in the recent dispute', and the Regional Committee had sent a 'letter of thanks' for their 'support and activity'. One flying picket had been elected as a steward.

UCATT Northern Regional Committee heard that employers were trying to 'offset' some of the wage award from the bonus. Jim French, convenor at Magnet Joinery in Darlington (formerly

Brown's), feared redundancies. The status quo would apply. The committee would put a £10 advertisement in the *Star* on the eve of the Labour Party Conference: 'Northern Region UCATT welcomes Labour and demands higher living standards at less cost'.

The *Charter* reappeared after three months. The Editorial Board had been 'up to their necks in the day-to-day activities of the strike, organising picketing, etc' and condemned national officials who 'betrayed the unity and solidarity of the strike'. It was a 'sell-out' and a 'con-trick'. The *Charter* stressed the role of strike leaders in Merseyside, Manchester, Birmingham and London. There were articles under the names of Bill Jones, Frank Marsh, Phil Beyer, Lou Lewis and Arthur Dale, but not Pete Carter. Dave Roberts was Charter Area Secretary in South Wales and Ian Stevenson in Sheffield, Rotherham and Barnsley. They were all CPers.

CHAPTER 6

Violence and intimidation

Chester and North Wales Area Action Committee

Back in June 1972 two elected UCATT Regional Council members were appointed to chair Chester and North Wales Area Action Committee. Alan Abrahams now worked on McAlpine's Liverpool Teaching Hospital contract. Charlie Jones was a joiner and Secretary of Shotton UCATT. UCATT officials Albert Prest and Lou Armour and the TGWU's Eric Roberts were also to attend. Local building workers were 10 percent organised and there were a lot of lumpers, so the Regional Action Committee selected three well-organised sites to come out on the 26th—Laing's Colwyn Bay Police Station, Holst's West End at BSC Shotton and Taylor Woodrow's Chester Telephone Exchange. Members at work were asked for £1 for the 'National fund' and one hour's pay—from 50p to £1—a week for the 'North Western Merseyside Strike Fund'.

According to Des Warren, Charter Area Secretary Billy Regan invited him to the first Chester meeting at the Bull and Stirrup in Upper Northgate Street on the 29th. He wasn't a steward and wasn't working, but Charter members were present and nobody objected.

They set up a 'Sub Action Committee' responsible for picketing. For the first few weeks they visited organised and lump sites with a good response. Prest and Armour received the cash at Chester Labour Club, sent it to Liverpool and distributed what was sent back. Prest said that three sites would be pulled out each week, but they weren't.

One subbie claimed a collector demanded money with menaces. The CID grilled him for two hours, but let him go. The workforce said that the boss was trying to set him up and promised a levy.

On 2 August Arthur Murray, a joiners' steward, and two other Holst's men were at the Sub Action Committee. Mike Williams, a joiner and UCATT member, was the unofficial bonus steward at Shotton, and in the absence of the secretary he took the minutes.

Dave Jackson, the Shotton TGWU Secretary and Federation Steward, was treasurer. Collectors had been told to use union cards for identification and buy receipt books, but the meeting 'strongly recommended' that 'credentials, collection sheets, etc be made available immediately!' They appointed pairs of collectors for the Chester, Wrexham, Deeside and Rhyl areas. Warren was one of those for Rhyl. He recalled that Regan asked him to go round with the pickets. Murray reported that men at the Padeswood sewerage site had agreed to appoint a steward and work a forty-hour week, but after a TGWU 'delegate' visited there 'seemed to be a break down in the organisation'. Pickets would visit the site after the meeting.

On the 4th Chester Action Committee called for a 'full escalation'. Murray told the Sub Action Committee that Prest was on holiday the following week, so strike pay would be held over. A Wrexham steward reported that the TGWU District Secretary, Henry Williams, had told managers that there would be a settlement by the end of the week. Williams had not attended Chester Action Committee meetings and if he did not attend the next one there would be a picket at his office. Murray and another picket had encountered some travelling men at Padeswood: 'To say that their reception was abusive would be putting it very mildly.' If the full claim wasn't met by 15 August 'all sites in the area will be pulled out on strike'. A telegram was sent to the UCATT EC demanding £30 a week.

On the 7th the Sub Action Committee heard that the EC was thinking about signing a deal and TGWU officials had told the press there would be a settlement by the end of the week. Pickets for a Greenfield site would meet at 7.30am next day. Pickets would also assemble at Wrexham Beast Market ('Details will be given in the morning.'). A demonstration at the UCATT office in Manchester had been moved to the 15th to coincide with a Liverpool demonstration.

On the 9th Chester Action Comittee reckoned that 3,000 men and 'at least 75 percent' of sites were out and 'this should be 90 per cent by the end of the week'.

John McKinsie ('Macky') Jones was born in 1947, left school at fifteen and did his national service in the Royal Navy. In 1967 he was a painter for Catherwoods at Shotton and by 1972 he was a UCATT steward. During the early weeks of the strike he collected money, but when Catherwoods were pulled out on 9 August he became the Deeside pickets' treasurer.

Barry Scragg joined the CP in Liverpool in 1968. In 1972 he was a bricklayer on Simon Carves' £53,000,000 coke ovens contract at

Shotton and Chairman of Shotton UCATT. He chaired the weekday picket meetings at 9.00am in Flint. Each picket got 50p a day. Jones recalled: 'People would say that such and such a site was working and that would be it.'

The £1,000,000 Padeswood contract had been picketed for a third time on the 7th. According to the *Liverpool Daily Post*, 'about 75 pickets' from Holst's wanted the 21 non-members to join the TGWU and threatened to burn down the caravans of eleven of their families. The agent called in security guards and dogs and the 'majority' of men returned next day, but did no work, even though there were no pickets. On the 9th the *Post* quoted the agent: 'Our men are on strike because they are terrified.' On the 11th the *Chester Chronicle* noted 'reports of intimidation with pickets threatening to burn down offices and smash machinery if workers did not respond to their call'. The picket leaders, 'believed to be some of the 200 construction workers on strike at Shotton', said they would return, though an anonymous Shotton TGWU 'spokesman' said the action was 'unofficial'.

On the 11th 1,000 met at Connah's Quay and voted for an all-out strike. The *Post* reported that the Wrexham bypass, school and council house sites were stopped and lump sites would be picketed.

The North West Regional Action Committee called for an all-out strike and on the 14th a 2,500-strong meeting at Connah's Quay voted in favour. According to Alan Abrahams, Regional Council members and officials were to call meetings to elect Action Committees of stewards, branch officers and 'leading members' in Chester, Shotton, Connah's Quay, Rhyl, Denbigh, Colwyn Bay, Anglesey, Oswestry and Wrexham. Delegates were to report to Chester every week about picketing and fundraising.

Ken O'Shea was born in South Wales in 1929 and left school at fourteen. He did his national service in the Royal Army Medical Corps. In 1972 he was a Monks ganger and was elected as Secretary of Denbigh TGWU. When the strike got under way he was elected as Chairman of Denbigh Action Committee and reluctantly agreed. According to Warren, O'Shea had worked two years in the past six or seven, because of blacklisting. According to one Denbigh lad, they had two or three ten-minute meetings a week and they sometimes went out with Warren, but there was no trouble.

McKinsie Jones recalled that up to fifty Deeside pickets went out at a time. Most stayed at the site entrance, while the leaders talked to the men before they went to see site managers. 'Barry would say, "I am so and so from Flint pickets. I am a member of the Chester and

The Flying Pickets

North Wales Action Committee and we... have been told
the strike by pulling the sites out".' Usually they got cooperat
if not, Scragg said: 'Fair enough, we will put the picket on and
supplies coming in here.' Murray was due to fly out to Palma on
16th, so Scragg and Jones went to Chester Action Committee.

John Llywarch was born in 1943. He did his national service in
the Royal Welsh Fusiliers and from 1962 he worked on sites on a
self-employed basis, joining a union if there was one. In August 1972
he was a ganger on the Wrexham bypass and after Deeside pickets
visited he joined the TGWU, signed other men up and was elected
branch secretary. He lived at Llanrhaeader near Oswestry, so after
the Connah's Quay meeting he met other Oswestry stewards and
volunteered to be Chairman of that Action Committee. On Monday
to Friday mornings they planned picketing and on Mondays,
Wednesdays and Fridays they held picket meetings. Llywarch split
them into two groups of about a dozen and they 'kept walking
around until we found a site that we saw that was working'. It was
'very peaceful'. Then they went out in cars to 'look for sites that were
working' further afield. 'If it was not too far away and a few men
were working there we would vote whether to visit or not'. For a
'long range trip' they asked Prest for cash and booked a coach.

Eric Tomlinson was born in Bispham in 1939, but his mother took
him back to Everton three days later. His father worked nights as a
baker and his mother cleaned pubs and worked in a washhouse. Eric
failed the 11-plus, but passed the 13-plus and went to Walton Technical College. He trained as a plasterer, passed his City and Guilds
exams and completed his apprenticeship in 1960. At some point he
met Alan Abrahams at the Carrington Power Station site, and became
a TGWU steward for a fortnight, but in 1968 he joined the National
Front. Plaster dust played havoc with his asthma, so in 1970 he got a
labourer's job on the Wrexham bypass. 'There were hundreds of men
on the site and only a couple of toilets, which were always blocked up
and stinking. Fellas would have to get cement bags and go behind the
bushes or in the middle of the fields.' 'One lad cut his head open
working down a ditch, but wouldn't go and get it seen to until his
lunch break because he was frightened of losing his job.' According
to Llywarch and Warren, Tomlinson was against the strike at first but
joined the TGWU after pickets visited and was elected as steward and
Chairman of Wrexham Action Committee.

John Carpenter was born in Bristol in 1935. He left school in
1950 and became an apprentice joiner. He spent six months in the
Royal Army Ordnance Corps and then worked in Ireland and

a joiner, vacuum salesman and stage illusion-
got a job as a joiner at Wrexham Borough
'ATT and in June he paid the £1 weekly strike
s steward and in July his members voted to
a local issue and after they went back they
vy. Tomlinson asked them to join the strike
was elected Secretary of Wrexham Action
... They advised on social security, made factory collections, organised meetings, discussed local issues on Wednesdays, gave
a report to the Chester meetings on Thursdays and reported back on
Fridays. Pickets—including lumpers—met at the Beast Market every
weekday morning to get 'directions' from Tomlinson: 'If I had two
sites that day to be done in the same time I would take a couple of
the older fellows and put them in charge of a couple of cars and I
would take the others and go to the other site.' There was no trouble. He sometimes took his two-year-old son.

What about Shrewsbury?

On 15 August a Rhyl lumper claimed that pickets told him and fourteen others to stop work 'or else'. A Tory MP was investigating and
a TGWU official was allowing work to go on: 'Building dispute or
no building dispute, road safety must receive top priority.'

By the 16th North Wales housing sites were stopped. A contractor told the *Post* that 75 percent of his men wanted to go on
working, but 'a militant gang of pickets going round the area' were
'provoking the trouble'. The police knew about two coachloads of
pickets, 'but there has been no trouble and workers seem to be coming out in sympathy'. A TGWU official told local authority workers
to work normally, but they were picketed out.

On the 18th Oswestry pickets visited Shrewsbury sites and were
'quite successful'. On the 21st the *Shropshire Star* reported: 'An anti-
picket force has been formed by Shrewsbury building workers to
defend themselves against pickets who have threatened to swoop on
sites in the town.' Subbies and lumpers worked there.

> Mr John Price on the Severn Meadows estate said he hoped to
> raise enough men to ward off the pickets and persuade them
> to leave.
> 'If the pickets come on the site, we will ring round and within
> ten minutes we hope to have enough men to get them to leave.

The Flying Pickets

'We hope to get the support of 300 to 400 men.'

He added: 'We do not want violence if we can avoid it. It is all according to how many they get.'

Mr Price... does not think that any confrontation will come to violence. But his force 'will fight the pickets if necessary'.

An Oswestry picket recalled that they felt 'really scared' to go back to Shrewsbury, given that there were 'just 40 of us'.

On the 21st, according to the *Post*, '350 building pickets gate-crashed a meeting called by small builders and sub-contractors' at Llandudno. 'Most of them had arrived in a fleet of coaches, from East Flintshire and Wrexham, but there were many with Liverpool accents.' CPer Bill Jones, 'Chairman of Merseyside Strike Committee', told employers that strike-breaking would not be permitted and, if necessary, they would 'call on the assistance of dockers and car workers'. 'Let me make it clear that whether there are police or troops to protect you, we will not tolerate scabs.' Des Warren added that a return to work would be 'a declaration of war'. 'If you choose to be scabs, we warn you—you've not seen anything yet.' They agreed to stop work for a fortnight. Forty police were present and did not intervene, but one employer told the *Post*: 'We have stopped under threats of violence and intimidation.'

Glyn Davies was a labourer at Shotton and worked with Barry Scragg. He was Secretary of Deeside CP. His notebook shows that between 21st and 25th August Deeside pickets visited sites and builders' suppliers right across North Wales. He also noted 'Calloghan', 'Watkin, Starbuck Jones' and 'McAlpine Telford scabs 300'.

On the 25th the *Post* reported that the NFBTE was 'compiling a dossier of strike violence' to send to the Home Secretary. UCATT refuted allegations of threats by pickets at Chester and Colwyn Bay, but they had stopped eleven sites in Shropshire.

Next day the *Post* reported that Fred Walker, the CP Chairman of Merseyside Action Committee, claimed that five companies had signed agreements and twenty were negotiating.

John Llywarch reported back from Chester Action Committee that the Shrewsbury issue was 'in the hands of the officials'.

On the 29th Wrexham Action Committee complained that TGWU officials Henry Williams and Ted Hughes had told workers and employers at one site that the strike was unofficial. They asked Williams to help to pull the men out, but he told them that they had no official standing and refused, so they asked him to phone the Wales Regional Office and held a two-minute 'sit-in' at the switchboard until he did. The regional secretary said the strike was official, they all went to the site and the workers came out. Williams gave Tomlinson credentials and he became the official 'spokesman' for the Wrexham pickets. Wrexham and other Action Committees met at Oswestry. Llywarch recalled that 'somebody was shouting, "What about Shrewsbury?"'

On the 30th Oswestry Action Committee went to a Liverpool meeting. The *Post* quoted Llywarch saying that one firm's concrete lorries would be blacked after the strike.

On the 31st McKinsie Jones got to the Bull and Stirrup before 8.00pm, but a Shotton steward handed over £282 so he took it home. Tomlinson recalls that he disagreed strongly with CPer Abrahams' proposal that they should allow employers who signed company agreements to restart, because it would undermine the dispute. Abrahams remembered chairing a 'regular' meeting of seventy, not all of whom were members, though they were all in UCATT or the TGWU. They heard a report about men returning to work in the Oswestry area, after being threatened with dismissal and blacklisting. Delegates from Wrexham, Denbigh, Rhyl, Chester and Ellesmere Port decided to meet at Oswestry Labour Club on 6 September.

On 1 September the *Chronicle* reported that the Wrexham NFBTE Secretary had criticised two firms for 'making individual agreements'. An anonymous UCATT 'spokesman' said that several medium-sized firms had done so. The police confirmed that pickets had caused no trouble.

By the 4th all Deeside sites and builders' suppliers were shut. Wrexham Action Committee let lumpers and managers attend their meeting and Abrahams addressed 400 people. Next day even Prest called for an intensification of the strike. 'About 60' UCATT pickets went to the Hawker Siddeley factory at Broughton.

Billy Regan had booked a coach from Colwyn Bay to go to Oswestry on the 6th, but 'no one from the Chester or North Wales areas knew which sites they would be picketing'. Oswestry Action Committee would decide where to visit. O'Shea agreed that Denbigh pickets would share their coach. Tomlinson booked a coach to Oswestry, but Carpenter understood that they were going to Shrewsbury. Oswestry pickets heard that Llywarch had booked a coach and Chester Action Committee 'had arranged a picketing to go down to Shrewsbury'. Scragg booked two coaches from Flint and one from Chester for a 'fishing trip' to Wrexham. What Ellesmere Port pickets did is unclear, but according to the

CP journalist Arnison, Abrahams (who was from Ellesmere Port) couldn't go to Oswestry because he 'had to report to a meeting in Liverpool'. Abrahams had been on peaceful pickets involving up to 3,000 and 'did not anticipate that 300 would cause any problems'. Besides, Warren was now Rhyl UCATT Secretary and an official Chester Action Committee 'spokesman'.

6 September 1972

At 9.00am on 6 September 1972 between forty and fifty pickets filled the coach that left Wrexham Beast Market. They arrived at Oswestry Labour Club at about 9.45am. Tomlinson recalled that all that Llywarch said was, 'thanks for coming', but 'there was nobody in overall charge'. Tomlinson asked the Wrexham driver to phone his depot to get approval to go on to Shrewsbury. An Oswestry picket recalled him saying: 'These men have been warned before about working and today we are going to get them out.'

At 9.00am a coach had picked up 39 pickets outside the Odeon in Chester. Two more boarded en route and filled the last seats. They visited a Wrexham site and the coach driver claimed that he heard someone threaten a tractor driver with having his legs broken. The two Flint coaches weren't full, but all three arrived at Oswestry at about 10.30am. McKinsie Jones recalled the meeting lasted no longer than it took him to eat a bacon butty.

The Oswestry coach held 38 pickets. One heard: 'We are going to Shrewsbury.' Another thought that Llywarch announced that they were going to Shrewsbury. Another heard that Shrewsbury pickets would take them round the sites. Another recalled that 'a ginger haired bloke got on to show us the way'.

At 8.00am twenty or so pickets met at Lenton Pool in Denbigh and O'Shea handed out 25p dinner money. The Colwyn Bay coach arrived with fifteen or twenty on board, so it left full. Regan recalled that O'Shea, Warren and others got off at a Llanrhaeader site and they reached Oswestry thirty minutes after the others left. Warren understood that 'Ginger' Davies was deciding the route.

The first five coaches reached the Oak Hotel on Mytton Oak Road in Shrewsbury about 11.15am. Pickets from the Chester coach turned over a dumper, a road-roller and a van on the nearby Kingswood site, broke windows and damaged building materials. A Denbigh picket saw Terence Parry, the son of the contractor, pull a twelve-bore shotgun from his car: 'The first one that touches me has it.' 'He had it pointing at the lads.' He was 'all het up' in 'a rage of a temper'. 'I think if anybody would have gone to him he would have fired it.' Another picket heard: 'The next bastard that touches the machines or throws stones gets this.' Pickets got hold of the gun and broke it. Carpenter carried the stock and Tomlinson the barrel. Inspector Douglas and Chief Inspector Gradwell arrived and police cars blocked in the coaches. Tomlinson showed them the gun and asked for a photograph to be taken, but they wouldn't agree. Parry wasn't cautioned. (He later claimed that the shotgun was in his car because he'd been pigeon shooting the night before and he got it out because he was 'terrified'.) Gradwell asked Carpenter to get the picket 'leaders' together and told them: 'You can approach men at work and attempt to persuade them to stop work, but you must not go beyond that.' He wanted to know their route.

Llywarch told Oswestry pickets that 'if this sort of thing goes on he was going home' and 'everyone around him was in that frame of mind', though a 'small hard core were not willing to be kept in the group and ran away from the main body'. One told him: 'The time for fighting with balloons is over.' 'Get your fucking babies back in the coach and get them home.' Oswestry pickets heard Llywarch say: 'Look lads, none of this to happen. We have never picketed like this before and we are not going to do it again.' 'You have to calm down a bit, no more running wild.' Tomlinson told Wrexham pickets to 'cool off'. Pickets on the Colwyn Bay coach thought Warren said: 'The police are here, you had better keep it down' or 'keep it calm'. 'Have to take it easy on the next site because we have got company, the police have arrived.' 'I think we all better cool down because we are not likely to meet another nutter with a gun on every site.'

The Chester coach driver felt that any violence was the result of 'individual acts,' but he had to ask a young picket to get rid of two bricks. This coach led the way to Galliers' site at the Mount. Police had warned the manager, Terence Callaghan, who told Scragg that he should 'fuck off' before he brought in the anti-picketing squad. Scragg and others tried to persuade him to let them speak to the men, but he refused and offered to fight Warren. Then an Inspector suggested that it would be better for him to agree to a meeting. Pickets damaged plant and kerbstones, but Regan and others addressed the workers 'in the proper manner'. They asked the pickets to leave while they thought about it and then agreed to strike.

The Chester coach, directed by the 'area organiser of the building union in the Shrewsbury area', led the way to Watkins,

The Flying Pickets

Starbuck and Jones's site at Severn Meadows. Warren got permission to speak to the men and told them that all the canteen was fit for was having a match put to it. There was a bit of shouting, but then the workers left.

At lunchtime Oswestry pickets told Llywarch about the visit to Telford. Some pickets went into the Dolphin pub. The Chester coach was booked until 1.00pm, but the driver thought he heard about Telford before he set off. (When he got back he found three bricks on board.) A lot of Chester pickets got onto the Flint coaches and six boarded the Oswestry coach. Carpenter recalled that the Wrexham coach was under half full, since twenty boarded other coaches.

After the Oswestry coach set off someone shouted that they were going to Telford. One picket recalled that 'there was somebody giving instructions', but it wasn't Llywarch. Another heard: 'Remember, peaceful picketing.' The Wrexham driver told Carpenter that they were going to Telford. Regan knew they were going to McAlpine's Brookside site at Telford New Town.

Pickets on the Chester coach caused some damage at Brookside, but Warren recalled that a senior policeman shook his hand and said: 'I would like to congratulate you on the way the meetings have been held.' They visited two nearby sites and 'apart from the shotgun incident, we had completed a normal day's picketing'.

When he got home Warren found two reporters waiting. They had been there since 2.00pm.

That evening a Kingswood lumper told the police that one picket 'waved a bar' at him and another broke a van window and put stones and sand in the petrol tank. He saw no shotgun.

The Wrecker

On 7 September the *Shropshire Star* headline was 'Mob rule! Terror on sites as pickets run amok'. Mr Galliers believed that the police were 'largely to blame'. 'It was like law and order had broken down and we were subjected to mob rule.' '300 pickets were chanting, "Kill, Kill, Kill".' Police had made no arrests, but claimed that some pickets came from Liverpool. Llywarch was quoted: 'The first site we went on to in Shrewsbury, a chap pulled a shotgun on us.' The reporter, Philip Jones, claimed that six coaches arrived at Brookside, including one from Liverpool. (There were five at that point and none from Liverpool.) 'Some brandishing sticks and bars, they marched three and four abreast' and 'blitzed through the site like a column of red ants'. Barbara Growcott condemned the '"rotten cowards" who attacked her husband'. He was in hospital 'with head, leg and back injuries'. 'From what I hear there were three of them that did this to him.' His workmates 'saw him being beaten up and wouldn't lift a hand to help him. It was left to an 18-year-old student to go to his assistance.' The Shrewsbury TGWU District Secretary, Derek Preece, believed that the pickets were 'probably nothing to do with a trade union at all but "thugs"' and was 'worried that the action will hinder hopes of a building site settlement in the town', since 'talks had been progressing well over the last week'. McAlpine's site manager was quoted: 'We don't think anyone in this country should give in to violence.' The police 'acted very properly'.

The *Shropshire Star* later reported that about a dozen Shrewsbury and Telford building workers waited for an hour on the 7th, but no UCATT official turned up. McAlpine's Regional Director was quoted: '50 men reported for work this morning' at Brookside 'but only 20 men remained'. Police 'hoped to make arrests'.

Eric Roberts, the TGWU official at Shotton, told the *Chronicle* that many small firms would 'go to the wall' if the strike continued.

On the 10th the *Sunday People* carried a picture of Warren, 'The Wrecker'. It stressed that he was a Communist and published his home address. The 'National Front' threatened to blow up his house and people phoned Elsa to say that they were going to rape her and kill her and the kids. Police told her: 'We are on duty 24 hours a day, Madam. If anything happens please let us know.' She took the kids to Bob Williams' farm at Abergele. (He was a steel-fixer, Secretary of Colwyn Bay UCATT and Des's friend.) Nick Warren recalled that his father got a shotgun and his friends had pick-axe handles.

On the 14th a Mount site subbie told police that pickets had 'used threatening behaviour' and one promised 'physical action' if they refused to strike, though he was 'not threatened personally'. When the picket 'spokesman' asked them to strike they agreed to do so 'for our own safety'. (In the margin the police typed 'G.7 Warren'.) He hadn't gone into the canteen for the meeting, but as the pickets came out they 'were chanting, "Kill, kill, kill!".' One picket ('D.2. Tomlinson') said: 'We're closing the job.' Another ('D.3 J.M. Jones') said, 'We're having you out.' The subbie saw no damage being done. (Six months later he fell off a platform that he'd erected with his labourer and broke his neck. The Department of Employment inspector found three flagrant breaches of safety regulations. His subbie was fined under £250.)

On the 19th, at Prestatyn, Warren disagreed with the terms of the settlement, but accepted the CP line and recommended a return to work. There was a 2,000-strong demonstration in Chester

Days later a Brookside lumper's statement was 'amended' by Inspector Powell. Another lumper claimed that 'G7' and 'G5' committed violent acts. His statement was dated six months later.

On 6 October the *Post* quoted Lord Shawcross's speech to the Magistrates' Association: 'I think it a pity that the Home Secretary of the time (Mr Reginald Maudling) said the kind of picketing that took place was lawful and that it was only occasionally that there were breaches of the law.' 'As one Chief Constable put it to me— "Of course it's a riot. Ordinary people are frightened... But what can I do. I have 500 policemen in my whole force. There are well over 2,500 people here, brought in by coach to intimidate men still at work".' Shawcross, a former Labour Attorney General and guest at McAlpine's 1970 Christmas party, added: 'The industrial violence of the past months was an "unlawful conspiracy".'

By the 11th Robert Carr, the new Tory Home Secretary, had seen the NFBTE's *Violence & Intimidation: A Dossier of Examples of Personal Violence, Injury, Arson and Damage During the Building Strike 1972*. He thought 'the real problem was enforcement', so he would discuss with chief constables 'what further action they might take to defeat such violence and intimidation in industrial disputes'. The right to picket was 'not a licence to intimidate' and 'sheer numbers' could 'constitute intimidation'. Maurice Macmillan MP told the Tory Conference that 'secondary picketing' and 'unfair industrial practices' would be referred to the Industrial Relations Court. He hoped the TUC would enforce a code of practice and quoted the General Secretary, Victor Feather, speaking against mass pickets.

On the 15th the *News of the World* carried photographs of Alan Tattam, Pete Carter and Lou Lewis: 'The strife makers exposed'. Shop stewards refuted the allegations, but the paper didn't print their letter. Tattam pointed out that the 'only evidence of violence' was of lumpers attacking pickets. George Smith had investigated alleged violence and intimidation by strikers, but found no proof. Gerry Kelly noted in *SW* that the *News of the World* claimed that Carter had been on a picket at a cement depot that didn't exist and Lewis had been a flying picket in South London, where they weren't used.

The *Morning Star* reported that at 2.00pm on the 20th men at a Bryant site in Manchester had agreed to work overtime. At 4.00pm the wages man arrived with security guards, dogs and four policemen. Site managers sacked 32 men and announced that they would bring in lumpers. A picket was organised and UCATT made it official. Management reinstated fifteen men, but they refused to cross the picket, which turned away eight lumpers and a steel lorry. When other workers walked off site, management sacked them too.

On the 25th the NFBTE published *Violence & Intimidation*, which reportedly cost £14,000. It claimed that 'the violence was the work of comparatively small, but co-ordinated groups of people who were well organised, well directed and well financed', including 'militant elements within and—we have every reason to believe—without the industry'. They 'succeeded in causing a degree of disruption far beyond that justified by their numerical strength', 'culminating in the events of notorious "Black Wednesday"—September 6—when building sites over much of the West Midlands were subjected to deliberate and well-directed attack'. Flying pickets were 'a serious menace to the health of industrial democracy in this country' and the dossier would 'assist the government to find ways of removing this threat to the British way of life'. The 'evidence' was from anonymous 'private' sources, managers and the press, which also relied heavily on anonymous sources. For the events on 6 September the dossier quoted the *Shropshire Star*, the *Birmingham Post* and the *Daily Mail*. 'Three workmen injured and, at Shrewsbury, the police seized a shotgun.' 'Most of the demonstrators were armed with pieces of timber, pick handles and other objects.' 'Men were dragged from scaffolds and assaulted with bricks and other missiles' and 'many' pickets 'were not building workers'.

The dossier didn't say that a manager had brought out the shotgun, or that lumpers had broken a picket's leg at Colwyn Bay, or anything about the vicious beating of Mike Shilvock, or the man who brandished a shovel at Alan Abrahams, or employers' blacklists.

The *Financial Times* noted that the dossier 'suggests the existence of a sinister plot without being able to substantiate the allegations'. Many incidents 'seem to be little more than the ordinary spontaneous angry behaviour that might be expected on a building site at any time'. It read 'more like a politically motivated pamphlet than a serious study'. Apart from the bosses' house journal, the *Economist*, the serious press ignored it altogether.

On the 31st a picket from Laing's Barbican site was charged with 'intimidation' under the 'Act for Amending the Law Relating to Conspiracy, and to the Protection of Property and for other Purposes', of 1875. (Benjamin Disraeli's Tory government had wanted to legalise peaceful picketing.) Days later, eight pickets were charged with 'wilful obstruction' of the police.

Do you know Des Warren?

By November twenty detectives from Gwynedd and West Mercia were based in the Grand Hotel, Prestatyn, led by Detective Inspectors Salisbury and Glover. The *Mirror* noted: 'Police chiefs have sent an elite corps of detectives to smash an army of pickets.'

On the 2nd the *Liverpool Daily Post* reported that Tory MP Robert Redmond claimed to have seen 'gangs following building workers on Merseyside and threatening them with violence unless they stopped work'. A friend had told him that a picket had told him that they wanted 'to destroy the constitution'. He did not want to start a 'witch-hunt' or a 'reds under the beds' campaign, but wanted to know who was financing the 'firm "Rent-a-picket"', which had 'something in common with the Provisional IRA in Belfast'.

On the 3rd Glover interviewed John Llywarch in the presence of Chief Superintendent Hodges. Llywarch recalled: 'if I said what they wanted me to say I would not even be charged.' Glover later admitted that he 'took detailed notes' and 'prepared' them 'into statement form'. Four Oswestry pickets who were Crown witnesses weren't charged. After five and a half hours in a police station a fifth agreed to become a Crown witness just to get home.

On the 10th the *Chester Chronicle* focused on the 'threat file'. Pickets 'claim they were victims of a "smear" campaign by the employers and others should relish the chance to clear their name'.

John Bithell refused to go to the police station. He was arrested. Witnesses claim to have seen him put sand in a dumper's tank, but photographs showed him doing nothing wrong. He refused to be a Crown witness. Police took photographs and fingerprints and let him out on bail.

Billy Regan recalled that most interviewees weren't read their legal rights and were told that they wouldn't be charged if they informed on others. A typical question was: 'How will your wife and children manage when you go down the line for two years?'

Police told Barry Scragg 'it would be the worse for him' if he did not go to the station. He refused. They interviewed his mother, who was so upset that she went to the doctor. A photograph of McKinsie Jones was on the wall of Holywell police station.

Mike Williams had four and a half hours of ruthless interrogation and was told that if he didn't name people who caused damage he would be charged. According to Warren, Williams was 'shown a photograph of a group of pickets, with an arrow numbered G7 pointing at my head', and asked: 'Do you know Des Warren?'

A steward who had been held for four hours in a police station was told that his charge sheet was going to read like the Kray Twins', for demanding money with menaces, but they were particularly interested in Arthur Murray. Police told another steward that if he didn't tell them about Murray he couldn't leave the station. Neither steward was charged. Murray's solicitor doubted whether it was serious, but he should refuse to cooperate with the police.

On the 14th Warren was arrested and cautioned. Glover told him he would get ten years for saying 'No comment'. Warren asked for his solicitor, but he wasn't available, so they released him on bail.

On the 15th Murray was arrested. A detective told his wife Margaret: 'It's not the police who are doing this. It's the government.' At the police station Murray phoned his solicitor, but he wasn't available. Salisbury wouldn't allow his brother-in-law to be a witness, so he refused to cooperate. Glover pointed to a book of documents and said that they were all about him, but declined to show them. Murray's photograph and fingerprints would be taken. He demanded to see a lawyer and they let him out on £10 bail.

Mike Williams bought a receipt book and a cash book for collections. On the 16th, £72 was collected for a 'West End Site Welfare Fund'. By the 24th money was coming in from SGB and Simon Carves. Williams opened an account at the Trustee Savings Bank in Shotton with £20. By the 29th there was £5 left in cash.

On the 28th Alan Abrahams was found guilty of assault. The judge at Mold Crown Court sentenced him to twelve months in jail—suspended for three years. (He subsequently won his appeal. The judge had failed to mention that he was the intended victim.)

On the 30th the *Post* reported: 'Detectives have seen nearly 800 people in a mammoth inquiry into alleged incidents.'

Most of the enquiries have been in Shropshire and North Wales and have lasted nearly three months. Claims made by employers in a dossier are among those which have been probed.

There have been allegations of physical attacks, threats to persons and to property, and of disturbances and damage. At least 14 building sites have been visited—some in Flintshire, Denbigh and Caernarvonshire—and a number of these featured in ugly scenes during the 14-week strike.

Most of those interviewed are building workers and the Director of Public Prosecutions will be considering whether to bring charges against several dozen. It is understood that the Home Office has been kept informed about the progress of the investigations.

A report was 'likely to be on the desk' of Sir Norman Skelhorn in 'a few days'.

Llywarch was asked to sign Glover's 'prepared' statement. Questions he answered with 'Yes' or 'No' were now statements. He didn't know Warren before 6 September and he didn't see Tomlinson that day. He refused to sign and was promptly charged.

The Shotton Welfare Fund paid £50 to Chester solicitors.

On 11 December a detective told Murray's wife that he could 'forget it'. On the 18th £40 was withdrawn from the Welfare Fund. Barry Scragg chaired a North Wales CP public meeting at Connah's Quay and Barry Williams, an ASB official, spoke. On the 22nd the Shotton Cash Book noted: 'All charges dropped at this point'.

On 26 January 1973 Wrexham and North Wales Builders organised the 'Hod Carriers' Ball' at Connah's Quay Civic Hall. The compère, 'Hobo Rick', was Eric Tomlinson. On the 30th the Chester solicitors told McKinsie Jones that they would close the file, since the matter was 'completed'. On 5 February the Welfare Fund's TSB account was closed. From the 9th the 'Building Workers' Savings Club' received 15p a week from 130 men and the treasurer opened a new TSB account. The crisis seemed over.

There will undoubtedly be more struggles to come

Back on 1 November 1972 UCATT North West Regional Council had publicised the fact that many lumpers were dodging taxes and signing on the dole. They backed 200 pickets at one of the seventeen Merseyside sites supplied by 'Mr Lump'—the subbie Derek Barnes—and asked the EC to make it official.

On the 17th the *Morning Star* reported that a company called SOS had begun supplying lumpers on Merseyside on a 'free agency' basis to get round the Inland Revenue's efforts to tackle tax evasion. Lou Lewis acknowledged that, during the strike, union members had been 'amazed' at 'how much lump, pure and simple, and tax evasion actually existed'. Of the *News of the World* smears he asked how could 'a small group of politically motivated people' stop 1,600 sites by violence and intimidation? If there was 'serious resistance' from lumpers, 'you only had to mention that the Inland Revenue might pay them a visit. There was no trouble after that.' As for *Violence & Intimidation*, the police had no evidence that violent workers 'went on a rampage through Staffordshire'.

In London the World's End and Lovell's strike committees had amalgamated. John Fontaine told *SW*: 'We can pump information about the struggle and appeals for sorely-needed finance on to every organised site in London. With a joint victory on these two sites, we will go a long way to breaking the blacklist and ending victimisation once and for all.' Cubitt had threatened to withdraw from a council contract unless they paid a substantial increase on top of the tender price, but the strikers were convinced that site mamagers engineered the dispute to try to screw money out of the ratepayers. On the 20th World's End workers won what *SW* saw as 'the most significant victory in the London construction industry for ten years or more'. They made management negotiate on bonus and won Fontaine's reinstatement. Lou Lewis would be the next joiner to start. Early in December a London rally raised £100 for World's End strikers. Fontaine had been victimised. UCATT didn't make it official but he was reinstated.

1972 had seen the most strike days since 1926.

In *SW*, Jim Nichol, the IS National Treasurer, announced an appeal for £30,000 'to expand our printing works to meet the increasing demands' and to help build 'rank and file organisations'. IS had printed 60,000 *SW* 'Specials' and tens of thousands of leaflets for dockers' stewards fighting for the Pentonville 5, 45,000 *SW* 'Specials' to help building workers 'build solidarity' and 'counter the lies of the employers and the national press,' plus IS's *Post Office Worker, Print Worker, Steelworker, Carworker* and *The Collier*, and the *Rank and File Teacher, The Dockworker, The Journalists Charter*, and *The Building Workers' Charter*. *SW* acknowledged: 'There will undoubtedly be more struggles to come'.

CHAPTER 7

I don't think you can keep politics out of trade unionism

Carr spells out rules on picketing

By January 1973 UCATT Midland Region membership had increased by over 2,700 in one year, mainly from picketed sites.

The *Charter* urged support for the Birmingham Conference. Pete Carter argued that the strike united employers and the lump would increase. Union leaders had no strategy, but it was the Charter's 'number one priority'. John Fontaine reported on the 'Success at World's End'. The Editorial Board explained that the four-month gap in publication was 'mainly due to pressure on the funds'. 'In spite of this and an expenditure of nearly £1,000 on the last three issues, we are able to enter 1973 with all bills paid.' (There was no printer's name.) CPer Arthur Dale was Area Secretary for Leeds.

SW noted that a World's End subbie had sacked five men, four of whom held union positions. They were reinstated after a day, but essential equipment was removed. The job was two years behind schedule and Cubitt wanted £1,000,000 from the ratepayers. Days later Fontaine was sitting-in on top of a crane.

Late in January 6,000 men from 42 Birmingham sites went on strike in support of Pete Carter and three others who had been sacked after refusing to work in the rain. A Disputes Panel instructed Bryant to reinstate them. Carter told *SW* that the labour agencies Manpower, Evergreen, Labour Force and SOS were at work in the city. Employers wanted rid of militants so as to casualise the industry before the next national negotiations. Mike Shilvock reported that they were trying to organise sites 'before they got off the ground'.

Tory MP Nicholas Winterton referred to picketing: 'New laws must be brought in or existing laws enforced, to ensure that the activities of anarchists and communist thugs are crushed.'

The Director of Public Prosecutions had examined the police report on picketing and recommended prosecutions for 'conspiracy' under the 1875 Act. (That October he refused to deny that British military personnel were torturing IRA suspects in Northern Ireland. He later had to resign over his treatment of Peter Hain.) Sir—later, Lord—Peter Rawlinson, the Attorney General, was responsible to the Tory Cabinet via the Lord Chancellor, Lord Hailsham. Rawlinson evidently told the DPP to act and the police had their instructions by 2 February.

On the 14th the *Liverpool Daily Post* headline was 'Carr Spells Out Rules on Picketing'. Picket 'violence, intimidation or threats made those responsible liable to prosecution'.

At 6.30pm that day two detectives called at Des Warren's home in Prestatyn. Elsa was out. They gave him just enough time to phone Bob Williams to ask him to come over to look after the five kids, the eldest of whom was eleven, and took him to Flint police station.

Rita Tomlinson recalled that Eric Tomlinson was watching *Z Cars* at home in Wrexham when two detectives knocked on the door. They read him his rights, drove him to the police station, took photographs and fingerprints and questioned him for hours about 6 September 1972.

Police took Ken O'Shea and Warren to Wrexham police station, where they found Tomlinson, McKinsie Jones, Llywarch and Carpenter. They were driven to Shrewsbury police station and put in separate cells. By 9.00pm O'Shea knew that he might face serious charges. At midnight Glover told Warren that he faced 28 charges. The others were interviewed for two to four hours and told that they might face ten years in jail. Next day the six men were taken to court in a police van flanked by motorcycles and charged. A lawyer secured their release. 400 building workers were outside. 500 had gone on strike at BSC Shotton. 'Car lads' drove them home.

The *Post* reported that eighteen men facing 178 charges were to be up at Shrewsbury Crown Court on 15 March. Seven others were to be tried in North Wales. That evening eleven more pickets were charged. Ten worked for Holst's at Shotton and three were shop stewards. Another picket was charged soon after.

Days later H Hannam, Sir Robert McAlpine's chief security officer and a former Chief Superintendent at Scotland Yard, reminded the Commissioner of the Metropolitan Police, Sir Robert Mark, of 'the various official and semi-official statements on the need for tough action against mass pickets'.

Kevin Butcher, a Shotton TGWU member, was charged with 'intimidation' at Kingswood on 6 September 1972. His Chester solicitors asked Mike Williams about him. Williams recalled that they were among the last to get to the top of the site, where the main body of pickets was coming back. So they followed. Williams saw a man 'bring a shotgun out of a car and give it to one of the pickets', who threw it 'over a bank'. He didn't see Butcher talk to site workers or adopt an aggressive attitude and they weren't there ten minutes.

Workers' Fight

Back in 1968 the International Socialists had been alarmed by Enoch Powell's racist 'rivers of blood' speech and became deeply concerned after some London dockers demonstrated in his support. They were keen to forge unity on the revolutionary left.

Ten or a dozen Manchester, Coventry and Teesside Trotskyists published *Workers' Fight*. They saw IS as 'a sizeable left centrist force'—wobbling between reform and revolution—that was basically 'Luxemburgist' but was 're-adopting piece-meal elements' of Trotskyism. IS was overly focused on economics, rather than building a Leninist party, but it was politically 'unstable' and organisationally 'loose', so they wanted to bring political 'clarification' to its leadership. According to IS's Jim Higgins, Tony Cliff let them join IS that November, though most EC members were against it. (He didn't explain why they let it happen.) Cliff successfully proposed a new organisational structure for IS based on 'democratic centralism'. Members would have full rights of internal discussion, could form factions and nominate candidates for a National Committee of forty elected at the bi-annual Conference, but a small 'Leninist' Executive Committee would be responsible for running IS on a day-to-day basis. *Workers' Fight* supporters elected two NC members. They later claimed to have recruited three more, including Andrew Hornung, who had joined IS in 1968.

By 1969 IS membership was over 1,000 and *SW* sales had 'vastly increased'. Cliff wanted full timers to work on the paper and organise in the regions and the EC allowed him to choose them. IS made a 'turn to the class' that mainly involved leafleting factories from the outside, though *Rank and File* was read by thousands of teachers. When the 'Trotskyist Tendency' continued to publish *Workers' Fight*, Colin Barker successfully proposed that their Manchester members should be corralled in a separate branch. The NC also put their half a dozen Teesside members into a separate branch, and by early 1970 that branch had three members, while the other IS loyalists' branch had eighteen. The NC reunited the branches and a 'Commission' limited the rights of factions to hold private meetings and express disagreements publicly.

In spring 1971 IS Conference banned probationary membership and the payment of separate dues by Trotskyist Tendency members. In October the NC voted 31 to three in favour of deciding whether the Trotskyist Tendency would become disciplined members of IS or leave. According to Cliff and Barker, their national membership had gone up from nine to 35. They claimed to have set up branches in Oldham and Bolton, with up to thirty members, though the NC had not recognised their Salford branch. The December Special Conference voted by 205 to 120 that the 'fusion' was 'dissolved' and gave Trotskyist Tendency members 28 days to choose one organisation or the other. Most left, but a few stayed. This had long-term effects on IS's internal regime, but it also had important short-term consequences for supporting the North Wales pickets.

In the *SW* dated 24 February 1973 Ewa Widowson from Manchester IS reported that the Shotton 'action committee' had seen no fighting on 6 September 1972. Even though 'about 60 police' had followed them around, they made no arrests.

The charges against them are serious. They include conspiracy (planning the picket), demanding money with menaces (making a collection), and intimidation (on blackleg building workers).

They are not charged under the Industrial Relations Act (a matter for the civil courts) but under the Conspiracy and Protection of Property Act of 1875. This is an attempt to isolate the men from their union, since the union will not normally give legal help to men charged with criminal offences.

The men are to appear before a magistrates court on Thursday 15 March. They are calling for an all-out stoppage in the building trades that day. All trade unionists must support this call. Against the united power of the working class, the bosses are helpless. But if they feel they can get away with this attack, there will be no end to the prosecution of trade union militants.

Donations and requests for information should go to Arthur Murray. On Sunday the 25th John Swain of Exeter IS wrote to Murray:

We wish to express our disgust at the criminal actions of the Police in arresting comrades who did so much to help win the building strike for workers & kick the bosses in the teeth, and offer you our support in fighting them.

If the Police & employers are allowed to get away with this sort of thing in Shrewsbury, the whole of the T.U. & Labour movement will be fast eroded all over the country.

We must join together to fight them—and we must win. Please let us know if we can help you in any way.

Swain signed the letter on behalf of the secretary, Paul Mackney.

Brian Rose-Smith, a London solicitors' clerk, sent 'Dear Comrade Murray' a cheque for £1 and would provide free legal advice. He was 'a socialist and a regular reader of "*Socialist Worker*".' Where was Liverpool IS?

According to John Bloxam of *Workers' Fight*, Cynthia Baldry was born in South Africa in 1949. Her parents were in the CP, but in 1971, after the family moved to England, Cynthia joined IS. When workers occupied the Fisher-Bendix factory in Kirkby she was assigned to go through the books. The Liverpool dockers blacked all Thorn products and the workforce staved off redundancies. Baldry was also active in rent strikes and the NUT. Early in 1972 she left IS and became a member of the National Committee of *Workers' Fight*.

Late in February 1973 Baldry and Hornung went to Shotton and helped the Shotton Joint Contractors Shop Stewards Committee to publish 'Police Charge Deeside Building Workers'. It stressed that the defendants carried out union policy, made the case against attempts to criminalise mass picketing and quoted the key charge.

That you on the 6th. Day of September 1972 at Shrewsbury on a building site known as Kingswood, wrongfully and without legal authority intimidated diverse people with a view to compelling those people to abstain from their lawful work, contrary to section 7 (1) of the Conspiracy and Protection of Property Act 1875 as amended.

It called for a one-day national strike and a Shrewsbury demonstration on 15 March. Donations should go to Mike Williams, Treasurer of the 'Building Workers' Social Fund'. It was printed 'by voluntary labour by Workers' Fight, 98 Gifford Street, London N1'.

The JCSSC leaflet soon reached Loughborough International Marxist Group, who sent £1. Stafford IMG asked for a speaker, guaranteed support from North Staffs Polytechnic Socialist Society and promised to make a serious effort to get the Trades Council's backing. Birmingham Rank and File Teachers and Portsmouth IS donated £3. York IS sent £8. York Charter raised £1.70 at its first meeting. It all went into the Shotton 'fighting fund'. Shotton Savings Club paid for thirty copies of the *Charter*.

On 5 March the *Post* reported that 13,000 Shotton steelworkers were to meet on the 8th and would be asked to strike on the 15th.

SW reported an angry lobby of the TUC's Steel Conference in Sheffield that included a large Shotton contingent. The chairman, Sir Dai Davies, refused to allow debate on motions for industrial action and all officials accepted the prospect of 50,000 redundancies. (IS's rank and file paper, *Steelworker*, calculated that it would be nearer 130,000.) *SW* acknowledged the Charter's successes in Birmingham and interviewed Ken Barlow. He had been 'very mild and non-militant' as an ASW official and 'believed everything could be dealt with by negotiation', but when he was appointed as UCATT Midland Regional Secretary in 1971 his patch was in a 'terrible state' and virtually all the members worked in factories and for local authorities. Thanks to cooperation between rank and file activists, elected Regional Council members and accountable appointed officials, there were now over 100 organised sites. 'We have managed to undercut the whole system of blacklisting and victimisation', and they maintained organisation as contracts ended and new ones began. He saw 'the need for true socialist control and planning of industry'. 'The employers certainly don't separate their organisations and activities from politics. And I don't think you can keep politics out of trade unionism.'

On the 8th, Albert Prest, the Chester-based UCATT official, told the Shotton mass meeting that he couldn't support pickets, because if they were found guilty of violence, as charged, the union would be seen to approve such behaviour. According to Warren, CPer Barry Williams was able to 'demolish his arguments and put the class position'.

The TGWU had pledged to support its arrested members. Jeff Douglas, a painter at Courtauld's in Greenfield, as Secretary of Flint UCATT, told officials: 'North Wales has been singled out by the state and the employers because they feel that we are weaker owing to our geographical difficulties in rank and file organisation.' The pickets 'should be defended by our union on *all* charges'.

Chester & North Wales Building Workers Committee issued a leaflet. It claimed to be backed by UCATT and the TGWU, repeated chunks of the Shotton JCSSC leaflet and added:

We of the contractors feel that the struggle is the responsibility of everybody here, that if the steel making stops here, a town will virtually die. We have learnt through experience that the only way to get anywhere is to make our presence felt and our grievances known and that the way to do this may lead to confrontation with the forces of Law.

They wanted a national strike on the 15th and for cash to go to Mike Williams. A 'North Wales Building Trade Workers' (Charter) leaflet—over Bob Williams' name—called for exactly the same.

We daren't touch this with a bloody barge pole

On 9 March the UCATT North West Regional Secretary, Eric Hughes, invited the 24 defendants who were due up at Shrewsbury to the Ship Inn in Flint. (Prest arrived, but they refused to begin until he left.) UCATT and the TGWU would give legal support to the defendants if they signed over their cases to the union solicitor. Warren, Tomlinson and O'Shea declined, but 21 agreed.

The Building Workers' National Delegate Conference took place on 10 March. North Wales Building Workers hired a bus and joined up to 600 delegates in Birmingham. (The *Charter* subsequently argued that attracting 300 fewer delegates than in 1972 represented a 'Total Success', since some didn't make it because of a train drivers' dispute.) The Conference was 'promoted' by the *Building Workers' Charter* and 'sponsored' by Charter Groups in Glasgow, Blackpool, Widnes, Runcorn and Warrington, Leeds, Bradford, Sheffield, Rotherham, Barnsley, Birmingham, South Wales and the South East, and also by London Building Workers, Merseyside Shop Stewards and Building Workers' Committee and Building Workers' Forums in Manchester, Wigan, North Staffordshire, Bolton and North Wales.

The Charter now included political and economic demands:

1   £1 per hour basic rate of pay for a five-day, 35-hour week with maximum differential of 5p.
2   Four weeks' holiday with full pay plus the retention of Christmas Day and Boxing Day as statutory holidays, and the introduction of New Year's Day and May Day as additional paid holidays.
3   A fully comprehensive pension scheme...
4   De-casualisation of the building industry...

5   Adequate safety and welfare regulations to be introduced and
     rigidly enforced in the building industry.
6   Democratise the trade unions by making:
     A) Delegate conferences policy making bodies.
     B) All TU officials submit themselves for election every three
        years and branch officials every year.
     C) The disbanding of selection boards.
7   Protection and recognition for shop stewards, with provision
     for regular meetings.
8   Establishing 100 percent compulsory TU membership.
9   Total opposition to the 'lump'.
10   The abolition of Working Rule 2B. Six day and Transfer
     clauses (which are used to victimise TU members) [by
     alowing employers to sack new starters in the first week].
11   The establishing of one fully democratic union for the
     building industry.
12   Full nationalisation and public ownership of the building
     industry.

It stressed the 'heroic efforts' of CP 'Charter Supporters' in 1972.
    Alan Abrahams was in the chair. Dennis Dugen stressed that the
Charter was not a challenge to the official union machinery, but Pete
Carter moved a 'Policy Statement' that challenged union leaders to
bring forward the rest of the 1972 wage award to June 1973, campaign for £40 for 35 hours, wage 'total war on the lump with
regional demonstrations and official picketing of lump sites' and
pledge support to the LCDTU Conference against the Industrial
Relations Act on 31 March, to help bring 'an end to this Tory
administration and a return to a Labour Government pledged to
Socialist principles'. The Editorial Board's amendment backed an
official Merseyside Committee 'Mass Lobby of Parliament' on 28
March to support Eric Heffer's Private Member's Bill against the
lump. It also supported regional activities against the lump to coincide with UCATT Midland Regional Council's official demonstration
on 18 May and its call for a national day of protest on 6 June. The
Charter's non-appearance during the 1972 strike was 'not from
weakness but because of the strength of the paper', since Editorial
Board members were 'involved at all levels', but it wouldn't happen
again. There was a need for 'greater participation by rank and file
workers' through letters, reports and articles; but greater paid sales
were required to justify printing the 15,000 copies called for in 1972.
The collection raised £536. (It was left to *SW* to report that delegates

supported 'moves to defend the 18 building workers from Deeside who are now on conspiracy charges for the "crime" of picketing'.)

That very day the UCATT and TGWU ECs withdrew support from the 24 North Wales pickets and sent Hughes to break the news. Next day—a Sunday—George Smith wrote to Hughes that the UCATT solicitor, John Williams, 'considers that these particular charges may take months to dispose of and would take us into legal costs beyond that accepted in the rules of the organisations involved'. The UCATT official Leslie Wood later recalled that Warren was 'charged on about eighty counts' and one EC member declared: 'We daren't touch this with a bloody barge pole'.

In the next few days Barry Jones, the East Flint Labour MP, assured Mike Williams that he had 'followed the debates on "lump Labour".' George Smith told Barry Scragg that the ECs had 'had legal advice on the lengthy and nature [sic] of the charges', and 'it would be doing the Building Unions a great disservice' to 'demonstrate or call a national stoppage in regard to these matters as the charges range from civil offences to criminal acts'. Prest called the charged men a 'bunch of hooligans' and 'only one step from the jungle'.

After paying £250 retainers to the Chester solicitors, and to Casson's of Salford, the Shotton Savings Club held £66. They needed more help. Liverpool dockers voted to come out on the 15th.

The Shrewsbury committal hearing

On 15 March the *Liverpool Daily Post* reported a 'big police operation for picket case'. Police leave had been cancelled, Abbey Foregate in Shrewsbury would be closed to traffic and officers were being drafted in from 'neighbouring counties'. (Some came from as far afield as Sunderland and Newcastle.)

At 8.00am police tried to turn back the defendants' supporters from Merseyside car plants, Liverpool docks, Shotton BSC and four Courtaulds factories, plus others from Prestatyn, Wrexham and Mostyn, as they entered Shropshire. Coaches of building workers came from Birmingham, London, Manchester, Stafford and Telford. A Wolverhampton coach was stopped six times. According to the *Post*, supporters were 'outnumbered two to one by 800 policemen', including 'a three deep line' behind 'temporary barriers', and 'not allowed within 50 yards of the court'. BSC Shotton was 'almost completely halted'. (A later Shotton leaflet noted that 'on the very route we marched along, there were fellow building workers working'.)

In *SW* Mike Flood Page reported that Shrewsbury 'looked like a cross between a ghost town and a police state', but 'despite repeated friskings and roadblocks, several hundred trade unionists joined the demonstration and marched through the town'.

In *Workers' Fight*, Cynthia Baldry's '1,000 Rally to Defend Pickets' noted that all the supporters' and the defendants' coaches were taken into a special car park. Police behind steel barricades lined the route to the Crown Court, police photographers were on top of the Wellington Monument, police surrounded the court building and police with dogs confronted defendants at the back door. McKinsie Jones's father was prevented from entering and his mother found herself in a public gallery that was supposedly too full for relatives, but not for dozens of police. Only six supporters were let in. There were more police in the body of the court. Baldry stressed there were 24 defendants, not only the six on 'conspiracy' charges, as reported in 'the capitalist press and the *Morning Star*'.

The six charged with 'conspiracy to intimidate' were John Mackenzie Jones of Flint, Eric Tomlinson and John Carpenter of Wrexham, Kenneth O'Shea of Henilan, Dennis Warren of Prestatyn and John Llywarch who had moved to Quoiseley Bridge. The other eighteen faced lesser charges. They were Alfred James of Fford Llewelyn, Bernard Williams and Bryn Thomas of Flint, Arthur Murray and Terence Renshaw of Bagillt, Graham Roberts of Mold, Patrick Butcher of Mostyn, Brian Williams of St Asaph, Michael Pierce, John Seaburg, Leonard Williams and Derrick Hughes of Denbigh, Dennis Morris, William Hooson, Peter Sear, Samuel Warburton and Malcolm Clee of Wrexham and Garry Davies, now living in Hove. They were all granted legal aid and £50 bail.

After the ten-minute hearing Pete Carter addressed a meeting outside. 'This is a political trial, and all sections of workers must respond. The parade of police is an indication of the fear that the ruling class has of the organised working class.' It was 'an effort by the Tories to back up the [pay] freeze by getting "public opinion" on the side of the ruling class against our trade union practice of picketing. The issue is a class issue and we must respond as a class.' 'We must work to put pressure on the trade union bureaucrats to get official support but we cannot afford to wait for them to act.' Then the 24 led a march through Shrewsbury.

The *Post* reported 'no scuffles' and police later escorted the coaches out of town. The Assistant Chief Constable of West Mercia had drafted in men from Stoke, Cheshire, Birmingham and North Wales, because 'advance information' had 'suggested that many

The Flying Pickets

more than the 400 to 500 demonstrators who turned up would' travel to Shrewsbury to 'disrupt the court proceedings'. There was no lawbreaking, so the operation was 'successful and justified'.

A Tory MP proposed that picketing rights should be curtailed and that strikers should get no social security benefits.

The *Guardian*'s 'How to "Rent" a Protest Demo' reported that '200' supporters were mainly 'local building trade unionists' with 'some help' from IS, the IMG and the CP. They and the SLL were 'probably the only' organisations 'with the discipline to call out the troops in the firm knowledge that the troops will actually arrive'.

SW quoted John Carpenter. 'It's not just me or the other lads here, it's not even just the 300,000 building workers who came out on strike last summer, it's the whole working class movement that's on trial here today.' 'We're not frightened about being put away for five years. We wouldn't be inside for five weeks.' *SW* reported the *Charter* call for a national strike on 25 April.

CHAPTER 8

The Charter Defence Committee

The Defence Committee

By mid-March 1973 cash was coming into the Shotton Savings Club from local sites and the balance was about £100. £10 went to the *Charter*. Local Charter members formed a 'Defence Committee'. It included Billy Regan, Secretary, Bob Williams, Joe Edwards (a joiner at Holst's), Ivor Lloyd (Chairman of Flint UCATT), Mike Reece (a bricklayer for Monks' at Greenfield) and Mike Williams as Treasurer. Shirley Williams photocopied a few 'collection sheets'. 'North Wales Building Workers' asked 'all trade union members' to support their 'brothers', 'morally and financially' via the 'Building Workers Social Fund'. According to Regan, they 'decided right from the start that we would be a non-political committee'.

The Joint Contractors Shop Stewards Committee's *Shotton Building Workers Solidarity Bulletin No 2* was printed by Workers' Fight in London. It noted that a picket carrying out union policy was in danger of being criminalised and the 'conspiracy' charge meant that 'the copper's word is evidence!' 'So far Law and Order has meant that they make the laws and we take the orders.' 'We have no faith in the courts run by the bosses and the police.' 'Our "leaders", the union officials, have been conspicuous by their absence.' 'The rank and file must act.' It wanted 'many more delegations' at Shrewsbury on 25 April and donations to 'Defence of Pickets'.

On 26 March Wigan Charter reported that thirteen local pickets had been fined up to £150 in 1972. After a 'great deal of pressure from the rank and file' the TGWU and UCATT had 'assisted in paying some'. They sent £7 (around £55 today) and 'expect to be sending you regular sums'. Someone wrote 'Leaflets' on the letter.

On the 27th a meeting at the Raven Hotel in Flint heard the official Merseyside Committee's leaflet about the 'Mass Lobby to

Parliament' on the 28th. Dave Jackson and Arthur Murray evidently went and Jackson was on a 'Delegation' to Sheffield, York, Rotherham and Leeds. The Savings Club sent £4 to the *Charter*. Ian Stevenson of the Editorial Board later reported that 'some shop stewards in Sheffield and Rotherham' were 'beginning to launch a campaign in your defence' with a public meeting. It was 'most important' that one of the 24 spoke. Leeds IMG knew of 'no Branch of the Charter', but building workers were 'willing to take the case up'. They planned a coach to Shrewsbury. 'Can you supply (i) 100 leaflets, urgently, (ii) a speaker for a meeting in Leeds?'

Preston LCDTU 'Steering Committee'—a TGWU docks steward, a member of the National & Local Government Officers' Association, a former UCATT steward and Ron Ralph, a former National Union of Sheet Metal Workers steward—sent the Defence Committee £28 from three building sites, transport workers, Harris College Students' Union, an AUEW branch, two NUT members and unemployed trade unionists. (UCATT, ASB and TGWU stewards, AUEW and EETPU convenors, AUEW, TASS and TGWU Branch secretaries, a TASS Office Committee Chairman, three members of NUT Rank and File and one NALGO member later signed a solidarity letter.) A Preston leaflet called for collections for the 'Shrewsbury Building Workers Fund' and solidarity on 'April 28th'.

On 2 April Kenneth Thomas was at Llanwrst Magistrates' Court and committed for trial at Mold Crown Court on 15 June. On the 3rd Glyn Davies was at Holywell Magistrates' Court, charged with 'intimidation' and 'assault causing actual bodily harm'. He was committed for trial at Mold. (Mike Williams was there to support him and after that evening's Charter meeting he noted: 'Get! Cards Printed with Defence of Pickets' and 'Pamphlets & Collection Sheets'.) On the 4th Peter Moroney was up at Ruabon Magistrates' Court and committed for trial at Mold on 15 June.

Near the end of the builders' strike the UCATT official John Broome had stopped a lorry on a main road outside a Stockport factory and spoken to the driver for nine minutes. The police charged him with obstructing the highway, but magistrates dismissed the case. The Home Secretary asked the police to appeal. Lord Hailsham had appointed John Passmore Widgery, a former soldier, as Lord Chief Justice in 1971. In 1972 Widgery presided over the whitewashing of the shooting of fourteen civil rights activists by the Parachute Regiment in Derry. On 10 April 1973 he and other Court of Appeal judges decided that Broome had committed a crime, because the Industrial Relations Act allowed pickets to use only voices and placards and they ordered the Stockport magistrates to convict him. (They fined him £25.) UCATT funded an expensive appeal to the House of Lords, which confirmed that Broome had a 'statutory right peacefully to seek to persuade a person not to work', but not to 'obstruct the highway'.

In August 1972 Peter Westwater had been a steward at the Padeswood sewerage site. Flint pickets visited, but couldn't do much about the travelling men who lived in caravans. These men asked Westwater to go to the Connah's Quay meeting on 14 August. He reported that if they failed to come out they would let their mates down. They refused. Westwater said: 'If the pickets come up here there will be bloody murder.' He was charged with threatening to murder.

The Crown Prosecutor was Frederick Maurice Drake. He was born in 1923 and educated at St George's School in Harpenden and Exeter College Oxford. During World War Two he was an RAF navigator in nightfighter squadrons and was awarded the Distinguished Flying Cross. He was called to the bar at Lincoln's Inn in 1950 and became a QC in 1968. Drake's supporting barrister, John Desmond Augustine Fennell, was born in 1933 and educated at Ampleforth School and Corpus Christi College Cambridge. He was in the Grenadier Guards from 1956 to 1958 and was called to the bar in 1959. In 1972, under the Tories, both Drake and Fennel were both promoted to the role of Recorders of the Crown Court.

On 14 April 1973 Westwater was up at Mold Magistrates' Court. Drake claimed that an hour after Westwater left, 'nearly 100 pickets' were 'stopped at the site entrance by two security men with guard dogs'. A ganger said that 'after a previous visit by about sixty pickets they stopped work' but 'decided to return on the Monday morning' and 'took the "bloody murder" remark seriously'. The site agent testified: 'One of them said to one man they knew where he lived and they would burn his house down.' Westwater's defence barrister, Geoffrey Kilfoil, stressed that his client was 'not one of the pickets who did damage at sites; not one of those thugs—non-union members and agitators among them, who turned up in buses, not one of those who threatened to burn caravans, wives and children'. The case was dismissed. Westwater was relieved. 'It was in no way a threat, but I used appropriate words to express the mood of a mass meeting of the action committee.' 'I would not have been able to get a job anywhere if I had been convicted.' (He got a job elsewhere.)

North Wales 24 Charter Defence Committee

Defence Committee Bulletin No 1 was drafted on the back of North Wales Building Workers collection sheets, probably early in April. It stressed the official nature of the picketing, underlined the seriousness of the 'conspiracy' charges, noted that the committal hearing had been postponed to 18 May and asked for solidarity. The 24's trial would start in October, last three months and cost £500,000 (worth over £4,000,000 today). The defendants' living costs would not be met by legal aid, so there was an appeal for 'funds'.

The printed 'North Wales 24 Defence Committee' leaflet gave Billy Regan's and Bob Williams' phone numbers, the addresses of the original members and those of Dave Jackson and CPer Barry Scragg. It was printed 'by voluntary labour at 98 Gifford Street, London N1.' (Workers' Fight wasn't credited.)

The *Charter*'s front-page headline was 'All Out' on May Day in support of the TUC-led general strike against Tory incomes policy. UCATT North West Regional Council and the Charter Conference had called on building workers to join the UCATT-TGWU London Action Committee lobby on 18 May. Pete Carter stressed that, while employers had agreed to ban the lump, 400,000 Tax Exemption Certificates were circulating and the Tories were trying to criminalise effective picketing. A photograph showed the 'Shrewsbury 24' on 15 March and claimed that 'nearly 1,000' building workers and '300' others demonstrated. Dennis Dugen conceded that there had been 'a period of post-strike exhaustion, and the *Charter* suffered,' but the Editorial Board needed 'more organised returns'. 200 delegates had attended a separate Charter conference in Scotland on 23 March. A correspondent thanked the *Star*, 'the only national daily that consistently supported our struggle'. (The *Charter* was printed by IS.)

Defence Committee Bulletin No 2 asked for a demonstration on 18 May and 'future action if all the charges are not dropped'.

We must recognise the trial for what it is—a political attack on our right to picket, to defend our standard of living and stand up to the Tories. It is an attack on all of us, the whole working class. We must respond as a class. We appeal for delegations not only from building sites, but from all places of work and unions.

The Tories aimed 'to strengthen the law—their law—against us'. 'They've been preparing the attack since last September, yet the police weren't ready to submit evidence to defence lawyers. 210

charges and 7 volumes of police evidence is still not enough for them.' The Denbigh defendants were now charged with 'affray'. The pickets had allegedly caused damage amounting to £1,400, yet the Inland Revenue lost £5,000 a week from Brookside lumpers. Defence lawyers would cost £250,000. As for 'our so-called leaders in the trade union movement', they had advised defendants to 'wash their faces and put on clean suits'. 'Our fight would be strengthened by official backing and we must continue to demand it. But we must not wait for it. We must act now ourselves and build rank and file support.' 'Organise through your branch, place of work, trades council, to get collections made and levies put on; to get tours of sites and places of work, and meetings, set up, and invite speakers from the Defence Committee'. The 'Defence of the North Wales 24' was 'organised and coordinated by a Defence Committee of North Wales Charter'. (The leaflet was 'Printed by voluntary labour at 98 Gifford St, London N1.' Workers' Fight wasn't credited.)

At some point Warren 'came into conflict with local CP leaders'.

> I felt we should have a national committee, operating from Liverpool, working for the broadest-based support. I felt that it should be made clear to the movement as soon as possible that it was not a legal attack on us personally, but a political attack on the movement as a whole. I was told by local Charter Movement leaders that there was no precedent for this situation, given what I felt were parochial arguments, and the defence committee got stuck in North Wales.

Yet he went along with the decision at the time. A 'North Wales 24 Charter Defence Committee' (CDC) collection sheet asked for cash to go to Mike Williams, Treasurer of the 'Defence Fund'.

On 16 April Ian Stevenson reported that Sheffield UCATT, TGWU and AUEW branches and students were forming a committee 'in defence of the Shrewsbury building workers'. They hoped to get 'at least 2 coaches' to Shrewsbury on the 25th. (*Bulletin 1* and *Bulletin 2* later brought him up to date.) Next day TASS Divisional Council in Birmingham pledged 'full support' for the 'Shrewsbury 18', called on their EC to raise the issue with UCATT and the TGWU and sent the Defence Fund £10. Leeds IMG planned a joint public meeting with the CP on 6 May. Soon after Leeds *Charter* announced a meeting that day. Pete Carter would speak and they hoped to get some of the charged men. CPer Arthur Dale sent a leaflet to his Shotton comrade Glyn Davies: 'Hope you can make it.'

The demand for a toilet roll remains a revolutionary slogan

Back in February 1973 Gerry Kelly reported in *SW* that the SOS Labour Bureau in Birmingham was supplying most big contractors with lumpers. It claimed it had 130,000 on its books. Kelly was one of six 'leading stewards' who had walked into the SOS offices, along with a TV crew. The stewards barricaded the door, told the staff that the office was being 'occupied' as a protest against the lump, leafed through the files and found that lumpers got no guaranteed basic pay, no holiday pay, no overtime rates, no notice of dismissal and no travelling expenses. Some bricklayers got 87.5p an hour while others got £1.25. After the police arrived, one steward noted down information about SOS's clients and gave it to a journalist. The police didn't charge anyone. A film of the occupation appeared on TV that evening, but the *Birmingham Evening Mail* didn't publish the names of SOS's clients.

On 17-20 March IS's conference heard that 746 of the 2,667 members were manual workers and 763 were white-collar workers. 750 had joined in the past twelve months, but only 467 had been members for more than three years. IS was 'breathing down the CP's neck' and some CPers had joined. 'Significant sections of the CP's rank and file, and on the whole their best militants, have come to regard us as part of the movement', while the CP leaders' 'trojan horse' in the union bureaucracy was 'a prison'. IS would build factory branches and a national organisation to link groups around sixteen 'rank and file' papers, including *The Building Worker*.

The LCDTU was taken out of mothballs. *SW* believed it failed to 'play any significant role' in the Pentonville 5 campaign or the struggle against the Industrial Relations Act. Its chairman refused motions from the floor. Was it a 'Stage Army or Fighting Force?'

On 31 March the LCDTU Conference was supported by four union executives (including the South Wales NUM), 26 district committees and 344 branches, but only seventy shop stewards' committees, including Shotton, McAlpine's Liverpool Hospital site, Shell Carrington and the Merseyside Docks. The Conference Declaration called for May Day strikes against the Tories' incomes policy.

IS's April *Internal Bulletin* noted that 200 comrades had been LCDTU delegates, but 'disparate elements of the CP ganged together to ensure that IS couldn't make an intervention'. The same thing happened at the Charter Conference.

On 19 April Pete Carter argued in the *Star* that some UCATT EC members were welcoming 'Bona fide labour only', yet there had been 'little improvement in site conditions since the days of "The Ragged Trousered Philanthropists". Most canteens and toilets remain appalling. Hot water, soap and towels remain a luxury. Drying rooms are near non-existent, those that do exist are inadequate.' 'The demand for a toilet roll remains a revolutionary slogan.' Heffer's anti-lump Bill could 'only be won on the basis of mass action and pressure' by 'a one-day stoppage with major demonstrations in every city' on 18 May. (He didn't mention SOS or Shrewsbury.)

That very day the DPP signed summonses for only *five* Birmingham stewards on charges of 'unlawful assembly' and 'conspiracy to trespass' and for the ATV crew members. UCATT Midland Regional Council learned that the Chief Constable had told the Home Secretary that his force was against the 'conspiracy' charge and Robert Carr delayed the summonses.

On the 23rd the *Star* reported that eighty Birmingham stewards aimed to give lump sites the 'treatment' by arriving unannounced, asking for the lump to end and, if that failed, putting on pickets and blacking supplies. UCATT North West Regional Council had distributed 5,000 copies of Heffer's Bill, asked stewards to lobby their MPs and booked two trains, each capable of carrying 500. They planned to black supplies to lump sites and called for local authority contracts to ban 'labour only'. The TGWU London Building Workers' Group had called for the lump to be a 'target' on May Day and organised a stewards' meeting to prepare for the 18th.

Engineering stewards at Courtaulds in Greenfield issued a leaflet, 'Why Are Millions of Trade Unionists on Strike on May 1st 1973'. It noted the 1972 strike but said nothing about the picket charges.

A London law collective sent the Charter Defence Committee (CDC) a 'Picket Special' leaflet for May Day. It listed the main attacks on picketing, including that in North Wales, and announced a picket of Marylebone Magistrates' Court to support two National Union of Public Employees pickets who had refused to tell fellow pickets to disperse. *Up Against the Law* and 'Defending in Court' gave useful advice on dealing with police, courts and judges.

The TGWU supported the 'Day of Action' on May Day and the AUEW instructed members to strike. An estimated 1,600,000 came out. (The LCDTU sponsors had now shrunk to 37.) Two of the 24 'tried to get assurances from a TGWU official at a Wrexham May Day meeting, which he avoided giving'. After a massive May Day demonstration in Birmingham, summonses were issued to the five stewards and the three ATV crew members.

117 redundancies were announced at Shotton, including eight of the 24. The Shotton Savings Club paid for 25 copies of the *Charter*.

On 7 May Arthur Dale told Glyn Davies that he had had 'a good dig at people' at the Leeds Charter meeting and several had promised to 'get various branches etc to write to the North Wales Committee'. 'I want you to get the Secretary of your Committee to write & I am assured of a good response' from Arthur Scargill, the leader of Yorkshire NUM. Dale also sent addresses for the Secretary of Leeds Teachers' Association and the Secretary of Leeds Trades Council, where he was 'hoping to get a resolution through... via UCATT'. (The TUC had abandoned its ban on CP trades council delegates.)

On the 8th a York Union of Shop, Distributive & Allied Workers steward, Trades Council delegate and IMG member told the person who spoke at a May Day meeting at the University that they had sent a letter to Glyn Davies. The writer had spoken at the Students' Union, which voted to donate £30 and provide a free bus to Shrewsbury for students and trade unionists on the 18th. The campaign was moving on to a York college and union branches.

SW reported the SOS stewards' 'conspiracy' charge, the Shrewsbury hearing and the London lobby on the 18th. There was 'no danger that parliament will bring the lump's reign to an end', because Peter Walker had been part of Slater Walker, which launched a firm of building contractors that relied on lumpers. He was now Tory Minister of State at the Department of the Environment, which was supposed to monitor public building contracts, yet factory inspectors had turned a blind eye to lumpers' breaches of safety regulations that led to the deaths of several workers. Marples Ridgway were fined £50 per death. UCATT was 'on its uppers', but while George Smith ordered branches not to give money to the Charter or other 'anti trade union' bodies, he had held merger discussions with the GMWU and borrowed £250,000. 25 UCATT officials now got £68 a week, plus expenses, and a new Ford automatic each year.

On the 9th the *Star* reported the CDC call for 'a big turn-up' at Shrewsbury on the 18th. Four coaches were going from Birmingham and others from Merseyside and North Wales. Sheffield and Rotherham Defence Committee's leaflet indicated that 'representatives' of Rotherham Trades Council, the NUM, UCATT, AUEW, TGWU and branch and shop steward committee delegates would organise a bus to Shrewsbury on the 18th. Those interested should contact Ian Stevenson or an AUEW official. Their collection sheet asked for cheques and postal orders to be made out to the Shotton Building Workers Social Fund.

Next day the *Star* reported a 'Big Build-Up for "Kill Lump" Lobby' in London on the 18th. North West sites and branches were sending delegates. On the 11th the *Star* reported that London Joint Sites Committee 'buses' would go to Shrewsbury on the 18th. After a meeting called by a Glasgow UCATT official, thirty stewards were 'planning flying picket squads as part of their campaign to stamp out the lump".' They would not notify sites in advance, but all construction union members could join the pickets on the 18th.

UCATT Midland Regional Council issued a statement about SOS. They could not condone law breaking, but the charges were the Tory government's response to employers 'baying for blood' after the 'humiliating failure' of the Industrial Relations Act. Criminal law was being used in 'a new way to discipline and repress militant workers', so this was 'an attack on trade unions and the labour movement'. The council had 'resolved to do all in its power to support the members and to be seen to be doing so'. A Birmingham Defence Committee would 'publish broadsheets and pamphlets outlining the progress of the case', raise money and arrange demonstrations. Support had come from trades councils, Labour Party organisations and 'other movements of the left'. The National Council of Civil Liberties' lawyers would undertake the stewards' defence. (This was all completely official.)

On the 14th the *Star* reported that Austin Motors stewards had supported Heffer's Bill. The London Action Committee had called on UCATT and TGWU members to attend the lobby and the London Joint Sites Committee was meeting next day to organise a strike. SOS was mentioned briefly. Five men would be up in Shrewsbury on the 18th, but committal proceedings against the rest had been adjourned to 15 June 'at the request of the defence'.

On the 17th the *Star* reported 'strong support' for a stoppage and protest in London from Wandsworth, Piccadilly and Olympia sites the following day. A few seats were available on what was now a single bus to Shrewsbury. Birmingham building workers were being urged to clock off at 10.00am to join an official march and meeting in the city. Thousands of leaflets had been distributed and UCATT Midland Regional Council wanted 'every man from every site on the march and every site identified by a banner'.

A Scottish Charter leaflet claimed that the North Wales Defence Fund had spent £1,000 on solicitors. Leeds Charter's leaflet noted that the case rested on 'photographic evidence collected by the *Special Branch*' and 'testimonies 6 *months after the event*'. It announced a meeting on 24 June. (Arthur Dale later told Glyn Davies about a

The Flying Pickets

'mass meeting of building *workers*' and would 'leave it to *you* to arrange with the Committee about speakers'.)

The Defence Fund held almost £1,000. £10 had come from a McAlpine's site at Wrexham, £15 from Bolton Students Union, £27 from Nottingham Workers' Fight and £31 from Wigan UCATT.

Of concern to all trade unionists

On 18 May the *Star* published an interview with Ken Barlow. 'Two years ago I was not convinced that the type of action that brings members on the streets was the best. But now I have no hesitation in saying that our marches, demonstrations and mass picketing have brought into being a new type of building trade unionist.' The Charter played an 'extremely responsible' role, 'complementary to the official one'. 'We need a combination of all these forms, plus the backing of the rest of the labour movement, in order to defeat the most determined attack of the building contractors to destroy our union.' The rule that allowed 'bona fide sub-contractors' was 'a Trojan Horse for the lump'—'never once have we found the employers in compliance'. Union rule changes took time, and Heffer's Bill had to be supported, but Midland activists 'go straight on to the sites where lump labour is suspected, give them a chance to employ direct or clear it off the job, and, if they don't, declare the site shut and place pickets on the gate'. They had 'an increasing army of pickets that maintain a rota, even if it closes an organised job'. The Shrewsbury trial was 'of concern to all trade unionists'.

The *Star* claimed that over 1,000 marched through Birmingham and 1,000 'extra' copies were sold on sites as well as on the London demonstration, where 'hundreds' of building workers and 'deputations' from Liverpool, Manchester, Scotland and Southend turned up at Tower Hill and were addressed by UCATT official Alan Tattam, even though the EC hadn't backed the demonstration. In Central Hall Westminster, Jack Henry was in the chair and 'won loud applause' when he recommended the *Star* as 'the only national daily paper which championed the building workers' cause'. Other speakers included Manchester and London UCATT officials, TGWU officials and CPer Pete Kavanagh. Eric Heffer wasn't confident.

Six Labour and eight Tory MPs were present in the chamber when the Bill was read. Idris Owen, the Tory MP for Stockport North, was a director of a construction company that used lumpers and a former NFBTE Vice-President. He led the attack. In the end, 56 voted in favour and sixteen against, but so many Labour MPs had gone home that the quorum wasn't achieved and the Bill fell.

A local paper reported the Shrewsbury committal hearing. Edward Williams, Derrick Hughes, John Seaburg and Michael Pierce from Denbigh were Shotton TGWU members and Kenneth O'Shea was Chairman of Denbigh TGWU. They were charged with 'affray' and 'criminal damage'. William Hooson from Shotton TGWU and Arthur Murray from Flint UCATT were charged with 'intimidation'. They were committed for trial at Mold Crown Court and released on £50 bail. 'About 40 people' were allowed into the court.

The *Star* reported that four coaches of supporters came from the Midlands, one from London and others from Liverpool and North Wales. There were building workers from Rotherham and Chester and 'delegations' from South Wales NUM, Morris Motors, Colchester transport workers, London and Glasgow electricians and Oxford draughtsmen. Trades Council banners came from Oxford, Colchester, Hammersmith, Kensington and the Cities of London and Westminster. Delegations came from Glasgow, North Wales, Merseyside, London and Leeds *Charter*, North Wales Area CP, South Wales University Labour Club and a 'host of International Socialist and International Marxist groups', including those from Colchester, South Wales, York, Leeds and Oxford. Bill Jones chaired a rally 'watched by about 100 policemen and plain clothes men'. He stressed that donations should go to Mike Williams. 'David Jack[son]', Chairman of the 'North Wales Builders' Liaison Committee', spoke, as did Ian Stevenson, Glasgow CPer Barry Docherty and a member of the South Wales NUM EC. 'Speaking for all seven defendants, O'Shea thanked the demonstrators', but 'could make no further comment'.

A local paper quoted the Deputy Chief Constable of West Mercia. 'Only a handful of demonstrators are trade unionists. The vast majority are young students. It's a case of "rent a crowd".' He had brought 200 police.

SW reported that police frisked supporters entering the court so thoroughly that 'initially they refused entry to the seven defendants'. The trials were 'engineered' by top construction bosses.

Glyn Davies wrote in the CP Wales Committee *Campaign Bulletin* that 'banners displayed by the participants from different unions, political parties etc transformed the mood of the 600 to 700 marchers, with shouts of "Solidarity with the Shrewsbury 24".' 'For June 15th when the 24 will appear again in court at Shrewsbury, a mass call is made for thousands of demonstrators to wave their banners in unison to convey the spirit of solidarity with the Shrewsbury 24, the Birmingham 5 and the lads who come up at Mold.' Deeside CP, 'one of our fastest growing branches', had recruited eleven new members.

The *Star* reported that 140 Birmingham Trades Council delegates regretted comments in UCATT's *Viewpoint* 'casting doubt on the role' of the *Charter*.

The CP Yorkshire District Organiser was 'deeply concerned' at the 'conspiracy' charges and asked the CDC for 'any literature which we can circulate in the labour movement'. The CP Political Committee's *Weekly Letter* noted that the London meeting had agreed that 'the next stage of the campaign is to pick a major contracting firm and launch a drive to turn the "lump" off its site'.

Dennis Dugen chaired a North Wales Charter meeting at Connah's Quay Labour Club and Jack Henry and Pete Carter spoke. The collection raised £20, but expenses, posters and leaflets (printed commercially by D G Owens & Co of Shotton), cost over £28.

On 25 May the *Star* reported concrete lorries had crossed a picket line in Birmingham and a mass meeting had called for blacking the company. (Barlow soon had a written assurance that their drivers wouldn't cross.) UCATT Scottish Region Conference delegates had called on the EC to 'mount a vigorous campaign on selected firms' against the lump, while 'rank and file militants' had narrowly won a vote to call on the EC to ignore the two-year agreement and claim £40 for 35 hours. Delegates hissed the chairman when he attacked the Charter and denounced Labour MPs who missed the vote for Heffer's Bill for 'the biggest stab in the back'. One argued that parliament wouldn't outlaw the lump and quoted Barlow on the need to fight on the sites.

SW reported that Barry Docherty in Glasgow had moved 'an emergency resolution on the "Shrewsbury 24" calling for full moral and financial support' from the EC.

By early June the Defence Fund had received £1,810. Simon Carves workers at Shotton collected £5, Bob Williams sent £5 from Colwyn Bay UCATT and Shotton UCATT and Swansea Trades Council both sent £10, as did a Liverpool UCATT branch. A Merseyside site sent £37 and Frank Marsh sent £49 from a site and a brickworks. £18 came from Bolton Institute students. British Aircraft Corporation stewards at Preston sent £20 via the local LCDTU. They were 'working on' Leyland Trades Council and Leyland Motors and planned a mass meeting early in July. The Junior Common Room at Pembroke College Oxford and the Association of

Scientific Technical & Managerial Staff at University College London both sent £10. Leeds IMG sent £10. York IS Busmen's Branch sent £9 and York University Students' Union raised £30. UCATT and TGWU stewards in the Glasgow area sent £55 via Barry Docherty. Could they have, 'by *return post*', 'any financial appeal leaflets' for Glasgow Trades Council on 6 June?

CDC expenditure had been £559 and the balance was £1,251. Mostyn Coaches wanted £26 for the bus to Shrewsbury. Owens needed £17.50 for 5,000 bulletins. Mike Williams got £1.18 for stamps. Glyn Davies (who wasn't a CDC member) and someone else got £5 apiece, evidently for doing a mail-out.

CDC *Bulletin No 3* noted that messages of solidarity and promises of delegations to Shrewsbury on 15 June had come from the South Wales NUM, Liverpool dockers, London hospital workers, Morris Cowley stewards, Glasgow building workers and trades councils in York, Colchester and elsewhere. It noted the SOS 'conspiracy' charges and announced that the 24 were to be split up for their trials.

On 6 June Ken Barlow issued 'An Open letter to the Labour Movement' on behalf of UCATT Midland Regional Council. The NCCL thought the 'unlawful assembly' and 'conspiracy' charges 'very severe', since they could result in prison sentences. Birmingham Defence Fund collection sheets were available from the UCATT office. Union delegations and banners were invited to a demonstration at Birmingham Magistrates' Court on 25 June.

The *Star* reported a UCATT branch motion for the London Regional Conference on 8 June that called for a campaign to end the lump, if need be by strike action. Another branch proposed asking the Greater London Council not to award contracts on a lump basis. (In the event Alan Tattam spoke and both resolutions were passed, as was the Regional Council resolution congratulating the *Star* and donating to 'the only working class newspaper left'.) The *Star* acknowledged the 'threat to the trade union movement' represented by the SOS charges and reproduced UCATT Midland Region's circular. Dave Jackson would speak at a London rally.

The CP Yorkshire Organiser asked the CDC to send 100 'leaflets' to the AUEW Sheffield District Secretary. Arthur Dale asked for 'official collection sheets' for Leeds factory workers and enclosed £2 from Menston Hospital NUPE. Edinburgh IMG was building a meeting with 'other left groups' and UCATT and TGWU 'militants'. Could they have twenty bulletins and go on the mailing list? Brighton IMG sent £1.50 from a public meeting. They were leafleting for a meeting on 27 June to 'inform the local labour movement' why it was 'important for all workers to defend the 24'. Cambridge IS sent £7 from the Students' Union and planned a meeting of 'various groups'.

On the 13th Jim Higgins issued a 'Branch Circular' on behalf of IS's EC, noting that the IMG were 'making approaches to IS branches in several localities calling for joint meetings in support of Shrewsbury building workers'. 'We do not believe that joint activity of this sort is more helpful to the Shrewsbury workers than our own efforts and provides a situation in which the IMG can divert some of our comrades into sectarian factionalism.' 'Local approaches to our branches should be politely but firmly rejected.'

Tony Cliff and his supporters now controlled the EC. By July he felt sure that there were major battles ahead and argued that IS could recruit 2,000 industrial workers in two years. According to Martin Shaw, a decision to stop circulating EC and National Committee minutes on security grounds was followed by six months without an *Internal Bulletin*.

CHAPTER 9

Make these pickets your direct concern

The real criminals of the building industry

On 15 June 1973 there were 160 police in Shrewsbury Crown Court. Forty were in the 'public gallery', others sat three abreast next to the dock and more were in the yard with dogs.

John Reide, defence counsel for eleven of the 24 defendants, got reporting restrictions lifted. The *Star* quoted Arthur Murray. He believed that the case was 'an attempt to bankrupt ordinary working people and smash the building workers' union', but the 24 refused to be 'pawns in a dirty political trial' and called on 'the movement and the working class of the country to come to our defence'. Des Warren recalled that Murray 'looked forward to the day when the real criminals of the building industry would be in the dock—the Laings, the McAlpines, the Wimpeys, the Bovis's'. The *Liverpool Daily Post* quoted Warren: 'Political trials of this nature will not intimidate or deter trade unionists of this country from striking, picketing and demonstrating to obtain social and economic justice.' 'We stand here facing charges of intimidation and conspiracy whereas we are the victims of a far greater conspiracy between the Tory government, the establishment, the judiciary and the police of this country to intimidate the working class to abstain from their lawful right to picket.' About forty supporters in the public gallery applauded, and did so again after Carpenter and Tomlinson spoke. The defendants pleaded not guilty to 280 charges

Defence counsel applied to have the trials moved away from Shrewsbury because the 'alleged happenings' on sites in the area had attracted much publicity and a local jury would have read the reports. There was also the inconvenience and expense of travel for the defendants, family members, friends and defence witnesses during a long trial. Crown Prosecutor Maurice Drake argued that publicity had been on a national scale and many of the 250 prosecution witnesses were from the Shrewsbury area. The magistrates refused the application, but released the defendants on £50 bail.

According to the *Post*, 'about 150 banner carrying demonstrators paraded outside the courtroom.' *SW* put the number at over 250: 'Preparations have to begin now to ensure that there is an even greater show of support for the men when their main trial begins in the autumn' and it was 'vital that trade unionists mount a massive demonstration' for the SOS stewards on 25 June.

Lambeth Trades Council had asked trade unionists to contribute to its 'Shrewsbury 24 Defence Fund'. The UCATT EC told branches that it took 'the strongest objection' and would raise the matter with the TUC. (George Smith was that year's TUC Chairman.) They must 'ignore' the appeal.

CDC *Emergency Bulletin No 4* noted that seven of the 24 were at Mold Crown Court on the 26th and wanted a 'Mass Demonstration'—'Bring Banners'—and 'a campaign of information and agitation'. 'Make sure that all Trade Unionists and working class movements know of the struggle of the North Wales 24 and what it is about. Let us have resolutions from branches and trades councils to make the EC and the TUC leadership come out and openly state that they back these lads.' 'Defence Committees' should 'liaise' with the CDC.

On the 23rd the *Star* noted 'big backing for builders' demo at Brum court' on the 25th and the Mold demonstration on the 26th.

On the 25th the *Star* reported that most LCDTU Conference delegates had come from engineering plants in Southern Scotland, Northern England—including Shell Carrington and Liverpool Teaching Hospital—plus the London Joint Sites Committee. The LCDTU planned a 'massive lobby' of the TUC Congress in September and a conference on Tory anti-union policies. It also 'urged the fullest support' for the 'Shrewsbury 24'.

That day 600 Birmingham building workers stopped work and 500 chanted 'Kill the lump' outside the court. Delegations came from the UCATT Midland and North West Regions, Birmingham Trades Council, Austin, Fort Dunlop, SU Carburettors, Rover, various engineering plants and several IS branches, including that at Chryslers at Coventry Stoke. There were also postal workers, medical workers and tenants. Arthur Murray represented the 24. After a two-minute hearing the eight SOS defendants got £100 bail.

Let's have no political nonsense here

On 26 June Bill Jones, as Chairman of Huyton and Kirkby Trades Council and the unofficial Merseyside Committee, wrote a long article in the *Star*. Every trade unionist had to understand that 'if the establishment can pull this one off' at Shrewsbury they would win 'what they could not achieve with the Industrial Relations Act'.

> The North Wales building workers have formed a defence committee. What they now need is resolutions to every union in the country, also to each political party, trades council, shop stewards' committee, TUC and members of parliament demanding that these building workers get even more support than the Pentonville Five.
>
> The various organisations are asked to keep in touch by contacting the North Wales 24 Defence Committee as to what help they need, and to forward without delay messages of support and most, important, cash donations to their fund.

Speakers were 'available on request for meetings in any part of the country'. 'Make these pickets your direct concern.'

The *Star* quoted Phil Beyer: 'We believe there is a lot of work to be done to get the workers on the shop floor to understand the change in tactics away from the Industrial Relations Act.' Isle of Grain Power Station stewards were sure that 'only an unconditional discharge' for the 24 would be 'acceptable to the movement'. 'Any support we feel we are able to give will be given.' The UCATT and TGWU ECs should call for 'nationwide industrial action' to defend the 24 in the same way as the Pentonville 5.

That day 200 police stood shoulder to shoulder outside Mold Crown Court and 100 more were inside. 300 building workers and students milled around and Cynthia Baldry took a collection. Then they moved off chanting 'Free the pickets'. In court David Turner-Samuels, a defence barrister, complained that the building had 'every appearance of being under siege'. Forty people in the public gallery clapped. Sir Hilary Gwynne Talbot, Presiding Judge on the Wales and Chester Circuit, told the jury: 'I don't expect you will be influenced whether there is one policeman or many.' Defence counsel challenged fourteen jurors, including a building contractor.

The trial involved eight men from the Denbigh area. John Seaburg, Michael Pierce, Derrick Hughes, Edward Williams and Kenneth O'Shea were members of the 24, but Colin Kelly, Gwyn

Roberts and Gwynfor Williams were not. They were charged with 'affray', 'criminal damage' and 'intimidating people with a view to compelling them to abstain from their lawful work' at Llyn Brenig Reservoir on 11 September 1972. All pleaded not guilty to 'affray' and 'intimidation' and five not guilty to 'criminal damage', but Gwynfor Williams, O'Shea and Hughes pleaded guilty to damaging a drill rig, a dumper and a telephone cable. All eight got £50 bail.

Drake alleged that they 'put on a display of force and violent conduct', pushing over drilling rigs and hurling rocks at machinery and site office windows 'to frighten and intimidate these workers, who were lawfully going about their jobs'. To 'compel others to join a strike by a display of violence or bullying' would lead to 'anarchy and the undermining of the very right to take industrial action'.

One Crown witness had seen 'the top of a drill rig topple over and heard windows being smashed'. He was asked to go to the police station. 'The way they interrogated me that night was to get us to condemn anybody. It was more like in front of the Gestapo during the war.' He later described his four hours' grilling. 'Well, they were out to trip you up. Like four constables sitting there and I was sitting here. *He* would start by asking me questions, then *he* would start, and then *he* would start again and so forth. They'd ask questions they'd already asked an hour before.' He asked to go home, but was told: 'Not before we have finished with you here.' They showed him a photograph with numbers linked to Tomlinson and Warren.

Drake asked witnesses about Shrewsbury and Telford. Defence counsel objected, but the judge let him continue. Des Warren was in the public gallery and noted that his name kept cropping up.

Detective Constable Thomas claimed that Seaburg had admitted hitting a man with a lump of earth. Defence counsel suggested that Thomas had told Seaburg that he had better cooperate or he would risk three to seven years in prison. Thomas denied it. (So did Inspector Powell.) Seaburg hadn't been cautioned or asked to read the 'statement' that Thomas drew up. He didn't realise that it was a statement and signed it just to get home, because he'd been there four hours and by midnight his wife 'would be wondering where I was'. Next day he went back to the police station and found that the 'statement' contained Thomas's words, so he retracted it. (He later insisted: 'The bottom end of my statement has been changed.' He hadn't seen Pierce 'running up the site waving a stick'. 'The first time I saw him carrying a piece of wood was when the police showed me a photograph.' And he hadn't seen anyone 'clobbered' with a brick by Tomlinson.) The judge allowed the retracted 'statement' to be used against Seaburg, but nobody else.

Gwyn Roberts had refused to go to the police station. DC Thomas had told him: 'You've got no rights in this case. I have got special powers to arrest you.' Roberts' mother was worried, so he went. 'At no stage was I cautioned.' He had glanced through the statement that Detective Inspector Salisbury had drawn up, but discovered later that 'words were put into my mouth'. Had Salisbury threatened to keep Roberts in the station for a week? 'Never, sir.' (Someone in the dock said 'Cor!') He also denied telling O'Shea to 'wipe that smile off your face or I'll take it off for you'. Edward Williams had refused to make a statement. Had Salisbury said: 'You will get two to ten or something on this affray charge'? 'No, never.' Williams testified that Salisbury showed him parts of John Llywarch's 'statement', but didn't say it had been retracted. The judge ruled that it was admissible evidence. (Salisbury later admitted that he wrote 'statements' from memory.)

Gwynfor Williams recalled that he got involved around 6 August 1972. He was working on a Rhuddlan road when 'a gang of lads who work for Monks' arrived. Ken O'Shea asked them to strike. 'There was no violence and no threats.' They had a meeting and agreed. Williams decided to 'go and picket peacefully as I thought it'd help to end the strike quicker'.

> At the Ellesmere Port meeting someone shouted that they were still working at Brenig Dam. The general feeling [was] that the bastards were still working, let's get them out. So two coachloads set off. When we got to the dam site we all got off and ran onto the site, pushing past a man at the gate to do so. We were all a bit wild… [I] ran to a rig and pushed it over. Saw others throwing stones and breaking windows. After about fifteen minutes back on buses.

After legal wrangling it was established that, to make the 'affray' charge stick, witnesses had only to say that they *feared* assault.

Colin Kelly explained that when the pickets first went to Brenig the workers agreed to strike, but when pickets returned the men claimed that they had heard that the strike was over.

O'Shea acknowledged that he had called the workers 'scabs' at the second visit, but he didn't agree with damaging machines. Union leaders 'sit on their backsides getting our money', but he was a proud member of the Charter. Loud clapping broke out in the gallery. The judge insisted: 'Let's have no political nonsense here.'

Drake claimed that Chester Action Committee was not 'part of the union'. Lou Armour produced a letter from George Smith that said that that the strikers could win if the 'impressive peaceful picketing carried out by a large number of members is continued'.

The *Post*'s 'Mold Court Hears about "Heavy Mob"' described 'A GANG of pickets', before acknowledging that they 'had talks with the reservoir workers' and that the plant operator was 'not afraid'.

On 12 July the jury cleared Kelly, Pierce and Edward Williams and acquitted the others of 'intimidation' and 'affray'. On the other charges, the judge had 'no doubt that you were each one of you genuinely motivated by the desire for higher wages, which you were perfectly entitled to be'. He fined O'Shea, Roberts and Hughes £15 and O'Shea, Seaburg and Gwynfor Williams £50. O'Shea told *SW* it was 'a great victory for the building workers and the trade union movement'. (The Savings Club paid the 'Car Lads'. The Defence Fund paid the fines and gave the men £3 a day.)

Back on 9 July three Holst's pickets, William Hooson, Arthur Murray and the Shotton TGWU Branch Secretary, William Hough, had been up at Mold charged with 'threatening to damage property' and 'intimidation' at Padeswood on 4 August 1972. Hooson was also charged with 'criminal damage'. All three pleaded not guilty.

Drake claimed that an 'aggressive band' of eighty pickets threatened to burn the caravans of fifteen men and inflict 'physical violence' on them, their families and cars, unless they stopped work. They shouted: 'Come out or we will come in and drag you out... We know the caravans you live in. We will burn them down if you don't stop work.' Two defendants said 'Ridiculous'. (The *Post* headline was 'QC: Pickets Threatened to Burn Homes'.)

The picket had begun at 7.15am. The *Chronicle* reported 'about 40 to 45 pickets' and the police were there when Murray arrived.

The only mention of burning caravans was when one of the employees, Mr Hicks, told him: 'If you burn our caravans down we can always find out where you live and burn your house down', he alleged.

Murray said he replied: 'I will know who I'm looking for, won't I?'

He said he then commented to Mr Hough, a member of Flintshire Fire Service, 'Billy, this nut wants to burn the place down. You had better get your hoses out.'

Murray argued with Buckle, the site agent. (Murray later wrote that Buckle was 'flying around trying to stir it up'.)

Buckle's brand new ledger had one column headed 'reason for absence'. The entries all read 'Fear of pickets'. Yet the workmen had not seen it, let alone signed it. Everything was in Buckle's handwriting. A workman who lived on site never knew about the threat to burn down caravans until he read it in the *Liverpool Echo* and said that Buckle had put the story in the paper. Buckle's friend, TGWU official Eric Roberts, had told him the strike was unofficial.

Hough was discharged and the jury found Murray and Hooson not guilty. Murray told the *Daily Telegraph*: 'We were only a sideshow.' The *Post* tacked the verdicts onto 'Court Hears of Pickets' Site Rampage', which referred to another trial altogether.

On 18 July Kenneth Thomas was up at Mold charged with 'criminal damage' and having 'intimidated divers people with a view to compelling these people to abstain from their lawful work'. He pleaded guilty to £10's worth of 'criminal damage' and the Crown accepted his not guilty plea on 'intimidation'. The Judge accepted that he had been 'carried away by his feelings' and fined him £15. (The Defence Fund paid that.)

Next day Peter Moroney, a Wrexham scaffolder, was up at Mold charged with 'affray' and 'intimidation' at Penycae in September 1972. He pleaded not guilty. Drake claimed he had led rampaging Wrexham pickets. The *Post* reported: 'A CROWD of building pickets ran onto a building site' and 'threw bricks through windows, tore down plaster and smashed tiles on roofs'. Moroney was acquitted. (The Defence Fund paid him £6 for the two days.) *The Times* estimated that the trials cost £45,000 (over £350,000 today).

Keep in touch with the North Wales Committee

On 26 June Bill Jones, Frank Marsh and Tony McClelland had attended the CP Merseyside Area Committee. After a report on the 'position in building workers leadership' they co-opted Alan Abrahams, Secretary of the party's Merseyside Building Group.

Next day the CP's *Weekly Letter* noted: 'The series of trials of building workers on conspiracy charges arising from picketing and activities around the campaign against the "lump" continues at Mold and Birmingham, with mass demonstrations at the courts, and a massive display of police strength.' No action was recommended.

1,000 Nottingham building workers responded to a Charter call to strike against the lump and in solidarity with the SOS stewards.

An *SW* builders' 'Special' was headlined 'The Lump Must Go'.

NFBTE negotiaters agreed a temporary arrangement for 'curbing the undesirable aspects of self-employment'. Contractors could 'register as being prepared to establish direct communication with union officials, provide them with information about sub-contractors, allow for deduction of union dues for wages and take steps to see that operatives are employed under NJC terms and conditions'.

On 7 July the *Star*'s 'Battle Spreads After Victory Against "Lump"' noted that two subbies had been forced off a London council site. Alan Tattam hoped to generalise this to other council contracts.

CDC members couldn't afford to take days off and lose pay, let alone shell out for travel and other costs. Dave Jackson was 'skint' and needed £16 train fare, 'at least £5 expenses' and 'two days' pay about £14.50' to speak in Brighton. He was advertised as speaking at a Reading IMG meeting and a Preston LCDTU meeting on the same night, but chose Preston and reported a '*Good General Turnout of Trades Unionists*'. He also spoke at Oxford and Belle Vue and at a meeting organised by the IMG and the SLL in Acton Town Hall, London, which raised £433. (The CDC paid Owens for 1,000 'Defence Fund Contribution Sheets', 1,000 letterheads and 5,000 copies of *Bulletin No 4*. £3 went to the *Star*.)

On the 9th the Charter's Scottish Area Secretary, Eamon Monaghan, told the CDC that a 'recall conference' to discuss the 'tactics and policy to be employed in support of the North Wales 24' had been 'an outstanding success with all the major towns being represented'. Six trades councils had called for support and Edinburgh Trades Council was calling the conference. A Glasgow defence committee would be the 'Co-ordinating Committee', and begin using UCATT procedure, 'mobilising' the TGWU and calling on 'rank & file committees' to publicise the campaign. They hoped the LCDTU would organise a West of Scotland stewards' meeting and factory gate meetings. UCATT Scottish Region had put out a financial appeal that would likely be successful because the regional secretary was on holiday and 'progressive' branches would respond 'despite the efforts of UCATT's EC'. They would need a speaker for '1-2 weeks as the movement begins to become more aware of the implications of this trial'. Monaghan noted that a CDC member had taken part in 'a movement that by and large conflicts with general opinion in Scotland and therefore may well do damage to the efforts put into the campaign'. Such speakers 'should be representing themselves rather than the defence of the North Wales 24'.

The *Charter* reappeared after a three-month break in mid-July. Its front-page headline, 'Great Victory', referred to the Mold verdicts, and exhorted readers: 'Step up the campaign in your area now.' 'Set up a defence committee in your area and involve not only building workers but trade unionists in other industries, trades councils, TU committees and branches.' 'Bring the maximum pressure on the UCATT leadership to come out in support of their members on trial', as the TGWU had done. 'Defend the right to picket by making sure every trade unionist, branch site, factory and workplace knows what steps are being taken in the campaign.' 'Financial aid is urgently required.' 'Useless' referred to national negotiations. 'From what we know of the agreement so far, it is not even the first step towards solving the problems of lump and labour-only sub-contracting.' Union negotiators had 'capitulated completely to the demands of the employers'. UCATT's *Viewpoint* had talked about 'unofficial groups' and claimed that collections were unaccountable, but Charter supporters 'don't live in ivory towers picking up nearly £35,000 a year on the backs of the membership'. Jack Henry had been elected to the General Council. Was the EC anxious about the two posts falling vacant shortly? The senior steward from the Isle of Grain site called on the TGWU and UCATT ECs to organise support for the Shrewsbury and Birmingham defendants along the lines of the struggle to free the Pentonville 5. Pete Carter referred to the many Labour MPs who failed to support Heffer's Bill as 'another ugly face of capitalism'. The UCATT EC had made no statement in support of his Bill or the demonstration and couldn't be relied on. Trafalgar House's profits had almost doubled to over £7,000,000, Wimpeys' had leapt to £14,000,000 and Redlands' had rocketed to £19,500,000. The Tory government gave 54 percent of construction work and 97 percent of civil engineering work to big contractors.

An interview with Dave Jackson appeared in the *SW* printed on the 17th. 'You cannot be an old man on the lump. You cannot take it.' The legal attack had come because the 1972 strike was won by 'effective picketing' and because employers 'knew we were planning a campaign to follow up our victory to clear out the lump and win the industry for trade unionism'. 'Without effective picketing, it is nearly impossible to win any struggle. That is what the employers and the Tory government is out to destroy.' 'This attack is every bit as serious as the Industrial Relations Act', and big contractors had twenty MPs 'on their books'. He stressed the importance of building

The Flying Pickets

a serious defence campaign before the October trial. 'What we're after is a response of the same kind and size as when the dockers were put into Pentonville if any of our lads are put in jail.'

On the 20th the *Star* reported that the CDC welcomed the TGWU's support and hoped UCATT would follow suit. Liverpool Trades Council was to ask a 'representative' from Merseyside shop stewards' organisations to serve on a 'defence committee'.

10,000 copies of CDC *Bulletin No 5* paraphrased Bill Jones's *Star* article and stressed that the trial 'will last from three to five months'. 'These men will have to cease work for this period and have to travel 106 miles each day. They will not be receiving any pay from work. The only money they *might* receive is for their wives and children from the Social Security.' Supporters should form defence committees, send money and 'keep in touch with the North Wales Committee'. (One copy was used for speaking notes, including: 'Heffers Bill Revival?' 'No chance through official movement to kill the lump'. 'Campaign against the lump through the *Charter*'.)

Swansea IMG indicated that the Defence Fund 'should be receiving a trickle of collection sheets from sites' because 'we have been round most of the main ones now'. They had put out three leaflets and were thinking about a bulletin 'as the trial comes closer'. Could they have 'any background info, plus snippets of news about harassment etc', and more collection sheets? York IMG sent the addresses of Kent, London, Essex, Hampshire, Northamptonshire and Yorkshire supporters who wanted bulletins. At a meeting 'to publicise the Shrewsbury 24' at a TUC summer school, the Assistant General Secretary (and ex-CPer), Len Murray, had claimed that the TUC could do nothing until UCATT or the TGWU asked them to.

On 23 July the SOS defendants were up at Birmingham Crown Court. According to *SW*, 250 building workers from all major city sites demonstrated and were addressed by the IS joiner, David Adshead, on behalf of the SOS Defence Committee. The case was 'part of a big Tory offensive against the working class movement', as was that against the 24. If the five stewards were committed for trial, 'we are going to make this a second Saltley gate'. The five stewards got legal aid and all eight defendants got £100 bail.

Robert Hugh Mais was born in 1907 and educated at Shrewsbury. He was called to the bar in 1930 and was a wing commander from 1940 to 1944. In 1948 he took an Oxford MA. He became Chancellor of Manchester, Carlisle and Sheffield Dioceses, and then a county court judge. In 1971, the Tories promoted him to the High

Court. He was knighted and made a Bencher of the Inner Temple and Fellow of Wadham College, Oxford. On 27 July 1973, at Birmingham Crown Court, he rejected the appeal for the 24 to be tried anywhere but Shrewsbury.

Defence Committees. I.S.

By early 1973 Crook UCATT had 165 members. It sent £2 to a Liverpool sit-in and £5 to the sit-in at Coles Cranes in Sunderland. It asked the local authority to ban the lump and wanted the campaign 'extended' by Labour Party and Trades Council delegates and it complained to the EC about the 'apparent ineffectiveness of proposals and letters', its 'growing remoteness' to 'rank and file needs', an 'authoritarian attitude' and the 'lack of democracy'.

UCATT Northern Region now had 800 stewards—a rise of 300 in six months. The Regional Committee agreed that the North East Coast Friendly Conference had 'no authority to use a title related to UCATT' and it was 'doubtful whether branch funds should be used'.

Crook branch nominated Dave Ayre as a regional auditor, sent £2 to support the Charter conference and elected Reuben Barker as their delegate. (He couldn't get there, 'due to rail dispute'.)

In March Dave Ayre heard Paul Foot, Laurie Flynn and left wing Labour MP Dennis Skinner speak at IS meetings. (Dave later went to a demonstration in support of the Clay Cross Labour councillors.) Crook UCATT discussed the upcoming trial 'for alleged picketing offences' and was concerned about 'the impartiality of police' and their 'use of discretionary powers against workpeople'. The branch heard about the TUC's 'general strike arrangements' and supported 'a meaningful protest against government policies on wages, prices, rents, pensions'. Members should 'lend their urgent support to the stoppage and events'. The branch asked the regional secretary about action regarding the second reading of Eric Heffer's anti-lump Bill.

> Concern was expressed at the apparent lethargic attitude being adopted at regional and national level in this respect.
>
> Concern was also expressed at the union attitude to the members being charged at Shrewsbury with picketing offences deriving from the last dispute, also at members being charged in Birmingham with the fight against lump labour.
>
> It was unanimously agreed that the general secretary be advised of members' strong views in this respect.

The general secretary replied that 'decisions taken not to defend these members, were due to constitutional constraints'. Branch members 'expressed concern' and wrote 'in the strongest possible terms' to ask the EC 'to reverse their original decisions in the interests of maintaining the confidence of members offering themselves for future duties'. The general secretary replied that the decision would stand. The branch sent £5 'towards meeting the legal costs of these members'. The UCATT Northern Regional Committee would 'co-ordinate a campaign' against the lump. A Crook meeting would be open to Bishop Auckland and Darlington members.

In May, Dave Ayre heard John Fontaine speak at an IS meeting. Early in June, Dave and Bill Kerris were Crook branch delegates at UCATT's Northern Regional Biennial Delegate Conference. Crook branch's motion argued that 'a campaign of action be implemented at both national and regional levels, with the aims and objectives of completely eradicating the system of lump labour from the construction industry', including 'the use of direct action.'

On 15 June, Andrew Hornung of Workers' Fight wrote to Mike Williams of the CDC about a meeting at the AUEW Hall in Middlesbrough to publicise the case of the 'North Wales 24'.

> Out of this meeting it is hoped that we can get a small committee together representing the branches and organised sites in this area (there being to our knowledge no *Charter* branch up here).
>
> At present those supporting the meeting are limited to members of the Workers' Fight group and the trade union branches of which they are members—Redcar 2 AUEW, Port Clarence G&MWU. All UCATT branches have been circulated as well as a large number of other branches. As the date draws closer we shall be leafleting the larger sites.

He was 'aware of the need to have some sort of authorisation' and did not want 'an endorsement of one political group'. (There seems to have been no reply.)

A week or two later Hornung wrote again. Middlesbrough Workers' Fight had distributed 1,000 leaflets about the picket trials. They had also raised the issue at Redcar AUEW, which held a collection and got the District Committee to write to the National Executive, the TUC and Teesside Trades Council, which also wrote to the TUC. By 'touring the sites in the area we have got some promises' to hear a CDC speaker and they could offer a day's fund-raising at stewards' committees. (The letter was marked 'I.S.' Billy Regan renamed his 'Miscellaneous' file 'Defence Committees. I.S.')

On 22 June, Dave Ayre attended a Charter meeting in Durham and on the 28th he was at another in Stockton. The *Charter* later reported that Dennis Dugen and Bert Smith had addressed over thirty convenors, stewards, branch officers and activists. They set up a Teesside Charter group and ordered 200 copies of the paper. The *Charter* welcomed this 'break-through' in 'the only major area left in the country, where there was no organised rank and file movement'.

On 3 July there was a meeting about the lump in Crook. On the 4th Crook UCATT 'expressed disgust' at the EC circular 'advising branches to ignore [the] campaign organised by Lambeth Trades Council for assistance for the Shrewsbury 24' and 'pledged a continuance of their solidarity and support for the campaign'. They discussed an appeal against the EC decision and agreed that 'further research into the feelings of other branches in relation to the rules would be undertaken'. Members were asked to 'offer their services for week-end picket duties' at lump sites. On the 5th Bill Kerriss sent £3 to the Defence Fund from Crook Trades Council. 'We wish you every success and will be watching the proceedings very closely.'

Jim French had attended the UCATT National Delegate Conference:

We opposed many EC recommendations and on the Wednesday thirty to forty men forced their way into the hall. George Smith jumped off the platform and ran towards them. They surrounded him, shouting and prodding all the time, and one EC member eventually called the police, who escorted the poor lads out. When Vic Feather, TUC General Secretary, tried to speak, some of us started whistling 'Awky Duck' in derision and he had to sit down. I don't think he finished his speech. The strength of feeling over what was felt by a lot of lads had been a sell-out in 1972 was tremendous. I read about the Mold trials in the *Star* and heard more about them from Dave Ayre. Dave, Charlie Lowther and I supported the ordinary lads who were trying to make a living and bring up their families. Not all of us had phones, so the *Star* and the *Charter* were vital links, because other national papers criminalised the pickets and portrayed the leaders as thugs, including the *Mirror*, which some lads believed was a working man's paper. How naive some people are!

On the 10th Dave attended a Charter meeting in Darlington.

At the weekend Crook UCATT members picketed two lump sites in Stockton. Dave was on one gate and Reuben Barker was on the other. They turned round several lorries. Dave recalls that one lorry driver asked Reuben what to do with his load of concrete before it set and was told to 'tip it ower that bloody hedge'. 'Then the police arrived and asked, "Who is in charge of this picket?"' Harold Hicks, the Teesside UCATT official and right wing Labour Party member, 'strode up like an army sergeant major and said: "I am, officer".' They promptly bundled him into the back of their van and drove him away. He never let us forget about this episode.'

On the 16th UCATT Northern Regional Committee congratulated the 'splendid activity of a small band' picketing Teesside lumpers and encouraged others to get involved: 'Modest expenses can be met.' Crook branch sought support to oppose the EC decision on the pickets to be tried at Shrewsbury. The regional secretary was asked to make 'a particular enquiry re finance'.

UCATT official and Labour Party member Russ King told Crook branch that the lumper picketing campaign 'was to be suspended over the holiday period', but there would be a meeting in Durham for all branches to 'participate in future policy'.

Stockton FTAT branch received a CDC leaflet. On 21 July they sent the Defence Fund £5 and would be taking up the issue with their EC. On the 28th Dave Ayre sent £6 from 'politically conscious people'. He recalls that most Charter meetings were now held in Darlington and Charlie Lowther did most of the organising.

Tommy Harrison, Secretary of Teesside Charter, told the CDC that they had had 23 present at their inaugural meeting (not 'over thirty', as in the *Charter*). They had been 'dishing out your bulletins' and could they have *No 6*? They had got their branches to write to the Northern Region and the EC 'asking them to support the lads but have been told that we are out of order bla. bla. bla!' 'We'll get around that somehow'. They planned 'another big Charter meeting' for 1 November and hoped Pete Carter would speak. Could they have a CDC speaker? Once they knew the names they'd get posters and leaflets printed and distributed. (Someone wrote: 'YES OK'.)

Jim French can't recall when he joined the Charter.

We needed it in Darlington because we were a long way from North Wales and needed contact with places like Liverpool. We also needed to represent as broad a front as possible, politically. We did what we could and everyone involved became much more political. In particular, we became much more aware of the things the right wing in the union and the Labour Party would do to win.

CPers, left wing Labour activists and IS members worked together.

Brother Jackson has been doing the rounds

By the end of July the CDC had received a total of £2,500. £1,500 went into a 'Building Workers Social and North Wales 24 Defence Fund' TSB account. During July £17 came in from Shotton, but that was the best from North Wales. South Wales NUM EC sent £25 and Cefn UCATT sent £50. Bert Smith sent £10 from 35 UCATT members on his St Helen's site. They would make further donations and convene a meeting to 'raise cash and give industrial support'. Wigan UCATT and Building Workers Action Committee both sent £10. Dunlop TGWU in Speke raised £100 and Lindsay Parkinson stewards in Ellesmere Port sent £119. Alex Weir, a UCATT steward on Turner's Police Headquarters site in Blackpool, sent £6, but promised a weekly levy. ('Brother Jackson has been doing the rounds.') British Aircraft Corporation stewards sent £20 from Preston. Heysham Nuclear Power Station stewards sent £22. (Someone noted: 'Ask if a speaker could be arranged.') Leyland Motors stewards sent £25. Leeds Trades Council and York IS both sent £10. Painters at Barclay Curle's Glasgow ship-repair yard raised £34. Lambeth Trades Council sent £90.

The *SW* printed on 31 July reported that the SOS ATV crew were charged with having 'created, promoted and participated in the incident with a view to reporting it', yet three journalists had not been charged. (*The Birmingham Evening Mail* reporter was now Press Officer for Devon and Cornwall Constabulary.) Keith Dobie argued that 'of course we must fight in and through our branches, trades council and union machinery to win support', but the TGWU's Jack Jones had said nothing in support of the Pentonville 5 and the TUC wasn't opposing the 'conspiracy' charges at Shrewsbury. The CDC 'must be supported by representative defence committees so that a national campaign can effectively co-ordinate for the maximum response'. *SW* reproduced the CDC's *Bulletin No 5* in full.

On 2 August, Cambridge Trades Council sent the CDC their wholehearted support. On the 4th the *Star* noted that Brighton Trades Council had heard a CDC speaker (Dave Jackson) and 'pledged full

The Flying Pickets

support for the 24'. A London Defence Committee planned a meeting 'open to all trade unionists'. Edinburgh Trades Council's meeting to 'mobilise support for the 24 and resist attacks on the right to picket' would be at the end of the month. On the 4th Betty Huffinley, the CP Secretary of Leeds Trades Council, told the CDC that they had called for a conference 'to discuss the implications of the Shrewsbury strike' in late September or early October. On the 6th the *Star* reported that workers at a Letchworth site had sent £50 to the SOS Defence Fund and £80 to the North Wales Defence Fund. Merthyr UCATT had called on its EC to 'give all support including financial aid' to the members on trial. UCATT Eastern Regional Council had urged the EC 'to make clear' that 'we intend to defend our members'. If a picket was sent to prison for 'conspiracy', the TUC must respond with 'action on a national scale'.

In the *SW* printed on the 7th, Dave Adshead reported that just before a Regional Disputes Panel ordered the reinstatement of two Birmingham hoist drivers, Bryant had sacked a convenor and six carpenters for 'not working' when they hadn't enough materials to work with. Two sites came out in sympathy, but a UCATT official got them back while the case went through procedure. An emergency meeting of the BJSSC called for flying pickets to bring out weakly organised and non-union sites and a mass meeting demanded an all-out strike if the men weren't reinstated. A National Disputes Panel agreed that Bryant had not followed the correct procedure, but the men wouldn't be reinstated. UCATT had accepted a new agreement. From 3 September nobody could be a steward unless they had been employed for a month. Employers would have time to use the blacklist and UCATT couldn't defend those they sacked.

On the 9th Dave Shepherd, Secretary of Hythe UCATT, sent the Defence Fund £5. They aimed to pull 'many stewards together to form a defence committee' and would pay for 1,000 copies of *Bulletin No 5*. Bill Jones forwarded £19 from the stewards at his Liverpool Corporation depot. They would take a weekly collection and 'the word' had 'gone out to other depots'. £100 came in from Alan Abrahams at the Liverpool Teaching Hospital site.

CHAPTER 10

The Liverpool Committee

UCATT and the Building Strike Prosecutions

On 13 August 1973 Simon Fraser, Secretary of Liverpool Trades Council, told the CDC about the 'Action Committee to fight on behalf of those involved in the Shrewberry [*sic*] Trials'. It would meet next day and he hoped 'a representative from your committee could advise us'. (Bill Jones was a Trades Council delegate.)

On the 14th the *Star* reported that nearly all the major London sites had backed a Charter and Joint Sites Committee meeting on the 16th. The Liverpool 'Shrewsbury 24 Committee' wished to co-opt stewards from 'some of the larger industries on Merseyside' on the 22nd. 'Preliminary arrangements' had been made for a Merseyside conference on the 29th and a national conference on 22 September.

Sheffield and Rotherham Defence Committee had collected over £190 from AUEW members, Rotherham Trades Council and IMG, IS and Labour Party members, but used £125 for buses to Shrewsbury and Mold and a 'Picketing and Repression' conference. They sent the Defence Fund £40. Sheffield Trades Council sent £38.

7,000 copies of the CDC's *'Bulletin No 5'*—ie No 6—noted that the TGWU was 'officially supporting' nineteen of the 24, but UCATT 'refuse to support their five remaining members'. (Had some switched?) UCATT members should 'make resolutions through their branches asking the union to support these men' who had 'suffered much with the impending trial hanging over their heads'.

On the 16th the *Star* noted that representatives from all stewards' committees and branches in the Merseyside area and 'action committees around the country' were invited to Liverpool on the 29th, when plans for the Trades Council's 'national conference to build up the campaign behind the "Shrewsbury 24"' would be 'finalised'. Fraser hoped to set up a 'national committee' to 'organise the raising of money and demonstrations on the day of the trial'.

On the 17th Fraser told Merseyside union secretaries and convenors that representatives from 'political parties' would attend the meeting on the 29th. Applications for credentials could be posted or 'handed in at the meeting'.

On the 20th the CDC told Norwich Trades Council that it was receiving 'assistance' from trades councils in Rhyl, Cambridge and Leeds, 'just to name a few'. However, 'we cannot, at this stage, inform you if one of the charged men can be present'.

In three weeks the Defence Fund had paid £330 to Barry Scragg, Bob Williams, Ivor Lloyd, Joe Edwards, Mike Williams, Bill Jones and Alan Abrahams for 'delegations' and the phone bills of Mike Williams, Bill Jones and Glyn Davies (who wasn't a member). Paying for stationery, leaflets and postage and the £10 for Margaret Douglas, who did the secretarial work, came to £127. £5 went to the *Star* and £50 to the Liverpool Trades Council Conference.

Partick UCATT had asked the EC to support the Shrewsbury defendants. When the EC refused, Southern Regional Council and seventy branches supported an appeal to the elected general council.

Mike Williams wrote to the UCATT solicitor, John Williams, and asked if he had 'advised the General Secretary not to defend our brothers'. On the 23rd the General Council, which contained at least five CPers, accepted the solicitor's advice—that 'in relation to the charges made, and the likely costs arising out of defence', the matter was 'outside the scope of the rules of the union'—by ten votes to four. On the 29th John Williams told the CDC that he couldn't disclose 'details of advice' to 'third parties or even to union members', unless the EC expressly asked him to. They hadn't.

The EC issued *UCATT and the Building Strike Prosecutions*. It noted that a 'campaign of criticism' was being 'carried out in the familiar pattern by the usual dreary people who by mis-representation abuse the sympathetic solidarity for workers in trouble existing in trade union branches and trades councils'. The Shrewsbury trials were 'major prosecutions', involving '22 workers [*sic*]' but the withdrawal of legal support had been influenced by 'the sub-judice legal situation'. The General Council had confirmed the EC decision because the rules did 'not allow legal aid for defence against criminal charges alleging misconduct in industrial disputes'. The 'interruption to earnings and the associated domestic costs' would 'not be provided for by state legal aid' and that would 'cause hardship'; but the EC had 'properly carried out its function, albeit in a highly emotive situation being foolishly exploited by some people for reasons other than helping the main victims'. They would 'return to the subject' when they felt 'free' of 'legal restrictions'.

The effect on collections for the Defence Fund was immediate. A Liverpool member sent money, but it would be 'the only collection from this site'. Merthyr branch condemned the EC, but made Dave Roberts go outside to collect £1.40. However, he had the addresses of South Wales NUM Lodge Secretaries and offered to send them bulletins. Raynes Park branch sent £2 and ten joiners at an Irlam Gilbert Ash site raised £10. Yarrow Shipbuilders stewards sent £200.

No speaker to attend political meetings

On 3 September the *Star* reported that the LCDTU was sending delegates to the Liverpool Trades Council Conference and urged 'full support for action' at Shrewsbury Crown Court on 3 October.

The earliest publicly available CDC minutes are for 5 September. Leaflets about the Liverpool Conference were to be distributed locally and Mike Williams would be the 'official treasurer of any fund set up'. Dave Jackson spoke about the LCDTU meeting and Barry Scragg about his trip to Sheffield. The Flint UCATT Secretary, Jeff Douglas, was now a member. He reported that Courtauld's stewards wanted speakers for a factory gate meeting. The 24 faced an additional charge of 'unlawful assembly'. Billy Regan proposed advertising the Shrewsbury demonstration in the *Star*. Another new member, Alan Abrahams from Ellesmere Port, proposed lobbying the TUC Congress about the UCATT EC circular, and Bob Williams would go there to distribute the next bulletin.

Owens' duplicated 500 copies of *Bulletin No 7*. It advertised the Liverpool 'Conference of all Shrewsbury 24 Action Groups, Trade Unionists and Trades Councils' and called for a 'National One Day Stoppage and a Mass Demonstration' at Shrewsbury on 3 October.

Regan wrote off for sixteen credentials for the Liverpool Conference and sent Worcester AUEW a leaflet about it. The CDC would send someone to speak at 'meetings organised by people such as yourselves'. Stockport Young Teachers could also have a speaker.

On the 11th Campbell Malone of Casson & Co, the Salford solicitors, felt that the key issue in the UCATT EC circular was whether they would give moral and financial support to the charged members and their families. He would ask George Smith to testify that Chester Action Committee had been an official body.

At some point Mike Reece's name was deleted on a copy of the CDC's *Bulletin No 1* and those of Bill Jones, Charlie Jones and Wyn Davies were pencilled in. (Davies was a TGWU scaffolder at Shotton and worked alongside his CP comrades Glyn Davies and Barry Scragg.)

By the 12th Wyn Davies had become the first TGWU member of the CDC and Bill Jones had come all the way from Liverpool. Mike Williams had to account for the non-appearance of an advertisement in the *Star*. Alan Abrahams suggested lobbying the Labour Party Conference and asking the Scottish NUM for support. It was 'most important that we get as many as possible from this area' to the Liverpool Conference and credentials applications should be distributed on sites. Bill Jones would speak at Stockport Trades Council, Barry Scragg at Manchester & Salford Trades Council and the Liverpool Conference and Dave Jackson at Basingstoke Defence Committee. The 24 were to be 'summoned' to the next meeting.

Cynthia Baldry told the CDC about a Workers' Fight meeting in Liverpool 'to gain solidarity for the North Wales 24'. Could a member of the CDC speak? (Someone noted: 'No speaker to attend political meetings.')

Mike Williams acknowledged receipt of £200 from the London Charter and was invoiced for 2,000 'Foolscap Contribution Sheets'. The Secretary of St Helens Defence Committee (set up on the 11th) asked for 'relevant information and addresses' and 'officially headed paper'. Their members had spoken at the Trades Council and an AUEW branch and collections were being made at some sites. (Days later, £52 arrived with a note on the printed notepaper of 'North Wales 24 Charter Defence Committee—St Helens'.) Blackpool Trades Council had received '"Shrewsbury 24" Committee' literature from Alex Weir, who urged them to liase with Preston, and recommended financial assistance, distributing leaflets to delegates and asking them to start a levy. Edinburgh IS sent the Defence Fund £5 after Bill Jones spoke at the Trades Council.

The *Star* noted that Midlands stewards and officials were to speak in Colchester in support of the 24. 'About 250' delegates to the Liverpool Conference included those from over fifty London sites, Tooting UCATT and the UCATT London Regional Council.

By the 19th Charlie Jones and Andy Kelly were CDC members. (Kelly worked for North West Painters at Shotton and was in UCATT and the CP.) Barry Scragg, Alan Abrahams, Dave Jackson and Bill Jones sent apologies. 'A number of the accused' were present and it was 'generally agreed there was a lack of communication'. Those who went see London QCs would get £10 and the CDC would try to get access to the residue of the Chester Action Committee strike fund. The 24 should try to attend the Liverpool Conference, but had to make their own way to Shrewsbury. They and their wives should claim social security and appeal if they were turned down. Mike Williams added that if any of the 24 needed 'help or information they would be welcome to call at his home to discuss this in private'. The 'accused' were told not to speak to reporters and then asked to leave. Bob Williams took the chair. If Scragg wasn't going to speak at the Liverpool Conference, Charlie Jones would. (Holst's had agreed he would be the next joiner to start, though redundancies were looming.) Regan produced a map of Shrewsbury with a proposed route. Members were to check if it was suitable and send a copy to the Chief Constable. The CDC was 'in full support of Chilean workers', but 'for political reasons it was thought that any resolutions regarding this matter would be best sent through the North Wales *Charter*'. (The Chilean army had overthrown the democratically elected socialist government, which had a policy very like the British CP's and the socialist movement was drowned in blood.)

Pickets on Trial

Early in September *SW* reported the 'wave of disgust' caused by the UCATT EC circular and welcomed Edinburgh and Liverpool Trades Councils' initiatives, but 'only widespread agitation' could make the Tories retreat.

The next *SW* reported that IS's National Committee had recognised ten new branches. The factory branch policy had proved successful and was to be extended. Jack Jones and Hugh Scanlon had instructed TGWU and AUEW members at Chrysler's Coventry Stoke factory to work machines repaired by scabs, and stewards had resigned, whereas Linwood Chrysler workers had gone on strike. IS had written to the CP, suggesting cooperation on the issue, but the *Star* had tried to disguise the TUC's rightward shift. The LCDTU had yet to speak out, but had booked a small hall in London for their conference, which would restrict the number of delegates. Given its leaders' previous 'hostility to criticism and any attempts to have a full, frank democratic discussion', and their record of provoking confrontation when challenged, it wasn't worth making a major effort to ensure a large IS delegation. IS delegates to the Liverpool Conference would press for strike action on 3 October and 'industrial members' would be 'urged to press now within their unions and workplaces for solidarity action'.

Geoff Brown had joined IS as an Oxford student in 1971, and was now in Manchester. He recalls a middle aged man explaining the trials, but Geoff had never heard of Mold and recalls 'a feeling of weakness with no idea how to respond to this crude piece of state repression'. John Hill of IS's Manchester District Committee asked the CDC for the availability of speakers from 24 September and for 'about 100 collection sheets' and 'any leaflets etc that you think might be helpful in preparing our own material'. 'We hope to be able to arrange a couple of site meetings, a couple of factory meetings, a town meeting mainly with building workers. Possibly also union branch meetings and college meetings.' (The CDC agreed to send a speaker for factory gate and union meetings, but it was 'not possible to send anyone along to a political meeting'.)

The mid-September *International Socialism* argued that the Shrewsbury trials were 'part of the back-up' to the Tory wage restraint policy, but they aimed to 'keep the attack on the right to picket out of the limelight until it is too late for militant action to be taken'. If there were no convictions, they wouldn't lose much face. If there were convictions, 'the trial would assume massive importance'.

> Fear of prosecution would then make workers think twice before engaging in militant picketing of any sort. The balance of power would shift perceptively in the employers' direction.
>
> Trade union leaders show every sign of allowing this manoeuvre to be carried through successfully... Yet there is little doubt that if the significance of the Shrewsbury trial is brought home to union activists, a storm of protest could develop sufficient to prevent any sentences being imposed...
>
> The best way to push the issue to the fore, is to try to ensure that a few powerful groups of workers strike in solidarity with the Shrewsbury 24 when their trial begins on 3 October.

On 19 September John Carpenter—one of the 24—was a guest at the CDC. He had a detailed report about a major contractor, the 1972 strike and the police. The CDC wanted no information 'leaked'.

Paul Foot, the IS printers and Laurie Flynn persuaded Jim Nichol to publish Flynn's *Pickets on Trial* as an IS document, but anonymously. In his Introduction, Alan Williams, a docker who led the struggle to free the Pentonville 5, insisted: 'We can and must prepare to do the same for the North Wales 24.' Flynn argued that the NFBTE's *Violence & Intimidation* had persuaded the Tories to seek to criminalise effective picketing. George Richards, a Chief Inspector in the Gwynedd Specials,

recently stood for election to the new Clwyd council and published an election address. On the bottom of the address Richards was obliged by law to state who printed it. 'Printed by George Richards' read his imprint.

In fact Chief Inspector Richards' address was printed by Sir Alfred McAlpine and Sons of Hooton, Cheshire. When this came out into the open, it naturally had to be investigated.

The nearby West Mercia force (who cooperated in the Shrewsbury case with the Gwynedd force) handled the inquiry. The police naturally decided that no action was required.

A major part of Gwynedd Police Force catchment area is Denbighshire. Chief of law and order for Denbighshire as elsewhere is the High Sheriff of the County. In April this year a new High Sheriff for Denbighshire was appointed. He is Mr Peter Bell, a director of McAlpine's and son-in-law of the late Sir Alfred McAlpine who was also Bell's predecessor as High Sheriff.

In fact the last nine High Sheriffs of Denbighshire have all been members of the McAlpine family. It could hardly be expected that they would not do their little bit to bring law and order back on the building sites of Britain, particularly when such profitable operations as the lump were threatened and when trade union organisation might mean that they had to abide by such expensive things as the safety regulations.

With the McAlpine octopus proving the missing link the police investigation of building workers' pickets went full speed ahead.

The Shrewsbury trials were part of the attack on workers' economic and political rights, so the struggle against the Tories, their friends in the judiciary and the police had to take place on three fronts.

With or without the support of the trade union leaders, the Tories must be made to understand that any attempt to intimidate workers and hamstring their ability to organise effectively will be resisted to the hilt. The only way to prepare the ground for that is to bring the issue home in every factory, mine and mill and every housing estate across the country.

Pickets on Trial called for strike action on 3 October, local defence and co-ordinating committees linked to a national co-ordinating committee. They should plan action 'in the event of serious penalties being inflicted by the court' and an all-out national strike in the event of jailings. It gave CDC addresses for donations and speakers.

On 21 September, police arrested George Caborn and seven other AUEW pickets in support of a victimised steward at Footprint Tools in Sheffield. The 'Sheffield 8' were charged with assault.

The Liverpool Conference

On 22 September the Liverpool Shrewsbury 24 Conference attracted 868 delegates from 370 bodies, including 86 UCATT branches, sixty TGWU builders' branches, fifty other TGWU branches, 31 trades councils, 28 AUEW districts and branches, 24 'defence committees' and twenty stewards' committees. The Liverpool Trades Council President, Eddie Loyden, warned that if the Tories succeeded it would 'present the trade union movement with an entire new set of circumstances'. The LCDTU's Kevin Halpin argued: 'Every issue on which trades unionists are campaigning should be linked with the Shrewsbury 24.' For the CDC, Barry Scragg stressed that police interrogations 'cast a shadow over the lives of the 24 and their families', who were 'still under harassment, with regular visits from probation officers'. All were blacklisted. 'We desperately need money. We estimate that it will cost us £30,000 just to pay the wages of the 24 for the duration of the trial.'

IS members circulated *A Programme for Action* that argued for strikes on the first day of the trial. 'Plans need to be made now on every site, in every union branch and in each locality to ensure that the campaign grows from strength to strength after October 3rd.' A 'National Coordinating Committee' of 'rank and file workers representing every region of the country' should build local defence committees (preferably as trades council subcommittees), arrange leaflets, speakers, meetings at factory gates and sites and levies. This should feed into national actions, led by the best organised sites, which had to be identified now. There should be monthly pickets of Shrewsbury Crown Court and of UCATT and TGWU headquarters, until they made plans for action in the event of fines or jailings. Any fines should not be paid. 'We have to make it clear that jailing any of the 24 will be resisted to the hilt. We must start organising now for national all out strike action till they are released.' 300 copies of

Pickets on Trial were sold. Keith Dobie argued: 'We have to build an organisation that can free the Shrewsbury 24 and defend the working class. Let's make sure that we do it off our own backs, not relying on the unreliable, union leaders.'

A 'Statement of Liverpool Trades Council' undertook to 'mobilise the whole labour movement against any attempt to convict them under capitalist law'. Unless 'Labour leaders break from the politics of capitalism'—and from Reg Prentice and Roy Jenkins, the 'agents of capital in the Labour Party'—workers would pay for the crisis. The last Labour government had 'proved that unless our leaders are proposing to tackle the power of big business' they would 'be compelled to attack the trade unions'. The TUC should 'prepare the movement to remove the Tory government' and to elect a Labour government 'pledged to carry out a socialist programme involving the nationalisation of the commanding heights of the economy to democratic workers' control and management'.

CPer Tony McLelland moved the 'Conference Resolution'.

1   A campaign throughout the country in support of the policy of the Shrewsbury 24 Committee.
2   Urge conference to set up action committees in every area possible.
3   A mass demonstration in support of the Shrewsbury 24 in Shrewsbury on the day of the hearing.
4   A mass demonstration and day of industrial action on 3rd October.
5   Fighting Fund to be set up to carry out the campaign.

The *Star*'s Jim Arnison noted two more points:

6   Gen[eral]. Council TUC support action in def[ence] of 24 & in defence of the T.U. m[o]'v[emen]t.
7   If sentenced—Concerted Action.

The first six were passed unanimously. The collection raised £1,000.

In the next few days Swansea IS asked the CDC for a speaker. (They refused.) Hull Building Trades Stewards Committee asked for a speaker to address a mass meeting in four to six weeks' time and 'a copy of your Weekly Bulletin' to duplicate and distribute. (The CDC agreed.) Dave Jackson and Ian Stevenson spoke in Salford, where two Association of Professional Executive Clerical & Computer Staff pickets had been charged with 'conspiracy' for stopping a manager. The

Defence Committee included the APEX Area Organiser, members of the NALGO EC and the NUPE Area Committee, TGWU, UCATT and AUEW stewards and two Manchester and Salford Trades Council delegates.

Crook UCATT 'expressed disgust' at the EC circular and an 'apparent disclaiming of responsibility'. Dave Ayre and Bill Kerriss's attendance at the Liverpool Conference was 'endorsed' retrospectively. Regional Committee was to be asked about 'possible payment of pickets in lieu of days lost, should weekday picketing be organised' against the lump. The Regional Committee 'urged upon the membership the need in their own short/long term interest to battle the lump on all fronts' and sent £50 to the North West Regional Secretary for UCATT members 'placed in a position of hardship' by the Shrewsbury trial. By the 26th the regional secretary had written to trades councils, the Confederation of Shipbuilding & Engineering Unions and most regional papers, and spoken on radio about the dangers of the lump. The Regional Committee agreed to 'utilise the lump write-up' in *Viewpoint* to make 'printed handbills for mass distribution', but refused to act on Crook's proposal for one-day picketing 'by rota' of lump sites, with expenses, as 'not being practical and likely to cause problems upon our membership'. Crook UCATT heard the Liverpool Conference Resolution and sent off their 'strong feelings' about the EC's attitude to the trial. Delegates to stewards' meetings would raise the issues of transport to Shrewsbury and an 'action campaign'. Dave Ayre recalls that Flynn's *Pickets on Trial* was 'crucial' for winning support.

It would be to your benefit if you attend

On 26 September John Carpenter took a Wrexham Department of Health and Social Security letter to the CDC. Defendants would 'be entitled to a Supplementary Allowance for yourself, your wife and your children', but 'no extra provision can be made for your travelling expenses to court. During any time you are not required to attend court you should return to work, if your job is being held open, or sign on at your local Employment Exchange, if it is not'. The cost of school meals and uniforms was up to the education authority. The CDC agreed to send copies of the letter to all of the 24. If they went to see solicitors, their 'wages' would be '£1.00 per hour', plus expenses. Mike Williams confirmed that 'all people who had been in touch' would be 'recirculated with up to date literature'. Collections were being made at Ince Power Station and they 'would be holding a meeting regarding a stoppage' on 3 October. Fords and Standard Motors stewards were being contacted. Alan Abrahams had heard 'bad reports' at the Cheshire Federation of Trades Councils. The CDC should get in touch with Hawker Siddeley stewards. Bill Jones was happy with his visits to Stockport and Bristol Trades Councils, but on 3 October he would be at a meeting addressed by George Smith. Dave Jackson reported that the local press and a UCATT official had been 'warned off attending' his visit to Havant Trades Council, but two coaches were 'being sent up' on 3 October. Three coaches would be 'sent' from Liverpool Trades Council and two from Shotton. Barry Scragg wanted 'to get around as many sites as possible in Shrewsbury & Wrexham to make sure they are out'.

The *Star* reported that the Liverpool Conference Resolution had been sent to all Merseyside stewards' committees. Ninety Liverpool Corporation building workers were going to Shrewsbury on 3 October. A 'number of sites' in Birmingham had agreed to strike and had booked buses. 700 Borough of Camden workers were to strike and one large site would join a London demonstration.

The CDC told the '24 lads' that the next meeting would be 'a full meeting of the North Wales Charter', so 'it would be to your benefit if you attend'. The Defence Fund was invoiced for 100 posters, 2,000 collection sheets and 7,000 copies of *Bulletin No 8*, headlined 'ALL OUT—October 3rd'. 'We ask you to organise fund raising through your branches, places of work, and trades councils.' If other defence committees were 'holding funds, would they please send direct to treasurer'. 'We have nowhere near enough funds.'

On the 29th the Greater Manchester Co-ordinating Committee of Trade Unionists held its first meeting. Bert Smith was chairman and his comrade Stan Brazil of the AUEW was secretary. The GMCC was based on 'delegates from shop stewards' committees, pit branches, chapels, etc' and would 'elect officers and a sub-committee of 8 elected delegates' to 'frame a constitution', call conferences 'periodically', set their agendas and invite delegates from stewards' committees and 'other trade union bodies'. It aimed to 'organise solidarity among workers in struggle and support those who suffer penalties through being involved in such struggles' and would 'meet the needs of the "24"' by holding a conference during their trial 'to assess the position'. A collection 'realised' just over £7.

Pete Carter sent apologies to the CDC-Charter meeting:

On Monday I already have 6 meetings getting support for the demo on Wednesday. The same is the case for Tuesday.

The response in Brum to the demo is good at the time of writing we have 15 major sites pledged to stop of which most will be making there way to Shrewsbury.

...Thursday would be a good time to hold a committee meeting. It would then be possible to review the situation and plan the next steps.

...I requested a supply of 1,000 copies of each bulletin for distribution in the Midlands. The last bulletin we received in Brum was No 4. I now notice that we are up to No 8 and we have only been sent 10 copies.

Could the CDC 'ensure we get a supply of all future ones'?

The *Charter*'s front-page article, 'Support the 24', echoed the Liverpool Conference Resolution. The demonstration at Shrewsbury would be 'the first of many'. Dave Jackson had done 'a fine job'. Alan Abrahams had spent four days in Glasgow at the request of the Glasgow Defence Committee and Trades Council. Bill Jones and Bob Williams had spoken at Edinburgh Trades Council and outside six sites. Eddie Nash acknowledged that Charter activity on Merseyside had not been at the pre-strike level, but 'a great deal of time' had been spent 'supporting the Shrewsbury 24' and the April meeting had been 'devoted' to the issue. The LCDTU advertised a Conference on 20 October. The *Charter* noted that the CDC had received donations from 'every part of the country, from every section of the labour movement and political parties'.

The Scottish NUM EC had sent the Defence Fund £100. (The Comrie Branch wanted a strike if any of the 24 were jailed.) South Wales NUM EC sent £50 and their banner would be at Shrewsbury. Rolls Royce stewards at Hillington sent £50. Ruston Paxman stewards at Newton-le-Willows sent £25 and promised two delegates for Shrewsbury. The Holst collection was £25. Mardy NUM sent £20. A London scaffolders' branch sent £15 and would be on the London demonstration. Preston Defence Committee expected NUPE and AUEW collections and were distributing collection sheets on sites and in UCATT branches. A London supporter hoped 'to bring a few mates from Fords' to Shrewsbury. IS member Tommy Healey at Standard Triumph on Merseyside sent his first monthly collection.

In IS's *The Building Worker* Tommy Douras of the TGWU welcomed the Liverpool Conference, but 'all union branches should give mass support to the initiative to make sure that this conference does not turn out to be another talking shop.' Cash should go to the CDC, but collections should involve agitation and propaganda. Three sites in Edinburgh had collected over £40 and Bill Jones had addressed over 100 delegates from sites all over Scotland. There was need for a campaign in the unions and for political clarity.

On 1 October the *Star* reported that Bill Jones had addressed 1,000 Liverpool dockers and they voted for a day's strike on 3 October. So had Alan Abrahams' Liverpool Teaching Hospital site, Francis Parker in Liverpool, Merseyside sites where the contractors were Mills, SGB, Monks and McAlpine, Bert Smith's St Helens site, Unit Construction at Runcorn, Shell Stanlow civil engineering workers, plus Birmingham Woodgate Valley and Priory Ringway sites. (It listed no strikes in North Wales.)

The CDC heard that Dave Jackson had won a place at Ruskin College. Des Warren and John Carpenter reported on social security problems: 'Every avenue must be explored regarding expenses.' There was a 'thorough' discussion of 'financial aid'. Alan Abrahams reported that the 24 would get £40 from the Chester Action Committee strike fund, but the CDC would continue to use its discretion. 'Concern' was expressed at less than £50 a day coming in, so 'fundraising' would be the 'main theme' at Shrewsbury. Speakers, publicity, collections and selling the *Charter* at the demonstration were discussed and 'a continuous picket would be arranged'. The Defence Fund had now received over £6,000. Half the £1,900 expenditure was for delegations. (Billy Regan noted: 'Bill Jones attend CP Branch meeting Glyn & Wyn.')

On the 2nd the *Star* reported that more London sites would strike next day. Six members of South Wales NUM EC and a delegation from the CP Welsh Committee would be on the Shrewsbury demonstration. 2,000 Liverpool Corporation building workers and 700 at McAlpine's Ince Power Station site would strike. The CP Merseyside Area Committee voted—but only by nine to six—that the organiser, Roger O'Hara, 'should be on the Shrewsbury rally'.

CHAPTER II

The first Shrewsbury trial

A nod and a wink

On 3 October 1973 there were barricades outside Shrewsbury
Crown Court and hundreds of police. Some wielded batons and
shields, others operated surveillance cameras and dog handlers
patrolled the footpaths. The *Star* noted delegations from London and
Lowestoft docks, Manchester engineers, Plessey workers, printers,
TASS and NUPE members, Cambridge, Portsmouth, Huddersfield,
Norwich, Preston and London students, Colchester CP and IS, Nor-
wich IS, several other IS branches, Aberystwyth Communist Society,
North Wales Charter and the CDC. Shotton JCSSC sent a coach.
There were building workers from Rhyl and Colwyn Bay UCATT
and all major regions. Six Birmingham coaches were 'crammed'.
Alan Abrahams, Bob Williams, Dave Jackson, Pete Carter and
Simon Fraser addressed 2,000 demonstrators.

The Court's ground floor windows were boarded up and remained
so through the trial. The *Sunday Times* noted that army buglers
played 'a ragged fanfare as the red-robed judge, Mr Justice Mais,
dodged the catcalls and boos'. Defendants' wives were searched
before entering the public gallery and police took names and
addresses. Defence counsel challenged this highly unusual procedure,
but Mais refused to act. As Mais left for lunch an empty Tizer can
'scorched past his ear with inches to spare'.

John Carpenter, John McKinsie Jones, John Llywarch, Kenneth
O'Shea, Eric Tomlinson and Dennis Warren faced 42 charges. Under
the 1875 Act the maximum penalty would have been a £20 fine or
three months in prison, but the Crown proceeded on three charges
under common law, which allowed for unlimited sentences:

for that you on divers days between the 1st day of July, 1972,
and the 31st October, 1972, in the County of Salop and
elsewhere conspired together and with others not before the
Court wrongfully and without legal authority to intimidate

those working on building sites in the County of Salop and elsewhere with a view to compelling them to abstain from their lawful work.

The National Council of Civil Liberties called the law a 'legal monster begot by political expediency and bred by lazy prosecutors, undemocratic in origin, uncertain in scope'. The Crown also alleged that all six 'unlawfully assembled with intent to carry out a common purpose in such a manner as to endanger the public peace' and 'unlawfully fought and made an affray'.

Tomlinson recalls that a deal was offered. If they pleaded guilty, the Crown would settle for a £50 fine and the unions would pay it, but that meant getting a criminal record and undermining the eighteen pickets awaiting trial. Llywarch recalled that his barrister was 'very insistent' about his pleading guilty to 'conspiracy' and 'unlawful assembly', because he would be let off 'affray', and 'he made it clear that I would not go to prison'. Had Llywarch done that, he would have compromised the others, so he told Sir Arthur Irvine, Labour's former Solicitor General, 'what to do with his dirty deal'. All six pleaded not guilty on all three counts and were granted bail.

Lord Hailsham had recently changed a five-century tradition. No information about potential jurors' occupations was available, so nobody knew if any builders were among those sworn in.

Drake introduced five defendants by surname, but pointedly (and inaccurately) referred to 'Mr Desmond Warren'. They were accused of 'ordinary criminal charges' and the case was 'not in any way directed against the right to strike' or 'the right of any person on strike or not to try by lawful and peaceful means to persuade others who are not striking to join their strike' by 'peaceful picketing'. 'Affray' applied to 'any gathering where there is a show of force, which, if continued, could lead to a breach of the peace'. The Crown had to demonstrate that 'unlawful fighting or a display of force accompanied by violent conduct' happened 'in such a way that ordinary, reasonable people' would be 'likely to be frightened and terrified'. On 'conspiracy', the Crown did not have to produce evidence of defendants 'sitting down or being present at some meeting where a formal agreement to terrify, to intimidate other workers was worked out'. 'Intimidate' was 'an ordinary English word'. The Crown had to prove that there was 'a compelling instance' that the six 'did at some time join together in one common accord', even with 'a nod and a wink'.

Drake described an 'expeditionary force' of '300' 'flying pickets', including some from Merseyside, that 'congregated at Oswestry' and 'descended upon' Shrewsbury, shouting 'Kill, Kill, Kill'. Then they 'frightened and intimidated and terrified numbers of ordinary workers'—'rather less than one hundred'—at Brookside. There were the 'most disgraceful scenes', including 'personal violence'. They visited seven sites 'between about half past eleven in the morning and, perhaps, four o'clock or quarter past four in the afternoon'. The six were 'among the leaders' and 'Mr Warren' was 'always in the forefront'.

Drake quoted Inspector Glover's 'prepared' 'statement' for Llywarch which included a report to Chester Action Committee on 31 August 1972 about lumpers being diverted to Shropshire sites. 'I was accused of being too soft.' 'We sat round a big table and people spoke from the back. It was chaos really. They did not say where they came from or who they represented.' A 'mass picket should be taken to Shrewsbury' from Colwyn Bay, Chester, Wrexham, Connah's Quay and Liverpool. Tomlinson 'seemed to be influenced by the Liverpool crowd'. On 6 September, at Kingswood, pickets were 'like madmen', 'smashing windows in machines, pulling scaffolding down' and 'a chap put a pick in the engine of a roller'. 'I saw a man on the roller being pulled by a picket on each arm. He looked absolutely terrified.' 'I can honestly say that I was terrified when I saw the way they swept across the site.' After the strike Llywarch had been voted out as branch secretary, because he 'condemned what happened' on 6 September, and Tomlinson was voted in. 'He was an agitator, encouraging and helping the pickets to cause damage.' He was 'one of the leaders with Warren', who 'was always shouting and wanted violent action'—'"To get in and throw them off"—straight in and bang!' Warren was 'one of the ringleaders: nothing was going to stand in his way.'

Drake acknowledged that Llywarch hadn't signed this document, but police would testify that he accepted it as 'a correct record'. He had quoted it to help the jury 'understand the evidence'. He also quoted O'Shea's statement. It was 'disgusting'. There was 'damage being done all round'. Yet why were there no arrests?

[T]here were never at any time of the day more than about a dozen or fifteen policemen going round these large sites—if they have a comparatively small number, then, if they try to act too hostile[l]y, they are unlikely to do any more than inflame the situation... They did not step in to stop the thing, they tried simply to control as much as they could and lower the temperature...

The pickets were a wild 'horde' and a disciplined 'detachment'. This organised chaos had several leaders and one 'ringleader', Warren. Drake would call over 200 witnesses. Most statements taken in 1972 had been 'misplaced'. (Many new ones had been signed in spring 1973. 400 out of 800 were available in court.) One exhibit would be a 'small album of photographs of various building sites'.

Warren's counsel, John Platts-Mills, challenged the idea that lumpers did 'lawful work', because they broke National Insurance, Income Tax and safety laws. If there had been a 'conspiracy', the Crown had to prove that it began on 31 August and went on until 6 September. An expert building engineer had recently found serious breaches of building regulations, including wobbling scaffolds, at sites picketed on 6 September 1972. (Mais insisted that breaches of the Factory Act were 'a far far call from the case here'.) In the early 19th century people at an illegal bare-knuckle fight were an 'unlawful assembly', but the charge hadn't been used in an industrial case after 1900. Did police escort an 'unlawful assembly' round Shropshire?

The mass of information in what was to be a three-month trial made the jury's job extremely difficult, so the account that follows uses the transcript, statements and other documents to reconstruct the Brookside picketing chronologically (see map on page 193).

PC Amies

PC Amies had been a West Mercia Constabulary motorcyclist based at Shrewsbury. On 6 September 1972 he heard about a 'picketing expedition' by radio and was to 'keep observation' at the Emstrey traffic island near the bypass. At 2.10pm five coaches came towards him from the Wrekin Cross direction. He radioed to headquarters and followed the coaches to McAlpine's site at Telford New Town. (That journey involved about eight miles on the A5 to Wellington and eight miles with a 30 mph speed limit. Allowing for normal delays, the veteran coaches will have arrived at Brookside at about 2.45pm).

Drake's supporting barrister, Desmond Fennell, produced a plan of Brookside estate, which was in the form of a rough ellipse and approximately 900 yards west to east and 800 yards north to south. He put the roundabout on the perimeter road in the 'north east corner'. Amies had followed the coaches as they 'came from the bottom left hand corner' off 'Dawley Road' and onto the perimeter road, turned right and carried on 'for about five or six hundred yards'. The leading coach stopped 'closest' to Site Office 3, while the fifth was 'quite some distance' behind. Fennell put Site Office 3 on the 'right hand side' or east. Then he produced an aerial photograph of the estate with the roundabout in the top left-hand corner and put Site Office 3 in 'the right centre' or south. In fact it was in the south-east, opposite Burtondale. A Crown witness testified that his picket coach entered Brookside from Southall Road in the west and stopped about fifty yards east of Blakemore. A policeman put the first two coaches 100 to 300 yards south west of Site Office 3. The Oswestry coach was in front and a Flint coach was second. McKinsie Jones's Flint coach stopped 'right south'. From where the Wrexham coach stopped Tomlinson couldn't see Site Office 3 around the bend ahead of him.

PC Amies saw the 'vast majority' of pickets—'about 150'—going 'like a swarm straight across' to where work was in progress. About twenty 'were running, some were shouting, and as they went across the site they trailed off leaving some ahead and some were walking taking up the rear'. Up to forty remained by the coaches. Carpenter testified that he walked along the perimeter road and saw about forty pickets and PC Amies, who told him that there was to be a site meeting. He walked 300 yards and found 'twenty or thirty' pickets at Site Office 3. McKinsie Jones went about fifty yards into the site, turned back to ensure that the cash was safe and then went onto the site, turned east and went down Burtondale to Site Office 3. Crown witnesses confirmed that Carpenter was 'on the road by us', but he, McKinsie Jones and Llywarch weren't 'given a chance to talk to site managers'. They were in PC Amies's sight from then on.

PC Amies drew up to the second coach and saw about twelve site workers in houses 'one floor' high. They ran away from the pickets 'very rapidly'. Fennell asked about 'pieces of wood'. 'There were considerable amounts of what I would think were off-cuts on the site.' Some 'leading men picked up pieces of these and were waving them as they ran up to the lads that had been building there'. Photograph J showed what he was describing. (It was taken elsewhere on the site.) Amies thought three window frames were 'pushed out'. When pickets 'went to the rear of these houses out of my view' he 'could hear brickwork etc being knocked about', but the men were too far away to be heard distinctly. Of the twenty 'leading men' 'half of them would be actually doing the damage'. (A Crown witness standing next to PC Amies couldn't see this, because of the houses in between.) Carpenter 'appeared to be in some sort of command', so PC Amies asked him to 'get some form of control to the mob' a quarter of a mile away. Carpenter 'said that without a loud hailer or some form of addressing these men it would be very difficult, which it would', so PC Amies radioed for a loud hailer. The first incidents happened 'two, three minutes' after he arrived. Reinforcements arrived ten minutes later—just before 3.00pm.

The Brookside lumpers

Clifford Growcott, a hod carrier, was working on Brookside Site 3 on the top house of the first block on the right of Blakemore, up from the southern perimeter road. They were 'expecting pickets' and at 'about half past two' his son-in-law told him that they'd arrived. He kept on working, but then 'a lump of hardcore flew over the top of the block' and 'hit me in the back of the leg'. There were 'twenty to fifty' pickets in front of the building, but 'quite probably they wouldn't have seen me'. Then there was 'a shout of, "There he is, fetch him off. Let's have the devil down."' They did not 'deliberately throw brick-ends at me' but he threw a brick at them. One picket started to climb onto the scaffold and Growcott 'tried to turn the ladder out with him on', but he 'got copped round the ankle and pulled off'. There was 'quite a bit of argey-bargey and a bit of pushing and shoving and a blow or two struck'. 'I saw a house brick lying close by' and 'went to grasp it', but a picket 'put his foot on my wrist' and another 'picked the brick up and hit me on the back of the head with it'. Then the pickets 'drifted off to a meeting down at the site office'. 'I must have followed them as best as I could'. He couldn't identify any assailant and he was on a photograph that 'must have been taken after the blow', showing no sign of pain, injury or distress.

In Growcott's statement of 12 March 1973 he had claimed he saw 'some blokes walking up towards the block', shouting, '*Come down*' and 'hardcore started to land around me. Some of it hit me on the leg.' One of 'about twenty to thirty' pickets 'grabbed hold of my ankles and pulled me off the scaffold'. He 'kept hold of the ladder and lowered myself down' and landed on his feet.

I do not remember much more because I was becoming more hazy. I went down partly on the ground under the scaffolding and they were all still around me. I thought I was going to have some more, so I went to grab hold of a house brick. I could not get anywhere near it and I remember one of them put his foot on my arm or fingers. There were different ones shouting and I remember some of them trying to stop it. I was pretty well out when I felt a blow to the back of my head. I was lying on the floor at this stage with men all around me. I got up to my feet, and a young student called Roger and some of the other pickets got the more violent element to leave me alone.

He couldn't see those 'who gave it me', even on 'extra photographs'.

Dennis Ralphs, a foreman, was erecting a scaffold near Growcott on Blakemore. 'About 2.15pm' he 'heard a lot of shouting' and saw 'about 200 men running across the site' 'carrying stones, sticks and iron bars'. (Later that became 'pickaxes, bricks and shovels'.) One picket shouted: 'Are you getting off the fucking scaffold?' and 'threw a stone at me'. (Later he said two stones were thrown and one 'hit the scaffold stanchions and bounced off into my face'.) He saw 'four other blokes' 'throwing bricks and roofing tiles at us' and they began 'climbing up the scaffold towards me'. He went round the other side, climbed down and saw 'fifty or sixty' men, 'ten, fifteen yards' away. Growcott had 'all blood coming from his head' and 'running down the side of his face', having been hit by a man with a brick in his hand. (Growcott 'had no wound or injury on the outside of his head which is detectable by a doctor'.) It 'could have been his nose' and he had 'made a mistake' about the brick. (Yet Growcott 'complained of no blood and no wound on his head'.). He had blood 'over his face'. (A policeman 'saw no blood and saw no wound'.) They 'carried him off the site'. (On a stretcher?) No: 'carried' was a 'mistake'. Ralphs couldn't identify an assailant and a photograph showed Growcott listening to pickets 'as calmly as can be'.

Ralphs had claimed in his statement that he walked down the site and saw 'three or four blokes' 'pushing breeze block and bricks off the scaffold'. Growcott was 'on the scaffold, walking towards them,' and one picket 'hit him on the side of his head. I can't say if the man had anything in his hand'.

Derek Butterfield, a scaffolding sub-contractor, was working with Ralphs. (Fennell helpfully suggested it was near where Growcott was 'thrown off the scaffold'.) He heard a brick hit the scaffold and saw 'swarms of men'—sixty to eighty—'coming up the site'. Some carried 'pick handles'. One told him to 'come off the scaffold' and called him a 'scab bastard'. Others knocked down brick walls and pushed window frames over. He heard no threats and saw no personal violence: 'Everybody more or less gathered their tools' and climbed down. He saw Ralphs *run* to Site Office 3 and walked down there. Then he sent Ralphs to find fifteen other lumpers up on Site 6.

James Griffin, a plumber, was working near Butterfield. 'About quarter to three' he saw coaches draw up on the perimeter road. '45-50' men came towards his scaffold carrying 'sticks' and 'about fifteen' stopped nearby. One threw a brick. Griffin threw one back and got 'about a dozen' in return. Trevor Clarke was on the other side of the scaffold. He saw up to sixty pickets, 'maybe one or two with a stick', but he saw no bricks thrown. He heard Griffin tell a picket he would 'wrap my hammer round your head'. William Barlow, a subbie, testified that that was when 'the fireworks started'.

Billy Regan later recalled that the Rhyl and Denbigh pickets 'split up into different groups to go around and tell the workers that a meeting was being arranged'. His group was 'stoned by workers up on the scaffolding' and 'a small minority of the pickets retaliated by throwing stones back'. Many of the 400 workers—four times the number that Drake had claimed were there—were drifting away.

Clive Jones, a bricklayer's labourer, was working on a tractor on Site 3. At 'about 3.00pm' five coaches stopped on the southern perimeter road. 'The next thing I saw was a group of pickets coming across the site from behind some trees. There would be about 50 men. When I saw them I drove off.' He parked behind Site Office 3, walked round to the front and saw Warren 'talking to a small group of workers near the site office'. A 'group of pickets opposite' were 'smashing in windows as they went along'.

George Garner, a glazier, was working on Site 3 above Brereton. At 'half past two' he heard a 'banging on the door' and saw 'fellows outside walking past with sticks in their hands'. One picket 'rushed in' and 'pushed me to one side'. 'He said, "You know what this is all about".' 'I said, "Yes", startled, and he said, "Well, come on then." And then the next thing I know the kitchen window shattered.' 'I had got the tools by the side of me in a plastic bucket and he kicked that in the air and scattered the tools all round.' Garner wasn't touched and saw nobody hurt, but he was 'Terrified'. Warren was 'very bombastic'. He had seen his photograph in the *Sunday People*.

Roger Castle, a joiner, was working on Site 3. Around 2.45pm, seven or eight men told him to 'get your fucking tools together'. 'You're on strike.' He said he wasn't and Tomlinson—who wore jeans and a white shirt and had a Welsh accent—told him: 'There's a fellow with the same attitude as you round the corner lying on the deck with a house brick on his head.' (Photographs show Tomlinson wearing pale trousers, a flowered shirt—it was pink—and a light cardigan. He has a Liverpool accent).

Barry White, a cable-layer, was up on Site 6. In 'between three and half past' a group of men, including Tomlinson, 'were telling us to "get off the site, the site is closed".' White's foreman heard: 'It is best you get off site before the other lot come.' They were 'vicious, shouting and waving sticks about and throwing stones'. He saw 'a bald Polish bloke', but couldn't identify him from any photographs.

George Oliver, a bricklayer, was working on Site 6 in the north of the estate when his labourer saw 'about 80' men coming up from Site 3 and 'about 200' altogether, 'breaking windows and 'pulling a compressor down the road and shouting, "You scab bastards".' 'Most' were 'armed with pieces of wood and bars'. One shouted: '"Get off the scaffold and go and collect your cards at the office", and we refused to go.' A picket got on the scaffold, spoke to the labourer and got back down again. The pickets shouted: '"You scab bastards get down", and we refused to get down then and the one got up and pulled the work down.' They still refused. 'If you don't get down we will come and pull the scaffold from underneath you.' 'Just give me time to wrap my line up.' 'Never mind your fucking line.' 'Get down.' He was 'frightened enough to get off the site'. (Was this the most frightening thing?) It was. (Then why had he 'failed to mention entirely any word of the scaffolding being pulled down' in his statement?) One man 'seemed to be the one who was doing a lot of talking' and 'I should have thought he was the leader'. He 'had seen him in the *People*'. (Warren's photograph was in the *Sunday People* four days later.) It was 'in a paper before he came onto our site'.

'About twenty to three', Oliver's labourer, Dennis Whittall, saw 'a gang of about 200 men coming towards us', pulling a compressor. There was 'a lot of shouting and noise going on and they was waving a lot of sticks and bars'. 'A gang of about 60 or 80' were 'shouting, "Get down, you bastards, get down."' One 'started to try and get us down' but 'we just kept on working.' He identified one man from a photograph who 'said that the site was closing down'. Another picket 'started pulling our work down'. 'I says to him, "Well, I am going to collect my tools and that now", and he says, '"You'll have no time to get your fucking tools, you have got to get off the site", and at that I got down off the scaffold.' As he and Oliver walked away pickets 'started to stone us', but 'I kept walking.' 'I was terrified'. Why didn't they run? And where were the police?

Wellington's finest

On 6 September 1972 Inspector Morris left Wellington police station at about 2.15pm, drove to Brookside and saw a meeting of '30 to 35' at Site Office 3.

PC Amies had sighted the picket coaches in Shrewsbury at 2.10pm. Morris's journey took other policemen ten minutes. To get to Brookside in fifteen minutes the coaches' average speed would have had to have been over 60 mph. So unless Amies let them average 90 mph on the A5 or exceed the 30 mph limit by 30 mph for eight miles, either he or Morris was mistaken.

PC Gandy left Wellington police station at 2.30pm in an 'omnicoach' with Inspector Meredith, two sergeants, four PCs and a cadet. They arrived at Brookside at 2.40pm and saw a police motorcyclist 'near the coaches'. (PC Amies had arrived at the south of Brookside around 2.45pm and then moved along the road).

Sergeant Hartland drove that omnicoach to Brookside with Sergeant Bastable, *five* PCs and a cadet. (Inspector Meredith had evidently been demoted.) They arrived at 'about' 2.45 and saw 'a dozen or so men waiting around', PC Amies, and 'a lot of people carrying tool bags', 'hurrying off the site towards the site offices'. (In his statement Hartland 'could hear glass smashing somewhere' but 'nothing too serious was happening'.) After 'a few minutes', Sergeant Theodore and PC McKeitch arrived. Theodore spoke to Hartland and Amies. He saw six or ten men, thirty or forty yards from ten or a dozen men near some coaches. Hartland then drove 'two to three hundred yards' to Site Office 3, asked where the pickets were and carried on in an anti-clockwise direction.

Detective Constable Davies was at Dawley police station at 2.30pm when he and PC Williams were told to visit local sites. They drove three miles to Halesfield and three more to Malinslee. (The second journey took five minutes, so they presumably arrived at Malinslee about 2.40pm). After 'about 20 minutes' they had a call 'to go immediately to Brookside'. (It wasn't very far, so they probably got there at about 3.05pm).

PC Williams recalled that they passed the Wellington omnicoach going the other way and stopped near Site Office 6—in the north. 'There were several people shouting "they're over there", indicating a side road into the centre of the site.' He 'could hear banging and the smashing of glass, and men shouting' 'further into the site', but 'no sign of disorder'. 'There were a few workmen just standing there, as if they wondered what was going on.'

DC Davies turned on to the site 'towards the shopping centre', parked and saw 'a large group of men, approximately 100-150', moving into the site' from Site Office 6, 'heading towards the Community Centre'. He saw 'groups of pickets, of two or three in number, breaking away from the main group and going into the complex of completed and partially completed buildings', 'visiting pockets of workmen' and 'shouting' 'Bastards', 'Scabs' and 'Blacklegs'. 'The main group of pickets were chanting, "Out, out."' He heard 'glass being smashed, but was unable to see anyone causing damage'. He saw a man 'assisting one of the local workmen down a ladder' with 'a cut above one of his eyes, which was bleeding profusely'. A picket said: 'I'm sorry about this mate, but some of the lads are upset, we've been out of work for a long time.'

Sergeant Bastable left *Dawley* police station with Sergeant Hartland. (So one of them was mistaken.) They arrived at Brookside 'about quarter to three' at Site 6—'I think it was Bembridge'—and parked 'not very far from the new school'. Bastable walked ahead of Hartland and saw 'about 150 men' 'near the centre' and 'several shouting', 'Come on lads, join us in the strike.' Men were 'near partly built houses', but no trouble—'none at all'.

Sergeant Hartland had driven to Site Office 6, parked and walked into the site with PC Price. '150' pickets were walking towards the school and 'an equally large number' were 'hurrying off the site carrying toolbags'. Pickets were 'chanting and shouting: "Scabs out, scabs out, come on out. There will be no fucking work here today".' 'About a dozen were carrying sticks.' (PC Price said they entered Burtondale. So one of them was mistaken.) They parked after 'about 300 yards', got out and split up. He saw no pickets for 'about three to four hundred yards', but then saw an 'unruly mob' of 'about 150' shouting 'Scabs out'. A man with 'blood covering his face' was descending a ladder and 'about three or four' at the bottom said, 'we don't want any of this.' 'Come on down, mate, you will be alright.' Pickets 'were all round and helping', so Price 'carried on after the main body'.

Sergeant Bastable 'ended up at Burford', returned to the centre and saw two men on a ladder leaning against 'a partly constructed building'. One was 'supporting the man who was above him', whose face was 'all bloody'. A picket was 'most concerned about it'. The injured man said: 'I only went to get my tools.' Bastable asked an officer—'I think it was Gandy'—to take the injured man away and then went with pickets 'towards a quadrangle' where 'the glass was all smashed in quite a lot of the maisonettes'. The 'main body of the crowd seemed ordinary, decent folk', but there was 'a nucleus of trouble makers' of 'about a dozen'. He couldn't identify one.

PC Gandy 'could hear men shouting, "Scabs out",' but couldn't see them.

> I remember glass being smashed some distance away. I saw a small group of about four or five men, who I assumed to be pickets, walking towards the direction of the shouting.
>
> There was a large high building ahead of me that was under construction, the noise appeared to be coming from the other side of the building.
>
> As I arrived at the rear of this building I saw a man coming down a ladder from the building. He had blood streaming down his face. There were several pickets at the bottom of the ladder and two of them appeared to be sympathetic and one of them said, 'I'm sorry mate, it's got out of control, some of these men have been on strike for over eight weeks and they'll stand no messing.'

The man 'declined my assistance and made his own way off site'.

Sergeant Hartland saw 'a number of door frames that had been pushed out' and 'eight to ten' broken windows. Then 'a man came to me and said: "Some bastard has thrown a brick and hit my mate on the head".' Hartland took the injured man to the omnicoach and 'handed him over' to PC Williams (not PC Gandy).

PC Williams saw about ten officers near the centre and 'about 30 or 40' men 'running or walking from the partly built houses'.

> I think these would be both workers and pickets. Certainly there was no damage being caused at this point, but I could still hear banging and glass smashing, coming from further inside the site...
>
> My reaction, about the persons running, was, 'What can we do about it?' and I cannot say whether any were frightened looking. They ran straight past us, got into cars parked near the shops and drove off.

Everything 'went quiet'. A few pickets remained—'a soft core who were not interested in charging around the site, but just there to make the numbers up'. He saw a man with 'a jagged cut above his left eye'. 'There was only one other man with him.' (The rest must

The Flying Pickets

have vanished.) He 'formed the impression that this man was a picket'. He said 'words to the effect "Sorry mate, it's just one of those things".' He arranged for a 'workman' to take the injured man home. Then he and DC Davies drove to Site Office 3.

Tomlinson had walked up between blocks of houses, towards the centre, and saw some dislodged, unglazed window frames. It was 'noisy', but no damage was being done. He walked past 'new stuff that was just going up on the fringe of the site', through 'partly built buildings to where only the foundations had been laid', and told some workers: 'All right, lads, you know there's a dispute on; let's have you down to the meeting.' Then he saw a man being 'taken to a policeman' by two pickets. That was Albert Blackham, who testified that about forty or fifty men were throwing stones and shouting: 'They were very noisy and a little wild.' 'They said: "Come down off there, you scabs, come on down, you bastards".' He and his mates climbed down, followed some pickets to Site Office 6 and decided to go home. Blackham went back for their tools. 'A couple of stones passed in front, and something hit me just above my left eye. My legs felt a bit groggy and I saw blood dripping on the scaffolding board.' The pickets who helped him were as upset as he was. (He needed two stitches.)

PC Gandy had gone 'about fifteen to twenty yards' when 'about twenty pickets came from my right', shouting, 'Scabs out, off, off.'

Some of them were armed with sticks. The man at the front of this group appeared to be leading them. He would start the shouting and the remainder would take up the chant and keep it up. He was about 5'7", 35 years, broad build, with a mop of light brown hair. He was wearing a shirt and trousers, but did not have a coat. I would say this man had a Liverpool accent. This man was obviously stirring the men up and the men following him were in an agitated and heated mood. They were a really rough looking bunch. Of the pickets I saw I would say that this group looked the most violent of the lot.

Following this group was a larger mob of about 100 pickets. Again I saw members of this group carrying sticks in their hands, but as they got nearer to me I saw sticks being thrown away. This group were also chanting things such as 'Scabs out', but they were not as vocal as the first smaller group.

I saw local workmen hurrying from the site, and the men were obviously frightened and this was visibly obvious.

His group 'were told to return to the police vehicle' and 'go around to the other side of the site and meet the pickets midway'.

Sergeant Hartland saw 'in the region of 80' pickets near the school and 'a number of brick ends and half bricks being thrown from the centre or front'. 'I believe it was eight 5ft by 4ft windows that were smashed'. He and PC Price 'walked into the pickets', who parted to let him through. PC Price heard glass breaking 'coming from the site all round me'. There were 'half a dozen to a dozen' policemen in sight, but about 150 pickets made him 'scared stiff'. He met no hostility. There was a 'solid block'—'about 100'—at the school and he heard 'the sound of breaking glass'. After a minute or two this group 'split as they went past' him. He stood still. (So either he or Hartland was mistaken.) He saw 'a wall of glass had been smashed'. A picket said 'something to the effect: "That's enough of that. There's kids in there".' (Tomlinson recalled saying: 'Pack that up, there's kids in there.') *One* pane was broken, but he saw nobody doing any damage. He saw pickets going 'back the way that I had followed them' and followed them again. He couldn't identify any of them.

Sergeant Hartland followed some pickets to 'a workman's hut to the right of the school'. Two workers 'immediately ran off', but 'three or four' were 'listening to what the pickets had to say'. (According to his statement, 'One big fellow with a Liverpool accent' was telling them 'what would happen if they didn't get off'.) 'A great number of workers were running off the site continually.' They were 'frightened men'. Some pickets 'appeared to be following a preconceived plan because they swept through the site'. 'I suppose 40 appeared to be the out and out militants.' 'Everyone seemed to be following' Warren, Tomlinson and Jones. He had 'never been so frightened'. (Why?) 'They totally ignored us; they brushed us aside as if we just were not there.' In his statement Hartland had acknowledged that police 'must have seen offences committed, but I would certainly not have instructed any of my officers to make any arrests. I would have feared for their lives.' As for the pickets,

> It struck me that they were following a pre-conceived plan, by the speed with which they moved, the way people causing damage were shielded by others. The hard-core militants, who were causing most damage and disorder, were quickly identifiable as a group, although I did not see them actually cause damage.

The Flying Pickets

He saw Tomlinson, Jones, Warren, Murray, Pierce and Warburton.

DC Davies noted that 'the main group of pickets disbanded into smaller groups who were running through the site shouting "Scabs", "Blacklegs" at local workers'. One picket (who he couldn't identify) told a worker: 'I remember you from another site, you scab, you were kicked off that site, I'll see you again, you scab.' Workmen 'were loading their tools into their vehicles and leaving'. He drove to 'where the pickets were likely to emerge opposite Brookside 3 Site Offices'. (He didn't mention sticks or damage).

Sergeant Theodore drove 'towards the centre' where the road 'bears left at a rather steep hill' and up an 'unmade' road (Burtondale). After '250 to 300 yards' he got out and walked in 'the general direction of the noise'. He saw 'approximately 150' men 'brandishing sticks', 'marching in file towards us from our right', shouting 'everybody out, get off the site.' He suggested to PC McKeitch that they should 'mingle with them' and they went down the hill together. McKeitch 'didn't see any stones being thrown or damage caused', but was apprehensive.

Inspector Collins ordered Sergeant Hartland to drive three PCs and a cadet round to the pickets' coaches. He went clockwise and the coaches 'passed me to go round the perimeter road', so as 'to turn round to come back'. (Photographs show that they had not turned round.) PC Gandy stayed in the omnicoach as pickets 'gathered in small groups in front of and opposite' Site Office 3. They were 'no longer rowdy'. He saw 'a lot of local workers packing their tools into vehicles and leaving': 'all the local workmen' were 'visibly shaken and frightened by what these pickets had done'. He couldn't identify one picket 'causing damage or using threatening behaviour'.

Under cross-examination, Sergeant Hartland admitted that he had not seen Warren, Tomlinson and Jones do anything wrong. They 'were walking back towards other police officers', none of whom he could identify. He could not explain why he was 'terrified' by men who ignored him. The meeting would be visible 'from one part of the site office but not from where I was sitting'. He didn't 'go up to the meeting' and couldn't say which men in photograph I were workers or pickets; but he acknowledged that several held bags, spare trousers, bait boxes and rucksacks.

Platts-Mills noted: 'Everyone saw the relish and delight and venom with which he pointed to the men in the dock.' Mr Justice Mais interrupted repeatedly, but Platts-Mills reminded him that two Crown witnesses had testified that pickets were 'sent away by Warren'. He called Hartland an 'irresponsible witness'. Another defence counsel described Hartland's evidence as 'deplorable'.

In the frame

Robert Craig took photographs at the Kingswood site in Shrewsbury, after the pickets left, and followed them to the Weir site. One suggested throwing his camera in the river. Another suggested throwing him. He didn't object to the defence seeing the photographs, but the *Shropshire Star* refused.

Philip Jones, the *Shropshire Star*'s senior reporter, was in Shrewsbury that day. At 'about 1.30pm' he heard by phone that pickets were 'on their way to Telford'. He left with the photographer, David Bagnall, reached Brookside, went eastwards along the southern perimeter road, returned to 'near the site office [3]' and saw 'about six coaches'. (The pickets had arrived in five coaches.) He saw 'small pockets of building workers and pickets standing in groups talking together'. Bagnall began taking photographs at 'about 3.00pm'. Bagnall claimed that he took the first of 'ten' photographs by 2.35pm. (The pickets had not arrived by then.) Police lettered them A to J and provided a list of 22 members of the 24—not including Hooson or Graham Roberts—who were identified by number on A, B, C, D, F, G, H and J. Llywarch and Tomlinson were listed as K and L in 'Album 3', which is not publicly available.

Platts-Mills got hold of *seventeen* Bagnall photographs—one was blurred and another was a duplicate—and produced fifteen of them when Drake was trying to discredit a witness. Bagnall had put them in chronological order.

1   A group of men are in front of huts on the other side of the perimeter road to the estate. Carpenter and McKinsie Jones are listed.
2   A group of men near a hut are closer to the camera. Carpenter is walking away. Jones isn't visible, but Growcott's hat is.
3   A group of men are standing near two huts. Carpenter is standing behind Growcott and both are facing Jones.

Growcott shows no injury or haziness. Nobody is running away.

Philip Jones talked with site workers and after 'about ten minutes' (3.10pm) he saw 'a column of pickets spread across the site': 'about two hundred' were 'moving in a body from the centre of the building complex towards the site offices and us'. It 'really frightened me and I returned to the car for safety. I could see that some of the pickets were carrying sticks and wielding them about.' Bagnall took three more shots:

4   A group of men are walking round the corner of roofed-in houses at the top of the fourth block on the right hand side of Burtondale. They include Clee, Morris, Warburton, Bernard Williams and Brian Williams.

5   A group of men are further round the corner. They include Butcher, Clee, Morris, Sear, Thomas, Warburton, Bernard Williams and Brian Williams.

6   A group of men are mostly standing still, including James, Murray and Bernard Williams. Some, including Crown witnesses, hold what appear to be sticks, ranging from about one to four foot long. There are no broken windows.

Photographs 4 and 5 were taken from near Site Office 3, about two hundred yards below. Bagnall then moved east to take 6, which shows the pickets about a hundred and fifty yards away. The telephoto lens makes the straggling group appear more compact, but even so they don't look anything like the 'column' that Philip Jones recalled.

The man with the iron bar

On 6 September 1972 Arthur Hartshorn, a lumper at the Kingswood site in Shrewsbury, was driving a road-roller when one picket 'attacked the petrol tank' and another began 'pushing some iron bar into the engine'. (Drake suggested that Tomlinson was 'busying himself' with an 'iron bar'.) Another lumper, William Wright, claimed that a picket threatened to ram an iron bar through his throat.

Keith Hitchen, a quantity surveyor at Brookside, thought 'the one carrying the iron bar' on photograph H was Clee. The lumper Dennis Whittall identified Clee at 'the front of the gang of men that come towards the scaffolding', 'waving a lot of sticks and bars', and picked out a man on photograph J. (Drake asked: 'You point to the man we know as Mr Murray, the man holding an iron bar?') 'I think that is the one that came up on the scaffolding.' The lumper Alan Hughes identified Murray on photograph J as the man he had seen with 'the bar of iron in his hand'. Stones were thrown. (He didn't mention that in his statement, or that his doctor found that he had some bruising but 'no serious injury' and was 'largely complaining of a boil'.) The lumper George Oliver identified Murray from photograph J as having a 'stick in his hand'. (Drake interrupted: 'That was a bit of iron bar he was carrying.') He also suggested to another Crown witness that he could be seen 'just to the right of the man with the iron bar in his hand' on photograph J.)

Tomlinson's counsel asked Terence Callaghan, site manager at the Mount site in Shrewsbury, to look at photograph J. Was the picket who entered his office 'that man with the stick'. Drake jumped in: 'Is he the man holding what appears to be an iron bar?' Defence counsel said, 'Yes'! Callaghan said that Murray wasn't in the office. Platts-Mills objected that 'what has been called an iron bar' was in fact 'a wooden thing'. Mr Justice Mais interjected: 'Wooden? There has been no evidence.' Platts-Mills argued that the man who carried a stick was improperly 'led' by Drake on the question of someone carrying an iron bar. Drake objected: 'No one said it was an iron bar.' Platts-Mills persisted: 'A number of witnesses said: "I saw the man with an iron bar".' Mais denied it: 'Nobody suggests that is an iron bar.' Platts-Mills insisted: 'It has been said, with respect.' (Only Hughes had claimed to have *seen* Murray holding an 'iron bar' at Brookside.) Mais noted that Murray was 'carrying an iron bar of some sort' on photograph J. 'That is what has been said in evidence.' Platts-Mills stressed that someone 'said it looked like an iron bar'. Mais changed tack: 'The man immediately ahead' of another picket—Gary Calverley—was 'carrying an iron bar of some sort. That is the evidence.' 'But that man has not been called and nobody has said it is not an iron bar looking at the photograph.'

When Drake cross-examined McKinsie Jones he raised the issue of a Brynford employer, Stanley Rawson, who had admitted pointing a shotgun at pickets on 16 August 1972. Rawson accused Murray of 'stirring up this trouble' and identified him from a photograph taken at Shrewsbury, but Jones pointed out that Murray was in Spain during the Brynford picket. Drake asked Rawson to identify a picket on photograph J who was 'between Mr James and Mr Murray', 'the man with the iron bar'. Drake asked Llywarch if he was in fear of violence from fellow pickets? 'No.' (At that point Murray entered the public gallery.) Drake asked Llywarch if he knew him. Not 'particularly.' Drake continued: 'The man we have seen pointed out in the photograph with the iron bar?' 'Mr Murray is just leaving the court room now. I was going to ask you if he was one of the people that you are afraid of.' 'No, certainly not.' (Murray returned.) Drake asked Llywarch if he saw him do any damage. 'No.' (Murray left.) Drake asked Tomlinson if he'd seen Murray at Brookside, 'armed with his iron bar?' He hadn't seen him there at all. In his summing up Mais said: 'There was a man with an iron bar, which seems to have been a man called Murray.'

The Flying Pickets

Warren's world record

On 6 September 1972 Warren had been an official Chester Action Committee 'spokesman'. He recalled that Alan Abrahams 'should have been the leader', but 'didn't show up'. There were 'several picket leaders' but there had been 'no decision taken about who was to address the men' at the sites.

Barry Scragg had walked 'right through the site' up to Site Office 6. (That was a quarter of a mile uphill and another quarter on the flat, not allowing for detours, and will have taken about ten minutes; so he arrived at Site Office 6 around 2.55pm.) He 'approached the agent in the normal manner and explained our case'. Mr Hammonds claimed that he 'had no jurisdiction to sign any agreement', so Scragg 'asked if it was possible to speak to the workforce'. Hammonds said they were all were self-employed, so Scragg 'would have to round them up'. (Hammonds later acknowledged his mistake. '50 percent of the men were labour only.') An inspector 'directed us to where the meeting was and thanked me for my cooperation'.

When Warren got off the coach he couldn't see a site office, so he went north up a bank, between Bishopdale and Blakemore. After about four hundred yards he asked workmen for directions, turned east, walked several hundred yards and went down to Site Office 3. Allowing for the hill, diversions and a pause to ask directions, he walked well over a thousand yards. Even at a brisk pace of three miles an hour that would have taken at least ten minutes, so he arrived at Site Office 3 at 2.55pm and was on photograph A, taken at 3.00pm.

The lumper Ralphs claimed that Warren wielded 'a pick handle' at Blakemore at 'about 2.15pm'. The lumper Garner saw him up on Site 6 at 2.30pm. The lumper Oliver saw him on Site 6 soon after 2.40pm. Hammonds spoke with him on Site 6. Sergeant Hartland saw him there too. The shortest route from the buses to Site Office 6 and then Site Office 3 is well over a mile. Nobody saw Warren running, so his walking pace must have been over six miles per hour, almost a world record. Or Garner, Oliver, Hammonds and Hartland were mistaken. Even Mais accepted that Warren wasn't on Site 6.

Warren recalled that at Site Office 3 John McCabe, the general foreman, 'tried to kind of smother me with, "I'll deal with you".' Warren went into the office to find the site agent, but there was no one there. He came out again, saw another picket and 'tried to get a bit of a meeting going to tell the workmen there would be a larger meeting'. There were 'about thirty to forty'. The lumper Butterfield saw him 'shouting and bawling' at McCabe before he 'stormed through the office' looking for the site agent. When he came out he 'seemed to climb on a box because all of a sudden he seemed to grow two feet'. He said that the next time the pickets came 'it just won't be walls we are turning over'; but then he began 'talking friendly'.

Inspector Meredith saw 'about three hundred' men at Site Office 3 at 'about two fifty'. McCabe told him that 'certain of their leaders' had 'gone in for a meeting' with the site agent. (How had Hammonds got down there so quickly?) Within 'two or three minutes' Meredith heard Warren 'call them all as brothers, to gather round and listen'. Warren recalled a workman 'said he had been hit on the head by something, or somebody has belted me' or he was 'belted around the head with a brick'. He saw no blood or marks, but apologised all the same. The lumper Growcott acknowledged speaking to Warren about the alleged assault and 'his attitude gave me the impression he wouldn't have done that himself'.

At 'about ten past three' Noel Egan, the clerk of works and a NALGO member, saw 'about twenty or thirty real agitators' 'to the right, mostly, of the First school' and 'about one quarter of a mile from Site Office 6 and the works office next door'. 'Others stood back and they were more peaceful', while 'about a hundred and fifty' 'gathered outside the office in a semi-circle'. A policeman 'of rank' 'chatted to them' and they walked downhill together, peacefully. Keith Hitchen was on Site 3 when, soon after 'half past two' he saw 'about fiftenn to twenty' men 'approximately seventy five yards away', coming from the centre of the site. Their numbers increased to 'approximately fifty' and 'ten, twenty possibly' were 'smashing windows' of houses and machines; but by around 3.00pm 'most of the workers' were 'at the offices'.

In his statement the lumper Clive Jones had said that he walked from Site Office 3 and saw 'a group of pickets coming towards me from the middle of the site', 'shouting and swearing and smashing windows. Some of them had sticks and pick handles in their hands.' He saw McKinsie Jones 'pick up a brick and throw it through a pane of glass in one of the houses'. (He was up to a hundred yards away and McKinsie Jones hadn't left PC Amies's sight on the perimeter road.) He saw Warren lead workers fifty yards into the site. He joined them, but 'was not threatened or injured'.

Chief Inspector Gradwell saw men 'about one hundred yards away from the site office' going to 'an assembly point'. PC Ball saw 'about two hundred' coming from 'the back end of the site' to a meeting 'about fifty yards from the road'.

The Flying Pickets

The site meeting

Crown witnesses confirmed that the site meeting began just after 3.00pm. PC McKeitch testified that 'local men had been drawn into the middle' and 'encircled by the pickets'. The main speaker said: '"Stand back lads so they don't feel intimidated".' Some 'moved right back and others moved away'. A Crown witness picket recalled Warren asking them to go to the coaches, 'so he could talk,' and 'the majority' did. Another remembered he 'told us to go back' and 'most' pickets 'stood on the side of the road' until the coaches drew up. Sergeant Theodore heard men 'on the fringe of the meeting' who were 'shouting reports after various things were said by the speaker' and pickets 'began to filter back towards the coaches'. Warren recalled anxiety about pickets being inhibited and saying: '"Now get back, right back out of the way, away from the workers", and they moved back and I think some went to the buses. A lot moved away to the back so the main bulk of the workers were in front.'

Detective Inspector Glover's 'prepared' 'statement' had Llywarch saying: 'After ten minutes to quarter of an hour' of arriving (around 3.00pm) 'the pickets came back through the site to the offices on the road'. Carpenter testified that he had left Llywarch near the coaches. Llywarch testified that he got back on the Oswestry coach with others and 'asked the driver to pull down to see what was going on' near Site Office 3. Crown witnesses saw him get off and go to the meeting with Carpenter, who passed questions to Warren.

PC Williams recalled hearing Warren saying something like: 'We want £30 a week for tradesmen, £27 a week for labourers.' 'You negotiate your bonuses before you start the job.' 'If you're on the lump, you're out.' 'If we find out you're back at work, we'll be back.' There were shouts of 'Scabs' and 'Get them out' from 'the back of the crowd'. 'The general tone was one of intimidation.'

A Crown witness recalled speaking with a man who claimed to have taken a knock on the head but was 'talking naturally'. He knew him as 'Growler'. When the main site meeting began this man said something like: 'I am just going up to see what is going on.' Warren recalled that site workers gave him 'some stick' and the man who had complained about being assaulted 'had a good go' because they were getting £50 a week, so why strike for £30? Warren said: '£50 a week and you couldn't get a pair of boots for your feet?' 'Your toes are sticking out.' 'Everybody had a laugh' at Growcott. About a hundred workers were 'listening to everything', but another hundred or so were hanging back. Warren got 'one of the lads to take over for a minute', went over and asked them: 'Why don't you come over and join the meeting and we'll have a full discussion and you can have your say and we will sort it out one way or another?' A 'couple of them came, but the bulk of them stayed where they were'. DC Davies saw the 'main spokesman' go to 'local workers' 'in front of the site offices' and heard him say that 'if they had anything to say they should say it to everyone'. PC Williams recalled:

> A group of Irish workers were across the road and they were shouting across to the meeting that they were earning more than £30 already. After a while, a number of pickets went over to them and said 'Come on then, get over there to the meeting.' They went on arguing for five to ten minutes and then the pickets rejoined the meeting, leaving the Irishmen where they were.

A 'blond haired lad' told the 'Paddies' they were 'finished anywhere unless they had their union cards'. He was in 'his early twenties, 5' 9", stocky—well built, shoulder length hair, not straight, but wavy, Liverpool area accent, wearing light coloured cardigan or pullover'. He couldn't identify him from photographs but insisted that site workers 'clearly did not know what hit them', that 'the whole business was purely and simply intimidation' and that it was 'obviously a pre-arranged plan to stop the workers by any means whatsoever'; yet 'I cannot say that any of them appeared to be actually frightened'. He identified eighteen pickets who were 'very much in evidence round the site, and at the meeting', but couldn't recollect one 'doing anything specific'. 'At no time on any of these sites did I see anyone carrying sticks or bricks' or damaging property. McKinsie Jones was 'generally argumentative'. 'It was not so much what he shouted from time to time, but the way he acted.' He was 'clearly a main organiser, but I cannot really say why'.

DC Davies heard McKinsie Jones 'asking for support for the strike' and 'for local workers to picket sites'. 'It will only take about a dozen of you to police this area.' They could increase wages and 'reduce the profits of firms like Sir Alfred McAlpine'. Two pickets were 'disgusted to find men still working in the area when they themselves had been on strike for eight weeks. They expressed concern at what had happened on this site, regarding damage, but blamed it on the workers who had not joined the strike.' Inspector Meredith recalled 'an orderly meeting' and there wasn't 'anything terribly wrong with the actual speeches'. PC Goodchild heard Llywarch speak. After a 'short meeting' the pickets 'started to clap their hands and it appeared to me that the site workers had decided to come out on strike, as they began to disperse among the pickets. I did not see any pickets threaten any site workers, although some of them were carrying lengths of wood in their hands.' He couldn't identify any stick carriers and none appear on the photographs.

One worker volunteered to be shop steward and three or four others agreed to help. A Crown witness gathered that a local Action Committee would try to get all the lumpers out on strike. Another left after he 'could gather they were agreeing' to do that. PC Williams recalled that Warren 'told them of a union meeting in Shrewsbury the following day'. Superintendent Landers understood 'some senior union leaders' would speak there.

Tomlinson apologised to Inspector Meredith about the damage. He replied: 'It is nothing more than the children do at any weekend' and 'the meeting had been conducted very well.' Warren recalled that a senior policeman 'shook hands': 'I would like to congratulate you on the way the meetings have been held.' Meredith recalled: 'I went to him. I sort of pushed my hand out more or less to sort of detain him, and he shook it, and I shook his, which is nothing more than I have done with people perhaps of the criminal fraternity.' 'I didn't know he was a criminal then.'

Inspector Morris believed that the meeting 'lasted perhaps ten minutes or a quarter of an hour' and ended at around 2.40pm, five minutes before the picket coaches arrived. Superintendent Landers found it going on when he arrived at 3.00pm and it ended after 'no more than four or five minutes'. Chief Inspector Gradwell thought it lasted 'about a quarter of an hour'. Sergeant Bastable thought about 'twenty minutes'. Inspector Powell reached Brookside at 3.15pm and was instructed to stay in the coach along with the other officers. He saw a meeting of 'about two hundred and fifty, three hundred' men that 'seemed quite orderly' and broke up 'quite orderly' soon after. The pickets walked past his coach to their own. Philip Jones testified that pickets started to come off the site soon after 3.20pm. Sergeant Hartland said 3.35pm. John Walsh, a trainee engineer, believed it began after 3.45pm and recalled 'two people carrying something, one was a stick and I think the other was an iron bar'. Inspector Meredith thought the meeting 'might have' ended at 4.00pm. Drake suggested 4.15pm. (Given that they visited two other sites, two miles away, before 4.30, he was clearly mistaken.)

Growcott was one of the last to leave. On the way home he 'felt really bad' and the driver took him to hospital because he was 'going drowsy'. 'I spent a week in hospital. I received bruising to my head and was treated for concussion. I was very sore all over. My eyesight was also affected.' Royal Salop Infirmary staff noted that he seemed 'very concussed, with severe headache and bruising on both arms', and wondered if he had a 'severe head injury'. He was 'slightly drowsy', had 'quite a lot of bruises on both arms' and 'posterior' and 'complained of pain on the left leg'. At Copthorne Hospital 'X-rays of his skull, left tibia and lumbar spine were all normal'. His pupils 'reacted minimally to light' and showed 'no clinical abnormality'. After a week's observation he was completely discharged. (Growcott later claimed that his hand had been stood on so hard that he almost passed out and that he was blind in one eye). Growcott's son-in-law, a Brookside lumper, 'didn't actually see anybody doing damage' and didn't see the 'assault' on Growcott, who 'looked frightened and distressed' and 'said he had been hit'. The son-in-law 'would rather not go to court' to testify.

The camera never lies

The reporter Philip Jones had been watching the site meeting for 'some minutes' when a man asked who he and David Bagnall were.

> When I informed him we were from the press, he said, 'Why don't you fuck off?' He also said something else which I cannot remember, to the effect that if we didn't leave he would use physical violence towards us to make us leave. This man left me in no doubt that he meant what he said and this threatening attitude worried me.
>
> We moved off for a short distance and stopped the car again, but this man ran after us so we moved off again. The photographer with me pointed his camera towards the pickets, which caused him to move behind a coach.
>
> We then returned to where the meeting was being held and stopped alongside the police cars, and almost immediately this same picket returned with another man.
>
> The second picket said, 'You'd better not take any pictures or I'll give you a permanent pair of sunglasses.' Then one of these two shouted to some other pickets, informing them that we had cameras. They were joined by three other pickets. All five men stood alongside the passenger side of the vehicle, therefore making it impossible to use his camera. They were leaning on

the vehicle and rocking it from side to side. I drove away a few feet, but the five men followed again and leaned on the car and rocked it, so I drove away from this location and returned some minutes later.

We parked at almost the same position and on this occasion another picket came over to the car and said, 'There are a lot of boys here, if you take any photographs your camera might get smashed.' There was no doubt in my mind that this was a definite threat. He had a foreign accent, possibly Polish. He was about 6'0", heavy build, going bald, but what hair he had was fair. I do not think I would recognise this man if I saw him again.

Where were the police?

Bagnall took more photographs.

7   A large meeting is taking place next to a house with its roof timbers in place (126 Burtondale). Warren is speaking. Warburton and Renshaw are also visible. The shot was taken from the direction of the perimeter road.

8   A car is moving along the perimeter road and a man is in the road between two coaches parked on the estate side. The shot was taken from the other side of the road.

9   Warren is addressing the meeting and he, Davies, Hughes, Jones, Llywarch, Morris, O'Shea, Renshaw and Tomlinson are listed. (Barry Scragg and Freddie Walker are also visible.) The shot was taken from the perimeter road, several yards north east of photographs 7 and 8, with a telephoto lens.

10 PC Gradwell and Inspector Meredith stand some way to the left of a large peaceful meeting. Between them and the camera a senior officer and two PCs are looking on with total equanimity. No worker shows terror and nobody holds a stick or 'iron bar'.

11 Llywarch appears to be addressing the site meeting and Carpenter, Hughes and Seaburg are in the audience.

12 A large group of men, including Pierce, Kelly and Edward Williams, is walking past the lower two houses of the same block as 126 Burtondale, going towards the perimeter road, where pickets are boarding coaches. The camera was behind at least two coaches and fifty yards away.

13 Men are walking along the middle of the perimeter road, going, south west, in between four coaches parked next to the site and a car parked on the other side, which are

pointing north east. A car is passing between them going south west. Beyond the coaches, pickets are boarding a fifth coach on the side of the road away from the estate. The camera was on that side of the road.

14   A few men, led by Pierce and Edward Williams, are walking past the third coach towards a Mostyn coach. One carries a jacket. The moving car had gone only a few yards.

15   Tomlinson and Jones are talking to Superintendent Landers.

Drake showed 15 (as D) to a Crown witness, asked about an alleged incident at Brookside and added that D had been taken 'shortly after the event'. Fennell showed D to PC Price and asked if he had seen Landers 'speaking to these two men'? He had not. Landers recalled speaking to Tomlinson and Jones, two miles away at Woodside.

Regan recalled of Woodside: 'There was shouting and throwing of stones from both sides' but 'a small minority of pickets' did that. Inspector Meredith told two pickets that 'if any more damage occurred he would hold them responsible', but 'things quietened down and there was no need for arrests'.

Drake and Fennell had omitted photographs 2, 3, 8, 10 and 13 and put the others in the order: 1, 5, 11, 15, 12, 14, 9, 4, 7 and 6.

A   Warren is addressing a meeting near Site Office 3.
B   A group of men is walking. One carries a piece of wood.
C   Warren is addressing the site meeting.
D   Superintendent Landers is speaking to Jones and Tomlinson.
E   A line of men is going to the coaches.
F   A few men are walking past the coaches.
G   Warren is addressing the site meeting.
H   A small group of men is walking along. One has a stick.
I   Warren is addressing the site meeting.
J   Three men are holding pieces of wood and a fourth an 'iron bar'.

According to this 'story', most pickets left the site as Warren was orchestrating a rising crescendo of violence amongst a 'hard core'.

Platts-Mills suggested that the sequence had been 'expurgated' by the Crown. Mr Justice Mais wanted the allegation withdrawn. 'The prosecution are entitled to produce such photographs as they desire, aren't they?' He also complained about the 'most astonishing expense' of making a new exhibit, but had to agree.

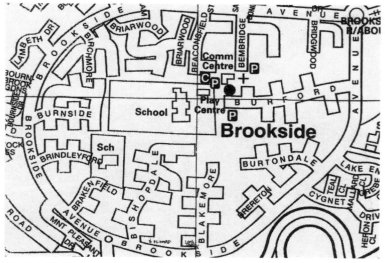

MAP OF SITE

I

A

2

3

The Flying Pickets

4   H

5   B

The first Shrewsbury trial   195

6

J

7

I

The Flying Pickets

8

9

The first Shrewsbury trial

10

11

C

The Flying Pickets

12   E

13

14   F

15   D

The Flying Pickets

Detective Chief Inspector Glover (as he now was) denied telling reporters that 'building employers were putting pressure on the government to bring about a prosecution' and 'the government was putting pressure on the police'. Platts-Mills asked Laurence Mansbridge of the *Border Counties Advertiser* about a meeting between journalists and a senior policemen on 27 September 1972. Had this policeman spoken about 'pressure' to secure a prosecution? They may have mentioned something like that. Mais asked if 'outside' pressure was being suggested. Platts-Mills insisted that he had only been asking if this had been the case.

Thirty three Crown witnesses had been on the picket coaches, yet none saw violence to people or heard any picket condoning damage to property. Several lumpers were serially mistaken. Police were at every site after Kingswood, yet none saw violence to people. Some claimed to have heard glass breaking and to have been told by other officers about damage, and a few claimed to have seen damage being done by individuals they claimed to be able to identify; but many were mistaken on a number of other important issues. One senior officer saw 'no damage whatsoever'. No picket was cautioned or arrested and no ambulances were called.

Platts-Mills pointed to a series of breaches of safety legislation in the photographs and argued that lumpers did not worked lawfully. If anyone was violent or caused damage, it was a minority on the Chester coach, and none of them had been arrested. The defendants had not known each other and had never been together as a group until 6 September 1972, so how could they have conspired? Mais interjected: 'You know very well, Mr Platts-Mills, that for conspiracy, they never have to meet and they never have to know each other.' Platts-Mills persisted. Mais threw his wig on the desk.

A copy of the police report to the DPP had been left behind in court at lunchtime by one of the Crown lawyers. One defence counsel told Jim Arnison about it, but he feared that it would be 'hearsay' evidence and the *Star* might be prosecuted. Platts-Mills questioned Inspector Powell, but he was non-committal. The former Chief Superintendent Hodges (now Assistant Chief Constable of West Mercia), wouldn't say that they had reached a 'firm conclusion' that the men who allegedly caused violence were on the Chester coach and dispersed amongst the other coaches before they left Shrewsbury. There had been 'comments made' that the Chester coach 'had contained a nucleus of men', but police had been unable to get any picket on that coach to give a statement. Yet he 'had no regrets', because their enquiries were 'quite conclusive'. Platts-Mills asked to see the report. Mais announced that it was a 'privileged document'. Platts-Mills suggested that Mais make a formal ruling or allow the witness to refresh his memory. Hodges mumbled and Mais demurred. Then Drake asked how Platts-Mills could put questions about a report he couldn't have seen legitimately and Platts-Mills let the matter drop. The report was strongly rumoured to say that any violence at Brookside was spontaneous and police had been unable to identify any instigators. They felt they had insufficient evidence to secure convictions on ordinary charges and that common law 'conspiracy' charges were wholly inappropriate.

Mais began summing up a case 'of considerable importance' to 'the public' on 13 December. The Crown claimed there was 'ample evidence' of 'agreement' and 'carrying it into execution'.

> Ask yourselves whether in fact what happened could have happened unless there had been organisation, unless there had been a plan, a common design. I must tell you that conspiracy is a matter of inference.
>
> It is seldom expressed in words still, less in writing, and it can be inferred from conduct, by words and by acts of those concerned...
>
> Now it is not necessary that all the conspirators should join the conspiracy at one and the same time. It is not necessary that they should all join at the beginning or that they all originated the idea...

After all, how could hundreds of pickets have found their coaches without leaders? McKinsie Jones wasn't at the Chester meeting on 31 August 1972 and there was 'some doubt' that O'Shea was there. Warren and Tomlinson were authorised 'lay speakers'. Mais didn't challenge Warren's claim that 'no one was ever asked by the police to call off the picketing', but if any defendant 'was participating or lending their support to aid in any violence or intimidation, or doing any damage, then they might be as guilty as any other man who was a party to violence and intimidation and did damage'. He confused the two Flint coaches with the one from Chester and insisted that Llywarch booked a coach from Oswestry to go to Shrewsbury and Telford on the basis of testimony from a single Crown witness and Llywarch's unsigned 'statement', in spite of his firm refutation in court. As for the lump—'whatever that may mean'—he was sure it involved 'working lawfully'. Defence counsel interrupted to correct his grossest factual errors. Mais said it was a long trial and he could not be expected to get everything right. Platts-Mills later recalled that Mais was 'the ideal choice for a trial of active trade unionists'. He 'showed a deep dislike for them all and clearly had no real understanding of the trade union movement'.

On the 18th the jury found all six defendants guilty of 'unlawful assembly', but O'Shea and Carpenter not guilty of 'affray' and 'conspiracy to intimidate'. Llywarch was not guilty of 'affray', but Jones, Tomlinson and Warren were. They hadn't reach a unanimous verdict on 'conspiracy' on Jones, Llywarch, Tomlinson and Warren, so Mais authorised them to return a majority verdict of ten to two. Next day Jim Arnison recalled that the jury foreman, a schoolteacher, looked 'shattered and unhappy'. They had decided by ten votes to two that Jones, Tomlinson and Warren were guilty of 'conspiracy', but Llywarch was not guilty. Arnison later heard that 'one somewhat dominant individual' had managed to convince others that the defendants would only be fined and get a 'slap on the wrist' and that the court official supervising them 'concurred'.

Tomlinson was confident that he and Warren might get off with a fine. He 'refuted with every fibre of my being' that his wasn't a political trial and looked forward to 'when the real culprits of these crimes, the McAlpines, the Wimpeys, the Laings, and the Bovis's, and all their political bodies, are in the dock facing charges of conspiracy to intimidate workers from doing what is their lawful right, picketing'. Warren had worked out his speech with Arnison: 'Every action taken in the furtherance of an industrial dispute is a political act' and the law was 'an instrument of the state to be used in the interests of a tiny minority against the majority. It is biased; it is class law, and nowhere has that been demonstrated more than in the prosecution case in this trial'.

> The conspiracy began with the miners giving the government a good hiding last year, and I hope they do the same this year. It developed when the government was forced to perform legal hocus-pocus in getting five dockers out of goal after they had only just been put there. The conspiracy was between the Home Secretary, the employers, and the police.

The 'working class movement cannot allow this verdict to go unchallenged'.

Mais said that 'deterrent sentences are necessary and justified'. He gave O'Shea, Carpenter and Llywarch nine months, suspended for two years, Jones nine months, without suspension, and Tomlinson two years on all three charges, to run concurrently. Warren recalled that the jury foreman stood up and asked: 'Can I leave this court?' He pushed his way past fellow jurors, exclaiming, '"It's disgraceful!" and left the court shouting, "It's disgusting, disgusting".' Platts-Mills—who was convinced that 'there could only be a fine at worst'—recalled that the foreman 'kept on shouting until he disappeared through the jury door. Another juror followed, showing his anger by slamming the door of the jury box.' Platts-Mills 'had never seen the like, and I don't think any of us had'.

Mais took ten minutes to restore order and then remarked: 'Well, we don't really need them any more, do we? Let the jury be discharged.' He singled out Warren as 'the leader and prime mover'. He was 'arrogant, vicious, and prepared to impose your views upon others by violence if need be'. Mais sentenced him to three years on all three charges, to run concurrently.

Elsa Warren was led sobbing from court. The jury foreman was in tears. He shook hands with Carpenter and O'Shea and explained that the jury had been split eight to four for over twenty four hours, but were 'led to believe that if found guilty there would be fines but no jailings'. He and one other juror lost a very heated argument.

In next day's *Guardian*, 'Bill Smith'—probably Bert—described the sentences as 'savage'. UCATT's Head Office would discuss the implications. Alan Abrahams hinted about industrial action.

CHAPTER 12

The Pentonville 5 movement will spring to life again

Building workers today, you tomorrow

By 1973 the number of British trade unionists had grown to 11,500,000. That year 13 percent were out on strike for an average of almost five days apiece. It was a boom year for construction. There were five vacancies for every bricklayer—ten in some parts of East Anglia and the south east—and three for every joiner and plasterer. Over 73,000 private contractors employed an estimated 400,000 lumpers. Winning political strikes wasn't easy.

On 3 October 2,500 Dundee and 3,000 Edinburgh building workers went on strike on the first day of the first Shrewsbury trial. Almost every large Merseyside site, all 2,000 corporation building workers, all 8,500 dockers and some engineers came out. So did eighteen major Birmingham sites and around 4,000 London building workers. 200 Higgs and Hill's Southampton General Hospital site workers went on strike, lobbied UCATT and TGWU officials—who gave no information because the case was 'sub judice'—and began a 50p weekly levy. The men decided that if anyone were jailed they would take 'action deemed necessary for their release'.

That evening police stopped the Colchester Trades Council coach outside the town as it returned from Shrewsbury. They claimed to be investigating an incendiary device in Woolworths, yet their main questions were about the 24 and they searched people's houses in the small hours. The CP Trades Council Secretary, other CPers and members of IS, the IMG and the Labour Party were released on bail, but had to report to the police station.

The NCCL condemned the police harassment. The CDC thought 'this action is typical of the harassment by the police of trade unionists, immigrants and progressives.' Barry Jones MP would be 'asked to raise the matter in parliament'. (He asked for the Tory Home Secretary's 'views' and donated £1 to the Defence Fund.)

On the 4th the CDC discussed the 'continuing of the campaign during the trial'. Pete Carter was a guest and the UCATT, TGWU and TUC lobbies were left in his hands. A daily picket of Shrewsbury Crown Court would be a 'huge organisational problem' and 'would not have the desired effect' if only a few people were there, but every UCATT and TGWU regional secretary and some regional committee members would be asked to organise a coachload of supporters to fill the public gallery one day a week. Trades councils in 'major industrial areas' should 'have all the buses stopped one week, a car factory next and so on', to 'keep publicity on the trial and let the powers that be know that the rank and file are right behind these lads'. Each night a defendant would contact a CDC member who would make 'regular reports' to the *Star*.

On the 8th, at an 'emergency' meeting, Barry Scragg became the CDC Chairman. John Llywarch's 'problems' had been sorted out. Scragg would see a defendant who was 'under excess strain due to domestic reasons and the pressure of the trial' and Joe Edwards would look into complaints about some defendants having 'more facilities than others'. Local financial support was weak. That week's income was £390, but £240 went to pay the six defendants' weekly 'wages' of £40 (about £320 today). There were Pete Carter's and Bill Jones's expenses, Billy Regan's phone bill, Margaret Douglas's wages and Ricky Tomlinson's visit to his solicitor. Owens had to be paid for five 'duplicate receipt books', 2,000 collection sheets, 10,000 'hand bills' about 'funds' and the bulletin.

On the 10th the CDC heard that the UCATT General Secretary, George Smith, refused to testify for the defence. Defence counsel advised against demonstrations outside court, in case the judge refused to extend bail. There were guests from Liverpool Trades Council. Tony McClelland suggested getting in touch with the wider shop stewards' movement and Simon Fraser had useful addresses. Alan Abrahams thought a mass stewards' meeting in Liverpool in November would be 'of great help'. After the guests left, he listed 'all Liverpool jobs that had agreed support for the 24'. Difficulties had arisen on the Ince site after a UCATT official visited. Bill Jones reported that Shell Stanlow workers had pledged financial support and to 'stop work if any of the 24 were jailed'. (The defendants' weekly wages were cut by £5.) A reference to the TUC in a draft bulletin was rephrased and solicitors would vet future ones.

Bulletin No 9 stressed that the 'employers and the state' were 'determined' to 'weaken the right to picket effectively'. 'It is essential that these lads are supported morally in the public gallery of the court so that they can see the rank and file are behind them. We urge you to do what you can in your area to organise a coach, mini-bus or even car full up to the public gallery.' 'Make collections at your branch, trades council and place of work. If you are on a large site or factory ask your stewards to invite a speaker.' If any of the 24 were found guilty, the Pentonville 5 'movement will spring to life again, and call on the TUC for their maximum support. Decisions should be taken now to this effect at shop floor level'.

The CDC explained to the LCDTU that the trial was 'an outright attack on the trade union movement'. If anyone was found guilty of 'conspiracy' they 'would expect to see the same rank and file action we saw when the five dockers were jailed' and the TUC giving 'maximum support'. Could a CDC speaker 'address conference'?

On the 17th the treasurer wanted the accounts audited by two people 'outside the committee'. None of the 24 or 'anyone who may be called as a witness should attend the public gallery'. A letter was to be sent to Bert Smith 'endorsing' a meeting for 'all trades shop stewards' in Manchester. Members of the 24 would get £40 apiece from Chester Action Committee. UCATT's fund might 'bring problems', but the TGWU should be pressured to follow suit.

Next day Billy Regan set out CDC policy in a letter to trades councils. If any of the 24 were sent to jail then 'the whole country must stop work until they are freed' and this 'must be far more widespread' than with the Pentonville 5. 'Building Workers Today—You Tomorrow'. The CDC had 'nowhere near enough funds'. 'Please organise weekly collections to support your right to picket' and 'demonstrations in your town to keep the case in the forefront'. The 'next stage of the fight' would be after the verdicts.

Regan thanked a TGWU dockers' steward in Liverpool. The CDC was 'having a little difficulty in getting over what a verdict against the 24 would mean to the trade union movement' in North Wales. He sent £10 to the *Star*: 'Reading the capitalist press then comparing it with the *Star* brings home to one just how biased the mass media is.' Could the treasurer's name and address follow the daily report? Zelda Curtis was delighted. The cash 'will greatly help to maintain the *Star* in fighting fitness for this bitter election battle now being waged'. The *Star* printed the treasurer's address.

£3, the use of some telephones and plenty of imagination

On 10 October Crook UCATT urged the regional council 'to support our members moral[l]y' and 'adopt' a family during the trial. Next day Manchester IS, who had tried to get a CDC speaker in September, heard that the CDC 'reiterated' its policy on political meetings. The next *SW* reported that prominent building industry trade unionists would speak at a 'Shrewsbury 24 rally'. They aimed to 'bring together as many socialists and trade unionists as possible to stress the importance of the trial and to show the men on trial that they did not stand alone', 'provide for the families of the men' and 'hear from trade unionists in other industries of the support and action that they are pledged to give'. Leaflets were available. George Smith was now a CBE for 'services to somebody'.

IS set out its perspective in *International Socialism*. EC member Chris Harman analysed the CP's decline, but acknowledged that their 7,000 active members had better roots in industry than IS.

> The short term aim of a revolutionary socialist organisation like IS must be to replace the CP as the main focus to which militants in industry look for a lead... by exposing the contrast between the CP's behaviour and what it professes to believe in. The best way to do this is by proposing united action to the CP leadership on important issues of principle in the class struggle on which it claims to agree with us.

SW reported that Southampton and Edinburgh IS building workers had organised for strikes and stewards in London's Royal Group of Docks had begun a campaign. IS had a programme:

1   IS members to raise the issue in their union branches and to send successful resolutions for publication in *Socialist Worker*.

2   Invite a speaker from the North Wales 24 defence committee to address the *Socialist Worker* industrial conference on 11 November.

3   Invite speakers from the defence committee to address IS branches, with IS speakers stressing the need for similar action to that over Pentonville.

4   Commission a special article for *Socialist Worker* on the technique of preparing for strike action along with improved coverage of the trial.

SW's editor, Roger Protz, reported that circulation had risen 'nearly 2,000 copies in the past three weeks' and branches should 'make a real effort to reach 35,000 copies by the end of the year'. Mick Marratty, Secretary of Hull Building Workers, commended *Pickets on Trial*. John Fontaine and Michael Fenn, a steward in the Royal Group of Docks and a key figure in *The Dockworker*, would address the North London Building Workers public meeting on the 23rd. Norwich IS's public meeting on 'Building Workers—The Way Forward' on the 24th would be chaired by a TGWU convenor.

On the 20th the IS Birmingham District Secretary, Colin Sparks, asked for a CDC member or a defendant to address factory and site stewards' committees, union branches, factory gate meetings and a public meeting. 'I cannot give you a detailed itinerary, as we would hope to arrange as many meetings as possible.' IS would provide accommodation and transport. 'Hopefully such a tour could provide considerable financial support' and 'serious commitment to other action'. Edinburgh IS had told him that Bill Jones was a 'very good presenter of the case'. Sparks recalls that IS had access to Longbridge and Lucas: 'Some CP convenors were relatively unsectarian and would welcome visiting delegations organised by IS.' The CDC replied that their policy 'right from the start has been any meeting as long as it is not political'. If Sparks 'could arrange public, factory gate, branch or trades council meetings' he would 'supply you with a speaker (possibly W Jones) on any date or dates'.

Alan Abrahams, Bill Jones and Jeff Douglas were CDC delegates to the LCDTU conference. It attracted 515 delegates, but only 35 shop stewards' committees. Jones felt that Abrahams 'got the main points over in the time allowed'. The Conference Declaration focused on the Tories' 'anti-union, anti-democratic, neo-fascist policies' and noted that 'prosecution of pickets' was part of a 'strategy of intimidation'. They applauded the 'courageous determination' of the Shrewsbury 24 and the Sheffield 8 'who refused to be cowed by the state organs of repression, and pledge all-out solidarity with them in their fight in every possible way.' *SW* reported that the number of delegates was under half of what it had been. An IS member had pointed out that if officials didn't give a lead then it was 'up to the rank and file to take the initiative in organising action'. The LCDTU was 'dominated' by the CP, whose policy of 'uncritical support for trade union leaders' like Jack Jones of the TGWU and Hugh Scanlon of the AUEW 'has disarmed and confused the trade union militants who follow that lead'; so 'far from being a pressure group pushing these leaders to the left', the LCDTU was 'a means of covering up and justifying their retreat'.

Dennis Dugen told the CDC about a *Charter* Editorial Board meeting in November, 'where some of the "Charter's" problems will be sorted out'. Item 2 on the agenda was: 'Initiate Campaign' and 'Stop the Trials—Change the Law'. 'Timing might be all important as that could read "Release the Building Pickets—Change the Law"—but we mustn't be too pessimistic.' They had 'ideas and plans equally as important as the meeting which floated the idea of a national conference' and a CDC delegation was 'essential'.

The UCATT North West Regional Secretary, Eric Hughes, sent £40 apiece for Renshaw, McKinsie Jones and 'R. Jones'.

On the 22nd the *Star* reported that the CP London District Organiser had told a Co-operative Conference that there 'must be a massive outcry' to 'win the release of the Shrewsbury 24' and tell the Industrial Relations Court 'to keep its hands out of union funds'. (The AUEW had refused to pay a £100,000 fine for defying a court order to end a long-running strike at Con-Mech Engineering in Woking, where management had sacked two stewards.)

Dennis Dugen and Bert Smith were guests at the CDC. Smith believed that their pressure had helped to establish UCATT's fund and pressure should be applied to the TGWU to follow suit. Bill Jones was, 'rather pleased' with his reception at Fords. His £5 donation to the LCDTU was endorsed. John Llywarch had 'sacked' his barrister after refusing to change his plea to guilty in return for a suspended sentence. Alan Abrahams gave information about legal aid and 'subsistence' that Llywarch had allegedly received from the TGWU. He was to be asked if this was true. A letter was to be sent to the AUEW in support of 'the stand they are taking'. Dugen had reported that the *Charter* was 'in financial difficulty'. That week's income was over £460, but half had gone straight out again. The print order for the next bulletin was to be 50,000 copies. *Bulletin No 10* paraphrased the CDC's trades council circular. 'Our brothers will still be on trial over Christmas, they all have families, it is up to us to see that they do not suffer any hardship.'

The *SW* printed on the 24th advertised a Hull mass meeting and a York Trades Council public meeting. All 5,000 copies of *Pickets on Trial* had been 'enthusiastically received in building sites and in factories' and it had been reprinted. A national meeting of IS building workers had noted that there were 'tens of thousands of workers who have not heard of the Shrewsbury trial', so there was to be 'a combined effort by IS branches everywhere to raise the issue on building sites and among industrial workers' through public meetings. Port of London stewards, two TGWU branches and two branches of the National Amalgamated Stevedores & Dockers would call for strikes if any of the

24 were jailed and the ASPD EC was being pressed to call a one-day strike against the trial and an indefinite strike in the event of jailings. Michael Fenn stressed 'the important support dockers had obtained from building workers and engineers when their five brothers were in jail', but 'the government and the Tory press had learned a lesson'. They 'gave massive publicity to the dockers' struggle and everyone knew what was at stake', but with Shrewsbury they were 'keeping dead quiet'. The dockers' release 'had been portrayed as a superbly-organised conspiracy backed by huge funds', yet a few stewards had started with '£3, the use of some telephones and plenty of imagination'.

Like most activists, Jim French got his information about the trials from the *Star*, the *Charter* and the LCDTU. 'In London, Alan Tattam and Lou Lewis would take me for a drink in the King's Head. UCATT's EC used to meet there and they would tell me tales about their antics. I also went to a couple of Party Building Group meetings in London, but was never asked to join.'

UCATT's Northern Regional Committee praised Labour Councillor Jim French for getting Darlington Council to rebuff an invitation to view Bovis show houses 'until it is employing men direct and not on "lump" labour'. £50 was to go to the UCATT Fund that was 'intended solely for the dependants' of men on trial. Branches should forward money to be sent on, but Crook branch's proposal to 'adopt a family' was 'impracticable'. A letter from 'another organisation'—the CDC—'suggesting a busload of trade unionists to attend a hearing' was not a 'possibility at this time'.

On the 29th George Smith told UCATT branches about 'the multiplicity of funds supposedly set up to aid building workers at Shrewsbury'. The EC had ordered the North West Regional Council to establish a 'Distress Fund' and 'if any donations are to be made for this purpose they could be made to a proper authorised committee'. Eric Hughes sent £40 apiece for eight Shotton TGWU members.

On the 31st the CDC heard that Warren and Tomlinson had 'expressed their reluctance to pay any fines' and wanted feedback on the issue. A response was postponed until after 'the next conference'. Llywarch was not getting money from the TGWU. Margaret Douglas had no access to a 'photostat machine', but Mike Williams would pick up the typed minutes on Mondays and make copies. The CDC 'had the task of approaching the broad TU movement'. It would 'co-opt' a TGWU member to pressurise the union either to set up a hardship fund or join UCATT's. The Defence Fund would pay for servicing vehicles 'to convey the accused to court'. The week's income was £1,130. Where did most come from?

On behalf of the more militant members

During October the Secretary of Stirling EETPU wrote 'on behalf of the more militant members' who were organising workplace collections. £10 came from Stirling Trades Council. ASTMS members in Fife Health Service had begun 'systematic' collections and, 'sponsored' by Kirkaldy Trades Council, had formed a Fife Defence Committee. They sent £25. Could they have a speaker—'preferably one of the 24'—for a week at the end of November, for site, pit, factory and college meetings, culminating in a 'mass rally'? (The CDC promised 'bulletin sheets and any other relevant information' and would 'certainly' supply a speaker.) £210 came from Paisley Rolls Royce stewards, £50 from Albion Motors stewards in Glasgow and £48 from a UCATT steward at Govan Shipbuilders. George Kelly, an IS steward at the Glasgow Corporation workshops, sent £5 and would do so 'for the next few weeks'. There was 'a possibility that we will continue this donation till the end of the trial'. He assured the CDC of 'physical support if necessary'. Edinburgh Trades Council wanted to issue a fortnightly leaflet to keep the movement 'aware of the progress being made at the Shrewsbury trials' and help raise money. 'If support on the scale necessary to bring victory to the Shrewsbury 24 is to be obtained' they could 'possibly raise this with Glasgow, Kirkcaldy, Aberdeen and Dundee Trades Councils.' (The CDC replied that their bulletins were monthly, but a fortnightly bulletin could be 'made up' from the *Star*.) Edinburgh University ASTMS sent £20 and there were collections from dozens of UCATT members. Four Scottish NUM lodges made contributions and the Scottish NUM EC sent £100.

Teesside Charter raised £9.50 and would 'put everything into the Shrewsbury 24 support'. 'We are in constant touch with Bert Smith' and 'are waiting word from him about Peter Carter'. (Carter and Smith often stayed with Jim French.) They had announced a CDC speaker in November and expected a good turnout, so could they have one? A Hull mass meeting would be open to all trade unionists. Could they have the 'Weekly Bulletin'? The Fellow Travellers, a left wing theatre group from Bradford, had given cash to 'comrades in Edinburgh who were collecting'. They sent a collection taken at a performance at Bradford University and planned to raise more on a tour of West Riding trades councils. Leeds Trades Council sent £66 and would support 'any future national conference' to 'discuss action on the Shrewsbury 24'. (Someone noted on the letter: 'Committee to be formed at EC'.) Delegates would hold workplace collections and 'collecting in some factories should start' soon.

Preston Defence Committee sent £200. There had been collections at a Preston site and an AUEW branch, three Blackpool sites and Chorley UCATT. Could Alan Abrahams speak in Preston and at Blackpool Trades Council? (He could.) They needed 'at *least* 100' bulletins. Their 'October Bulletin' listed Charter activities and noted support from Padgate College and Harris College Students' Unions, Leyland CP and Preston IMG. The only way to stop such attacks was by using the full strength of the movement, 'if necessary by striking'. NUM North West Area offered help. A Bolton NUT member needed 'a few hundred copies of the latest bulletin'. A Bolton TASS branch, Bolton Trades Council and Bolton East Labour Party donated. So did TASS Divisional Council. A Rochdale worker apologised for a small contribution but was arguing for 'sympathetic action in case of conviction'.

In Manchester Dave Beck collected 50p a week from nineteen men at a Fram Gerrard site and persuaded his deputy convenor to include 150 copies of the CDC bulletin in the mail-out. He also collected at two other Fram Gerrard sites and his Swinton UCATT branch would collect throughout the trial. Bert Smith, a member of that branch, spoke to Swinton TGWU Branch Committee. They donated £100. After CDC delegates addressed a mass meeting, Shell Carrington TGWU sent £50. Carrington Trades Council, Partington AUEW, the mainly AUEW Gorton and Openshaw Shop Stewards' LCDTU and Manchester University CP all donated £10.

Maurice Turner sent his first collection from Cooper's site in Skelmersdale. Regular collections were taken at some Liverpool Corporation sites and at a Monk's site on the Rock Ferry Bypass. Engineers at the Bass Charrington site in Runcorn collected £88 and electricians raised £32. Dare Construction stewards sent £30 and Frank Marsh forwarded £80 from Unit Construction. Would it 'be wise to show ourselves outside the Court House or is the money more important at this stage?' (Getting the TUC to 'pledge maximum support' and 'funds' were 'more important'.) Ford Halewood stewards sent £100 via Simon Fraser, who asked for 'all your literature' to be 'reprinted' and 'issued to all of our shop stewards and trades councils in different parts of the country'.

In Birmingham, the TGWU 5/909 branch sent £50.

A Norwich TGWU branch sent £14. Lowestoft College Students' Union wanted collection sheets for themselves and local factories, and speakers. UCATT stewards in Felixstowe sent £14: 'We intend to organise more strongly on your side in this area in the weeks ahead.' Chelmsford IS needed a speaker for a public meeting designed to set up a defence committee. (The CDC was 'unable to send speakers to any political meetings'—'this has been our policy throughout the campaign after seeking advice from our solicitors'.) Stevenage Trades Council planned a meeting. Was someone local 'prepared to come along'? (The CDC asked Londoner Lou Lewis.)

The Works Committee at McInerny's Finsbury Park site in London sent the proceeds of a 'site appeal' and hoped to raise 'at least that each week'. Jim Hiles sent £68 from exhibition workers and others at Olympia sent £32. Paddington NUR sent £22. Lambeth NUT sent £10. Tower Hamlets Town Hall NALGO wanted a 'spokesman' for their AGM. (They got Lou Lewis.) East London activists were dismayed at the 'very poor turnout' from their area at Shrewsbury on 3 October. Nobody went from Fords and the sole contingent was from Warnes Rubber Company. A UCATT convenor, a TGWU steward, a Tate and Lyle steward, Vic Turner of the Pentonville 5 and someone from Fords printed 3,000 leaflets and fifty collection sheets. The 'central task' of the thirty-strong 'Ad Hoc' Barking and Dagenham Defence Committee was winning 'commitment to take strike action if any of these men are jailed'. UCATT's London Regional Organiser would place the CDC's letter 'before the Regional Committee'. The NUM General Secretary, Lawrence Daly, 'cannot as a general rule deal with matters such as you raise other than through the appropriate national union or unions.' (The CDC had asked for the addresses of NUM lodges.)

Reading IS sent £12 for Dave Jackson's expenses. £42 came from AUEW members at Gatwick Airport. Southampton IS sent £7, the Trades Council collected £8, and the University Students' Union donated £100. The hospital site sent £65 and wanted a speaker. (They got Bill Jones). The UCATT South West Regional Secretary 'would consider it more appropriate if you directed your letter to the General Secretary'.

NUM lodges, TGWU branches and stewards' committees in Swansea, Neath, Aberdare Joint Unions Committee had been 'very active in support of workers in struggle both locally and nationally (making substantial contributions to the Fine Tubes struggle, for example, as well as providing pickets)'. Could they have a speaker? (They could.) The CDC asked a Colwyn Bay TGWU convenor if he 'would allow a speaker to address your shop stewards'.

Money was coming into the Defence Fund from different parts of the country, but patchily, and almost always from one-off donations, rarely as a result of regular workplace collections. Several individual CPers and IS members were making a serious effort to win strike action in the event of jailings, because of the industrial and political consequences of the criminalisation of mass picketing; but there was no nationally-co-ordinated strategy or effective leadership

We need a workers' party

On 1 November the CDC told supporters that the campaign was 'well under way and the response we are receiving from the whole trade union movement is terrific'. 'We have sent speakers to almost every part of the country and have received letters by the thousand.'

Six CPers—Bill Jones, Alan Abrahams, Barry Scragg of the CDC and Bert Smith, Pete Carter and Lou Lewis—had done most of the speaking. The CDC received about 200 letters. The Defence Fund issued 687 receipts. The average donation was £13 and going down.

At the CDC on the 7th Bill Jones argued that what mattered most was winning TUC support. The defendants 'wanted more support in the public gallery', so there would be a delegation. Bill Jones and Alan Abrahams would speak at Stockton, Blackpool, Hull, Preston, Fife and Bristol. Abrahams wanted 'changes in the record keeping'. The draft bulletin received 'changes and additions' and only 20,000 copies were ordered.

That evening Dave Ayre reported to Crook UCATT about the 24 and the official 'hardship fund'. The branch sent £10.

On 11 November 2,800 people attended IS's Industrial Conference in Manchester. Tony Cliff

> rammed home the message that the struggle ahead was about more than just rank and file organisation.
>
> 'To mobilise millions we need strong rank and file, movements—plus a central cog to bind them together.'
>
> 'We need a socialist outlook', he declared, 'so that militants think, I'm a socialist first, a miner second, a socialist first, a docker second', and so on.
>
> The rank and file papers created in recent years could not survive without IS politics—even though our members are in a minority on their editorial boards.
>
> He ended with a ringing call that won sustained applause: 'We are fighting a political battle. We need a workers' party.'

SW believed the conference made IS 'an integral part of the working class and a force to be reckoned with'. *The Collier, Post Office*

Worker, Rank and File Teacher, Carworker and *NALGO Action News* would sponsor a 'Rank and File Movement' conference.

The CDC met on the 13th. (Bill Jones and Alan Abrahams weren't present and so there were no delegates' reports.) The defendants were 'in good spirit', support from Scotland was 'very satisfactory', Tomlinson and Warren's car repair bills would be paid, but volunteers were needed to stuff envelopes.

Dennis Dugen reminded North Wales Charter about a Charter meeting. 'Bring any cash for sales so we can produce next issue.'

On the 16th the Shotton Welfare Fund account was closed and the last £50 went into the Defence Fund. Total income had been £11,262 and expenditure £4,005. £2,165 had gone to members of the 24. Speakers' expenses—now listed separately—were £672.

On the 20th Manchester & Salford Trades Council asked the CDC if collections were made in factories and workplaces and if 'official collecting sheets' had reached 'district officers, for distribution to stewards and other sympathisers'. If not, they'd be happy to help.

Next day the CDC heard that two defendants had 'managed rather well' in the witness box and counsel 'had no objections' to 'orderly' support in the public gallery. Billy Regan wanted someone else to draft the next bulletin 'to avoid too much repetition'.

Soon after Regan told a supporter: 'It seems to be going pretty well for the first six.' There was 'little or no concrete evidence against them' but 'we must look forward to what happens if the worst comes to the worst and one or more are jailed'. 'If the pledges of solidarity are anything to go by', it was 'certain' that the Pentonville 5 movement 'will spring to life again!'

In the *SW* printed on the 27th Dave Adshead reported that industrial action was being organised for the Birmingham SOS trial. Requests for speakers, donations and messages of support should go to UCATT's Midland Regional Office. Roger Rosewell—now IS's Liverpool organiser—argued that the Shrewsbury trial was 'not about truth or justice but about politics, and politics will determine its outcome'. 'The campaign to organise a wave of strike action if any of the accused pickets are jailed... cannot just be left to chance or until after the judge's final speeches.' The 'only way this attack on picketing can be defeated and the 24 defended' was by 'militancy of the type and on the scale' that freed the Pentonville 5:

Regular publicity for the 24, starting now, fortnightly, leaflets or bulletins, are needed that explain the issues at stake in the trial and include up-to-date reports both of what is going on in the courtroom and of how solidarity is developing.

Ideally these bulletins should be issued by shop stewards' committees. But where this is not possible then either trade union branches, IS workplace branches or groups of militants should take on the responsibility themselves.

Meetings were important, especially 'mass meetings at which decisions to strike if the 24 are jailed can be taken'. IS branches should ask for CDC speakers, leaflet workplaces, get speakers to shop stewards' meetings and factory gates and sell *Pickets on Trial* in union branches. *SW* added: 'All trade unionists and their families' were welcome at an *SW* rally in London on December 17th. The proceeds would go to the families of the 24. (IS sent the CDC a ticket, asked for a speaker and gave two 'phone numbers.)

Dennis Dugen told the CDC that the Greater Manchester Co-ordinating Committee had booked a hall on 19 January for a conference 'as important as the Liverpool one in planning the future action'. Manchester & Salford Trades Council was sponsoring it, but 'the onus is on the Rank & File to organise it and make it a success and it could be the springboard to a national campaign'. (The CDC would be 'turning up in full force'.)

Alan Abrahams could not be present at the CDC on the 28th, so someone had to pick up cash from the Liverpool Teaching Hospital site. A mini coach of London supporters had heard John Llywarch give evidence. He was to be asked about £40 that he had reportedly received and his TGWU membership status. The *Guardian* would not be thanked for reporting the trial, but Barry Scragg's letter to the *Star* was endorsed. If defence counsel agreed, it would be sent after he appeared as a witness. It was 'impressed upon all present how important it was that this committee should be represented outside court' in Birmingham when the SOS 'conspiracy' trial began.

In November the CDC received £2,700 and spent £1,060. The TSB 'Building Workers Social & N Wales 24 Defence Fund' account was closed. Over £7,260 went into a TSB savings account.

The International Socialists have been very active

In November Hillington Rolls Royce stewards had sent £100. Three Scottish NUM lodges and Yarrows stewards all donated £50. Glasgow NUJ and the AUEW at Sunbeam Electric in East Kilbride sent

£20. The Edinburgh TASS Divisional Organiser sent £25.Newcastle Student Branch of IS was planning a meeting and hoped to get round the rules on payments to 'outside groups' and donate '£100 or so'. When were speakers available? (They were asked to organise a 'non-political' meeting.)

Hull TGWU Heavy Chemicals Branch asked for 'collection sheets and any available propaganda' and the University Students' Union promised a collection. £240 came from the BSC River Don Works and £10 from NUM members at Kellingley Colliery. Barnsley IS miners had raised the issue, only to be blocked by officials, because the CDC was an 'unofficial body'. Dave Gibson, the Barnsley IS Secretary, passed on contact information for NUM lodge secretaries and asked about speakers. (The CDC promised a speaker for a 'mass meeting'.) Huddersfield AUEW stewards sent £36.

Rick Gwilt from Longsight Direct Works and Dave Beck both sent £10. Swinton UCATT voted £20 to the UCATT fund, but 'our policy is still to send site collections direct to you [CDC]'. Sale UCATT donated £12. £10 came from a retired UCATT regional organiser and Francis Shaw stewards. Shell Carrington stewards sent £75.

Bass Charrington at Runcorn sent £85 and Monks' site at Rock Ferry £35. St Helens Miners Emergency Fund sent £30. Liverpool Teaching Hospital site sent £100 and five corporation sites made collections. Birkenhead Trades Council and a Costain site at Bootle both donated £20. Tommy Healey had encouraged Standard Triumph TGWU stewards to make collections and they were sending a delegation to Shrewsbury. Shell Stanlow stewards sent £190. 'If there is any way in which you think we can assist you please don't hesitate to ask.' Simon Fraser had distributed collection sheets. He had spent over £350 of the £800 collected at the conference on posters, leaflets and advertising and was 'duplicating and sending out literature to trades councils every day'. He would 'endeavour to finalise everything before the end of this year and let you have the balance'.

Birmingham ASTMS Divisional Council donated £100. Pete Carter spoke 'on behalf of' the CDC at Wolverhampton Trades Council, which set up a Defence Committee, donated £5 and would write to affiliated unions urging them to support the Shrewsbury 24. A UCATT Midland Region leaflet stressed their lawyers' opinion that successful prosecution of the Birmingham 5 would mean that 'conspiracy' could be used against any protest, occupation or even union meetings. The had the support of Birmingham, Coventry, Wolverhampton, Derby and Stoke Trades Councils, UCATT, TGWU, EETPU and other union branches and activists at many factories. 'All welcome at the demo' outside court. A member of the IS 'cell' at Balliol College Oxford needed copies of *Bulletin No 9* and assured the CDC that the 'overwhelming majority' of local IS members worked on sites and in factories, mines and docks. He took some credit for the 'many collections' sent and was confident that students—who were occupying the university—could raise a 'great deal more support'. (The CDC stressed that 'union, trades councils and factory gate' meetings were 'the only type we can attend', but 'the International Socialists have been very active in raising support and finance'.)

Norwich Trades Council sent £55 plus £50 from affiliated branches. £61 came from an Iver site.

McAlpine's workers at Nine Elms in London collected £110, after Bill Jones, Jack Henry and Alan Tattam addressed them. Jones spoke at Cubitt's Battersea site and raised £50. Sunley's Sloane Street site managed £16 and £50 was collected at four other sites, though that from McInerny's site in Tottenham might be the last for some time, because they were 'on total strike against the blacklist'. Tattam passed on a cheque from some pickets. Hayes TGWU sent £25. ASTMS's NEC donated £500. Hillingdon Trades Council contacted ASTMS members at EMI, who sent £10. They had been central to the dockers' campaign in 1972 and assumed that if any of the 24 were found guilty then 'we must do another "Pentonville Five" and get them off'. The Society of Graphical & Allied Trades sent £23. John Carpenter sent £291 from dockers, via *The Dockworker*, as did Lennie Alexander. Michael Fenn noted: 'If the worst happens we'll do our best to get you all the support we can in the docks.'

Southampton General Hospital site sent £125. Many men asked how the trial was going, but wouldn't read the *Star*. Bristol Rolls Royce stewards sent £97 and the SOGAT branch £50. After a Bristol Defence Committee meeting, Tony Robinson understood that 'each request for money' would be 'the beginning of a discussion'.

> I collected about a fiver from a Workers' Educational Institute meeting—you'd have been very moved, I think, to have seen people who obviously have a hard time making ends meet giving so generously and without fuss; another seven quid came from friends—teachers, TV and radio directors, mums, writers; and the rest came from a meeting of actors in London.

Actors faced the lump, yet Equity leaders had disaffiliated the union from the TUC and registered under the Industrial Relations Act. He had raised the Shrewsbury issue at a union meeting and knew he could count on members of IS and the IMG, but the chair ruled a collection out of order, so he collected outside: 'What took me completely by surprise was the warm-hearted support I got from other people both on the platform and in the hall.'

South Wales NUM EC sent £40.

There's a lot of people don't know what's going on

On 1 December Barry Jones MP forwarded a Home Office letter on the Colchester issue to the CDC. The Chief Constable had 'reason to believe' that one person 'might be able to help them with their enquiries'. The Chairman of the Police Authority added: 'So long as the police have reason to believe that searches in certain areas may well lead to finding the culprit they must be permitted to carry out these searches. I am assured by the Chief Constable that such action as the police took was solely in pursuit of this objective.'

IS issued thousands of 'Defend the Right to Picket. Support the Shrewsbury 24' leaflets. Convictions would be 'very serious indeed'.

> The five dockers were released from Pentonville last year because tens of thousands of trade unionists went on strike.
>
> That is what is required NOW.
>
> All trade unionists should follow the lead of the dockers in London and Liverpool, car workers at Standard-Triumph and building workers in Glasgow and Edinburgh who are actively campaigning for an all-out stoppage if any of the defendants are sent to jail. They should raise the issue urgently in their shop stewards' committees, district committees, trades councils and in their union branches, and get a firm commitment to industrial action in support of the Shrewsbury building workers and organise for large financial donations for the families who have been suffering real hardship during the trial.

Donations should go to the Defence Fund via Billy Regan's address.

In IS's *The Building Worker* John Fontaine stressed that the trial was a 'Frame Up'. 'We must start to organise now to fight back in the event of jailings or fines', without relying on officials. The UCATT circular 'read more like a prosecution case than a defence of workers' rights' and they had failed to get rid of the lump. The editorial argued that the Shrewsbury trials were 'rapidly developing into the most severe attack on trades unionism for decades'.

The GMCC Conference sponsors included Manchester District Confed, Manchester, Stockport and Ashton AUEW District Committees, stewards' committees where the AUEW was influential, TASS Divisional Council, APEX North West Area Council and Manchester & Salford and Stretford Trades Councils. There was no support from UCATT or the TGWU. A circular about a meeting on 15 December stressed that 'unions and bona-fide TU organisations not on our sponsored list' could send delegates. The Secretary of Manchester & Salford Trades Council volunteered to pick up and mail out 200 Defence Fund collection sheets.

On 3 December almost a thousand building workers on six Birmingham sites went on strike. Thre hundred people, led by Pete Carter, demonstrated outside Birmingham Crown Court beside the CDC banner. All eight SOS defendants pleaded not guilty. Next day defence counsel insisted that the occupation was in furtherance of an industrial dispute and protected by the 1875 Act. The prosecution conceded. The judge directed the jury to acquit the five stewards on the 'conspiracy' charge and the ATV crew on both charges. On the 5th the jury cleared the stewards of 'unlawful assembly' and next day the Birmingham 5 went to support the defendants at Shrewsbury.

SW carried an interview with Margaret Llywarch. On the first day of the Shrewsbury trial she had had an operation and was expecting John to visit, but the judge sent the defendants home. 'That's when this whole business really hit me.' 'I never knew anything about trade unions and what have you before all this. I know about it now.' 'There's a lot of people don't know what's going on.' George Kelly reported from Glasgow.

> We raise it at every shop stewards' meeting. We've sold a good number of IS pamphlets explaining the background and we've collected money regularly.
>
> We're a wee but disappointed at the lack of initiative among some trade unionists who really should be getting stuck in. To this end our Shop Stewards' Committee has sponsored a city-wide collection in Glasgow on Saturday to get money for the defence committee and to publicise what's going on.
>
> If it comes to it—and we must all prepare for the responsibility—we're going to have to organise stoppages to defend these men.

John Fontaine stressed that a 'bad result' not 'followed by organised resistance would be a complete disaster for every trade unionist'. 'We can't stand aside if the men are jailed. There's only one answer the trade union movement can give—everybody out.' London Royal Group of Docks stewards were going for an all-out strike.

All out for money

By December the New University of Ulster Labour Club had sent the Defence Fund £28. The CDC asked Fife Defence Committee to accept a three-day speaking tour, since 'the demand for speakers' was 'so great that we are having a struggle now to cope with them all'. The Fife tour was cancelled. 'Most of the places where we were planning to take speakers have either not replied to our requests or sort of shrugged their shoulders.' Cumbernauld Trades Council raised £29 from a street collection and forwarded £10 from a factory. Glasgow Corporation stewards had a weekly levy and planned a street collection. Norwich Trades Council would picket Shrewsbury Crown Court. Could they have a speaker on 11 January? ('Every endeavour to send a speaker.') City of London & Westminster Trades Council sent £28. Prestatyn UCATT sent £21.

Only part of the CDC minutes for 6 December is publicly available. Defence counsel thought the trial was 'progressing very well'. Barry Scragg thought that 'if the worst came to the worst we should make sure we could immediately call to life a movement on a far greater scale' than over the Pentonville 5. Llywarch was a TGWU member, but would get a letter about an interview he had given to *SW*. No interviews should be given 'unless they were authorised'. 'We therefore strongly advise that you contact whoever you gave the interview to and ask them not to print anything until the committee have vetted it.'

Laurie Flynn had reported the trial for *SW*. When he couldn't get to Shrewsbury he used Reuters and the Press Association and phoned local reporters, John Llywarch and John Carpenter.

The CDC's *Bulletin No 11* ridiculed the idea that the trial wasn't political: 'Who's kidding who? Anyone who has sat up in the public gallery will inform you that it is a political trial.' It was 'nearing Christmas and the six lads now on trial all have families'. 'Why not form a Defence Committee in your area? Organise a public meeting to give publicity to the trial, raise the matter of support in your branch.' 'When the trial of the first six is over we still have eighteen more to defend.' 'Funds are urgently required.'

The Flying Pickets

Billy Regan told Dennis Dugen that in the event of guilty verdicts the CDC were hoping to 'get immediate stoppages on a far greater scale than the Pentonville Five' and 'we can rely on you to do your best in your area'. He told Bert Smith: 'If you yourself or anyone you think suitable manage to attend' a Burnley meeting, 'please send the bill for any expenses'.

On the 9th Hackney Trades Council told the CDC about a meeting on the 11th to set up a London Defence Committee.

With an eleven days holiday this Christmas for almost everyone, it will be very difficult to mobilise quickly. I shall never forget the speed at which we mobilised over the Pentonville Five—but in the circumstances, such speed will hardly be repeated... Much will depend on the response we get this Tuesday. I feel that the building sites are ready, but we will have a lot of work to do with other workers. I will direct our principal concentration on the four Hackney bus garages and Liverpool Street railway station. But we must also get the press out...

If guilty verdicts came, 'we will do all we can'.

Edinburgh University CP, ASTMS, Labour Club, Science for People, Socialist Medicine Group, IMG and Women's Liberation aimed to get a contingent to Shrewsbury and were planning a rally with prominent union speakers. Could they have a speaker? (Edinburgh Defence Committee 'will supply you'.)

Blackpool 'Local Action Committee' had held its first meeting. Blackpool and Preston supporters would lay on transport to the next mass demonstration at Shrewsbury. £50 had been collected at a social and three sites. (Many of Alex Weir's letters went into Regan's 'IS' file, but he replied: 'If it goes against us we will be calling on your support.') Manchester University Students' Union sent £99. Kirkby Union of Shop, Distributive & Allied Workers stewards had donated, but two *SW* readers thought it 'important to go round the canteen in our breaks with a petition' to raise money and give 'a bit more publicity to your trial and campaign', since 'most people had heard or read something about the trial' and 'quite a lot didn't really know what it was all about'.

The headline of the *SW* printed on 11 December was: 'Pickets Trial: Get Ready to Act.' It celebrated the Birmingham 5 victory, but 'the lump continues, and so does the Shrewsbury 24 trial'. Unions must take 'strike action if any of the 24 are jailed.'

On the 12th Barry Scragg told the CDC that Barry Jones MP 'had said in so many words that he did not want to get involved with the 24'. 'The Pentonville 5 movement must make sure that any appeal is immediate,' since 'we cannot see the lads in jail over Christmas'. He had not given the letter to John Llywarch, but reminded all six defendants of the committee's policy on 'interviews etc' and they should 'abide' by it in future. Defence counsel had asked Bill Jones not to organise a demonstration outside the court or send large delegations to the public gallery. Jones gave notice of the Charter Conference. The *Charter* would appear after the trial. (That week's income was £1,415, but one appeal could cost £1,000.)

Bill Jones persuaded eight Burnley UCATT members to try to get the Trades Council to call a joint public meeting with Nelson & Colne Trades Council. Jones also forwarded £85 from an ICI Runcorn steward and spoke at Leicester Trades Council. The collection raised £28, but his expenses were £15. East London Defence Committee sent £75. The collecting box was back at Merthyr UCATT, but the cash went to the UCATT Hardship Fund.

Back on 6 December the IS National Treasurer, Jim Nichol, had taken £24 to the *Star* for ten days' advertisements for the *Socialist Worker* rally, but it hadn't appeared by the 10th. The *Star* asked Nichol and Paul Foot about the CDC's response. On the 12th Bill Jones told the CDC that the *Star* had asked him 'if they could print an advert from a group of International Socialists' who were planning a meeting and collection. He had told them that 'this committee could not endorse the ad and asked them not to print it'. Billy Regan told Laurie Flynn that they would not sponsor the event or send speakers. What went in the *Star* was between the paper and 'yourselves'. The *Star*'s editor, George Matthews, promised to look into the matter and the CDC wished IS 'every success'.

On the 17th over 900 activists attended the rally. Gerry Kelly, Tony Cliff and Laurie Flynn spoke. Jake Thackray sang. Sandra Kerr and John Faulkner—'The Combine'—performed 'tough and funny sketches' and 'pilloried the "law and order" gibberish of the building bosses'. The event raised £940. Next day Matthews told Foot that he had 'discussed the advert with colleagues' and returned the cheque.

The last *SW* of 1973 was printed on the 18th. It told readers to 'prepare for industrial action if any prison sentences are imposed'. 'Information on the final outcome and any sentences can be obtained from IS head office' by phone.

Next day Jim Nichol went to Shrewsbury and was 'completely horrified' by the sentences. 'There was a limited campaign going on',

The Flying Pickets

but IS 'set out to up the profile of the whole case'. He sent the Defence Fund £100 from the rally for each of the six defendants' wives and hoped to send £200 more.

Crook UCATT expressed 'strong concern at the vicious sentences imposed on the Shrewsbury building workers, criticising in particular the lack of response from the EC'. It unanimously resolved to ask the EC to 'convene urgently and immediately a special National Delegate Conference to formulate the defence for the remaining eighteen members awaiting trial, and also secure the immediate release of those imprisoned, with a move to organise strike action if necessary'. The Northern Regional Committee and the local MP would be asked for support and the matter 'placed before the next meeting of the trades council, with a view to involving the whole of the movement, with TUC support'.

The CDC was due to meet, but no minutes are publicly available. Bill Jones later acknowledged that up to then they had been 'all out for money'.

CHAPTER 13

The Shrewsbury 3

Godfather Behind The Campaign Of Violence

On 20 December 1973 the *Daily Mirror* carried a photograph of Des Warren, the 'Godfather Behind The Campaign Of Violence'. UCATT official Albert Prest claimed that 'students, young socialists and extremists' 'tried to take over the union and promote violence' in the 1972 strike. The TGWU's Ted Hughes alleged that 'a small private army' 'terrorised' his staff at Wrexham. They 'were not union men. In fact, they frightened good union men.' 'It all smacked of paid agitators.' He referred to Warren's 'gang of pickets'.

Warren wasn't in Wrexham on the day that Hughes referred to. John Carpenter, who was, challenged him. Hughes claimed that the *Mirror* interviewed him before the verdicts, yet he refused to put the record straight. Three months earlier he had confirmed Carpenter and Tomlinson as official Chester Action Committee members and described their pickets as 'always carried out in a peaceful manner'.

The *Star*'s 'Savage Sentences for Pickets' quoted Warren and Tomlinson's speeches from the dock. The CDC was 'considering issuing a call for immediate strike action throughout the country in all industries'. The LCDTU called for 'swift and massive support' and 'a massive turnout' to lobby the TUC General Council's meeting with Tory ministers. London site delegates had lobbied the new TUC General Secretary, Len Murray, who could not act until the TGWU's Jack Jones raised the matter in January. UCATT's George Smith was looking at the possibility of bail. Labour MPs Eric Heffer and Dennis Skinner were raising the sentences in the Commons.

That day Arthur Murray was charged.

On the 21st the *Star* headline was 'British Labour Mobilises Against Picket Jailings. Eruption Demands "Set Them Free".' 'Leading the action were more than a dozen sites and factories in North Wales', where 'thousands of engineering, transport and building workers launched a united protest strike' in response to a CDC call for 'immediate, spontaneous action by workers throughout the country'. There was a mass meeting at the Raven in Flint that day. Standard Triumph stewards at Speke had formed 'a sub-committee for the defence of the 24'. Liverpool Trades Council had been asked to 'broaden' a CP demonstration on the 22nd. Merseyside Confed would discuss action. Glasgow Trades Council had asked the Scottish TUC and London TUC for 'united, militant mass action'. 100 Paisley engineering shop stewards had resolved to do 'everything possible' to free the three jailed men. An AUEW EC member called for mass actions. South Wales miners would discuss 'many telegrams and suggestions' on Christmas Eve. Liverpool Corporation workers would strike after the holiday. UCATT EC condemned the sentences and would consider the verdicts on 9 January.

On the 22nd the *Star* reported that 'Shotton Action Committee' had called on the TUC to 'mobilise action to free the three'. Liverpool Teaching Hospital site would support any call for action from their stewards. Stockport engineering stewards had called for a one-day strike and the AUEW Construction Section and others had demanded the recall of the TUC. 200 Edinburgh building workers had demonstrated outside the Scottish Office. Fifteen London UCATT officials had signed a petition calling for the sentences to be quashed. The LCDTU's Kevin Halpin had addressed 'several hundred rain-soaked demonstrators' outside the TUC-Tory talks and called for a repeat of Pentonville. Lou Lewis added that thousands of leaflets were being printed and there 'would be a mass meeting early in the new year'. Bristol Trades Council had voted for a one-day strike on 7 January. The Manchester conference was on the 19th.

Seventeen leading members of the ASB, AUEW, TASS, the AUEW Foundry Workers, EEPTU, the Educational Institute of Scotland, the Fire Brigades Union, NUJ, TGWU and SOGAT sponsored a march to the Glasgow NFBTE office and chanted 'Free, free the Shrewsbury 3'. George Kelly told the CDC that they had not been 'supported by the wider trade union movement and a certain important political organisation'—the CP.

By next day the Preston Defence Committee's 'policy statement' was in the hands of affiliated branches. 'Resolutions should be passed condemning the imprisonment of pickets, the use of conspiracy charges against pickets, and urging that action must be taken to secure the release of the 3 building workers.' They would 'shortly be sending details of further national actions'.

Flint UCATT unanimously agreed that Prest should be charged under Rule 31, Section 1. 'Surely he must realise that not only will such statements jeopardise their appeal, but also prejudice the trial of the other 18 yet to take place.' North Wales building workers had been 'burdened' with him 'for far too long'. He should be sacked.

Mike Williams wrote to IS to express his 'sincere thanks for the very generous donation' of £600 (almost £5,000 today). The six wives also sent their thanks. The CDC had called 'on every trade unionist in the country to protest in every way possible' to get the three jailed men 'released from the clutches of the oppressive class'.

On Sunday the 23rd Elsa Warren, Phil Beyer and Pete Carter were guests at an 'extraordinary meeting' of the CDC that aimed to get a 'picture of the happenings to date and make our plans for the future'. Alan Abrahams deplored Hughes's statement and Prest had to be removed from office. On the sentences, telegrams should go to MPs and the Home Office and a postcard should be distributed nationally. UCATT's North West Regional Council should discuss a programme of action to secure the three men's release and union officials 'must decide whether they are going to fight with us or against us'. Bill Jones had moved a motion on behalf of the CDC at Liverpool Trades Council on the 20th, but had opposed the parts of an ASB motion that argued for a one-day stoppage and councils of action. At a Liverpool meeting on the 22nd there had been a call for a one-day stoppage, but the dockers were waiting for building workers to move. Some Merseyside sites wanted to go back to work after Christmas, 'but they must be out in the new year.' Manchester sites would be out on the 24th. Jones reported that Bert Smith believed that when UCATT's EC 'see things moving they will have no alternative but to move too'. One UCATT official had called for a stoppage on Merseyside on 3 January. So far, the CDC had been 'out for money', but now 'every ounce of our energies must be used to free the lads!'

At least one page of the minutes is not publicly available, but according to Des Warren, the DHSS had deemed Ken O'Shea to be on strike with the rest of his workmates and wouldn't help after the trial. 'The CDC discussed his request and turned it down.'

When the minutes resume, Pete Carter blamed national union officials and the capitalist press. He wanted a conference of officials to discuss action and an immediate Charter conference. The 'only way to release the lads was action on the scale of a general strike', but 'I don't think we should call for immediate action' since 'we cannot afford a split'. Bill Jones reminded him that the CDC had 'always called for immediate action if any were jailed' and defence committees 'all over the country' were 'waiting for us for a lead'. Abrahams' phone hadn't stopped ringing and people were asking what the CDC was going to do. They should call for a 'mass stoppage' on 3 January. Carter accused them of underestimating the size of the task, but Jones insisted that 'if it were not tackled now it would die'. The *Charter* Editorial Board was going to discuss the issue. Abrahams insisted: 'What we should be busy with, is organising the flying pickets again.' He was against setting a date for the movement to join in, since union officials and the TUC would be discussing that question and 'we do not want any conflict'. The CDC agreed that Lou Lewis would be asked to double the print run of the *Charter* and the Defence Fund would underwrite any loss.

Emergency Bulletin No 12's headline was 'Savage Sentences Passed at Trial'. 'If the state or ruling class wish, they can use this case law to find any strike committee guilty of conspiracy and any picket line guilty of unlawful assembly.' It was 'a vicious Tory attack on building workers' and 'the whole trade union movement'.

> We call on every trade unionist in the country to take strike action for the immediate release of the building workers, [since] failure to do so will further strengthen the Tories in their attack on wages and conditions in every industry. That we call on the TUC to have a recall conference to discuss this important matter and urge that the National Building Workers Union meet to discuss the implications of the trial.

'We did it with the Pentonville 5 and we can do it again.'

Jeff Douglas later told Des Warren that it 'took weeks for the initial impact to wear off' in the CDC. 'The emotion, frustration and disillusionment was enough to make anyone pack it all in.'

Free the Three

On Sunday 23 December Birmingham area UCATT officials and convenors issued a declaration on Shrewsbury: 'We believe that this trial was politically motivated' and 'constitutes a most serious threat to every trade union and trade unionist in the country'.

On Christmas Eve the *Star* reported that Manchester stewards had called for 'the maximum protest action and stoppages'. Leaflets with extracts from the speeches from the dock would go to all sites on 3 January 1974 and 'an appeal will go to all other trade unionists in the Greater Manchester Area to join a demonstration' on the 7th. Liverpool Trades Council called for 'maximum protest action'.

UCATT's Midland Regional Council had sent the jailed men a 'pledge of support to win their freedom'. Ken Barlow had 'never felt so bitter' and demanded 'the maximum fight mounted throughout the labour movement'. The LCDTU 'pledged to do its utmost'. Stan Brazil's address was given for credentials to the GMCC Conference.

On Friday the 27th the *Star* headline was 'Merseyside to Stop Over 3-Day Week, Pickets ALL-OUT "FREE THE THREE" DRIVE'. 'Nationwide action is to be taken in the next fortnight to secure the release of the three North Wales building workers.' The CDC had 'supplemented its earlier—and still operative—call for mass strike action by trade unionists throughout the country' and wanted telegrams calling on the TGWU and UCATT to 'win TUC leadership of the national campaign'. The CDC would distribute 20,000 of the 24,000 copies of the *Charter*. Telegrams 'against the sentences and for the three's release' should be sent to the Tory Home Secretary. 100,000 postcards 'to be signed by trade unionists' had been printed. (They were addressed to 'Dear Mr Carr' and read: 'I find the sentences imposed on the building workers in the Shrewsbury trial unbearable. I urge that you take action to bring about the dropping of the charges and the release of the men.') A 'massive response' to the CDC call was 'being planned over the whole Christmas holiday'. 'Today building, engineering, transport, steel and other workers are expected in big numbers at a meeting at the Raven, Flint, at 11am, to decide on how they will continue and extend the campaign of industrial action they launched before Christmas.' Liverpool Direct Works and the London Defence Committee would meet on the 28th—those wishing to attend the latter had to phone Lou Lewis—and there would be an 'open meeting' for Wigan trade unionists. Glasgow building workers would meet on the 29th. Manchester site meetings on 3 January would prepare for a demonstration on the 7th. Liverpool Confed and the TGWU-UCATT committee called for a one-day strike 'about the second week in January'. Ken Barlow aimed to organise an all-Birmingham stewards' conference before the end of the month.

The CDC heard that there were no pickets at Shotton, so a delegation would meet the stewards. Barry Scragg acknowledged: 'Maybe we have made some mistakes along the line regarding the timing of the verdict, but every effort must be made to get as many of the major sites stopped' by 4 January. 'From then on we must involve the whole trade union movement.' If action were not underway by mid-January, they 'would have to do some re-thinking'. The 'girls' at Courtaulds would strike 'whenever we asked them'. Jeff Douglas had organised a meeting at the Greenfield factory on the 4th and would draft a leaflet calling for a mass meeting at Connah's Quay Labour Club that day. (£600 of that week's £1,691 income came from the *Socialist Worker* rally.)

Billy Regan told supporters at the Southampton General Hospital site that 'real action will be around the 10th of January'.

On 29 December the *Star* announced: 'The protest movement developing all over the country will now be directed towards winning bail, pending the appeals.' Wigan site meetings on 2 January would appeal to the trades council to 'organise a united campaign for the release of the three'. Liverpool Trades Council had called a stewards' meeting on the 3rd. Appeals would be lodged on the 4th. The TGWU Building Group EC would meet on the 7th. Bert Smith had invited Wigan trade unionists to attend the Manchester demonstration on the 7th and to send delegates to the lobby of UCATT's EC on the 8th. Bail applications would be in by the 11th.

Stan Brazil invited GMCC 'sub-committee' members to a 'Building Workers'' meeting in Hulme Labour Club on 3 January. Manchester & Salford Trades Council would 'fight along with us' and its EC had invited Labour MPs to the conference on the 19th.

Next day's CDC minutes aren't publicly available, but the *Star* reported their call for 'national co-ordinated action' and 'a return to work on January 2 of all building workers in North Wales pending calls for further action including strikes, lobbies and deputations with, as a first step, the winning of bail for the three men pending their appeal against the sentences'. They 'urged an early meeting' of the *Charter* Editorial Board and were sending delegates to the Liverpool Trades Council meeting on 3 January.

Des Warren later heard that O'Shea, Carpenter and Llywarch went to the CDC, 'ready to play an active part in the campaign for our release', and were 'astonished to be told that the only work they could usefully do' was 'address envelopes!' They 'broke from the Defence Committee' and spoke on IS platforms.

Alex Weir told the CDC that a Blackpool 'Action Committee' had been formed on 9 December. Motions had gone to two UCATT branches on the 10th, asking them to ask the North West Regional Council to 'initiate industrial action' in the 'event of any convictions or heavy fines'. On the 20th a mass meeting on Weir's site passed a similar resolution and sent it to Manchester UCATT, a Wigan TGWU branch, Blackpool NUSMW and the 'completely reliable organiser' of Blackpool UCATT. 'It would not be politic for us... to strike without some official backing', but 'if this does not happen rapidly, say, within a week of a return to work, we would hope that an escalation of strike action from Merseyside, Manchester to Wigan would give us the incentive to escalate strike action'.

On New Year's Eve the *Star* reported that a joint Glasgow Defence Committee and LCDTU meeting attracted '100 or so' building workers, factory and shipyard stewards and delegates from Glasgow and Edinburgh Trades Councils. Barry Docherty stressed: 'No organisation would be barred from taking part in the campaign which would be mounted, but before anyone takes any decisions we must agree to co-ordinate activity.' 'Building workers at many sites have been asking when do we down tools in support of the three lads. What we have got to get is the membership of the four main unions in the building industry demanding a stoppage on this issue' and 'giving unqualified support to obtain the three lads' release'. He quoted *Emergency Bulletin No 12*. The *Star* added that a 'packed emergency meeting' of London CPers had agreed to distribute the speeches from the dock to building sites, 'heighten demands' for the recall of the TUC, organise a 'big lobby' of the AUEW National Committee on 3 January and 'make January 15 a massive day of demonstration and lobby of parliament called by the London Trades Council'. Elsa Warren hoped 'the judge chokes on his turkey'.

The solicitor Campbell Malone told Warren and Tomlinson that applying for bail earlier than the 11th was undesirable, since 'support for you is growing, but only slowly because of the holidays', though it would 'be given impetus by meetings which will be held this coming weekend'. He discussed costs with Billy Regan and Barry Scragg and asked the Defence Fund for £1,650 of its £10,000.

We could not expect a spontaneous reaction

IS Treasurer Jim Nichol had become 'very friendly with a number of defendants'. He visited Tomlinson, sent him *SW* and he 'ended up with a little readers' group'. Marlene was 'suffering from both her husband being in prison and financially' and 'bringing up two kids in a place that was virtually derelict'. 'We raised some money to keep body and soul together' for her and Elsa Warren. During the *SW* printers' traditional holiday they came in to produce 20,000 free leaflets for the London Defence Committee and 20,000 IS leaflets calling for immediate strike action over the Shrewsbury jailings.

In summer 1973 the NUM had introduced an overtime ban in support of its pay claim, but the Tories were determined to make workers accept cuts in real wages, because of inflation. By late

The Flying Pickets

December power station coal stocks had dwindled and the Tories published a 'Three-Day Work Order' that obliged firms to specify three days each week for using electricity and banned them working longer hours. It came into effect on New Year's Day 1974.

SW was printed on New Year's Day. Rita Carpenter thanked IS 'on behalf of' the 'united wives' for their 'wonderful contribution'. 'Without your support and one or two others, I am sure nobody in this country would have known that this most suspect trial was taking place.' John Llywarch had explained to his eldest son that their 'crime' was to 'hurt bosses' profits' and that 'justice is corrupt'. *SW* noted that several North Wales factories, including Courtaulds at Holywell, had gone on strike on 19 December, a Myton's site in Edinburgh had struck on the 21st and McAlpine's and Laing's sites had supported their demonstration. Edinburgh Defence Committee had called an all-industry shop stewards meeting to organise action. A photograph showed the demonstration outside the Glasgow NFBTE offices on the 22nd, where the TASS convenor at John Brown Engineering had read out a letter to employers: 'We pledge ourselves to fight until our three brother trade unionists are free and we have restored our right to picket.' York IS building workers' branch had held a public meeting and bus workers had spoken about the need for industrial action. Other photographs showed Royal Group of Docks stewards, NALGO Action Group and IS members picketing a TUC meeting, and Lovell's workers and the NUM General Secretary lobbying the TUC-Tory meeting. Liverpool Trades Council's stewards' meeting on 3 January and the CDC's 'call for national co-ordinated action to free the three' should be 'the start of the action aiming at general strike proportions to secure the release of the Shrewsbury Three'. The speakers at a London Defence Committee meeting on the 4th would be the President of North London TASS and UCATT's Alan Tattam. All London IS members were to attend. On the 11th Liverpool, London and Hull dockers were to decide what action to take and building workers in three major cities had pledged to strike. 'Every trade unionist worth his or her salt has a duty and a responsibility to take up the struggle to release the martyrs of Shrewsbury' and defend the eighteen awaiting trial. '*If that struggle is not waged with the utmost determination, then others will be next for the railroad, the frame up and the prison cell.*' IS members must 'make a major effort' to get strike action on the 15th, given the UCATT and TGWU ECs' 'flurry of inactivity'.

On 2 January the CDC's first agenda item was 'Return to Work'. Howards' Greenfield site had 'not yet returned'. Barry Scragg hoped that the Liverpool stewards' meeting would agree to a 'stoppage', but the meeting in Connah's Quay Labour Club on the 11th would 'just be greater Merseyside' because of 'other arrangements made in other areas'. More of the 24 were likely to be up at Shrewsbury on the 14th and he doubted that they could get support for both events, so they should call for delegations to Shrewsbury on the 15th. Credential forms had arrived for the GMCC Conference on the 19th. (Sponsors now included Radcliffe and Stockport Trades Councils, Urmston NUSMW, the ASB District Committee and UCATT No 1 BD.) A 'full discussion' took place on the three men who hadn't been jailed and it was agreed to stick to 'previous policy'. Any CDC member 'who had suffered because of the extraordinary meetings over the Christmas period' would get an 'ex gratia payment'. Dave Jackson reported on his activities in Oxford and offered to speak elsewhere. Jeff Douglas was to contact him every week after he went back and Jackson would be the delegate to the LCDTU Conference on the 19th. The *Charter* Editorial Board was unlikely to meet before the 26th, but there would be no CDC bulletin 'for the time being'. Scragg announced a meeting in Bagillt on 7 January. Alan Abrahams would speak 'in a personal capacity'. (The leaflet slogans included 'Free the Shrewsbury Three' and 'A General Election Now!' The meeting had been organised by North Wales CP and the leaflet included an application form for party membership.)

Crook UCATT heard that Ernest Armstrong, the local Labour MP, had indicated his 'inability to help these trade unionists due to constitutional constraints'. (He was a Labour whip.) George Smith sent the branch 'Seasonal Greetings'. Bill Kerriss reported on 'the context of the proposed resolution' to the Trades Council. It urged a recall TUC Congress 'to bring pressure to bear in order to consolidate action for the release of the imprisoned trade unionists'.

On the 3rd the *Star* announced: 'Shrewsbury Three drive building up.' A strike on the 15th would be proposed at the London Shrewsbury 24 Committee as 'the start of strike action aiming at general strike proportions'. Alan Tattam would speak. Birmingham UCATT, TGWU, AUEW, NUSMW and ASTMS officials had petitioned the government, 'demanding the immediate release of the Shrewsbury Three on the grounds that their arrest and trial was politically motivated in order to intimidate the whole of the British trade union movement'. They planned a city-wide meeting on 3 February and were contacting councillors and MPs. Stewards from three Fram Gerrard sites in Manchester, chaired by Dave Beck, would lobby the UCATT EC. They planned a one-day strike on 8 January. 'Representatives from all sites have been asked to report to a meeting tonight in Hulme Labour Club.' Beck added: 'We will urge a continuing campaign aimed at winning the release of the three lads in prison and as an immediate aim, the granting of bail pending the appeals.' The *Star* plugged the GMCC Conference.

Billy Regan told CDC supporters that the sentences 'could not have come at a worse time, and no doubt it was planned to happen that way'; but they were welcome to attend the GMCC Conference and 'details of most meetings' were in the *Star*. There was 'plenty of support'. Regan told George Kelly that 'because of the nature of the building industry and the holiday period, we could not expect a spontaneous reaction as we saw for the Pentonville Five'.

Dave Roberts hoped to put an emergency resolution at Merthyr Trades Council and his Labour MP wanted further details. UCATT South Wales Regional Council had condemned the sentences, called on the EC to 'initiate' a demonstration and asked the TUC to participate. 'This is, in my opinion, not strong enough, but we must realise that this area is very incompetent, and right wing'. He had raised the issue with four Labour MPs and 'influential union leaders', who promised cash. Four South Wales NUM officials were to lobby the Court of Appeal. (The CDC replied: 'The campaign for their release is building up, but as you say it is much too slow.')

Thirty Birmingham building workers set up a defence committee to build an all-out strike. Ken Barlow later told Warren that 'support began to build up among the rank and file' until

> Trades Councils from all over the region joined the campaign—including the East Midlands, previously considered to be a 'moderate' area. Rallies, conferences and meetings of workers from varied industries were held in Nottingham, Lincoln, Mansfield, Sutton-in-Ashfield, Mablethorpe, Newark and other places. Shop stewards from many factories called for action and when speakers addressed meetings at Longbridge and Rover-Triumph plants, the shop floor response was one of anger against the imprisonment of the pickets.

He was sure that if Glasgow, Liverpool and Manchester had acted with the Midlands, they could have spearheaded a serious campaign.

4,000 Manchester Corporation Direct Works employees voted to strike on the 8th and to send a delegation to lobby the UCATT EC. In London eighty building workers from Barking and Dagenham Defence Committee confronted Len Murray. No union leaders had raised the issue formally with the TUC General Council.

It isn't easy to become subservient overnight

On 4 January Des Warren had been sent to Bedford Prison, Tomlinson to Stafford Prison and McKinsie Jones to Ranby, an open prison. Warren wrote to Elsa: 'I am on 7 days punishment at the moment, and I'm afraid I've lost 3 days remission... it isn't easy to become subservient overnight.' He hadn't seen the *Star*, which was 'the only paper that tells you what's going on', but he'd had two copies of *SW*. Carpenter and Llywarch were 'busy all over the country' speaking at IS meetings and 'being used as a recruitment gimmick'. The 'object' was 'to *unite* the working class', but 'after one of them has spoken an IS organiser will stand up and slag everyone in TU movement and point out that only they (the IS) have the answer'. He spotted 'another cock-up': 'They've printed "£600 sent to families", the [D]SS will love that, see how they keep trying to ease the Defence Committee out? causing splits all the time, if they send you money give it straight away to the DC'. (He later acknowledged that he had 'never knowingly met a Trotskyist', but they were 'always portrayed by CP leaders as "splitters" and "provocateurs",' and he took the line uncritically.)

The CDC had persuaded Nottingham Shrewsbury Action Committee not to demonstrate outside the prison, but they supported the demonstration at Stafford Prison. Billy Regan told Alex Weir that they were 'organising mass action', but the timing of the verdict and the three-day week made this 'no easy task'. He stressed the Merseyside strike on the 11th and the GMCC Conference on the 19th.

On the 5th the *Star* noted that the two hundred and fifty stewards and 'representatives of the North Wales building workers' at the Liverpool Trades Council meeting had pledged to strike on the 11th. They called on Liverpool Trades Council to reconvene the national delegate conference and on the TUC to organise a general strike and to call for a general election. However, 'many delegates pointed out that a one-day strike was not enough to free the three' and 'a campaign for all-out action was needed'. The Manchester strike had now been moved to the 11th and its organisers called for 'maximum representation' at the GMCC Conference. Bill Jones agreed with Bert Smith: 'The rank and file must bring pressure to win official action by the unions.' He plugged an LCDTU meeting on the 19th.

On the 7th the *Star* noted that Elsa Warren and the children would have to travel over 200 miles and stay overnight in order to see Des in Bedford. The London Defence Committee had called for lobbies of the UCATT EC and TGWU Building Group meeting next day.

The CDC asked George Smith of UCATT and Jack Jones of the TGWU to 'take action to get our brothers out of jail'. 'It would seem that the union leadership have not realised' that trade unionists 'can be jailed for official picketing'.

Next day the TGWU's Building Group unanimously agreed that the trials were politically motivated, the sentences were 'barbarous' and the three must be released immediately. They called on their EC to 'raise this as a matter of urgency' with the TUC 'with a view to a national campaign' so as to pressurise the Tory Home Secretary to abandon further trials, get the Labour Party to promise to legislate to prevent 'conspiracy' law being used against workers and give picketing 'a proper legal status'. They backed strikes on the 11th, called for a 'full and complete stoppage' on the 15th and hoped that 'a unified front can be established between the unions concerned, including the establishment of an official joint fund'. Money 'collected in support of the Shrewsbury workers should be directed into the official union collection organised by the North Wales Divisional Office' and members should 'disregard other appeals'.

The TGWU North Wales Officer, Jim Griffiths, asked the CDC for 'information indicating the financial support' to TGWU members. The Chester-le-Street TGWU Branch Secretary condemned Durham pickets' use of non-union bus drivers in the 1972 strike. Billy Regan 'fully agreed', but surely they wouldn't use that failure to 'follow trade union principles to the full stand in their way of pledging support for 24 members in North Wales who did'. Could they discuss it again? No. The TUC had 'machinery to deal with these matters', so there was 'nothing further to discuss'.

On the 9th the *Star* carried a photograph of Alan Abrahams addressing a 200-strong lobby outside the UCATT EC, which would seek joint action with the TGWU and back regional campaigns. Ken O'Shea and John Llywarch had been on the lobby, along with people from Liverpool, North Wales, Manchester and 'many' London sites. The TGWU Building Group had given Llywarch 'a warm welcome'.

TGWU delegates from Flintshire and Denbighshire branches voted for a one-day strike. TGWU and UCATT branches called for the withdrawal of the charges against other pickets and for union leaders to launch a national campaign to release the jailed men. UCATT asked the TUC to help them protest to the Home Office.

The CDC heard that Bert Smith had told Alan Abrahams that 'if there was a response from regions' then the UCATT EC 'could call for a national stoppage'. Barry Scragg read out the TGWU Building Group circular. Bill Jones complained about the 'inconvenience' caused by their decisions and Abrahams felt that 'the work we have been doing to secure the release of the lads has all been undone by the official movement stepping in'. Scragg thought the strike on the 11th should go ahead in North Wales: 'It must be seen that this area is moving.' Charlie Jones argued that they should ask for 'full support' for the London demonstration on the 15th. (No decision was recorded.) The TGWU's Jim Griffiths would be told that the CDC 'could give no information pending appeal'. Bert Smith had indicated that the lads' branch secretaries should appeal to the UCATT Fund for the appeal costs. 40,000 more postcards would be ordered. The *Charter* should be out next week and two people from London who enquired about making a 'documentary film' had been 'checked out by various members' and 'found to be OK' Bill Jones 'explained the background' to his *Star* article. 'Disappointment and concern was expressed by all the committee after hearing the activities of Bro's Llewark and Carpenter.' The books must be 'recovered immediately'. (That week's income was £1,374.)

Take stock, be vigilant and fight back

In the *SW* printed on 8 January, Derek Watkins, one of the Pentonville 5, wrote about the need to 'take stock, be vigilant and fight back'. *SW* argued that the Tories and employers were going on the offensive, yet most union leaders were '*running for cover*'. Granville Williams analysed the NUM's 1972 victory and stressed that the three 'will be free only if we organise the same way'. John Llywarch insisted that it was 'vitally important that trade unionists know how ordinary trade union activities can be turned into criminal offences'. He would tell 'as many people as possible' 'how the trial was conducted and how the police investigation was conducted. These are things that are not known in the trade union movement, because no one has been able to speak out openly'. *SW* announced that from the 11th there would be '*Socialist Worker* Free the Shrewsbury Three!' meetings in Coventry, Manchester, Liverpool, Wolverhampton, Nottingham, North West London, Birmingham, Glasgow, Edinburgh, Leeds, Sheffield, Hull, Teesside and Tyneside to offer 'major rallying points in the working class movement for the demand to free the three jailed pickets'. The halls held up to 500, thousands of leaflets had been distributed and the meetings would be 'a central part of the IS effort to build stronger socialist organisation at the heart of the working class movement'. IS speakers, including Tony Cliff, Roger

Rosewell, Glyn Carver (the former Workers' Fight member and now Manchester organiser), Bob Light and George Kelly, would 'draw the political lessons of the trial' and 'link it with the overall attack on workers' liberties and living standards'. John Carpenter or John Llywarch would speak. Both would appear with Paul Foot in Birmingham: 'Special canvass squads have been touring two of the city's biggest council estates, introducing people to *Socialist Worker* and telling them about the rally. Last weekend 89 copies of *Socialist Worker* were sold on the Castle Vale estate alone.' Many tickets had already been sold in Glasgow.

Llywarch recalled that he, Carpenter and O'Shea toured London sites rallying support for strikes on the 15th 'as a first step towards further action to free the three'. Because of appalling coverage in the capitalist press there was 'a lot of arguing and convincing to do'.

On 10 January the *Star* reported that Llywarch and O'Shea had spoken at two Trollope and Colls' sites. One workforce voted for a day's strike on the 15th and the other voted for a half-day strike. Liverpool Trades Council had moved their demonstration to the 15th.

York Trades Council had decided to 'adopt' one of the jailed men and York Defence Committee welcomed nominations from the CDC. (Someone wrote 'Unnecessary' on the letter.)

On the 11th the *Chester Chronicle* reported that 'more than 2,000 building trades workers on Deeside are expected to stage a one-day strike' on the 15th to protest about the jailings. UCATT delegates were to meet at Shotton and were expected to support the stoppage. In the event a Connah's Quay rally supported striking on the 15th.

Some Merseyside sites came out. 25 Manchester sites struck and 800 marched, including delegations from the AUEW Manchester and Stockport District Committees and GEC Openshaw AUEW. AUEW Manchester District Secretary John Tocher asked Stan Brazil for GMCC Conference credentials for himself and GMWU, EETPU and ASB officials. Brazil told him that a TGWU official had declined to speak and Eric Hughes of UCATT hadn't replied. They had a CDC speaker and Pete Carter. Would Tocher speak?

In London 300 building workers lobbied the Court of Appeal, which allowed the three jailed men to appeal against conviction, but deferred the decision about an appeal against sentence.

Dave Jackson heard from the CDC that Llywarch and Carpenter were speaking for IS. Could he speak at Oxford Trades Council?

On the 12th the *Star* reported that a Liverpool Trades Council Recall Conference would be held on 2 February. It quoted Bert Smith: 'We now need a joint national and regional campaign to win the release of the lads and to demand the abandoning of the charges against the other 18 building workers.' Lou Lewis argued for a 'tremendous turnout' in London on the 15th.

Dennis Dugen reminded the CDC about the *Charter* Editorial Board on the 26th. Could they 'bring some of those postcards which are an excellent idea'? They'd 'bought hundreds of stamps and stuck them on and we get the 3p off the lads and post them ourselves'— 150 on the 11th alone. 'I do not have to impress on you how vital this meeting will be the week before the recall conference'.

On the 13th Flint UCATT told Eric Hughes that McKinsie Jones' wife had received the £100 he sent. The 'initial cost' of his appeal was 'in the region of £1,000' and 'neither he nor his family can raise this amount'. Could it be paid by UCATT's distress fund? Instead of responding, Hughes replied to their letter of 22 December. The 'charge' against Prest was 'not in conformity with General Rule 31' and 'should have been related to Clause 1, Sub-Clause (1) and stating the branch to which the person being charged is a member'.

On the 14th Bill Jones arranged for the three jailed men to receive the *Star* and committed the Defence Fund to pay.

Bob Light and other London Royal Group of Docks stewards had recommended striking on the 15th and the majority against was 'far from overwhelming'. 'Had the campaign started to move immediately the three were imprisoned the vote might have been very different. As it was, it seemed as if dockers in the Royals were being asked to stand alone again.' 'The vote might have been different again if the speaker' from the London Defence Committee 'had been there to explain the case in full. But he didn't bother to show up.' Liverpool shop stewards had 'recommended to a mass meeting of their men to work normally'. Only building workers could 'take events by the scruff of the neck and build up the momentum' as they had done for the Pentonville 5.

CP membership had risen by around 1,000 in 1971-1973, but began to falling. Yet in January 1974 Ramelson argued that they had 'more influence' in the labour movement than ever. Ten percent of trade union officials were estimated to be CPers, including several EC members and the Presidents of the Associated Society of Locomotive Engineers and Firemen and the NUT.

On 15 January the *Star* announced that CPer Arthur Utting had been elected to UCATT's EC. In London, Alan Tattam came second.

The 3,500 at Tower Hill included building workers, dockers, ASTMS, Association of Teachers in Technical Institutions, AUEW, EETPU, NALGO, Civil and Public Services Association, the National Society of Operative Printers and Assistants, NUR, NUT, Society of

Lithographic Artists, Designers, Engravers and Process Workers, SOGAT, TASS and the TGWU, London, Camden and other trades councils, TUC Congress House staff and CP, IMG and IS branches. Alan Tattam spoke: 'We have got to turn the pressure on for a recall of the TUC.' John Carpenter 'brought greetings from North Wales building workers'. 'The fight has got to be carried throughout the whole working class.' They marched to the Commons where Labour MP Norman Atkinson told them that they were working on how to stop the 1875 Act being used as a political weapon, but Labour MP Stanley Clinton Davies stressed that the case was 'sub judice' and so an attempt to raise it would be ruled out of order.

At that day's North Wales demonstration Dai Francis of the South Wales NUM EC backed the CDC. The Liverpool demonstration attracted 2,000. Confed and TGWU banners were there, but only one TGWU official. Eddie Loyden and UCATT officials called on the Tory Home Secretary to release the three and on the TUC to intervene. Blackpool Trades Council demonstrated at Shrewsbury at the start of the second picket trial. 1,000 TGWU and UCATT members on the Humber Bridge site went on strike. At a Teesside demonstration, the Confed called for a strike on the 21st and on the Trades Council to mobilise support.

According to *The Building Worker*, UCATT's Scottish Regional Secretary had told stewards that only the TGWU supported industrial action and sent an official round to tell members not to strike. At the last moment he instructed members, including those who had been billed to speak, not to turn up. 300 marched, including workers from one McAlpine and two Myton's sites, ASLEF, SOGAT and Fife and Midlothian NUM. The speakers at Leith Town Hall included the Edinburgh Trades Council Secretary, a member of the Scottish NUM EC and Frank Drain of UCATT and IS.

The *Star* claimed the Edinburgh marchers represented 'almost 100,000 trade unionists'. 600 had turned up at the joint Glasgow LCDTU and Defence Committee demonstration from three city sites, sites elsewhere, Chrysler, Jarrows, Scotstoun Marine, Marathon, Govan Shipbuilders, Polkemmet NUM, SOGAT, Springburn Works, Corporation electricians and Strathclyde University Students' Association. The speakers were two TGWU officials, a member of the Scottish TUC and the Vice-President of Scottish NUM.

Bert Smith later acknowledged that up to 40,000 workers 'all over the country' stopped work on 11 and 15 January.

IS's Tony Cliff wanted *SW* to focus on the 'ugly face of capitalism', aimed mainly at workers without much experience of the trade union movement and including articles written by workers. He anticipated a sale of 70,000 to 80,000 in two years' time. The *SW* printed on the 15th reported John Llywarch's speech to 200 at the Merseyside *Socialist Worker* rally. Ten building workers joined IS.

The credibility of this committee

In the first half of January 1974 Tyburn Post Office Engineering Union donated £20 to the North Wales Defence Fund. London and Westminster Trades Council forwarded £22, Fords stewards at Langley raised £23, Harlow ASTMS sent £25 and an Olympia worker collected £25. Paddington ASTMS voted £30 to colleagues on strike, but they sent it to the Defence Fund. ASTMS Division 15 donated £50. Jim Hiles sent £68 and Stevenage UCATT £100. A Waltham Abbey site collected £115 and planned a weekly levy. Oxford Defence Committee donated £20 and Leicester Trades Council £29. Swansea Trades Council sent £22 after hearing Phil Beyer, 'a representative of your committee'. Pete Carter forwarded £50 from Mike Shilvock, £99 from one Wolverhampton and six Birmingham sites and £200 from the Birmingham Defence Committee. Liverpool Corporation depots, Inwood site painters and Wigan UCATT all donated £20. Workers at Dare Construction at Runcorn sent £27. An Ellesmere Port site raised £90, Liverpool Teaching Hospital site sent another £100, Shell Stanlow scaffolders managed £114 and Townson's Birkenhead site £400. Manchester Direct Works TGWU raised £85 and Swinton TGWU £135. Leeds Trades Council sent £20 and Hull TGWU £56. Edinburgh University ASTMS donated £20, the Textile Workers' Union £20 and Edinburgh Trades Council £60. A Scot sent 50p of his £7.75 weekly pension: 'What a pity the old judge didn't choke on his turkey.'

By 15 January the Defence Fund balance had recovered to over £10,000, but average weekly income had gone below £500.

On the 16th the CDC agreed to lobby UCATT North West Regional Office in Manchester on the 25th and support a parliamentary lobby on the 30th. Alan Abrahams would 'take Mrs Warren to Blackpool'. They couldn't 'stop' the film-makers, so they should give 'guidance'. The next bulletin was to be drafted before the *Charter* Editorial Board. Members of the 24 who were not yet on trial should ask their union branches for expenses. McKinsie Jones had got legal aid. O'Shea would get expenses for going to London, but Abrahams wanted a 'fresh policy' on 'who is entitled to money'.

Bill Jones argued that Carpenter and Llywarch were 'being used by the International Socialists for the furtherance of their own political platform' and 'pointed out again the harm it could do to the credibility of this committee'.

Flint UCATT called on the North West Regional Council to play an active part in the campaign by 'fully supporting' the Liverpool Recall Conference, 'calling for a mass lobby of parliament before the 1st February' and asking the TUC 'to co-ordinate national industrial action to secure their release and the dropping of all charges'. They told the EC that Graham Roberts was blacklisted. He and Terry Renshaw had had £40 from the Chester Action Committee fund, but there was an 'immediate need for financial aid' to reimburse their committal hearing expenses. They sent a revised complaint about Prest. (George Smith replied that Prest 'must be conceded' the 'same freedom of speech as it is claimed by others on this particular subject' and 'too often press statements are only portions of what have been said and sometimes taken out of their context'. The complaint under Rule 31 'does not properly constitute a charge under general rule 32'. Eric Hughes indicated that Prest would have to explain 'alleged statements in the national press'.)

On the 17th Dave Ayre and Bill Kerriss went to the Spennymoor Trades Council meeting. Crook UCATT heard about the Teesside Charter Group's proposals for a defence committee, but made no decisions. Reuben Barker recalls: 'We got plenty of conversations going, but trying to stimulate some action was hard work.'

Next day the *Star* quoted the General Secretary of Kent NUM: 'the miners would not surrender'. The AUEW Divisional Organiser pledged his members' support for the Shrewsbury 3.

300 were on UCATT Southern Region's official march through Southampton including delegates from Portsmouth Naval Base UCATT, other UCATT branches, Vosper Thorneycroft, Davy Power Gas, university students and three IS branches.

On the 19th 163 credentials had been issued for the GMCC 'Conference in Defence of the Shrewsbury 24'. About 100 turned up. Scragg and O'Shea represented the CDC. Some delegates argued it was 'essential that a mass movement be developed with national co-ordination'. The Conference Declaration acknowledged that what was required was a repeat of the industrial action that led to the release of the Pentonville 5, but it settled for repetitions of the 'action already taken by thousands of workers' to be channelled 'through their executives' to pressurise the TUC to lead 'a national stoppage to release the Shrewsbury 3'. It also called on the 'labour and trade union movement' to 'condemn the savage sentences imposed', on 'progressive elements within the legal profession' to 'help in the drafting of such documents that will achieve changes' and on Labour MPs to carry the 'fight' into the Commons. Where no shop stewards' committees existed, defence committees should be formed and hold meetings to 'explain the facts'. It also endorsed the parliamentary lobby and the Liverpool Recall Conference.

Next day the *Star* reported that delegates from Wales, Scotland and 'many parts of England' had attended an LCDTU meeting on the 19th. They called for 'action committees' of building workers with subsidiary committees based in factories, pits, other workplaces and union branches. The Shrewsbury issue should be on the agenda of a recalled TUC, and building union leaders would be 'pressed to carry out their financial commitments'. They supported the lobby of the Court of Appeal on 1 February and the Liverpool Recall Conference. Dave Jackson told the CDC that Jim Hiles was 'circulating the Liverpool conference to all the people on his book'.

CHAPTER 14

The only way to free the 3

There was no principle at stake

On 22 January 1974 the CDC heard that John Carpenter had returned the mailing list, but neither he nor John Llywarch had been contactable. Margaret Llywarch said that John 'was a member of the organisation in question' and 'would not cease his activities'. The solicitor Campbell Malone would point out the 'dangers'. An IS member had 'quoted the amount of funds we had' and talked of 'a split'. (The week's income was £433, but two thirds went straight out again.) Barry Scragg warned about being 'extra careful in future when discussing finance'. The London NUJ Book Branch wanted to 'adopt' a jailed picket. Laurie Flynn had suggested McKinsie Jones, but recommended that they contact the CDC. If they 'insisted' he should be 'adopted'. (Billy Regan later told the branch 'it would be better for the money to come to this committee' and offered a speaker to 'put the facts over'.) Two members the National Film School Action Group were asked upstairs. (Their treatment for *Free the Six* drew on IS's *Pickets on Trial*.)

Emergency Bulletin No 13 was headed 'Free the three "Political Prisoners".' 'Every trade union branch throughout the country should send resolutions' to their EC and the TUC, 'demanding action to secure the release of our brothers' and give 'full support' for the Liverpool Recall Conference and the parliamentary lobby. The CDC welcomed the TGWU and UCATT decisions about industrial action and their call for the TUC to develop a national campaign. It urged the Labour Party to get involved. (40,000 copies were printed).

George Smith read a research brief on the Shrewsbury issue drawn up in consultation with UCATT's solicitor. It set out 'where UCATT might go from here both from the point of view of joint action' with the TGWU 'and unilaterally with regard to recovering the initiative in this difficult situation and so preventing other interested parties from going off at half cock to the extent that has already happened'. The convictions 'were of a criminal nature', so to appeal 'would be more or less to condone the behaviour of the Shrewsbury pickets', but 'to appeal against *sentence* is a more reasonable alternative'. There was 'no principle at stake'.

On the 23rd the TGWU and UCATT ECs agreed to ask the TUC to 'make urgent representations' to the Tory Home Secretary for 'an immediate review' of the Shrewsbury sentences.

Blackpool supporters were thinking about producing rock with 'Free the Three' in it and asking Paul Foot to write a book. Would the CDC produce a badge? Padgate College of Education Students' Union was to strike and hold a 'teach-in'. Could they have Bill Jones, Alan Abrahams or Pete Carter to speak? ('Alun will go.') The University of Wales Communist Society wanted a speaker. (Yes, if a meeting could be arranged by Aberystwyth Students' Union. 'Best Communist Wishes'.) Could Burnley Anarchist Group have a 'competent speaker' for a meeting that 'could result in the formation of a local defence committee'? (No.) The Treasurer of Burnley Defence Committee, who was also Secretary of Burnley UCATT, wanted to know about the 'monies received to date' and 'help given to members and families etc'. (Billy Regan told him that the money was used to help the families and the books were 'audited regularly by lay building workers'; but 'for obvious reasons (social security etc) we do not publish the amount collected or paid out'.)

Dave Jackson addressed 100 people at Oxford Trades Council, alongside NUM, NUPE and AUEW speakers. A defence committee was set up and a request sent off for the recall of the TUC. He also spoke to about ninety people at Barking and Dagenham Defence Committee. The police paid a visit, asked for a list of speakers and the attendance figure and informed them that they would be reported to the Special Branch. Jackson was going to the Liverpool Recall Conference with the Ruskin Defence Committee and had been invited to address the National Union of Students Oxford conference and Bristol Defence Committee. (Someone wrote: 'IS?' on the letter, but the CDC approved. Jeff Douglas told Dave Jackson: 'Everyone seems to have given up the idea of starting an unofficial movement on the lines of the Pentonville Five and are resigned to the fact that it will have to be done through the official movement.')

On the 24th the *Star* reported that Pete Carter was 'coming off site work for three weeks with the agreement of UCATT, the TGWU and Birmingham Trades Council'. He would 'co-ordinate the campaign

The Flying Pickets

for the city's conference to initiate a stronger fight to release the Shrewsbury Three' by 'winning a wide representation of the city's trade union, labour movement and shop floor workers'.

UCATT Midland Region and the Midland TGWU Building Section announced a meeting in Digbeth Civic Hall on 25 January. 'Every building worker should attend this meeting to hear *the truth* about the building workers jailed at Shrewsbury.' They were 'not calling for a day's stoppage', but for a 'full house' in working hours.

The *Star* later reported that 400 Birmingham building workers left work on the 25th and were addressed by Ken Barlow, Bob Williams, Arthur Utting and Phil Beyer. Beyer's proposal to call on UCATT and the TGWU to organise industrial action was unanimously agreed. The meeting backed the parliamentary lobby and the Liverpool Recall Conference. So did UCATT's North West Regional Council, which had also called on the EC to convene a meeting of regional committees to establish a 'Joint Campaign to Free the Shrewsbury Three' and a joint fund. If the appeals were rejected, 'a call for industrial action' would receive their 'full support'. Eric Hughes sent cheques for UCATT members of the 24.

On the 29th Barry Scragg told the CDC that John Llywarch 'had no intentions of discontinuing his present activities'. Scragg had pointed out 'the harm he could be doing to the appeal and the other lads on trial', but he 'was not concerned about individuals'. Llywarch 'was of the opinion the work he was doing was for the benefit of the whole trade union movement'. Bill Jones reported that 'complaints' had reached Jim Arnison 'regarding certain speakers addressing meetings supposedly representing this committee'. It 'seemed they were Bro's Llewark and Carpenter'. A statement would be put in the *Star* and the *Guardian* 'making it clear' that they 'do not represent this committee or the lads in jail' and Alan Abrahams would 'try to get something to that effect on Granada'. Scragg had found Marlene Tomlinson 'apparently distressed'. She turned down an offer of help but agreed to contact the CDC 'if the need arose'. George Wright, the TGWU Regional Secretary in Wales, wished to see 'monies received' from TGWU branches and a list of TGWU members who were 'supposed' to have received 'donations'. 'Bro J' would 'have a word'. Jim Shepherd, the TGWU Building Trade Officer in Liverpool, was a guest. He reported on a meeting with Jack Jones and EC members about the residue of the Chester Action Committee fund. O'Shea would receive expenses for visits to TGWU offices. £10 was to go to the *Star*. Abrahams would speak at the Liverpool Recall Conference. Dugen would be resigning from the *Charter*, which was 'in desperate need of funds'. CDC copies 'must be circulated on a wide basis and not let go to waste'. Joe Edwards reported that CDC bulletins were 'taken down almost as soon as they were put up' at Connah's Quay Labour Club.

Two *Militant* supporters in Liverpool wanted to write to the three jailed men. (The CDC sent only Jones's home address.) Bob Askew of Manchester Polytechnic ATTI reported that their four delegates to the GMCC Conference were 'amazed by some of the details relating to conspiracy charges'. Two delegates were going to the Liverpool Recall Conference. Could they have a speaker? (They could.) Nottingham Action Committee to Free the Three included people from Stanton-Staveley Iron Works, Long Eaton Trades Council and two Nottingham Labour Party Wards. They had asked the Trades Council to convene a conference to co-ordinate further action. Could they have a speaker on 28 January? (Regan needed 'two or three weeks notice'.) The TGWU National Building Trades Officer asked if any CDC members were in Solidarity—a libertarian socialist organisation founded by expelled SLL members in 1960. Their *Defend the Shrewsbury 24, But Don't Trust the Union Officials* was widely circulated in London and included the Defence Fund Treasurer's address. (Hee dissociated the CDC completely.) Jim Deakin of *The Collier* sent £3. (Regan sent bulletins and a *Charter*.)

The *Charter's* headline was 'Shrewsbury Victims—Mass Campaign To… Free The Three'. 'Mass action at sites, docks, factories, rails, etc' had led to a threat of a general strike and the release of the Pentonville 5, but the Shrewsbury campaign had to be based on the official TGWU call for a one-day stoppage and the 'go-ahead from UCATT for regional activity'. Readers should 'immediately join and mount' the 'mass campaign' of 'mass meetings and stoppages of work on every site and workplace', hold 'emergency meetings to plan action in every branch and trades council', send resolutions to union committees and raise cash. The speeches from the dock filled the back page, except for an announcement for the Liverpool Recall Conference. The *Charter* was no longer printed by IS, but by the CP's Farleigh Press.

Viewpoint's headline was 'UCATT Executive Supports Action To Free Shrewsbury Three'. Reportedly, Smith failed to get it withdrawn, but the EC issued *UCATT and the Shrewsbury Trials* to 'clear up any misunderstandings resulting from various interpretations being put on' the article. The trials 'cannot be viewed as an attack on picketing in general' or on 'peaceful picketing', since 'the accused at Shrewsbury have been found guilty of having agreed beforehand or on the picket itself to carry out personal violence or damage to property, or to intimidate individuals'. So 'the clear issue was whether there had been assault, damage to property, physical intimidation or the intention to do any of these'. No union 'should or could support its members committing acts which are obviously of a criminal nature and which are contrary to the union's instructions'. UCATT and the TGWU might ask the TUC to appeal to the Home Secretary for 'a review of the severity of the sentences'. An approach 'could profitably be made to the Labour Party to ensure that the next Labour Government will clarify the law on picketing and, *if necessary*, review' the use of the 1875 Act 'in situations of industrial dispute'. The TGWU-UCATT joint fund 'does not, of course, imply that UCATT condones the behaviour of these pickets', but 'we have a moral responsibility to ensure that the effects of these savage sentences on innocent bystanders are reduced to a minimum.'

Political prisoners

The *SW* printed on 22 January was almost all about the jailed pickets. One photograph showed John Llywarch and Ken O'Shea talking with CPer Jack Collins of the Kent NUM EC, who noted that the Shrewsbury sentences had come as the NUM overtime ban began to bite. The Tories were 'attempting to disarm the working class movement and isolate the fighting leadership', but hadn't dared to arrest miners. Elsa Warren reported that when she couldn't see Des at Bedford, she rang the Home Office to ask where he was: 'They refused to tell me.' (He had been moved to Walton Prison in Liverpool on the 17th and to Stafford Prison on the 22nd.) They were 'political prisoners' and 'the government wants to try and stop news of the movement's support reaching the men and to stop demonstrations at the jails.' *SW* insisted: 'We need action—not words.' It quoted John Carpenter: 'Pious resolutions against the jailings were not sufficient. What was needed was a real campaign among the rank and file of the unions.' 'Every area should organise a defence committee.' *SW* argued that employers were pushing the Tories into helping them prepare a cut in real wages across the board and were 'resorting more and more to the Special Branch, the police and the tanks'. There was 'a great abyss between the crisis in society and the consciousness of the workers'. A Labour government would have to 'carry out their pledges'. 150 people heard Llywarch and Carpenter at the Coventry *Socialist Worker* rally and Charles Llywarch, aged five, collected over £70. Rallies were to take place in London, Cwm, Pontardulais and Maesteg. NUM officials would chair and O'Shea, Jim Nichol, leading NUM and AUEW activists and Lew Adams, Secretary of ASLEF's London District Council, would speak. The Combine would entertain in North West London and IS's Alex Glasgow in Sheffield. Tottenham UCATT were organising a 'Benefit Social'. Vic Turner of the Pentonville 5, Gerry Kelly of UCATT and Dave Jackson would speak at Barking.

Dave Ayre had been elected to the UCATT Northern Regional Committee. On the 24th they discussed the 'extremely grave—and in the view of many, harsh decision' at Shrewsbury. They would produce leaflets and organise a meeting of stewards and branch delegates on 20 April to consider 'how to end if possible or diminish' the sentences. The TGWU, GMWU and FTAT would be invited. The EC would be asked to 'approach the TUC with a view of a considered determined approach to government'. On the 26th Dave attended his first *Charter* Editorial Board meeting in Manchester. He apologised to the CDC for sending £1.50, but hoped it would be the first of many collections. 'Pressure is also building up on official trade union movement' to 'move them from lethargy'.

The *SW* printed on 29 January reported that Llywarch and Nichol had addressed thirty members of Cwm NUM, Nichol and Margaret Llywarch spoke at a 'packed meeting' at Pontardulais that raised £15 and 24 people heard John speak at Clydach and collected £28. (Nichol recalls that he and Marlene Tomlinson 'spoke at six o'clock every morning to miners at a series of pits in Wales'.)

Over 400 people had filled Digbeth Civic Hall in Birmingham to hear John Llywarch and Paul Foot. Llywarch stressed that 'IS have led all over the country in organising to free the three. They're a fantastic group—they need your help and you need them.' Six people joined. At another Digbeth rally, Carpenter told a large audience that in 1872 jail sentences for 'conspiracy' were cut after a massive campaign. 'We've got to go back to industry, go back to our schools and colleges and places of work and organise ourselves in action committees to "Free the Three".' 'We've got to talk about a National Defence Committee.' Gerry Kelly wanted an all-out strike and delegations to the Liverpool Recall Conference.

Pete Carter spoke to Austin stewards, who supported the Birmingham Defence Committee meeting on 3 February. Wolverhampton AUEW District Committee invited Carter to address their quarterly meeting. Granville Williams, then IS Organiser in Birmingham, recalls that Dave Adshead and Gerry Kelly worked well with Carter and there was mutual trust and respect, as there was in the AUEW Broad Left. Carter didn't appear to be under pressure from the CP and they all used the CP's *Star* Club for a late drink.

George Kelly chaired a *Socialist Worker* rally of 300 in Glasgow. Foot and Llywarch spoke. Llywarch also spoke at 22 meetings at building sites, railway workshops, pits and engineering factories there and in Edinburgh. Edinburgh IS had increased its *SW* order to 1,100 and needed 200 more on the Friday. Over 300 were sold to miners. IS booked Leith Town Hall and 400 people turned up for the rally. IS organiser Alice Murray chaired, Foot spoke and Llywarch got a standing ovation. The financial appeal was made by the convenor of the strikers at a McAlpine site, who stressed that the collection would be split between the Defence Fund and the *Socialist Worker* Fighting Fund. £100 was raised and twelve people joined IS.

Carpenter spoke to 100 people in West Middlesex, where a huge Ealing hospital workforce pledged support for action to free the three. He also addressed 200 people in East London, where Lew Adams of ASLEF stressed the importance of the industrial action on the railways. At both meetings Laurie Flynn argued for building a socialist party capable of stopping picket trials.

SW knew of fifty IS branches that had issued leaflets and won industrial action after the jailings, but 'organised leadership' was 'woefully lacking'. The UCATT official in York was 'very slow off the mark' and 'doesn't take the issue at all seriously', but a defence committee was set up all the same. The IS National Secretary, Dave Peers, had been going round sites with Llywarch and Carpenter. Organised sites 'where previous meetings had been held' were 'much more responsive' and 'it was up to IS' to 'help them get around as many sites as possible'. The campaign would not end with the Liverpool Recall Conference, though delegations were a 'top priority'. The IS Building Workers' Fraction would caucus beforehand.

SW's print order was 37,000. Rob Clay and Rab Jeffrey reported an 'astonishing rise' in interest in Teesside and Southampton and John Charlton knew of 600 sales at Yorkshire pits. Tony Cliff argued that IS were 'the only people capable of straddling the abyss, but we are just not big enough'. Llywarch would speak at a Darlington rally.

On the 30th Crook UCATT heard that Spennymoor Trades Council wanted to 'be associated with any campaign' likely to win the men's release. Dave Ayre complained at the Northern Regional Council's 'lack of initiative'. *Viewpoint* had caused confusion by first 'implying that regions were authorised to take action' and then 'last minute reactions' 'suggesting reversals of policy'. The CDC and Liverpool Trades Council had sent information about the Recall Conference. Llywarch was to 'give his impressions of the issue' in Darlington, Teesside and Newcastle. Crook UCATT would organise a public meeting with Crook Trades Council to 'outline the case of the Shrewsbury 24' in the context of the general economic crisis.

The Building Worker, 'Voice of International Socialist Building Workers', called for defence committees 'based on genuine trade union bodies' to finance speakers to argue for industrial action. 'We have a responsibility to fight until they are free.' Llywarch's speaking tour had convinced him that 'everybody seems to be completely ignorant of what has happened in Shrewsbury' but they were 'keen to know'. 'There is a great need for leaflets to be printed so that people know exactly what has gone on. I think in the near future we must consider an all-out national strike to get these lads out.' 'The whole movement needs a fire lighting under it.' 'If people are to be pulled out they have to be argued with, given facts and convinced. This means that site and factory meetings must be organised.' Delegates should go to the Liverpool Recall Conference 'armed with pledges of commitment to total strike action until the three are freed'. He would speak at an IS meeting sponsored by Greenwich Trades Council that aimed to launch a defence committee. A Coventry AUEW branch had sponsored a meeting at which he and Gerry Kelly spoke to thirty stewards and branch officers. Shop floor collections and donations from trade union branches had already come in. Coventry Radiators stewards would hold regular collections and a 'huge social is being organised at Chrysler Ryton'. A tour was being arranged. Factories could 'adopt' members of the 24 'to bring home even more clearly the issues on the shop floor', but strikes were 'The Only Way to Free the Three'.

In the second half of January, Llywarch had sent £45 to the Defence Fund from the Glasgow *Socialist Worker* rally. Leeds Central IS sent £39 from an AUEW Left Unity meeting addressed by Carpenter and Arthur Scargill of the NUM. Lanchester Polytechnic Students' Union sent £100. Lowestoft Trades Council raised £20 after an IS member spoke. UCATT's London Regional Secretary forwarded a £31 branch collection. IS sent £10 to the CDC for Carpenter and O'Shea's travel costs and forwarded £85 from the EETPU London Press Branch. The Defence Fund's January's income was £2,921, but £3,215 went out.

Underhand

On 31 January the *Star* reported 450 credential applications for the Liverpool Recall Conference, including those from from Merseyside car factories, Scottish factories, shipyards and docks, London sites, TGWU branches and the South Wales NUM EC. Underneath was Jim Arnison's 'Shrewsbury Three and the IS':

> The North Wales defence committee yesterday condemned the methods of the International Socialists in the campaign to free the jailed Shrewsbury pickets.
> A committee statement refers to the fact that the IS is writing to organisations offering speakers on the campaign, and says: 'This is a cheap and unprincipled means of attempting to recruit to this political organisation.'
> Two of the three men who received suspended sentences, Mr John Llywarch and Mr John Carpenter, are being offered as speakers by the IS.
> This, says the committee, is in violation of a decision taken by the committee that none of the three would be used in this way.
>
> UNDERHAND
>
> Messages from the three in prison have made clear that they recognise only speakers approved by or from the committee as speaking on their behalf.
> 'Only harm can be done to the lads now in prison, those at present in court at Shrewsbury and the others awaiting trial as a result of the underhand methods being used by the International Socialists', says the committee.
> 'John Carpenter and John Llywarch are not speaking on behalf of the defence committee but for the International Socialists.'

The *Star* printed no messages from prison, no evidence of IS offering speakers and no such CDC 'Statement' has yet come to light. Warren was a CPer; but there was no evidence of him or McKinsie Jones asking anyone to speak on their behalf. Tomlinson recalled that Marlene told him about the 'Shrewsbury Independence Fund' set up by building workers and supported by IS and about Carpenter and Llywarch speaking at meetings around the country. He was delighted that she had spoken and joined in the protests.

That evening Dave Ayre heard Carpenter and Llywarch speak in Eston. *SW* reported that two of the 100 people at the 'Free the Shrewsbury Three!' rally had given out leaflets criticising IS and Llywarch. He asked if anyone would care to voice their disagreements, but the leafletters didn't speak up, so he asked people 'to hold up their hands if they thought that his conduct was in accord with the principles of the working class movement'. 'All except two held up their hands and no one responded to a request to raise their hands if they disagreed.' The two abstentions were from the CPers who handed out the leaflets. (Tomlinson read this report in *SW* and asked to be classified as a political prisoner.)

Lou Lewis sent the Defence Fund £345 from the London Shrewsbury 24 Committee. Ian Stevenson apologised for Sheffield Defence Committee having 'fallen behind', but 'about 70' shop stewards and trade unionists would 'start up' again. Their leaflet about that day's Court of Appeal lobby argued that the way to free the three was to pressurise the TUC. (In the event thirty of the 100 at the lobby were from a Hackney school. Small delegations came from two sites, Camden and Southwark Trades Councils and Croydon District AUEW. Lord James scheduled the appeals for 19 February, but turned down the bail applications.)

Dave Peers wrote an 'Open Letter' to the CDC on behalf of IS:

We cannot understand why you did not write directly either to us or to John Llywarch or John Carpenter before speaking to the press. Not only are your allegations completely unfounded, but they can only serve to damage the whole campaign at a time when the maximum unity of all sections of the working class movement is required to get these trade unionists released.

...We have not written to any organisations offering speakers on Shrewsbury, and the *Socialist Worker* rallies at which John Carpenter and John Llywarch have spoken have been openly advertised as IS meetings and all money collected at these meetings is divided equally between the *Socialist Worker* Shrewsbury Campaign and the Defence Committee. Both John Llywarch and John Carpenter make no secret of the fact that they are members of IS and surely they are entitled to address meetings of their own organisation. What is '*underhand*' about that?

When John Llywarch and John Carpenter have spoken at site meetings, trade union branches or shop stewards' committees they have done so not on behalf of the North Wales Defence

Committee but in their own right. But they do insist at these meetings that any money raised in the collections or trade union donations be sent directly to your committee. Their intention has been simply to bring home to other trade unionists the importance of what happened to them and the other Shrewsbury pickets and to build support for the movement to get Des Warren, Ricky Tomlinson and John Mackinsie Jones out of jail. They know that you disapprove of what they are doing and that you have tried to stop them, but they have brought the message of Shrewsbury to thousands of workers in dozens of meetings over the last few weeks. Through their efforts hundreds of pounds has been sent to your committee. They have taken [a] personal risk in doing this, because they are on suspended sentences, but it was THEIR decision to undertake the campaign. It is their contribution to bringing about the release of their three brothers in prison, and IS is proud to be able to assist them in this. What would you have them do—sit at home and do nothing?

We intend to continue the campaign to release the Shrewsbury 3 by every means at our disposal. This is our clear duty as socialists and trade unionists. But we would prefer to do this *in unity* with the North Wales Defence Committee, and we cannot understand why you have chosen this time—on the eve of the Liverpool Trades Council's Shrewsbury Conference—to launch this unprovoked attack upon IS and the two Shrewsbury defendants. We would welcome the opportunity to refute these charges in front of your committee in the hope that we can achieve united action in our common aim.

On the 2nd the *Star* noted that IS had 'admitted' that Llywarch and Carpenter knew that the CDC 'disapproves' their speaking at IS meetings. 'Des Warren Angry over "IS antics"' quoted his 4 January letter to Elsa. It claimed that all six defendants had 'agreed that those who walked out of the court should place themselves completely at the disposal' of the CDC. In fact Warren had written: 'Carpenter asked me what they should do if they got out and we (Ricky and me) didn't. I told them to put themselves at the disposal of the NW defence committee 100 percent.' He didn't say they agreed.

'Shrewsbury and the IS—Our Reply' noted that 'a successful campaign to free the Shrewsbury three and to prevent further sentences will require unity of all sections of the left and the trade union movement.' 'Regrettably, some people have been trying to prevent this unity coming about, using methods that can only cause dissension and confusion' and 'seem to have persuaded the North Wales Defence Committee into issuing a statement to the *Morning Star* about the activities of the International Socialists which is both untrue and a threat to the unity of the campaign'. IS had printed and distributed 100,000 leaflets on the issue.

> The main thing now must be to step up the campaign against the jailings. Surely, every organisation that cares about Shrewsbury—whether it be the Communist Party or the Labour Party or the International Socialists—has a right and a duty to organise meetings on the issue. It is regret[t]able that a few odd individuals seem more concerned with stopping activity than with initiating it.

Llywarch and Carpenter had a right to speak at IS meetings and it was 'quite right' for Barry Scragg to speak at a CP rally (at CPer Arthur Jones's parliamentary candidature launch in Merthyr).

The *Star*'s 'United Action Planned for Shrewsbury 3' claimed that 800 delegates turned up at the Liverpool Recall Conference on 2 February. They agreed to picket the Court of Appeal on the 19th and give 'mass support' for a parliamentary lobby and to hold a 'national day of action' on 18 March in a form 'to be decided by meetings of workers at factories, docks, building sites, etc'. The TUC, TGWU and UCATT would be 'called upon to recognise the day of action as official policy' and conferences would be held in London, Birmingham, Coventry, Leeds, Bristol, Sheffield, Newcastle, Glasgow, Edinburgh, Dundee and Aberdeen. Regional committees would 'consult with the unions what the next steps in the campaign shall be'. The collection raised over £1,500. The London Shrewsbury 24 Committee were to 'put a full-time worker on the campaign'.

SW reported several CPers' speeches. Alan Abrahams had insisted that 'the day of action in March had to be of the same order as the massive TUC demonstration against the Industrial Relations Act. Sporadic outbursts of action here and there were not enough.' Lou Armour 'appealed for the maximum unity in the campaign' and 'realised how frustrated people felt' at no official lead from his own union'. Pete Carter 'stressed that there was a tremendous amount of confusion in the working class movement'. The 'lack of publicity on the nature of the charges and the course of the trial meant that the field was clear for papers such as the *Daily Mirror* to weigh in when the verdicts came out'. John Deason of St Helen's Trades Council (and IS) was 'absolutely clear that one-day stoppages would not get the lads out of jail and that the TUC would only move if the massive pressure was built up'. The campaign 'had to build towards pro-longed industrial action'. Willie Lee, a Chrysler Linwood AUEW senior shop steward (and IS member), tabled an amendment on action, but CPer Bert Smith backed the original motion.

Who has called the meeting?

Early in February Oxford IS wanted to distribute CDC bulletins to building workers, but had received none since November. (The CDC apologised, but put 'IS' on the letter.) The Coventry AUEW Divi-sional Organiser needed a copy of each CDC bulletin and 'a balance sheet showing how the donations received have been distributed'. (The CDC was reprinting thirteen bulletins and would 'publish an account at the end of the campaign'.)

Bolton UCATT and Council of Action planned a public meeting on the Shrewsbury trials. Could they have a CDC speaker? The Pres-ident of Westhoughton UCATT asked again. Billy Regan asked: 'Who has called the meeting?' 'Is it of a political nature? ie Labour Party, International Socialist, Communist, etc' 'Where is the venue?' He required an assurance that the council was 'not run by a political group' and that the meeting would be 'non-political'. The UCATT members explained that the council was 'political and industrial & embraces any or all trade unionists and invites anyone whatever their political beliefs to involve themselves in its organisation'. If 'the jail-ing of pickets is a political act (as stated in your own leaflet)', then 'any meeting supporting the pickets must be a political meeting'. The council was 'not run by any political party' but had 'members of *var-ious* political parties from the Labour Party to the Socialist Labour League'. Most were 'ordinary workers and tenants'. Their public meetings were usually attended by 50 to 100 people and they were 'the only organisation in this area to fight for support for the jailed pickets'. A UCATT Trades Council delegate had raised the matter without success. (Someone put a large tick on this letter.)

Union branches at Imperial College in London had arranged for Llywarch to speak, but the ASTMS branch secretary felt that the *Star* had offered 'evidence that he is likely to misuse our hospitality'. Could he see the CDC 'statement'? Regan replied:

> This committee, the three lads in jail, also the lads on trial and due for trial have said that it is not their wish that Bro's Llewark or Carpenter go speaking round the country on our behalf...

The fact is that they are being paid and used by the International Socialists to further their own political beliefs. We have had reports from meetings they have attended all following the same pattern and ending with an IS official running down different sections of the working class and trade union officials. This committee believes that unity is needed to release our brothers and that the tactics of the IS can only bring about splits in the movement.

He gave no evidence to support any of these claims.

On the 6th Barry Scragg told the CDC that Marlene Tomlinson had complained about 'the state of her home' and he had asked her to 'obtain an estimate'. Bill Jones said they were 'not in a position' to 'go spending large sums of money on house repairs'. He would speak at Wigan, Stoke and Padgate, but speakers were required for Bracknell, Birmingham, Kent and Preston. He would discuss having a paid speaker with Simon Fraser and draft a 'stock reply' for queries about the Defence Fund. Four Flint UCATT members who received money from the Chester Action Committee fund wouldn't have their 'wages' cut. The North Wales Charter Chairman would be paid for 'work appertaining to this committee'. Andy Kelly became Deputy Treasurer. Mike Williams could open a Nationwide account, but Scragg's signature would be required on cheques. A 'large cheque' from IS 'could not be cashed owing to a mistake in the date'. (The Defence Fund had received almost £2,400 in two weeks and held over £11,000. This is the last publicly available treasurer's report.)

Dave Jackson had been invited to speak by Preston AUEW and Trades Council. Bill Jones, Alan Abrahams and Lou Lewis said he should go, but he needed the train fare: '200 people expected to attend.' Brent Trades Council wanted to set up a defence committee—'it won't be a political meeting'. Oxford Defence Committee was 'building up slowly'. NUM members at Ruskin had asked for help in picketing Didcot Power Station: 'Hope we don't get lifted.'

Ashington NUM were 'prepared to donate' if the cash was 'earmarked for the wives and children of the imprisoned men'. (Regan assured them that the wives' 'expressed wishes' were 'that all donations should be made to the fund' and they sent £100.)

The NUM reported that a national ballot showed 81 percent support for a strike, which would involve picketing coal supplies to power stations. On the 7th Edward Heath called a general election.

Next day Dave Jackson reported on the Bristol meeting.

John Carpenter was there but he saw me in the pub first and asked not to make it a 'Political Meeting'. This was obviously what we wanted as disruptive meetings do little good and a lot of harm. I was introduced as from The Charter Defence Committee & Liverpool Trades Council; and I asked them to endorse last Saturday's meeting [and] fortunately Carpenter went along with this.

A TGWU official had said his union 'would make all action official'. The meeting called for pressure through official channels, a regional conference and workplace meetings and collections before the London demonstration. It was 'dominated by the IS'.

No. 24 Divisional TASS Women's Sub-Committee asked Bob Williams, on behalf of the London Shrewsbury 24 Committee, if he would pass invitations to the wives of the 'Shrewsbury Three' to talk to women trade unionists about 'solidarity with the Shrewsbury building workers'. (Elsa Warren's acceptance went from Billy Regan's address.) Doncaster Trades Council would 'give full support', but it 'would not be possible to hold a meeting on the Shrewsbury 24' because of the election. (The CDC could 'fully understand'.)

Prestatyn UCATT and Tottenham UCATT sent the Defence Fund £100. £337 went into the Nationwide. The TSB account held £9,824. £10 went to the *Star* as a 'small token of our appreciation for the truth and sincerity you have shown towards our brothers'.

Don't think I'm being overly critical

Back in spring 1973 Pete Kavanagh had joined an EETPU picket at St Thomas's Hospital site in London. When police stopped four pickets from approaching a coach carrying scabs, Kavanagh tried to get through. He was found guilty of assault and obstruction, fined £20 and ordered to pay £20 costs. He appealed to the High Court.

In January 1974, at a picket at Art Castings in Nuneaton, the President of the TGWU branch was near Jack Sprung, a Coventry activist, when he talked to a lorry driver. Sprung moved in front of the lorry. 'The next moment I looked round and four officers were manhandling Jack' and, 'as if by a pre-arranged signal, police reinforcements who had been concealed in a van came flooding round the gates'. 'I have never witnessed such violence.' Two of Sprung's sons were there. One was filming for Cinema Action. All three were charged with 'threatening behaviour likely to cause a breach of the peace'. Jack was also charged with assaulting a policeman and his sons with obstructing the police.

On 3 February Lord Widgery ruled that police had been correct to anticipate a breach of the peace in Kavanagh's case. It was 'a fallacy to suggest that a picket had a legal right to approach a driver'.

Days later, a prosecution lawyer in the Sprungs' case argued that the decision proved that the Industrial Relations Act didn't give a right to picket. A policeman had limited the number of pickets to six and another had decided that Jack Sprung wouldn't be one of them. The prosecution had difficulty in making the charges stick and the case was adjourned, but the sustained efforts to criminalise effective picketing through judge-made Common Law was becoming clearer.

SW reported that Carpenter and Foot spoke in Blackburn. IS had three branches, two industrial branches and 'the makings of one' in both Preston and Darwen. Marlene Tomlinson was a guest. The £68 collection was split between the families and *SW*'s Fighting Fund.

Ricky was in solitary. The governor told him that 'there had been a demo, controlled by the IS, but it had passed off peaceful'.

Bill Jones told the *Star* that the official Merseyside Committee would decide on the day of action. The CDC asked Labour parliamentary candidates to pledge to demand the Three's release.

On the 13th the *Star* reported that 'almost 300 delegates representing thousands of Midlands workers' had applied for credentials for Birmingham Trades Council's conference on the 16th.

> There will be men and women from post offices, railways, sheet metal workers, printers, transport drivers and miners. Six trades councils are sending delegates as are the engineering union district committees in Wolverhampton and Birmingham. The transport union district committees of Wolverhampton and Derby are appointing delegates.
>
> Building workers' branches and ASTMS members from Hereford, GKN and GEC will be there and 15 full-time trade union officials have agreed to attend.

UCATT Midland Regional Council found the EC circular 'fraught with contradictions' and urged them to reconsider their position.

Crook UCATT read a CDC bulletin and wrote to the EC 'outlining criticisms of the statement' and their 'increasing lack of confidence' after the failure 'to adopt firm and positive policies' to free the three jailed pickets. Crook and Spennymoor Trades Councils' joint support meeting would be in March.

A Leicester UCATT member was aware of 'a lot of concern' about the campaign. The 'group most active in this struggle is the International Socialists', but the CDC 'does not appear to be as active as necessary'. Could they give him 'an idea of the sort of activities that your committee is presently engaged in', 'what struggles you envisage' and 'clarify your relationship' with the UCATT fund? 'Don't think I'm being overly critical, but over this last two months when addressing meetings on Shrewsbury, I've face[d] a bar[r]age of questions on these very points.' (Regan replied that members had been 'travelling the country week in & week out for more than twelve months speaking at meetings and raising funds'. Moreover, 'none of the families' had 'suffered any hardship while their husbands have been on trial or in prison', so 'the lads and their families are fully satisfied with the work we have done'.)

Ricky Tomlinson heard that 'the welfare were going to try to take the children' away, but he was confident that Marlene would fight.

Guilty of trade unionism

Back on 14 January eighteen of the 24 had surrendered bail, but the trial of nine was deferred. The other nine—Malcolm Clee, Derrick Hughes, Alfred James, Dennis Morris, Michael Pierce, Brian Williams, Samuel Warburton, Arthur Murray and Garry Davies (who had refused to become a Crown witness)—were charged with 'affray' and 'unlawful assembly'. Some were also charged with 'assault', 'criminal damage' and 'intimidation'.

His Honour Judge Richard Michael Arthur Chetwynd-Talbot was born in 1911, went to Harrow School and Magdalene College, Cambridge. He was called to the Bar at Middle Temple in 1936 and was a Major in the King's Shropshire Light Infantry from 1939 to 1945. He became Recorder of Banbury in 1955 and a Bencher in 1962. In 1972 the Tories promoted him to Circuit Judge.

Arthur Murray later wrote that 'the fantasy and character assassination that the *Daily Mirror* and the rest of the gutter press were churning out' made things very difficult for the defendants. 'I was promised that if I pleaded guilty to unlawful assembly the judge would not send me to prison.' Eight pleaded not guilty on all counts, but Dennis Morris pleaded guilty to two charges of 'unlawful assembly' and the crown prosector, Drake, withdrew the 'affray' charge. (All except Morris received Defence Fund wages.) All nine got bail.

Drake and Fennell proceeded on the 'affray' and 'unlawful assembly' charges on 6 September 1972. Drake spoke of a 'terrifying scene of violence and intimidation' by '300' pickets who left 'a trail of damage while shouting abuse and threats with the object of compelling workers by terror to stop work'. A Shrewsbury 'worker'—actually a boss—'was so terrified at what was going on that he got out a shotgun he kept in his car for clay pigeon shooting and pointed it at some of the pickets.'

The manager at the Mount site in Shrewsbury, Callaghan, claimed that pickets shouted 'Kill, kill, kill'. (He denied that it was 'Kill, kill, kill *the lump*', but acknowledged that nobody was hurt.) A lumper claimed to identify Murray from a photograph because he had 'a nice crease' in his trousers, but denied giving a statement. (He was mistaken. It didn't mention trousers.) Police had shown another lumper his statement, which said that Murray was 'smartly dressed'. (A photograph shows that he was casually dressed.) A couple who lived at Kingswood claimed that they saw a picket throw a paint can at a worker, but neither could identify this alleged assailant.

Police showed Mrs Drake (no relation) some photographs before she testified. Defence counsel objected, but the judge ruled that the police could show witnesses photographs and statements. Mrs Drake had locked herself in an office toilet at Brookside, yet claimed she saw one picket carrying a stick. (Under cross-examination she admitted that one of the men she had picked out on photographs wasn't the one she identified in court.) Most Crown witnesses were Brookside lumpers. Nigel Roberts saw a 'good 200' pickets. (His statement said 'more like 100'.) 'It was my mistake.' Dennis Ralphs said a piece of tile bounced off the scaffolding and caught him above the left eyebrow. He saw a dozen men throwing stones, two or three holding sticks, a worker pulled off a scaffold and a van overturned. (He acknowledged that only one man might have carried a stick.) Derek Butterfield said that Pierce had a 'club' and pushed 'walls' over, but admitted that he was thirty yards away and couldn't see what Pierce was doing. Mr Butler called the pickets who ordered him out of the house a 'wild horde'. Yet they stepped aside at his request to let some women cleaners leave. He had told a picket that 'if he came into my house I'd shoot him with my double-barrelled 12 bore'. He 'knew his name was Warren'. Leslie Pritchett saw Davies throw a concrete block through a window. (He had said a 'half brick' in his statement and he could be mistaken about identifications.) George Francis saw Clee brandishing a stick. (He looked at his statement and accepted his mistake.) Graham

Marshall saw Clee with an 'iron bar', but only on a photograph. (At the first trial he *thought* it was Clee.) Two witnesses identified Clee. They hadn't done so before. George Oliver thought Arthur Murray had an 'iron bar' on a photograph, though he hadn't seen him holding one. (At the first trial he said Murray had a 'stick'.) Dennis Whittall was not sure that Murray came onto the scaffold. Police had shown Alan Hughes photographs. He was shown one in court. He couldn't find Warren. Then he picked the wrong man. Finally he spotted him. (Like most Crown witnesses, he had seen the *Sunday People*'s 'Wrecker' and the *Daily Mirror*'s 'Godfather' articles.) He claimed that Murray smashed a JCB windscreen. (Defence counsel proved that the glass was undamaged and asked him to read his statement.) 'It must have bounced off the roof.'

At the first trial PC Price could identify nobody. At this trial Sergeant Price testified 'how powerless and scared stiff he felt among the crowd of pickets'. PC Williams saw no damage being caused on Site 6 and nobody carrying a stick, but he saw Clee, Warburton, Pierce and James at the front of the site meeting, where workmen were intimidated. (The *Shropshire Star* photographs show that several relaxed policemen were only a few yards away and nobody looks intimidated.) The unpromoted Sergeant Hartland ordered no policeman to make arrests, because he 'would have been putting their lives in danger'. Murray, Warburton and Morris (along with Warren, Tomlinson and McKinsie Jones) were leading a 'mob'. The reporter Philip Jones saw a column of about 200 pickets moving through the site, some carrying 'sticks' or 'bars'. 'It was a frightening sight.' (He had been up to 200 yards away.)

The *Morning Star* reported that Drake asked Murray if he condoned violence. 'I condemn any form of intimidation but there is also legal intimidation as you know.' 'You have pointed out to every witness that I had an iron bar.' The steel rod produced in court would not be found on a building site. The *Chester Chronicle* reported that Murray 'did no damage, did not climb onto the scaffolding or throw a stone or a piece of machinery. He did not carry an iron bar at any stage, or see anyone else with one.' A photograph showed a piece of wood in his hand, but he picked it up and put it down 'in a couple of seconds'. (Nobody saw him do damage.) *SW* reported that Drake tried to get Davies to admit that since he did not turn the pickets back then he 'must have been rampaging across the site'. Drake's '"get them at any price" approach showed time and time again'. (Davies hadn't gone onto the site until he was asked over to the meeting.)

On the 29th Clee and Hughes pleaded guilty to 'unlawful assembly' and Drake did not proceed on 'affray', 'intimidation', 'criminal damage' and 'assault'. They were bailed until sentencing. (Barry Scragg later told the CDC that he and Murray 'tried their best to change their minds'. Clee and Hughes received no more wages.)

Next day the Crown withdrew the 'affray' charge against James. *SW* stressed that Drake 'had been unable to produce a single witness to identify James as being involved in any alleged offences'.

The judge summed up on 11 February. Next day the jury found Davies not guilty on all charges. Warburton was guilty of 'unlawful assembly'. Williams, Pierce and Murray were guilty of 'unlawful assembly' and 'affray'. On the 13th the judge insisted that what had happened was 'deplorable'. 'Terror was imposed on other people by a display of force' and 'it must be made clear that such conduct resulting in terror simply cannot be permitted, whether that conduct arises out of an industrial dispute.' This 'violent conduct which terrorises, reinforced by large numbers—simply must stop'. He gave Morris, Clee, Hughes, Warburton and James four months, suspended for two years, and Pierce, Williams and Murray six and four months, to run concurrently. A cry of 'Disgraceful!' went up in the gallery.

SW pointed out that to be guilty of affray you had to be part of 'a display of force such as to frighten a reasonably courageous man', yet Drake had claimed that simply being in a crowd was 'contributing' to a 'display of force'. 'The whole trade union movement must now pass judgment—on these vicious laws. It must rally to the defence of these men, who are being victimised and persecuted to discourage the others, to dissuade other strikers from adopting the tactics necessary to win strikes.' They were 'guilty—of trade unionism'.

The last nine members of the 24 awaiting trial were invited to the CDC. Barry Scragg summed up the cases of those found guilty at the second trial. Bill Jones wanted an 'all-out effort' to involve local MPs. After the defendants left, the minutes were 'passed around'. Alan Abrahams reported that 70 to 100 people at Camden Town Hall 'could have been better' but the rail strike 'made it difficult'. Cinema Action lacked funds to complete their film so the CDC would attend a viewing. Eric Heffer would be asked about sympathetic Labour MPs. Billy Hough had audited the accounts. Elsa Warren's house was in a 'terrible condition', so accommodation would be rented until it was repaired. No money should go directly to the wives of the six jailed men. (The Defence Fund held over £9,000.)

CHAPTER 15

The Shrewsbury 6

Despite the general election campaign

On 15 February 1974 the *Star* reported that mass meetings at major London sites had voted to strike over the Shrewsbury jailings on the 20th. UCATT and the TGWU backed the Court of Appeal lobby.

Almost 300 people applied for credentials for the Birmingham Trades Council, TGWU and UCATT Midland Region conference, 'Trade Unions—A New Attack'. On the 17th only 200 turned up, including 81 from the TGWU, 52 from UCATT and 42 from the AUEW. A Labour councillor chaired and the Labour Leader of West Midlands Metropolitan Council spoke. Delegates demanded that a Labour government should free the six men and stop 'conspiracy' law being used against trade unionists and backed the parliamentary lobby. The collection raised £280. (Next day the CDC Treasurer sent a receipt for £284 for the residue of the Liverpool Conference collection.)

Bert Ramelson told Des Warren that 'despite the general election campaign we are trying to keep the issue of your release and the political consequences of your conviction alive'. 'I hope you don't mind that at election meetings I have read your letter to me to the audience and it has had a tremendous effect.' 'PS. Pete Kavanagh is now working full time for three weeks to organise a London conference on the campaign.'

On the 19th Warren, Tomlinson and McKinsie Jones appealed against their convictions for 'conspiracy' and O'Shea, Carpenter and Llywarch against their convictions for 'unlawful assembly' at the Court of Appeal in London. According to the *Chester Chronicle* O'Shea was a labourer, Carpenter was a foreman joiner and Llywarch was a 'contractor'. Outside the court 'about 150 trade union demonstrators' conducted 'peaceful picketing'. Inside, the men's counsel attacked the trial judge, Mais. One complained about his 'sheer inability' in his summing-up. He had put the prosecution case as if there was no other case to consider and dismissed the defence case in one sentence.

'It was like water wearing away a stone', Mr Rhys-Roberts said. 'The Jury were left with the Crown's case. In drawing attention to the conspiracy he never said: 'It is for the Crown to satisfy you that there was a conspiracy and each one of these men was a conspirator.' What he did was put it the other way round: 'Can you say they weren't?'

That 'shifts the burden of proof to the defence'.

On the 20th the *Star* carried photographs of Marlene Tomlinson, Rita Carpenter and the CP candidate for Tooting, Lou Lewis, outside the Court of Appeal. Penrhiwceiber NUM, Austin's stewards, Shotton steel workers, 'many trades councils' and a 'huge contingent of building workers' had been represented.

SW argued that the trade union movement must 'rally to the defence of these men, who are being victimised and persecuted' to 'dissuade other strikers from the tactic necessary to win strikes'. (The paper's print-run was 46,000, and the 'vast majority' were sold. Liverpool IS's order went up to 1,000, Edinburgh's and Leeds' to 1,400 and Glasgow's to 3,000.)

Elsa Warren was billed to speak at a CP meeting at Connah's Quay with Reuben Falber, the Party's Assistant Secretary, Dai Francis of South Wales NUM (who sent a substitute) and Barry Scragg, 'in a personal capacity'. The *Chester Chronicle* reported that Elsa Warren 'told an audience of 70 that she was living in a semi-derelict cottage in need of extensions and repair, and furniture and carpets had been sold to buy food for her five small children'. After the meeting, Scragg refused to have his photograph taken for 'a reactionary paper.' 'Mr Bob Wilson'—possibly Bob Williams—tried to prevent Mrs Warren from speaking to the press', but she told the *Chronicle* that she was 'living on social security'.

Next day Lord Widgery, Lord Justice James and Mr Justice Kerr were satisfied that the 'conspiracy' convictions should stand, but the six men's counsel could raise further points in the week beginning 4 March—after the general election.

That evening the CDC minutes were read out and agreed. There is no list of members present. The meeting lasted two hours but the minutes take half a page. Bill Jones (CP candidate for Swansea East), Pete Carter and Lou Lewis were producing a 'broadsheet'.

By the 22nd Imperial College London NUPE branch had heard Llywarch speak. 'We found his comments extremely interesting and will do all we can to get this branch actively supporting the campaign to free the six lads in gaol.' They were 'disturbed' about the CDC's 'quite unwarranted' comments. 'Clearly John is not in the pay of the International Socialists in any subversive sense, and meetings where IS speakers have joined him on the stage have been advertised as IS rallies.' £9 was enclosed 'in the hope that the lads' families will be looked after' and that the CDC 'will be working seriously to get the six out of gaol'.

IS sent a further £45 to the Defence Fund, which paid CPer Frank Foley for two days' speaking 'on behalf of' them in Dundee. Ron Sinclair of Sale UCATT thought the postcard campaign 'a waste of *time & money*'. The 'only thing the Tories do understand is mass action'. (The CDC replied that its 'main purpose' was to get people 'to find out more about the issue'. 'We fully appreciate that Carr would pay little attention.') Merthyr UCATT had a collecting box in their meeting room, but the money went to the official fund. Dave Roberts was 'engaged in the election campaign' and 'hoped that a change of government will help in the release of the lads'.

Harold Wilson reportedly had discussions with the TUC and took legal advice: 'we are going to change the law at the end of the day.'

On the 23rd, John Carpenter was billed to speak with Jim Clarke of the NUM at an Earlestown and St Helen's IS meeting.

On the 26th the *Star* announced that ten delegates had been elected to a UCATT-TGWU London Region Conference to discuss 'conspiracy' law. Labour MP Norman Atkinson would speak.

There's no plaster on the walls and there's rising damp

The *SW* printed on 26 February had an interview with Marlene Tomlinson. 'Ricky was going to do up the old cottage where we live. There's no plaster on the walls and there's rising damp.' 'I stuck it three months like that, carrying the babies to bed to save them from the wet floor.' She had stayed with the Carpenters and then her father. *SW* added: 'Last week Marlene and the kids sat in at the council offices, demanding they find her a house. At 5pm she got word that they had one waiting for her and she could pick up the keys.'

Graham Roberts appreciated the CDC's support. (The CDC 'does not blame anyone for pleading guilty'.) Carpenter told the CDC that he 'would not be associated with any statements' that Llywarch made against the CDC and 'At no time have I recruited for IS', or claimed to represent the CDC. He had received 'messages of support' from Ricky Tomlinson, via Marlene. 'Neither do I feel my action in gaining support and donations was anything but right.'

George Wright noted that some TGWU defendants had 'not yet received any financial assistance' and he needed 'clarification'.

The UCATT Northern Regional Committee discussed the trials and asked the EC to 'approach the TUC with a view of a considered determined approach to the government to end such infamous practices in the name of law, including the earliest possible release of those convicted'. Leaflets would be produced and briefing meetings held for stewards and branch delegates after the election, with invitations to the TGWU, GMWU and FTAT, to see 'how to end if possible or diminish the sentences' and 'the infamous implementation of out of date law'. Crook UCATT had Charlie Lowther's agreement to a 'Shrewsbury support meeting'. Members were urged to support the 'National Day of Action' and the parliamentary lobby. Lumpers were working at a local sewerage site.

The minutes of the CDC meeting on the 28th are not publicly available, but TGWU members Butcher, Roberts, Sear and Thomas received £14 and Bernard Williams could keep the £10 he held. Carpenter was thanked for 'taking the trouble to attend' and his 'cooperation in the matter we discussed was fully appreciated'—'we would like you to attend a meeting at Burnley Trades Council on March 12th to speak on our behalf', all expenses paid.

The Nationwide held £1,200. In February £1,100 had been paid into the TSB but over £1,500 withdrawn, leaving £9,160. Only the three men yet to be tried and the six in jail were getting wages.

A Shrewsbury Prison warder told Murray, Pierce and Brian Williams that they should try to get moved to an open prison. The probation officer told them that there was no chance, because of the 'affray' conviction, but the warder suggested that they ask for permission to petition to the Home Secretary. The governor agreed. On the 27th the senior warder asked them to cancel their petitions because they were being transferred to an open prison. They agreed to do so as they left. On the 28th Murray was woken before the bell. His bedding and possessions were thrown on the balcony and he wasn't allowed to shave. The three men were taken to Drake Hall open prison. The probation officer wore a Labour tie and was listening to the election results. He 'had heard on the grapevine that the trial was a carve up'.

The Tories had called an election on the issue of 'Who Governs Britain'. The Labour manifesto 'Social Contract' with the unions appealed to left reformists, yet Labour got 500,000 fewer votes than in 1970. They won 301 seats, but the Tories got 296 and the Liberals 14. The 44 CP candidates got 32,000 votes—barely half the number in 1970—and no seats. Sales of the *Star* had begun to fall.

Stan Brazil told the GMCC that since the election results gave 'no clear return of a Labour government' it was 'vitally important' that the Appeal Court lobby was a success. 'Anything less than a massive turnout will be interpreted by the politicians that the trade union movement are not concerned with the 'Shrewsbury 24' and 'the chances of repealing the 1875 Conspiracy Act will diminish.' Merseyside Joint Construction Unions booked a train.

Warren and Tomlinson asked to be transferred to an open prison and be classified as political prisoners. Both requests were refused, so they went on hunger strike and asked to see the Board of Visitors. The governor told the Board that 'maybe' the two men would get a transfer and then moved them to single cells.

There is no category of 'political prisoner' in this country

On 1 March Arthur Murray appealed against his sentence.

On the 4th the *Star* reported that Warren and Tomlinson were taking only tea and looked pale and worn. They had been locked up on Friday nights and not allowed out until Monday. They were allowed half an hour's exercise and the food was 'atrocious'. That day the Tories and Liberals failed to do a deal and Wilson became Prime Minister. The UCATT Distress Fund sent £100 for Murray. (His wages were cut by £100.) Tomlinson began writing poetry.

On the 5th the Court of Appeal judges allowed McKinsie Jones, Tomlinson and Warren's appeals against conviction on 'affray', because the offence 'continued only so long as the essential ingredients of fighting or showing of force' continued, and 'when it terminated the offence ceased'. Mais had been responsible for 'an error in the law'. The Court upheld Jones's 'unlawful assembly' conviction, refused all six men's appeals against sentence, fixed no date for Warren and Tomlinson's appeals against conviction and refused bail. O'Shea, Carpenter and Llywarch would apply for leave to appeal to the House of Lords. O'Shea told *SW*: 'This is a disgrace. The decisions were all cut and dried before anyone came into court.' There was a conspiracy—'between police, employers and the courts'. 'If the Labour government was 'worth a pinch of salt then they will repeal the conspiracy laws and free the pickets'.

The Drake Hall librarian refused to let Murray and Williams pick up their copies of the *Star* from the library. They complained to the deputy governor. He laughed, walked away and had the papers put with the personal property that they could recover only on release. They complained again, presumably to the governor, and were allowed to pick up the papers at the gate. They had to hand the old one in first and promise not to show it to other prisoners, but that promise wasn't kept. Days later Murray was charged with abusing a warder and put in the 'Block'. The Deputy Governor wouldn't let him call witnesses and cut his earnings by £1.

Warren and Tomlinson had been taken back to Stafford Prison, but they got their copies of the *Star* on the day of publication.

On the 6th Ken Barlow was a guest at the CDC. The minutes are not publicly available. Next day John Carpenter was 'very pleased' to speak at Burnley and 'go anywhere and do anything to help'.

The *Star* quoted Len Murray. TUC General Council members had spoken of the 'very severe sentences' and would express 'concern' to the new Labour Home Secretary, Roy Jenkins, but they would not call for the six men's release.

On the 8th the *Star* reported that eighty stewards at a Glasgow Trades Council conference had called on Jenkins to move Tomlinson and Warren nearer home. Barry Docherty criticised the UCATT Scottish Regional Committee for 'placing obstacles in the path'. George Smith would speak at the UCATT-TGWU conference.

The AUEW's John Tocher told '*all trade union officials concerned*' in Manchester that a meeting about the 'Shrewsbury 24' had been arranged at the request of UCATT and the TGWU, with 'a view to obtaining the release of the imprisoned members'.

TASS No 16 Divisional Council was 'a little concerned' at the CDC's 'apparent reluctance to issue a balance sheet' and would send future collections to the 'Shrewsbury 24—Coventry Action Committee'. In a letter sent to Regan's address, Elsa Warren was invited to speak to London TASS members. After 'some difficulty' getting her home address, King's Cross ASTMS sent her £2 a month. Alex Weir reported that 180 people came to the Blackpool concert: 'The Trades Club hasn't had a night like it for years.' Carpenter spoke and 'we got the message over to a much larger section of the local trades unionists than we have ever managed previously'. The singers included a Labour agent, a Labour councillor who was a UCATT branch Chairman and the wife of the CP Chairman. They raised £90. UCATT and AUEW branches had passed resolutions calling for 'Free the Six'. Weir had offered a speaker to eighty union branches and ordered 150 'Support Shrewsbury 24' pens.

The CDC told George Wright that Jim Shepherd would reply about payments to TGWU members. If Wright had difficulty contacting him, they would be happy to pass on a message.

SW's 'Make Labour Free the Jailed Pickets' argued that now was the time to press for the repeal of the conspiracy laws and the release of the six men. Llywarch was to speak at an IS meeting in Bolton on the 21st and in Glasgow on the 23rd. (*SW* sold 30,000 copies.)

The *Star* reported that the Labour government proposed 'to eliminate the abuses arising from the "lump".' SOGAT's Scottish Group Council had called for the release of the six men and the repeal of the conspiracy laws. 500 delegates would attend the London UCATT-TGWU conference, including all regional officials, 'Every major union district committee and trades council' and every NUM Area. Elsa Warren would speak. She and the children had moved three times in eighteen months and were in 'a semi-derelict cottage'.

The CDC agreed to book a coach to catch the Liverpool train on 20 March. (Barry Scragg asked that 'TU organised coach services be given first opportunity for future transport'.) Elsa Warren and Pete Kavanagh would go to the London NUJ Book Branch dance. Dennis Dugen had 'covered all the expenses to date' for the *Charter*: 'you will have to find out where this cheque should now be paid in to.' Ken Barlow and Lol Irwin (a UCATT Midland Regional official and Labour Party member) were guests and received a 'bulk order' for lapel badges. An article 'asking that no demonstrations be held outside any of the prisons' and an advertisement for the lobby would go in the *Star*. *Emergency Bulletin No 14* stressed that '£15,000 is still needed to carry on the fight and to see that none of the families concerned suffer any hardship'.

The Crook UCATT meeting attracted forty, including some from the Crook Woodworkers, Barnard Castle and Billingham branches. CPers Charlie Lowther and Norman Temple of the AUEW spoke.

Hackney Teachers' Association heard Margaret Llywarch speak and 'decided almost unanimously to "adopt" a family'. Could the CDC advise them? (The CDC and 'all the wives concerned' were against it: 'Having the money in one fund… helps to finance the campaign for the release of the lads' and pay 'for bulletins, speakers travelling the country and legal costs'.)

The CDC told Peter Moroney: 'I believe Bro W Jones has explained to you the importance of the monies coming direct to the fund and I am glad to hear you agree.' Bolton UCATT wanted someone to speak with an NUM member. They got 'Bill & John'.

Mary Abbott, Secretary of Rossendale Textile Workers' Union and a leading CPer, asked the TUC Women's Conference for a Defence Fund collection. Marie Patterson of the TGWU ruled that it 'would have to be taken outside the hall, because of TUC policy' but CP and Scarborough Trades Council delegates collected £23.

The Oxford and Ruskin Defence Committees' joint leaflet advertised free seats on a coach to London on the 20th. Car stickers and lapel badges were being printed. Dave Jackson asked for a speaker on 1 May, since 'most of the people in this area have seen me more than once'? (The CDC was 'sorry you have not been receiving copies of all the minutes but we have had trouble getting them photostated'.)

On the 16th the *Star* reported that Glasgow Trades Council had reserved a few places on a sleeper to London for the 20th. Delegates had been elected on Manchester sites and factories and engineering unions were giving support, but there were spare seats on the UCATT train. UCATT stewards from South Yorkshire and 150 miners representing every Welsh lodge would be there. The *Charter* Editorial Board had invited London, Birmingham, Manchester and Merseyside Areas to 'form a conference committee'.

The *Star* later reported that only half of those with credentials attended the UCATT-TGWU London conference on the 16th. Pete Kavanagh was in the chair. Eddie Marsden acknowledged that 'only mass action could win freedom for the Shrewsbury Six'. The NUM's Jack Collins agreed. 'While these lads are in jail, we are all in jail.' Les Wood, UCATT Assistant General Secretary, argued that the EC couldn't act because the solicitor 'advised there was no provision to do so in the union's constitution'. (Barry Scragg later reported continuous booing.) Alan Tattam stressed that the 'way to win justice for all building workers was through the elimination of "the lump".' Elsa Warren called on union ECs to take up the cause.

SW reported 'plenty of rhetoric' from Tribunite Norman Atkinson, but he had 'declined to give any commitment as to what the new Labour government would do about releasing the jailed men and repealing the anti-picketing laws'. On the platform, only Collins 'attacked the shameful role' of the UCATT EC. Delegates gave 'maximum support' to the parliamentary lobby and 'called again' on the TUC 'to take up the struggle'. Llywarch would speak at a Buxton IS meeting on the 24th.

John Carpenter drove Marlene Tomlinson to visit Ricky, who noted that she was 'a bit put out' over the hunger strike, but didn't try to talk him out of it. Carpenter was speaking 'all over the country' and would try to sort out her house.

On the 18th Labour MPs sent printed postcards to the CDC, acknowledging 'receipt of your communication'. Syd Bidwell replied: 'I support your demand for the release of the Shrewsbury Six.' John Prescott wrote: 'I fully support your cause but will be at another meeting. Sorry.'

Next day the *Star* reported that 'representatives of over 20,000 Rolls Royce aircraft workers' had called for a pardon for the six men and Sheffield engineering stewards had called for their release.

Dai Francis told the CDC that South Wales NUM EC and lodge delegations would be in London on the 20th and asked for 'a chat'.

The CDC heard that some of the 24 had had cheques from the TGWU. They would be asked to hand them over. Volunteers were needed to bring the Warrens' house 'into a decent condition'. Marlene Tomlinson 'had had to move to a council house'. The CDC would deal with 'any problem regarding excessive rent'. Every bulletin would be reprinted. A cheque had gone to the new Charter National Secretary. A group was invited upstairs to show a film.

The Home Office told Warren and Tomlinson: 'There is no category of "political prisoner" in this country.'

On the 20th Barry Jones MP told the CDC that he would 'be available in the Commons tho[ugh] I've got a debate later'. Dennis Skinner wrote: 'You have my support. Good luck.'

The *Star* reported that the GMCC train brought delegates from AUEW Manchester and Ashton District Committees and Gardner's, GEC and Shell Carrington. Dai Francis, Ken Barlow, Barry Scragg, Simon Fraser and Bert Smith addressed 2,000 people at Tower Hill and demanded the immediate release of the six men. A Merseyside contingent of 400 marched from Euston. 3,000, including hundreds of building workers and over 250 Welsh miners, lobbied parliament. Elsa Warren, four of her children, Marlene Tomlinson, McKinsie Jones's parents, John and Rita Carpenter, O'Shea and Llywarch were present. In the Commons there were sharp words for Tribunite MPs. Norman Atkinson 'had to be careful of interfering with the men's right of appeal'. The lobby asked Warren to discontinue his hunger strike: 'We are confident we will be able to obtain your release.'

On the 22nd the Court of Appeal rejected McKinsie Jones's application to appeal his 'unlawful assembly' conviction to the Lords, since 'no point of law of general public importance was involved'. O'Shea, Carpenter and Llywarch withdrew their applications, but Warren and Tomlinson's were left on file, pending appeals against 'conspiracy' convictions. Their appeals against sentence would be considered later. They came off the hunger strike.

The third Shrewsbury trial

Late in February the last nine defendants were due at Shrewsbury Crown Court, but William Hooson understood that his charges had been dropped and Edward Williams, John Seaburg and Terry Renshaw would be tried later.

Kevin Butcher, Graham Roberts, Peter Sear, Bryn Thomas and Bernard Williams were told that if they pleaded guilty to 'unlawful assembly' all other charges 'will be dropped'. They pleaded guilty. Butcher was told: 'the mere fact that you are of a big build could constitute an affray'. He pleaded guilty to 'threatening behaviour'.

The *Chronicle*'s 'Flying pickets: five men dealt with' described defence counsels' speeches in mitigation. Butcher 'never took part in any assembly, but remained consistently with a friend.' There was no evidence against Roberts apart from 'his own admission'. Sear 'engaged in peaceful picketing and thought the visit to Shrewsbury would also be peaceful'. Thomas was 'involved in youth work'. Bernard Williams was 'a man of previous good character, and lived with his widowed mother'. Judge Chetwynd-Talbot said that 'the conduct seen on the sites must be discouraged by the court'. He gave Butcher three months, suspended for a year, and the other four six months, suspended for two years.

Late in March, Terry Renshaw, John Seaburg and Edward Williams were on trial at Shrewsbury. Renshaw spent the first day in an armchair with a broken leg, but was excused until he gave evidence. They had pleaded not guilty to 'unlawful assembly' and 'affray'. *Bulletin No 14* noted that a defendant was told that if he didn't plead guilty to 'unlawful assembly' he would 'definitely receive a prison sentence'. He refused: 'Another two charges were added.'

Drake alleged that 'a minority' 'put on a display of violence and terror' at Shrewsbury sites on 6 September 1972 and repeated it at Brookside 'with renewed force and vigour'. A Kingswood lumper was hit on the shoulder by a clod of earth and saw windows, drainpipes and machinery damaged, but most pickets were peaceful. Seaburg testified that he wanted to withdraw his 'statement', because the police altered it, but a detective had told him that it was 'out of his hands'. (*SW* noted that Crown lawyers had been 'making much' of his alleged admission 'that he threw a lump of dirt'.)

The *Chronicle*'s 'Court Told of an "Unruly Mob" of Pickets', quoted Sergeant Price on why he hadn't intervened at Brookside: 'Not with the numbers we were in. I was scared that they would turn on us', though most pickets were 'peaceful and inoffensive'.

Renshaw, the Chairman of Flint UCATT, testified that he and other official pickets had asked the Brookside manager's permission to call a meeting. He refused. After a brick smashed a window, Renshaw apologised and explained that the men were heated after weeks on strike and a long day's picketing. The *Post* reported:

'We just turned and walked off with bricks showering round us', said Renshaw, adding that he turned other pickets away.

Mr Drake: 'It must have been a frightening experience to get showered with bricks, entirely unprovoked, by the workers.'

Renshaw: 'It was not very nice.'

Mr Drake: 'The Shrewsbury workers ought to be on trial here, not you?'

Renshaw: 'I think they should be, yes.'

Renshaw added that much of the evidence was 'a lot of rubbish' and 'grossly distorted'. He said that he had listened to more lies in the court than he had previously heard in a lifetime.

The judge directed the jury to find Renshaw not guilty on one charge of 'unlawful assembly' and two charges of 'affray', but they found him guilty on a third 'affray' charge. Williams was not guilty of 'affray', but guilty of 'unlawful assembly'. Seaburg was guilty of 'affray' and 'unlawful assembly'. The Crown offered no evidence against Hooson and the judge discharged him.

On 22 March the judge called the Brookside incidents 'deplorable'. 'A lot of law-abiding citizens were gravely terrorised.' He sentenced Seaburg to four and six months in prison, to run concurrently and gave Williams and Renshaw four months, all suspended for two years. The 'intimidation' and 'criminal damage' charges remained on file. 22 of the 24 now had criminal records.

Seaburg and Williams received £50 from the TGWU. Their Defence Fund wages weren't paid for the first week and were cut to £20 for the second, but Renshaw was paid even when he wasn't in court. Jeff Douglas told Warren that Renshaw 'wanted to make a speech from the dock but they would not let him, he was sick'.

These men should receive the queen's pardon

Late in March, Marlene Tomlinson thanked the CDC for the 'Holiday' cheque. She had told Barry Scragg that she wanted to know what was going on, so why wasn't she told about the

Stafford Prison demonstration? Carpenter would 'act for' her at the CDC.

The London Federation of Trades Councils asked for the addresses of the six men. (The CDC replied: 'Some of the families are living in temporary accommodation' and 'one family has moved address', but 'do not hesitate to write care of the above address.')

Labour MP Syd Tierney was pleased to have met Scragg. 'I hope the present government will concern itself with the 1875 Act.'

Scottish Labour MPs had been 'very widely approached' by the movement on the question of 'the savage sentences imposed on the "Shrewsbury Five [sic]".' They urged Roy Jenkins to transfer those in closed prisons to open prisons near their homes 'on humanitarian grounds', until their sentences were reviewed. It was 'generally felt that these men should receive the queen's pardon'.

SW believed that most Labour MPs' lukewarm responses showed that the minority government wouldn't free the six men or change the law. Llywarch and Foot would speak at Chelmsford. SW also reported that the Home Office 'take the view that there should be an amendment of the law to allow peaceful picketing, which permits vehicles to stop but does not include intimidation or violence'.

UCATT's Northern Regional Committee discussed the upcoming meeting on Shrewsbury, which was to be addressed by UCATT's solicitor, Owen Parsons. They agreed to ask the Northern Group of Labour MPs for 'their assistance in having the law in relation to picketing amended'. A new Regional Council member, Jim French, was to second a motion at UCATT Conference.

Crook UCATT 'expressed dissatisfaction' at the EC reply to their protests and their 'entrenched and negative attitude' and read a CDC circular. They would ask three Labour MPs—Ernest Armstrong, Tom Urwin (a former AUBTW official and now MP for Houghton-le-Spring) and Eric Heffer—to seek a Royal Commission, a Parliamentary Departmental Committee of Investigation or a National Tribunal of Inquiry.

The CDC heard that a collection from a Monks site was going to one of the six men's wives. Scragg would 'make enquiries'. Members of the 24 were allowed into the meeting. Bill Jones reported that Warren was 'in pretty good condition', but wanted books for himself and Tomlinson and reports on CDC activities. Jeff Douglas would write 'regularly to the six lads' and send them a £1 postal order. Tomlinson's biggest concern was his house. A vote about a separate fund was 'not carried', but Carpenter 'would try to raise money for repairs through contacts he had made'. Bill Jones asked everyone to work for a large attendance at the Liverpool Charter Conference on 27 April. Those involved in the last trial would be 'treated the same as all the others had been'. (£300 was withdrawn from the TSB account, but Hooson's name was queried.)

The TGWU's Jim Griffiths told the CDC that the TUC was approaching the Home Secretary, so 'there is a need for a discussion to take place' to discuss 'the future use of funds collected to help the members involved'. (It took weeks to agree a date.) The CDC assured a supporter: 'Not one of the 24 lads or their families have suffered any financial hardship.' 'The wives of the six lads in prison are being looked after in the best possible way.'

Warren heard that the CDC was 'as active as ever'. Supportive letters were coming in daily and Carpenter went to meetings 'where two speakers are needed'. UCATT wasn't giving support, but they hoped to change that at the June Conference. Ken Barlow, Pete Carter and Lol Irwin had been guests at the CDC on 'a number of occasions' and were 'doing a good job'.

Warren and Tomlinson discovered fraud by 'screws'—prison officers—at Stafford and were transferred to Sudbury open prison.

In March eleven donations accounted for £1,815 of the £2,230 that went into the Defence Fund. London NUJ Book Branch sent £49, Renfrew Babcock's and Wilcox AUEW £50, Harlow Trades Council £90, North London Polytechnic Students' Union and University of Lancaster students £100, Kirkby IPD £136, South Wales NUM £150, EETPU London Press Branch £140, Liverpool Teaching Hospital site £200, Ince Power Station site £400 and the ASTMS EC £500. Over £1,320 went out, leaving almost £10,000.

CHAPTER 16

It's action, not words, that counts

Sympathy won't get my brothers out of jail

The IS-backed Rank & File Organising Committee Conference in Birmingham on 30 March 1974 attracted 600 credential applications from 318 union bodies, including 249 branches and forty combine and shop stewards' committees. 500 delegates from 270 union bodies turned up and two-thirds were manual workers, including 51 engineers (mainly the car industry and including two district committees), 37 from transport, 32 from teaching, 22 from NALGO, twenty from ASTMS, sixteen from printers, fourteen from public employees, seven from construction, five from the NUM and nineteen from trades councils. Many were from groups around IS's rank and file papers and half weren't IS members. Yet, all thirteen members of the London-based Organising Committee were in IS and only four of the seven manual workers attended consistently. *Flashlight*, *The Dockworker* and the *Charter* weren't represented.

Dave Adshead told delegates that officials were blocking the formation of a rank and file committee in Birmingham, for fear of embarrassing the Labour Party. 'Of course we must work in the official union structure, but we have also got to organise mass pressure to keep full-time officials in line.' Terry Horan and Frank Drain reported that Edinburgh union officials were 'completely out of touch'. There had been strikes, but 'no co-ordination', and 'a rank and file movement was so important'. Edward Short MP had told Eric Bright that Labour would repeal the 1875 Act, except for 'conspiracy'. John Llywarch 'castigated union leaders and Labour politicians for their refusal to fight'. 'Sympathy won't get my brothers out of jail. It's up to you, the rank and file, to force the issue. We have to organise for strike action. It's action, not words, that counts'. He a motion proposed supporting 'all moves' to win strikes:

Conference condemns the Labour government's failure to free the imprisoned Shrewsbury pickets and calls on the government to do so immediately. Conference believes that trade union pressure and militant action can free the Shrewsbury defendants. Conference therefore pledges to link up with all other bodies organising for the release of the pickets.

All delegates present pledge to campaign in their trade union bodies to invite the Shrewsbury defendants or representatives from the North Wales Defence Committee to speak on what has happened.

Conference empowers the organising committee to publicise as widely as possible in the trade union movement the need for collections, the 'adoption' of the families of the defendants by trade union and shopfloor bodies.

Conference instructs the organising committee to keep all delegating bodies informed of all developments in the case, and to work for the maximum support for industrial action, lobbies and other action inside the movement.

Next day the *Star* attacked the 'Trotskyist Rival' to the LCDTU.

SW stressed that the Labour government 'will almost certainly *not* free the Shrewsbury Six' and published Laurie Flynn's guide to the trials to help win difficult arguments. *The Building Worker* carried articles about Shrewsbury, UCATT and 'the fight ahead'. IS building workers would meet in Salford on the 20th.

The *Star* reported that Jenkins had told the TUC that it was 'constitutionally impossible for him to intervene'.

George Smith told Flint UCATT that the EC was 'pressing' the TUC to take up the sentences with Jenkins. Eric Hughes sent £100 for Terry Renshaw and £120 apiece for Margaret Murray, Rita McKinsie Jones and Elsa Warren. (They gave it to the Defence Fund.) Barry Jones MP told Glyn Davies: 'I cannot see signs of release', but 'we are pledged to repeal the Industrial Relations Bill and to end the "lump" and... *amend* the law on picketing'.

Over 200 delegates at the Wales TUC signed a petition calling on the Labour government to repeal the 1875 Act and 'secure the immediate release of the Six', including 43 names from the TGWU, 21 from the AUEW and TASS, twenty from the NUM, eleven from the GMWU and seven from UCATT, a few from other unions, three members of the Labour Party Young Socialists, one AUEW Divisional Organiser and Mick Costello of the *Star*. (Costello was born in 1936. He went to Manchester University, became President of the Students' Union and joined the CP in 1956.)

Next evening the CDC heard that Len Murray was one of 'the very few that didn't sign'. MPs were to ask Elwyn Jones, the Lord Chancellor, if he 'could possibly constitute an enquiry'. Barry Scragg thought that 'interest in the campaign was dying off'. Deeside Trades Council and Shotton Action Committee would decide what was to be done on May Day. The person passing money from a Monks site to one of the six men's wives would be told about CDC policy. They discussed closing the Defence Fund.

Glyn Davies was meant to be up at Mold Crown Court in July 1973, but got his case deferred to 4 April 1974. He pleaded not guilty to 'intimidation' and 'assault occasioning actual bodily harm'.

Kenneth Humphreys, the site agent at Greenfield sewerage plant, had told police that when he arrived on the site on 24 October 1972 two men said that they'd been given a start by steelfixing subbies. 'M Jones' was Des Warren, 'The Wrecker' in the *Sunday People*. Humphreys phoned the police. 'Warren' 'became aggressive' when they arrived and Humphreys 'realised' he had refused to start him the day before. 'Warren' and 'J Barton' gave the same Prestatyn address. They started work, while Humphreys went to check with the subbies. When all three returned, 'Warren' and 'Barton' left.

Next day the two men asked Humphreys to sack the lumpers and employ them 'direct'. He threatened to have them evicted. 'Warren' looked set to 'try the strong arm stuff', so Humphreys called the police. After they arrived, the two men asked to be paid for their work. Humphreys refused and escorted 'Warren' off site. 'Warren' said: 'I'll see you, your wife and family. Right.' That afternoon Humphreys saw 'about twenty' pickets and three, including Billy Hough and Terry Renshaw, came on the site.

'Warren' returned next day. Humphreys contacted UCATT official Albert Prest, who sent a message that the men should 'carry on working normally' because the picket was 'totally unofficial'. When Humphreys approached 'Warren', he said: 'Bugger off or I'll put your teeth down your throat.' On the 28th Humphreys saw 'approximately 20 men in a bunch' and 'pushed my way through'. 'Ginger' 'spat deliberately a number of times into my face uttering threats of further violence' and a half brick flew past his head 'from the direction of Warren and three other men'. Then the police arrived.

Two days later Detective Constable Roberts took statements from Greenfield lumpers. One claimed to have seen 'Warren' with a poster reading 'Kill the lumpers', but no scuffles or spitting. Another saw Humphreys pushing through 'between thirteen and twenty' men and identified 'Warren' from photographs. A third said that pickets had remained at the site entrance 'most of the week'. He had seen up to 'twenty or thirty' on site, but Humphreys was protected by his employees.

DC Roberts's undated statement said that on 21 November he and Detective Sergeant Griffith interviewed Glyn Davies at his home in Central Drive, Shotton. He had denied being at Greenfield and was cautioned. Next day Roberts took another statement from Humphreys, who claimed that Davies was 'Ginger'. Coincidentally, he had seen him in Central Drive the day before.

On each witness statement Davies had written 'Absolute' and on the claim about being cautioned he wrote 'LIES'.

In court Humphreys claimed that Davies 'put his shoulder into me and started bouncing me into five or six others' and then 'started to spit all over me'. Davies had asked workers to protest against the blacklist in a friendly way, and after Humphreys pushed him, he left.

Davies was found guilty of 'assault'. The judge told him he 'would have been going to prison without any question' if he had been guilty of 'intimidation', but spitting and jostling were out of character. He gave him a conditional discharge for two years and ordered him to pay £25 costs. (The Defence Fund paid the fine and two days' wages. The *Star* ignored the trial of the secretary of Deeside CP.)

What we have not achieved

On 8 April the *Star* announced that the Glasgow Defence Committee would lobby the Scottish TUC to support freeing the six pickets. A UCATT official, a TGWU official, the Trades Council Chairman and the Govan Labour MP (and one-time Trotskyist) Harry Selby urged that letters be written to Jenkins. There would be a Glasgow conference.

Next day the *Star* noted that Tribunite MPs were receiving a 'large number of protests' about the failure to free the 6 and had asked to meet UCATT and the TUC. The Governor of Stafford Prison asked Tomlinson if he wanted to go to an open prison. 130 people at a Chelmsford IS meeting heard Llywarch speak. 'Before I met these people, I was doing it on my own.' They should join IS.

SW advertised the UCATT Midland Region badge. Elsa Warren and Labour MP Audrey Wise would speak at the Stafford Prison lobby. A 'Free the Shrewsbury Six' Conference in Aylesham, sponsored by Southdown NUM, was open to trades councils, unions, political organisations and observers. Llywarch would speak at an IS meeting in Ashton-under-Lyne and there would be a lobby of parliament on May Day. The Sheffield TGWU District Secretary was blocking efforts to start a campaign in support of the jailed pickets.

On the 10th the *Star* reported that Stafford Trades Council had invited labour movement organisations to picket the prison.

Nottingham Trades Council wanted a CDC speaker. (They got Bill Jones.) Tribunite MPs lobbied Labour's Attorney General, Sam Silkin. No Labour MP, including their own, had replied to Crook UCATT. A Charter Conference circular was read out.

The CDC minutes are not publicly available. Dave Jackson received a copy to 'fill you in sufficiently for the time being'. He was trying to 'get delegated' to the Charter Conference and 'if I cannot get credentials could you make sure that somebody is there with some'. He needed expenses for the Iver meeting. (Someone wrote: 'PLASTER ABOUT THE SAME AMOUNT AS BEFORE.')

On the 12th Lord James decided that Arthur Murray's sentence was 'correct in principle and not too severe', in 'the light of the behaviour of others who were part of the assembly'. Warburton's acquittal on 'affray' didn't mean that Oliver or Whittell's evidence was unreliable in relation to Murray and the fact that Seaburg's sentence was different did not mean that that Murray's was wrong. (Murray, Pierce and Williams got to know that their applications for leave to appeal against sentence had been refused on the 20th.)

On the 13th the *Star* noted that the West of Scotland LCDTU would lobby MPs to demand the six men's release.

On the 16th Jenkins told Scottish MPs: 'It would not be proper of me to comment' or 'seek to intervene' while appeals were pending.

I have the power to recommend the exercise of the Royal Prerogative of Mercy to set aside a conviction or to remit part of the sentence, [but] it would be contrary to long-established practice for me to contemplate such interference unless there were some significant new facts or circumstances which the courts were able to consider; and as I understand it this is not the position in these cases.

McKinsie Jones was due for release in June and would 'probably remain' at Ranby. After Warren and Tomlinson's appeals were 'finally determined' he would consider a transfer to an open prison, though they might go 'further away from their homes'.

A lobby of various conferences

On 17 April Bob Williams told the CDC his concerns about the Stafford Prison lobby: 'If any trouble broke out, Warren would be blamed.' Enquiries would be made about £100 that Mike Pierce's wife had received from the TGWU. 400 badges had arrived and would sell at 5p. A CDC delegate would go to Glyn Davies's *Star* meeting. Bert Smith, a guest, argued that 'part of the future campaign would involve a lobby of various conferences'.

On the 23rd the *Star* advertised *Release the 6 Defend the 24*, which argued that the Labour government 'provides the basis for a reversal of "union bashing" policies'. It quoted the disowned *Viewpoint* article, the TGWU Building Group's Jim Shepherd, UCATT EC member (and CPer) Arthur Utting, Liverpool Trades Council's Simon Fraser and the Leader of West Midland Metropolitan Labour Party. It also offered a programme:

1 Hold meetings and plan action of support in every trade union branch and trades council.
2 Resolutions to your EC, Regional, District or Group Committee and local MP
3 Take up with your local Labour Party the question of the immediate release by the Labour government of the six jailed building workers.
4 Through your union and trades council demand that the TUC acts to campaign for the 24.
5 Send messages and letters of support to those in jail and their families.
6 Send donations to help the campaign and to assist the dependants.

The leaflet was 'Published by the North Wales Defence Committee, Colwyn Bay'. (The CP's Farleigh Press printed 25,000 copies.)

The Times noted that the TUC would not press the issue.

Only seven CDC members heard that the UCATT Fund held over £3,000, but there was no information from the TGWU. Bill Jones had put a May Day advertisement in the *Star*. A coach would go to the Liverpool demonstration. CDC members would go to the London lobby and 'every effort must be made to secure employment' for the four men due for release. *Emergency Bulletin No 15* noted that a 'full account of monies collected' would be published 'at the end of the campaign'. 'Please make every effort to send delegates' to the

LCDTU May Day parliamentary lobby, the UCATT and TGWU conferences and the Charter Conference.

Cambridge Defence Committee had 'long since collapsed in the face of almost complete apathy and disinterest' from the 'local trade union movement' and 'hostility & downright opposition' from some quarters. Alex Weir hoped that a few Blackpool delegates would go to the May Day lobby and there would be another Blackpool social. York Defence Committee suffered from a 'lack of background knowledge' and thanked Bob Williams for agreeing to speak on May Day. He could help them tackle Alex Lyon MP.

Dave Ayre attended an IS *Building Worker* meeting in Manchester. Crook UCATT heard that the EC had 'vetoed' Owen Parsons' speech to stewards on picketing law. Dave was elected as a delegate to the Charter Conference.

The Charter Conference organisers claimed 'over three hundred' delegates. Alan Abrahams was in the chair and Eddie Nash was elected as National Secretary. Eddie Loyden MP, Simon Fraser and Jim Shepherd spoke. Bert Smith had ten minutes on the collection, which took fifteen minutes. The Conference Resolution was debated for two hours. Lou Lewis took twenty minutes on the *Charter*. Bill Jones introduced a CDC statement that he had written with Barry Scragg. 'Without the Charter Groups we would never have been able to carry out the work we have done', but 'what we have not achieved' included failing to get the six men out of jail and to win full support from the UCATT EC. After 'a very good statement of intent' by the TGWU National Committee, other officials had shown a 'lack of support', and Labour MPs couldn't shift Jenkins. The CDC wanted May Day demonstrations to demand the release of the pickets and a 'massive lobby' of the UCATT Conference on 19 June. This and the discussion lasted forty minutes. Elsa Warren and Marlene Tomlinson urged delegates to keep on fighting.

Des Warren had written to Eddie Nash and wished him 'every success' with the Charter Conference. He made a 'few points which I feel strongly about'. 'Surely one of the Tories' main reasons for choosing the building industry must have been the weak, cowardly, treacherous anti-working class leadership that we're sad[d]led with'. He wanted a change of leadership and the constitution behind which it 'lurks committing acts of treachery with apparent impunity'. They used the constitution to 'thwart all attempts at progress and protect corrupt and incompetent officials', who should face regular elections and be subject to immediate recall. All settlements should be ratified by the members. The TUC called for 'wage restraint', but workers were 'sick' of them and of union leaders who 'grow fat on their regular monthly salaries plus expenses, drive around in their union provided car, get sun tanned on their frequent holidays and face retirement on their union pensions, all provided for by a membership that is continuously sold out and forced to accept a standard of living very much lower'. They were 'so insulated from the consequences of capitalism as suffered by the rank and file that they have come to accept it'. He put the blame for still being in prison on the UCATT EC, 'just as surely as if George Smith had the key to Stafford prison in his pocket'. (Nash told him there was no time to read his letter.)

Billy Regan told a supporter: 'Five of the committee members attend meetings all over the country to speak on the case and we also use a number of people we know personally.' He apologised to Dartford Trades Council for a month's delay: 'We are having to make a programme of speakers due to demand for May Day demonstrations etc.' He told Christopher Hitchens of the *New Statesman* and IS: 'We have always had ample speakers.'

Mary Abbott reported that two Birmingham UCATT members distributed *Release the 6* at the TWU Conference. Labour Foreign Secretary Jim Callaghan refused to meet a delegation and 'repeated in parrotlike fashion that he was opposed to violence being used when picketing'. (He had signed over frigates to the Chilean Junta that was responsible for 3,000 murders and disappearances.) She explained that the six men weren't in jail for violence and sent *Release the 6*: 'He had better come into the lobby on May 1st', or she 'would release his statement re violence which sounds hollow re Ireland.'

On the 30th UCATT's Northern Regional Committee asked the EC to discuss 'a national petition being organised with a view of supporting the maximum desirable change in the "picketing" section of any act as anticipated in the Queen's Speech' and press for the release of 'victims of the Shrewsbury trial'. They asked the Northern Group of MPs to 'support any legislation to restore reasonable but effective use of picketing'.

During April, Tilmanstone NUM and the London Defence Committee both sent the Defence Fund £100. Triumph Motors No 2 stewards sent £105 and Townson's site at Birkenhead raised £300. About £1,300 went into the TSB, but expenditure was around £2,200. The balance was £9,000. The Nationwide held £2,500.

In April a CP Political Committee draft report to the EC argued for 'undogmatic but firm and principled handling of the ultra-left, particularly the IS' This was 'of great importance' where they were 'part of a wider group of organisations in the mass movement'. 'In factories and in Labour movement rank and file activity we need to consider and apply in accordance with the circumstances the lessons of the *Builders' Charter Movement* and Shrewsbury 6 campaign'.

The Shrewsbury 3

Early in 1974 Des Warren's barrister John Platts-Mills and Jim Arnison of the *Star* were both writing books about the Shrewsbury trials. On 12 February Jeff Skelley of Lawrence & Wishart told the CDC that they were publishing Arnison's account. Would they buy 1,000 copies and pay on delivery for a 'substantial discount'? It was 'good, hard-hitting stuff', would 'do the campaign a power of good' and 'produce a substantial profit'. On the 18th Bert Ramelson told Des Warren that he had 'just read' a 'booklet on your trial' which 'I am sure will have a ready sale and big effect on the activists in the movement'. On 5 March the CDC asked for a copy for 'perusal'. What discount would there be on 500 and 1,000 copies? Skelley offered 40 percent off 1,000, or a 'bit less' on a smaller number. On the 27th Barry Scragg told the CDC that the 'draft' was 'very good'. The CDC would like Arnison to write about the second and third trials and by 3 April an 'amendment' had been made. The CDC confirmed its order. (Bill Jones had already plugged it in the *Charter*.) On 29 April the CP Merseyside Organisation Committee checked that Progressive Books had ordered 50 copies.

Bob Campbell reviewed *The Shrewsbury Three: Strikes, Pickets and 'Conspiracy'* in the *Star* on the 30 April. It had been written in March and 'concentrates on the trial of the first three [*sic*]'. The 'rank-and-file defence committees have toiled long and hard to raise the consciousness of the trades unions on this issue with only limited success. Any further dragging of feet by the official movement, by the building workers' unions, by the TUC, will be seen as outright betrayal of the imprisoned workers.' The 'combined strength of the working class' would 'secure the release of the Shrewsbury Six'.

The Shrewsbury Three was published on May Day and sold for 45p. Its cover showed the first six defendants and other members of the 24, but the caption noted only Warren, Tomlinson and O'Shea not Carpenter, Llywarch or McKinsie Jones.

Bert Ramelson's *Foreword* argued that the first Shrewsbury trial had 'probably been the most serious in its implications for the labour movement this century'. Warren and Tomlinson's 'spirit has not been broken'. Ramelson quoted Warren's 9 February letter.

The Flying Pickets

Arnison criticised the original Shotton defence committee's 'attitude'. '"We accept help from anybody" seemed reasonable enough until it was realised that some of the factions which became involved were more concerned to espouse instant revolution and engage in crazy ultra-left antics than with the urgent task of gaining support from the trade union movement at every level.' The Charter was 'unofficial' and there was 'always the danger that the rank and file body will begin to see itself as the alternative to the established trade union organisation', but that was 'a malformation usually brought into the movement by the lunatic left and especially that section consisting of people with little knowledge of the working class at first hand or even of work itself'. This 'dangerous trend showed itself in the Charter movement, but fortunately there was sufficient control in the hands of the experienced down-to-earth shop stewards and rank and file workers to prevent it being disrupted by the super-lefts'. When the unions 'did not officially become involved' with the CDC campaign it 'became a matter of urgency to bring the campaign within the orbit of the broad labour movement', and, 'thanks to Liverpool Trades Council', this was achieved. 'Apart from Warren and Tomlinson, none of the twenty-four arrested men appeared to have had any real experience of the trade union movement.' Llywarch had no experience 'until the strike'. Arnison claimed 'a close personal relationship with the defendants' at the first trial and especially Warren and Tomlinson, who stayed at the Warwick Arms, because 'it was too far to travel each day.'

Tomlinson had been a steward for a fortnight before 1972. Carpenter, Jones and Llywarch became stewards before he did. O'Shea had been blacklisted. Murray had been a steward for years and Renshaw was Flint UCATT Chairman. Tomlinson lived near Wrexham. Carpenter went back each day. Warren's family was at Henllan. So was O'Shea's, but McKinsie Jones left Flint at 6.00am, picked O'Shea up and drove to Shrewsbury and back every day.

Arnison's two-paragraph '*Postscript*' mentioned that Murray, Pierce and Brian Williams 'steadfastly refused' a deal at the second trial and Renshaw, Seaburg and Edward Williams did so at the third. He didn't mention Llywarch's crucial refusal of a deal, the names of twelve of the twenty four or those of the eight tried elsewhere—not even his comrade, Glyn Davies. If it was about pickets who went to prison, why wasn't it *The Shrewsbury 6*? If it was about being tried at Shrewsbury, why not *The Shrewsbury 24*? And if it was about all those tried for picketing, why not *The North Wales 32*?

It's action, not words, that counts

Ramelson had approved the booklet by 18 February, after the jailings at the second trial. Arnison concluded that 'judge-made anti-trade union laws must be revoked, and the laws of Conspiracy and Unlawful Assembly be removed from application to industrial relations and trade union activity'. By May Day, shuffling political responsibility onto the TUC and the Labour Party had been CP policy for almost two and a half months.

Just keep your nose clean and leave it to us

On May Day the CDC was cancelled due to 'pressure of work', but the treasurer paid £270 for 1,000 copies of *The Shrewsbury Three*. Flint UCATT told the EC that it was 'unbelievable' that they could be 'so naïve' as to believe that the trials weren't an attack on the right to picket. Their Distress Fund 'conscience money' came 'twelve months too late'. The EC must meet a delegation from local branches, including people who picketed on 6 September 1972 and some who had been tried, as soon as possible. (The EC would consider the letter and forward the result 'in due course'.)

Next day York Trades Council reported that Bob Williams had 'inspired' them to 'redouble their efforts' and asked for five copies of *The Shrewsbury Three*. The CP Merseyside Area wanted Progressive Books to produce a circular about the booklet for union branches and district committees. Blackpool supporters had distributed *Release the 6* to 250 delegates at the TASS conference and 'IS lads' had arranged for them to collect £35.

Murray and Pierce were advised that their appeals were preventing Labour MPs from acting. On the 7th the *Star* reported that they wouldn't appeal. The CP North Wales Area urged the Wales TUC to 'honour its promise to give urgent practical consideration to the task of freeing the Six and securing the repeal of the 1875 Act'. 'Everything possible' should be done to sell 'thousands' of copies of *The Shrewsbury Three*.

Next day Crook UCATT heard Eric Heffer MP's correspondence with the Home Office and supported the Trades Council motion against 'Lump Labour and Private Employment Agencies' for the Divisional Labour Party Conference. Dave Ayre and Bill Kerriss reported on the Charter Conference. The branch sent concerns about harassment in Stafford Prison to the Home Office.

The CDC heard that Ken Barlow needed £100 for badges. The jailed pickets would get minutes and a £1 postal order each week and all 24 a free copy of *The Shrewsbury Three*. CDC members had taken one each. John Carpenter had thirty for sale and members of the 24 had taken twenty one. Audrey Wise would be asked to sell copies to Labour MPs.

In the next few days Burnley Trades Council needed a speaker. (The CDC wanted a week's notice and plugged *The Shrewsbury Three*.) Stan Thorne MP felt it would 'need massive pressure from the rank and file' to repeal the 'conspiracy' laws and release the 'Shrewsbury lads'. (The CDC asked if he and 'any of your colleagues' would meet 'three people off this committee'.) Bert Smith took Ricky Tomlinson a copy of *The Shrewsbury Three*.

The CP's Farleigh Press needed £209 for printing *Release the 6*. Lou Lewis sent £25 from the EETPU for 5,000 copies and the Joint Sites Committee would pay for 5,000. The posters were free, but could £11.40 go to the *Star* for adverts? He sent a letter to Elsa Warren that had reached him after it had 'been round the houses'.

Dave Roberts was now Chairman of Merthyr UCATT. They were hoping to set up a defence committee and 'wish to work in conjunction with your committee'. Billy Regan replied that 'most other committees' consisted of 'any interested trade unionist'. 'They organise meetings in their areas' and 'keep up the pressure' on MPs. The *Star* had 'always been most helpful'. The badges went 'like hot cakes' and they also had copies of *The Shrewsbury Three*.

The *Star* noted that, 'stimulated' by *The Shrewsbury Three*, the Lancashire Association of Trades Council was demanding that the North West Regional Association convene a meeting of Labour MPs to get the pickets out of jail. Arthur Davidson, Labour MP for Accrington, acknowledged that 'concern did exist' about 'the long delay before proceedings were brought', the 'delay in bringing the trials at Shrewsbury' and the 'protests of members of the jury' at the first trial. He would write to Roy Jenkins. So would Charles Morris, a Manchester Labour MP. The TASS EC was pressing Jenkins to act, since the case was not now 'sub judice'. The CP Merseyside Area wanted branch and site sales of *The Shrewsbury Three*.

On the 15th the CP Political Committee's *Weekly Letter* noted a 'very good response' to *The Shrewsbury Three*. The 3,000 copies sold 'will help to give a much needed lift to the campaign'. The Wales TUC was to press the 'British TUC' to 'take action to secure the release of the six pickets'.

The CDC minutes are not publicly available, but the treasurer opened a 'B[ui]lding fund' TSB account with £1,000 from the Defence Fund and there are notes about building materials.

Regan told Blackpool Trades Council that they could have Bill Jones to speak and was happy to oblige Manchester & Salford Trades Council. (The secretary had resigned and the president, a leading CPer, hoped to invite a speaker in 'early autumn'.)

Dave Jackson 'went down very well' at a Bristol meeting, which called on the ASTMS EC to pressurise union-sponsored MPs and voted £50 to the Defence Fund. CPer Mary Abbott got 'thunderous applause' at the Annual Conference of Trades Councils. If a Tory government 'could produce an Official Solicitor to get the dockers out of jail then surely this Labour government could do something to get these lads out'. CPer Beryl Huffingly, Secretary of Leeds Trades Council and the Yorkshire Association of Trades Councils, successfully moved a resolution against police harassment of Colchester supporters. Jenkins had 'got to get his finger out'.

The *Star* noted that forty 'representatives' at a Cardiff conference had set up a 'Campaign Committee' to organise for the UCATT Conference lobby in June. The Shrewsbury issue would also be raised 'in a big way' at the Labour Party Conference in September.

Bill Jones visited Des Warren, who asked 'what the plan was':

> He looked at me blankly, not understanding what I meant. Well, I told him, there is the mobilising of the movement outside for our release, and what part do we play here? How do we fit in? What's the tactics? He asked again what I meant. Thinking to shake him I said: 'What do you want us to do? Capture the governor or what?' He was horrified. 'Jesus Christ! Don't do anything like that. All you've got to do is just keep your nose clean and leave it to us.'

Warren asked to see the CDC minutes, but they didn't arrive.

Ultra-Leftism in Britain

By March 1974 IS had 3,310 members, of whom 1,155 were manual workers and 550 were 'non-professional' white collar workers. Another 750 workers had signed membership forms in the past year but hadn't been integrated into the organisation. 56 factory branches had been established and 38 continued to function with 300 members. Roger Protz argued that *SW* had to maintain its focus on 'advanced workers', but the EC wanted to shift its orientation. During April the National Committee removed Protz and Jim Higgins from *SW*'s Editorial Board and installed Paul Foot as Editor.

The next *SW* front-page headline was '140 Years of Law and Order'. Under 'FREE THE SIX!' were the names of the six agricultural labourers transported in 1834, allegedly for swearing an illegal oath. 'THEIR REAL CRIME' was to organise a farm workers' union in Tolpuddle. A second list named the Shrewsbury 6. 'THEIR REAL CRIME' was to organise a building workers' union in North Wales. Inside, Neil Davies of UCATT asked about the recent Charter Conference: 'Why all the excitement?' There were 200 delegates and the discussion about why the *Charter* hadn't appeared 'any too regularly' was full of 'excuses'. The organisation 'hasn't functioned for over a year' and was 'clearly going to need a lot of effort to get it back on its feet'. The lump was 'bigger than ever and the basic rate is one of the lowest in any industry'. There was a 'great lack of concrete discussion' about how to get the pickets out of jail. John Llywarch would speak at Barnsley and Brighton.

In the next *SW* Llywarch told 'How I sacked Sir Arthur Irvine'. He was to speak on '*Socialist Worker* and the struggle for socialism' at a Wigan IS meeting. *SW* advertised the meeting again on the 15th, but that was the last time that he was billed as an IS public speaker.

The CP's *Ultra-Leftism in Britain* acknowledged that the number of people involved 'must be a considerable one'. Three organisations 'with *Trotskyist* origins'—the Workers' Revolutionary Party, IS and IMG—were 'the main organisations in terms of influence and membership'. The WRP had 1,000 to 2,000 former SLL members, but a 'very limited base in industry'. IS membership was 2,600—not the claimed 3,500—because of 'faction fights and expulsions', though *SW* was now 'a much more effective and well produced paper'. They accepted Foot's claim that the January and February print runs averaged 40,000, that the election week issue's was 52,000 and that 70 percent were sold, including a 'fair proportion' in industry. IS presented problems for the CP in white collar unions and some trades councils and 'could conceivably become a problem in some of the main unions if we are not responding to developments as we should'. IS had a 'base' and EC members in the NUT, NALGO, ASTMS and the CPSA. *Rank and File*, *Casecon* (for social workers) and *NALGO Action News* had 'quite a wide circulation and influence'.

During May, after what Ian Birchall recalls was 'an extremely stormy two-day meeting' of the IS National Committee, the EC still hoped to 'reconcile the different currents in the organisation' and postponed the conference until September.

On 18 May Greenwich Trades Council and the South East London Defence Committee's *Bulletin No 1* listed support from Lewisham &

Deptford Trades Council and Southwark Trades Council for a 'representative c[ommit]tee based on local trades unions'. No affiliation fee was required and they had a plan:

A Publicity and propaganda in the area with leafleting sessions, etc, aiming to get more people involved, and information on to the shop floor.

B We hope that shop steward committees will be able to arrange factory meetings for which we can supply speakers. Public meetings will also be arranged.

C Fund raising by means of factory collections, etc—funds both for our jailed brothers' dependants and for the campaign.

D We aim to build links with other London Committees, and also to work closely with the official national body (the N Wales Defence Committee).

E It was felt at the meeting the first vital step in our campaign is to mobilise massive support from this area for the *delegate* Conference of the Labour Movement called by *Clay Cross Labour Party* at Westminster Central Hall on June 8th...

This Conference will discuss 'the whole question of Conference decisions and policies of the Labour government', including Shrewsbury, and a large turnout for it will be crucial in extending the campaign through the unions and Labour Parties, thereby putting pressure on our national leaders.

They wanted 'information, lists of speakers, planned activities, etc'. (The CDC had 'a number of very able speakers in your area'.)

Some of the 24 had received nothing

On 22 May John Carpenter told the CDC about a 'fund to support the families of the jailed lads'. Barry Scragg 'made it clear that the committee did not go along with the idea' since it was 'obviously politically motivated'. TGWU officials 'Bro Griffiths' and 'Bro Morris' were invited into the meeting. The demand for *The Shrewsbury Three* was 'very good' and 'close on 100' had been sold at a branch secretaries' meeting in Liverpool. More badges would arrive soon. Speakers were allocated for Central Hall, Westminster (Barry Scragg, Charlie Jones and Elsa Warren), Shipley (Bob Williams), Stockport (Bill Jones) and Kirkby (Bert Smith). The UCATT fund held £2,834.

Defence Fund 'grants' were 'still being made and an extra grant would be given to cover holidays and rehabilitation'. The Wales TUC petition had been sent to Harold Wilson, Jack Jones and George Smith. Scragg explained that the Wrexham meeting would be 'a kind of local branch' of the LCDTU and was 'the first of many', while the Cardiff LCDTU meeting 'would assist in getting support' for the UCATT Conference lobby.

Griffiths acknowledged that the CDC's efforts 'were recognised all over the country', but 'reports had reached him that some of the 24 had received nothing'. The three funds caused 'a great amount of confusion' and the campaign was 'at a critical stage'. The CDC could have details of the TGWU fund if they gave details of theirs. Morris added: 'If [Michael] Foot gets his way the [1875] Act will be repealed' and the TGWU would 'put on pressure until it is'. Jim Shepherd, a guest, had suggested months ago 'that the three parties get together'. 'All the confusion had arisen because the officials had once again stepped in too late'. Bill Jones noted that the CDC had been 'hard at it for 18 months' and its only mistake was 'being too nice' to UCATT and the TGWU. If everything had been left to them, 'everyone would have been in a hell of a state now'. UCATT had 'continuously ducked, dodged and weaved'. He hoped that Griffiths and Morris would 'get help from the official side and if possible arrange a meeting with Jack Jones'. Griffiths claimed that they had called in their solicitors as soon as they knew that the men were being charged and if Jones repeated what he had just said in public 'it would be a disservice to the TU movement'. Mike Williams pointed out that the Shotton JCSSC had hired the 24's solicitors. Charlie Jones noted there was money left in the old Chester Action Committee strike fund. Griffiths stressed that some of the 24 had joined the TGWU after the strike and a distinction had been made between those released and those in prison. Billy Regan felt that there was 'no comparison' between the amounts going to UCATT and TGWU members, but the Defence Fund 'had seen everyone ended up equal'. Scragg concluded that 'if the official movement would step in firmly now' the campaign 'could soon be over'.

The CDC decided that the Carpenters and Bert Smith would get expenses and 'Berwyn Roberts' would be 'co-opted' to help with bulletins and 'clerical work'. 20,000 copies of the next bulletin 'would be sufficient'. *Emergency Bulletin No 16* stressed: 'The rank and file are campaigning for their release', as were 'many' MPs.

Sadly there has been the stumbling block all along the way—UCAT [T] and TGWU executives. They have, from the offset, refused to support any campaign for their defence or their release, in fact they have done their utmost to dampen any support from the official movement even to the extent of publishing a book to justify the Executive's non-action on the issue.

The CDC had asked to meet the UCATT EC 'to put them clearly in the picture concerning the picketing and the trial, but they have constantly refused to meet us'. They '*must* be made to change their mind on the issue' and 'fall in line with the wishes of the membership'. There should be a 'big turn out' by 'the whole trade union movement' for the mass lobby of the UCATT Conference.

For four weeks from 22 May Brian Williams's 'wages' were 'NIL'. On the 24th UCATT's Eric Hughes sent Margaret Murray £220.

On the 26th the *Star* reported:

Mr Jim Arnison, author of the book 'The Shrewsbury Three', told a meeting of trade unionists at Wrexham last night that the way was open for the judiciary to find a way of releasing Mr Warren and Mr Tomlinson and put right an injustice.

The trade union and labour movement would step up its campaign for their release along with that of their colleagues.

The movement would also strengthen the demand that conspiracy and criminal laws should never again be used against trade unionists…

Warren and Tomlinson's appeals against conviction might not be heard until October, but their appeals against sentence were due on 3 June. The three at Drake Hall were due to be released on 12 June and McKinsie Jones would be freed on the 18th.

Clay Cross Labour Party sent a 'VERY URGENT!' letter to the CDC about their conference at Central Hall Westminster on 8 June. The first item on the agenda was: 'We demand the immediate release of the Shrewsbury 6.' Could they have 'Elsie Warren'? (Regan was 'approaching' her but promised Barry Scragg and Charlie Jones.) Regan told Marlene Tomlinson that the CDC had 'done all they can to make sure that everyone concerned is treated equally' and 'would appreciate it therefore if you could confirm what Bro's Griffiths & Morris has said is true'. Would she also send 'details of the amounts received' from the TGWU? York Trades Council was organising a Shrewsbury 6 Conference. Could they have advice and two speakers, including 'one of the men that was originally charged' to describe 'how the dice were loaded' to Alex Lyon MP? They were getting good press coverage and Yorkshire TV might run a story. Could they also have more posters and copies of Arnison's book? (The CDC would 'try to arrange for one of the charged or jailed pickets to be present', but there were 'legal difficulties'. Bob Williams and Mike Williams would bring posters and books. Could they invite a local union official and a 'prominent' MP—'Audrey Wise for example'?—and put 'an advertisement or two' in the *Star*?)

SW reported that the 'Shrewsbury Dependants Fund' would be 'administered separately from the Rank and File Conference Fund' and 'give money to the imprisoned and blacklisted workers and their dependants, by subscribing to the North Wales Defence Fund'. They wanted weekly collections of 5p or 10p and had 'collecting sheets and information about the facts of the case, news, demonstrations, etc, as well as an up-to-date balance sheet'. The treasurer, Ossie Lewis, was a member of SOGAT's P & T Group EC. The sponsors were Albert Luck of the SOGAT EC, Jack Collins of the NUM EC, Dick North of the NUT EC (and IS), Joe McGough, UCATT convenor at Dunlops in Speke, and John Llywarch.

The CP *Weekly Letter* insisted: 'If there is no reduction in their sentences, the pressure on the government must be increased considerably' with 'full support' for the UCATT Conference lobby.

On the 29th the Charter's Eddie Nash was a guest at the CDC. Barry Scragg introduced Berwyn Jones (not 'Roberts'), a bricklayer and former Secretary of Holywell UCATT. The Defence Fund would pay the 24's National Insurance stamps when they had been on trial and in prison. The jailed men would get assistance when they left prison, to be reviewed weekly. Further information was required from the TGWU before a decision could be taken about 'rehabilitation grants'; but due to 'the unprecedented rise in the cost of living, grants would be increased as from next week'. The three at Drake Hall were 'all in good spirits'. Warren and Tomlinson were 'much happier' and accepted the CDC's decision on parole, though Warren was 'concerned about the condition of his house'. Scragg pointed out that the CDC was 'not set up to finance the building or rebuilding of any person's property' and any decision would have to be made 'in consultation' with him. Manny Cohen's invitation to a fundraising meeting for the *Star* to meet George Matthews was 'in order'. Berwyn Jones suggested cutting the number of leaflets, but Nash offered to circulate them to area secretaries. More badges and books had arrived and Ivor Lloyd would try to get local libraries to buy

The Shrewsbury Three. Blackpool Trades Council would show a film and sell badges and books at the UCATT Conference. Mike Williams and Jeff Douglas would be delegates at Warren and Tomlinson's appeals and Elsa Warren and Marlene Tomlinson would be 'contacted'. John Carpenter's name was on an advertisement for a Shipley Trades Council meeting, so 'various' CDC members had agreed to send Bob Williams, too. Similar future invitations would 'require consultation'. Mike Williams noted that the Carpenters' expenses had not yet been paid. Nash reported that 'Bro Dirkin' from London was 'writing an article to counteract' the UCATT EC booklet, which would be published 'subject to the approval of the committee'. There would be a lobby of the TGWU Conference.

On the 31st the *Star* noted that the CDC 'disowned' a circular 'purporting to be aimed at raising money for the dependants of the imprisoned building workers'.

In May, Dave Jackson sent £50 to the Defence Fund from Bristol ASTMS. John Broome collected £56 at the Annual Conference of Trades Councils. CPSA Conference delegates collected £63. £70 was raised at a Kirkby social. Leicester University Students' Union sent £84. £88 came from the EETPU London Press Branch. A Liverpool Corporation site sent £100. The London Federation of Trades Councils sent £110. £145 came from collections and events in Blackpool. The EETPU at IPC magazines sent £220. The London Shrewsbury 24 Committee sent £259. Eleven contributions made up over £1,000 of the £1,630 received. £3,310 was withdrawn from the TSB. £136 of it was for 500 copies of *The Shrewsbury Three*.

We aren't throwing the towel in

On 3 June Warren and Tomlinson's appeals against conviction could not be heard, because the trial transcript wasn't ready, so the judges postponed the hearing and released them on £500 bail. According to the *Star*, they 'insisted that trade unionists must not be complacent and must fight to scrap the convictions and to abolish the conspiracy laws'. That day's GMWU Conference demanded that the Labour government free the jailed pickets, that 'conspiracy', 'unlawful assembly' and 'affray' shouldn't be used in industrial disputes and the right not to cross a picket line should be written into contracts.

The CP Merseyside Area Committee was briefed about the '*Ultra Left*'. IS had roots in NALGO, the NUT and the 'working class'. '*International Socialism*' [ie *SW*]—'well presented rubbish'—sold

'35-34,000', but had reached 50,000. The CP Manchester Area Secretariat noted: '*Shrewsbury Book*'. 'Campaign good.'

Warren had begun converting a run-down pair of cottages at Hen-llan and Elsa and the kids had moved in during the trial. Two rooms were habitable, there was no proper cooker and the tap was in the backyard toilet. Bob Williams did what he could, but Elsa and the kids had spent the winter in a tiny wooden chalet with a one-bar electric fire and no bathroom and were now in a caravan. Tomlinson found Marlene and the kids 'surviving on donations and charity'.

SW reported that Warren wanted TGWU and UCATT leaders to 'start earning their corn'. He would 'tackle the executive of my union, UCATT. They are a bunch of cowards. They have done little or nothing to defend the members when we were under attack.' Eddie Prevost found Arnison's *The Shrewsbury Three* 'very weak'.

> When a communist writes a book you would think some attempt would be made to offer explanation and criticism of the mistakes made in the unsuccessful campaign to free the jailed men. You would expect some suggestions about what can be done now to get the jailed trade unionists released and how to rid the working class of the conspiracy laws.

Prevost assumed that the 'lunatic left' meant IS, yet IS wanted to construct 'a detonator to the wider trade union movement' so as to 'try to begin change in the unions to make them more democratic' and 'more efficient instruments of workers' demands'. The 'whole attack on the left' was 'a cover up for the inadequacies of the CP's political perspective'. Arnison was uncritical of the CDC, which 'signally failed' to explain 'the truth about the Shrewsbury trials and organising a rank and file movement to mobilise in the unions for the release of the jailed men'. The booklet helped Prevost better understand his 'drift away' from the CP. 'Because of its reformism' and 'its pursuit of positions in parliament and the union machine', he had been 'a communist without a purpose, going nowhere until I joined the International Socialists, a small but growing revolutionary socialist organisation'. Four pickets 'languish in jail, and others may join them in the future unless we workers build a democratic rank and file movement with a more sensitive trigger mechanism—one which will fire the trade unions into action'.

On the 5th Crook UCATT read their Labour MP's Department of Employment letters. Parliament could not 'interfere with the judgments of law'. Eric Heffer sent a reply from Dr Shirley Summerskill at the Home Office 'denying any harassment to imprisoned Shrewsbury workers'. The CDC's 'pamphlet' was read.

Warren, Tomlinson, Carpenter, Renshaw, Bert Smith and Arnison were guests at the CDC. Pete Kavanagh had asked if Warren or Tomlinson could speak at a TGWU London Region meeting and they agreed, but the CDC wanted legal advice. The guests were asked to leave. Mike Williams wanted guidance on winding up the Defence Fund and 'an audit by prominent people in the labour movement'. Warren and Tomlinson had received £80 for 'immediate expenses'. Discussion 'concerning house repairs and possible costs' reached 'no firm decision'. Carpenter would get expenses. The guests were allowed back in. Carpenter asked if he could speak at an IS meeting to 'justify his condemnation of their proposed fund'. Barry Scragg noted that they couldn't stop him speaking in a personal capacity. The UCATT Conference lobby would go ahead. The cost of the 'Shrewsbury film' would be met. 'Because of the heavy agenda'—'House repairs etc'—the next meeting would begin an hour earlier. £10 would go to the *Star*.

Warren recalled feeling that the CDC 'exuded complacency and had not the least conception of mobilising workers or tapping their initiative'. They had turned down Elsa's suggestion that the pickets' wives should be organised, but she and the kids had picketed the Home Office all the same.

The CP *Weekly Letter* celebrated Warren and Tomlinson's release as 'a triumph for the campaign' and one that 'lends added importance to the conference being held next week', which 'must become a spur for stepping up the whole campaign to quash the sentences' and the 'conspiracy' laws. On the 7th Tomlinson, Warren and George Matthews were at a North Wales Area CP meeting. Warren was quoted in the *Star*: 'On the occasions when I was unable to get the paper in prison I felt completely lost.' (CP Merseyside Area wanted a 'push' on sales of *The Shrewsbury Three*.)

On the 10th five London Trades Councils and five sites sent delegations to lobby the TUC at Congress House. Next day forty people from the docks, print unions and the EETPU London Press Branch lobbied Len Murray, who agreed that the 1875 Act 'must go': 'further representations' would be made to Jenkins.

Regan told Dave Jackson: 'It would be wrong to keep up the appeal' when 'we have ample to sustain the campaign', though 'the pressure must be kept on right up to the appeal' and 'we aren't throwing the towel in'.

On the 12th Arthur Murray, Mike Pierce and Brian Williams were released. The *Star* carried a photograph of them with June Williams

The Flying Pickets

and Valerie Pierce. Arnison wrote: 'All three walked out of the prison this morning carrying their copies of the book, "The Shrewsbury Three", and Mike Pierce had a copy of Tuesday's *Morning Star*'. Williams said: 'We would like you to pass on to the *Morning Star* our appreciation for the way it has campaigned for us and to thank all those who have demanded our release and are still fighting to get the sentences quashed.' Murray said 'that a statement would be issued' after they 'consulted' with the CDC.

Warren and Tomlinson were on the platform at the TGWU London Region Conference, though the legal advice was that they 'should be extremely careful as to the contents of their speeches'.

The CDC decided that Warren was to be advised not to speak at a Birmingham CP rally. It 'would be more appropriate to talk about the amending of the conspiracy act' rather than its repeal. 'All six lads would be invited to the next meeting.' No house repair grants would be made, but money handed over by the 24 would be returned, up to £400 apiece. The Defence Fund would close on 1 August and the CDC would meet fortnightly.

The *Charter* reappeared with a headline of 'The New Claim'. It advertised *The Shrewsbury Three*, the UCATT Conference lobby and a meeting organised by North Wales Building Workers, where Pete Carter would outline Charter strategy, Alan Abrahams would report on UCATT Conference, Eddie Nash would speak and there would be a film about the 'Shrewsbury 24'. Ron Edwards was Charter Area Secretary for Manchester, Barry Docherty for Glasgow and Joe Edwards had taken over from Billy Regan in North Wales.

Harlow Trades Council needed a speaker. (Regan referred them to Lewis.) Could Chelmsford Trades Council have a speaker? (Regan told Lewis: 'None of the committee are able to make it.')

On the 18th McKinsie Jones was released. He got a job at Shotton and a council house in Flint. All six pickets were out of jail, but two were on bail.

CHAPTER 17

The Shrewsbury 2

Doubts about the present IS leadership

By 1974 the oil crisis precipitated the first worldwide recession in 45 years and UK wages were rising rapidly. The Labour Chancellor of the Exchequer (and ex-CPer) Denis Healey, tried to impose a 'monetarist' policy of wage control and limits on public spending, but with mixed success. Tony Cliff wasn't the only socialist who was convinced that the crisis was going global.

In the June IS *Internal Bulletin* Steve Jefferys listed disputes in which 'IS supported rank-and-file organisation and IS comrades played a significant role or distinguished themselves'. It read 'like a current working class history'. (Shrewsbury came eighth.) IS should aim to have 5,000 members by 1975 and at least 2,000 should be manual workers. There should be eighty factory branches: 'We are challenging the CP', but the development of 'a workers' leadership' was uneven. The Building Workers Fraction had 'approximately 70 members scattered over the country', with 'strength in small pockets' like York, but the situation left 'a lot to be desired'. 'Many of the militants we have are of the best and toughest quality. But the traditional independence of the industry coupled with doubts about the present IS leadership means the IS fraction is classed as being of the same tar' and they 'see their prime activity as working in their local area, and not attending national meetings'. The fraction should be 'an organisation of revolutionaries (thinking, active Marxists)' and not 'a collection of good trade unionists who can be IS supermilitants'. There was 'resistance' to 'the super-star system, as, eg, the case of cde J Fontaine' (who had left IS to join the CP with no explanation). 'Regional schools must be organised' and 'discussion should not be centred totally on the industry'. 'Perspectives for the Building Industry' noted it was 'very quiet at moment in London'.

Sense of demoralisation mainly over ineffectiveness of Shrewsbury: (a) 1972 dispute, although a victory, led to exhaustion of militants and cynicism amongst rank and file, (b) little lead by Communist Party, etc for a long time over Shrewsbury. Great demoralisation over cynical attitude of UCATT Executive. Great faith placed in EC elections to gain left control. Left lost—vote being challenged at the moment. Also verdicts at Christmas, the miners and election also side-tracked attempts to activate sites.

Barely a quarter of the cost of the six issues of *The Building Worker*—with print-runs up to 2,000—was covered by sales, so it had been replaced by *SW* 'Specials': 'We didn't really have enough on the ground to take on the CP and we are going to have to fight harder and put more work into the Building Workers' Charter', which was looking to UCATT Conference 'to re-activate the Action Committees over the new claim'. Pay was the key issue, but the 'campaign against the lump will be heightened and offer some opportunity for our members to make an impact'. The IS EC antici-pated a major recession in the industry over the winter and the 'concentration of militants on local authority jobs'. The strategy should be 'to build a base for confrontations in 1975'. (CP leaders got hold of this document and noted the references to York Trades Council and 'doubts about the present IS leadership'.)

On 13 June Dave Ayre attended a CP social and on the 20th he was a delegate to the UCATT Conference. The delegates debated a motion from Lou Lewis's branch: 'Conference severely censures the Executive Council for its failure to wholeheartedly defend our members, uphold trade union rights, or to alert the whole trade union movement to the need to actively defend the 24.' Alan Abrahams's branch's motion crit-icised the EC's handling of the welfare and financial needs of its members amongst the 24. Warren and Tomlinson's release should be made permanent and laws limiting the right to effective picketing should be amended or annulled. The EC was urged to win the support of the Labour Party and the TUC Conference. A Southampton branch motion criticised the EC for having 'failed to grasp the full implications of the trials'. George Smith failed to get these motions remitted, but managed to get them discussed in private. No delegate spoke up for the EC during a three-hour debate and only a few voted against. Dave recalls: 'CPers agreed with me, privately, about various issues, but then they'd say "Thoo's a Trot" and go to the CP caucus. When it came to the vote they always took the party line.'

SW reported that delegates had decided that the wage claim would be £1.50 an hour for craftsmen and £1.40 for labourers, plus a 35-hour week, but Smith had indicated that the position of the minority Labour government would have to be taken into account. *SW* believed that the EC 'got off lightly', because they weren't forced to launch a campaign on picketing rights.

On the 22nd John Carpenter spoke at the York Trades Council Conference. The film, *Free the Six*, 'went down really well' and North West Spanner Theatre was 'well received'. York University Defence Committee's motion, condemning the 'increasing violent use of police, particularly the Special Patrol Group, against pickets and demonstrators', was sent off to Roy Jenkins.

On the 26th McKinsie Jones was a guest at the CDC. He reported that Carpenter hadn't told anyone that he'd been invited to speak at York, but he hadn't spoken on behalf of the CDC and was writing a book about the trials. The CDC would have 'no part' in it. Bill Jones wanted members of the 24 to let the CDC know if they were asked to speak. The freed men would get a 'rehabilitation grant' of £500 and their wages, but Elsa Warren's phone bill was queried. The UCATT Conference lobby had had a 'good attendance' and Alan Abrahams had done a 'tremendous job'. Wyn Davies took fifty copies of *The Shrewsbury Three* to sell at a conference, Ivor Lloyd and Joe Edwards took ten, Andy Kelly took eleven, Bob Williams took twelve, Barry Scragg took 24, someone took 48 for North Wales CP and Jeff Douglas paid for three. (During June £682 was put in the TSB account and £4,920 withdrawn, leaving £2,888.)

On the 28th George Smith told Flint UCATT that Conference decisions 'will be given full consideration by the Joint Committee'.

Dave Jackson told the CDC that the LCDTU Conference talked about 'the dropping of the sentences against the lads'.

An LCDTU circular noted that 'nearly 100' delegates passed a Conference Declaration welcoming the Labour government 'as a working class victory over Toryism'. It looked forward to Labour winning a bigger majority and being 'committed to solving Britain's crisis in the interests of working people' by 'adopting and carrying out policies that challenge the power and rule of big business'. It also called for 'an all-out campaign by the trade union movement' to end the lump and urged the TUC and Labour Party

> to press for the annulment of all laws, statutes and legal precedents which impinge on the rights of trade unionists to effectively picket or conduct a trade dispute and demand the removal of the threat of conspiracy from trade unions. The trade union movement must insist on the quashing of the

sentences on the Shrewsbury pickets being urgently carried out in view of the pending appeals. We declare our determination to work to keep these lads out of prison.

The LCDTU would lobby the TUC Conference in September.

Make way for men with ideas and energy

Bert Smith's 'Thoughts on Shrewsbury' appeared in the CP's July *Labour Monthly*. He acknowledged that 'many have asked, and no doubt historians of the future will record the question: "Why was there no spontaneous action to release the Shrewsbury pickets?"' The movement had struggled against *In Place of Strife* and the Industrial Relations Act for four years. The first sentences came two days before an eleven-day Christmas holiday, the industry was 40 percent organised and stewards were 'unable to call mass meetings overnight'. Up to 40,000 'all over the country' struck on 11 and 15 January, but the three-day week and the NUM strike 'overshadowed the fight to free the lads'. UCATT and TGWU leaders 'failed to recognise the implications of the charges' and 'became committed in two different ways'. 900 delegates at the TGWU Conference supported the 24, and 'it was considered by most to be only a matter of time before a similar movement developed to that which released the Pentonville Five', yet 'everybody waited in vain, because it was only an empty gesture to pacify the angry delegates'. He hoped the Labour government would 'redress the injustice' and repeal or amend 'conspiracy' law. Meanwhile, *The Shrewsbury Three* was 'helping to keep alive the interest needed if we are to win freedom for those who have been jailed'.

On 3 July Barry Scragg heard about discussions between Labour Party officials (including the General Secretary), government law officers and the Home Secretary, at the TGWU's request. The government was 'reviewing' the law on common law 'conspiracy' and the Labour Party was pressing 'hard for early action', but Jenkins did 'not consider it proper to comment on the decisions of the courts or to intervene in any way *while appeals are still pending*'.

On the 10th McKinsie Jones, Arthur Murray, Terry Renshaw, Des Warren and Brian Williams were guests at the CDC. Connah's Quay Civic Hall had been booked for a celebration on 2 August, but this was felt to be premature. McKinsie Jones and Barry Scragg would speak at Greenwich Trades Council, Bob Williams at Nottingham

Trades Council and Lou Lewis at Bracknell Trades Council. Four of the freed men would get another week's wages, but Warren and Tomlinson would get two weeks' because they 'may be better unemployed'. Two-thirds of Elsa Warren's phone bill would be paid, but this was the last payment to 'anyone outside the committee'. Bill Jones announced that since CDC meetings were 'dealing with more or less routine matters, he would be leaving the committee until September', though he would speak at public meetings. IS wanted to hire the 'Shrewsbury Film', but this was 'against past policy'. (Soon after the CDC let Brighton CP have the film for the cost of the postage.)

SW announced that a 'Socialist Worker Builders Special' would be 'out next week' with coverage of UCATT Conference, the pay claim, the lump, the 'super-slump', Ireland and racism. 'All IS branches to sell on sites'. (On the 20th it was still 'out next week'.)

On the 17th Dave Ayre and Jim French were at UCATT's Northern Regional Council, where 'satisfaction' was expressed that members were out of prison. The EC's action in taking the issue to the TUC General Council, and possibly to Congress, was endorsed.

Crook UCATT bricklayers' and woodworkers' branches merged. They elected all the bricklayers' officers and heard a CDC statement.

£850 was withdrawn from the Defence Fund's TSB account, but only part of the CDC minutes for the 24th is publicly available:

Because of the problems the cash received by Bro's W Jones and E Nash had caused (house repairs) it was agreed that Bro R[obert] Williams hand the cheque back to Bro Warren and the committee would reimburse Bro's Jones and Nash to the same amount. Various members of the committee expressed their disgust at the outcome of something that was done as a good turn.

The treasurer should handle the tax issue. Barry Scragg and Bob William's car service costs would be met. £10 was to go to the Star.

Thanks to Tony Ledgerton, the steward at a Liverpool site, and the men on the waiting list for jobs there, Warren and Tomlinson went to the front of the queue. The men already employed threatened to strike if they weren't given a start. The two men had to travel fifty miles, used false names and worked as labourers for two months. At weekends they made Warren's cottages habitable.

Beryl Huffinley of the Yorkshire Association of Trades Councils wrote to Bill Whittaker of the Lancashire Association about 'our joint action re letter to Smith'. She had 'full support for the action and for future developments' and would 'send a list of names etc'.

Whittaker sent a list of his EC members to Barry Scragg: 'The names *underlined* are the best.' Simon Fraser of Liverpool Trades Council heard that Bill Jones had 'had a chat' with Billy Regan about a 'National Co-ordinating committee'. Fraser was willing to help.

On 30 July, Joe Edwards called a meeting to discuss the 'Future role of Charter in N Wales'.

Discretion is being exercised

On 1 August the CDC closed the Defence Fund. It held £1,400.

On the 7th Kevin Butcher, McKinsie Jones, Murray and Renshaw were guests at the CDC. Bill Jones turned up and reported that the 'National Co-ordinating Committee' would meet in Liverpool on 14 September. A 'number of prominent people in the Labour move-ment' were 'willing to attend'. The names of Audrey Wise MP and Jim Hiles of the LCDTU were put forward, but Barry Scragg argued that it shouldn't be 'overcrowded'. McKinsie Jones had asked about Tomlinson's 'remarks' at the last meeting, but Carpenter had 'denied all that was said' and 'would attend the meeting tonight to clear mat-ters up'. (He didn't arrive.) Bill Jones reported that a UCATT Conference resolution had been accepted for the TUC Congress agenda. He had sent 190 copies of *The Shrewsbury Three* to the CP's Central Books in London, because they had run out. The CDC would order 100 'Keep the Two Out' posters. Bill Jones and Alan Abrahams would visit Warren. Bill Jones believed that there would be criticism for using the Defence Fund to finance the 'Welcome Home' buffet. 'People are bound to say that the...' (The rest isn't publicly available.)

Jeff Douglas apologised to Dave Jackson for not writing since mid-June and sent the CDC minutes. They were planning 'a national co-ordinating committee ready for the appeal in October.' 'There has been some criticism from some of the 24, but Bill Jones or Barry Scragg would put him 'in the picture'.

On the 13th Billy Regan hoped Ken Barlow and Eric Hughes 'would consider it favourably' if Regional Council members were asked to sit on the National Co-ordinating Committee.

Simon Fraser had been 'asked by a few people to call a meeting of specially interested persons' and 'invited less than 20' trade union-ists, MPs and 'lawyers'.

Campbell Malone believed that the campaign to repeal the 1875 Act was 'a bit of a "red herring",' but the use of 'unlawful assembly' was 'very dangerous for future pickets'. Support was growing in the Parliamentary Labour Party, but 'discretion is being exercised so as to avoid any risk or prejudice to the appeal'. Labour MPs thought that Jenkins wouldn't intervene before the appeals.

On the 21st there were no guests at the CDC. Carpenter had returned 32 badges and three copies of *The Shrewsbury Three*. Tomlinson had sold ten copies and had ten left. Peter Moroney had four left. The money Carpenter sent would be checked to ensure that it was correct. Conversations with Warren and Tomlinson about Carpenter and the London Docks were reported. An apology was to go to Bletchley Trades Council for the non-appearance of Dave Jackson. Bob Williams would speak at Oxford Trades Council. 'London lads' were to be contacted about Cambridge Trades Council. Barlow, Fraser and Jim Shepherd had been told about the Defence Fund audit. At least five CDC members should go to the TUC lobby. Bill Jones had written an article for the *Star*. Tickets for the 'Welcome Home' dance had been sent to the 24—apart from Derrick Hughes—plus Glyn Davies and Colin Kelly. The CDC would 'assess the situation' on the 29th. *Bulletin No 17* noted that the UCATT EC had been 'instructed to gain the support of the TUC and Labour Party'. It asked supporters to 'make sure your union supports' the campaign and put 'pressure on your local MP'.

The *Star* reported that Bill Jones had appealed, on behalf of the CDC, to 'all trade unionists' and 'particularly TGWU members', to 'bring pressure on their own union to support the Shrewsbury resolution' at the TUC Congress and to give 'mass support' for the LCDTU demonstration and lobby. UCATT's EC were 'urged to win support'. There would be 'a social and buffet for representatives of all the many thousands of trade unionists who have taken and are taking part in the fight for the Shrewsbury 24' on 7 September as 'a mobilising effort to rekindle the struggle' to keep the 2 out of jail. 'The 24 and their families will also be invited'.

A group putting on entertainments in South Wales clubs to raise the issue reported that when they sold tickets they were 'always confronted' with 'Who are the Shrewsbury Six?' Could they have 'one of the main people involved'? (Regan had nobody available.)

SW noted that the Building Workers' Conference was cancelled.

Dave Ayre attended the *Charter* Editorial Board on 24 August. The Charter's front-page headline was 'THIRTY BOB AN HOUR'. The UCATT EC was not implementing Conference decisions and Pete Carter argued that they should 'get out of office and make way for men with ideas and energy'. The lump was widespread. 'Pressure undoubtedly' led to the 'unexpected release' of Warren and Tomlinson and 'pressure and action is the only guarantee to make sure they will stay out and FREE'. The *Charter* thought it 'timely' to publish a 'short profile' of the 'rank and file trade unionists' on the CDC and listed their official union and trades council positions.

On the eve of the Labour Party Conference a Birmingham delegate to the 1973 TGWU Conference, writing in *Labour Monthly*, denied that they had agreed to give moral, financial and legal support to the 24. Bert Smith pointed out that the TGWU Building Committee had voted for 'moral and financial support' and had asked a delegate to raise 'the principle of legal representation' with his regional secretary. Neither decision was challenged at the TGWU Conference Standing Orders Committee or Liverpool Trades Council Conference. UCATT's motion for the TUC Congress called for Warren and Tomlinson's 'continued freedom' and 'an examination' of the 1875 Act. He hoped TGWU delegates would support it.

Bill Jones told Mike Williams that Alex Weir had told him about John Llywarch's claim that the Defence Fund did not 'finance' him during his trial. Williams told Weir that Llywarch had had expenses and wages for meetings with solicitors and the committal hearings, £10 to attend court on 3 October 1973, £40 for the first week of the trial, £35 a week while it lasted and throughout the Christmas period and a Christmas gift of £100. His claim for van maintenance was met (less the £10 gift), though the van turned out to be his brother's, 'a *lumper*'. It would be 'a little involved' to prove that Llywarch received £600, but Weir could ask the auditors or himself for details, or Blackpool Trades Council could meet the CDC.

George Smith moved the UCATT motion at the TUC Congress:

Congress demands that every step be taken under existing legal provisions to ensure that no building worker tried at Shrewsbury be held in jail any longer.

Congress asserts that the sentences imposed on the building workers at the 1973 Shrewsbury trials were savagely excessive, having regard to the nature of the dispute and the evidence of provocation from lump workers and others. Congress concludes that the charges were pressed only because the strike was successful and because the employers were anxious to intimidate the workers concerned.

Congress demands a review of the existing law as to peaceful picketing and particularly requires satisfactory curbs on the use of conspiracy charges in strike situations.

(He didn't challenge the convictions.) It was passed unanimously. Len Murray insisted that the TUC General Council 'would continue to examine the changes which were needed' to picketing law. CP Industrial Organiser Bert Ramelson's relationship with Jack Jones had deteriorated. CPer Ken Gill, the TASS General Secretary, withdrew the motion criticising the Social Contract so as to placate Hugh Scanlon and help bring about a merger with the AUEW.

The Shrewsbury 24 National Co-ordinating Committee

On 4 September the CDC asked Mike Williams to attend a preliminary meeting of the 'Shrewsbury 24 National Co-ordinating Committee' to pay expenses. The transcripts of the first trial were ready and if the appeals succeeded the SNCC would press for a pardon. Bob Williams had been asked about tickets for the 'Welcome Home'. Tomlinson's four brothers wanted to go 'in case any criticism was made about Ricky or Des'. Barry Scragg said that 'noone would be criticising anyone and no political speeches would be made'. If the Tomlinsons phoned, tickets could be left at the door.

On the 7th £500 went into the TSB account and £44 was sent to the *Star* for advertisements. Leading trade unionists, Labour MPs, the press and TV were invited to the 'Welcome Home' Buffet Dance 'in honour of the 24'. Carpenter sent apologies.

Warren saw nothing to celebrate. 'I didn't see a victory and my family didn't have a home.' He understood that Llywarch, Tomlinson and McKinsie Jones also stayed away. Several Rhyl CPers who 'were critical of the lack of activity of the party over the Shrewsbury issue' had 'found difficulty in finding out what was going on'. They were 'hoping to have some discussion at the dance', but there were no tickets available. When they found out that a lot of tickets hadn't been used, half the Rhyl CP branch resigned. Warren told Liverpool Trades Council they 'would be making a big mistake if they allowed George Smith and Jack Jones to call the shots'. They decided to 'delete from the minutes all reference to my presence'.

On the 14th Simon Fraser was Chairman and Ken Barlow was Secretary of the 'preliminary' SNCC. Bill Jones, Barry Scragg, Billy Regan and Mike Williams represented the CDC. Also present were Bill Whittaker, Peter Gorman (President of Leeds Trades Council) and Jack Rogers (UCATT, Merseyside). Apologies came from MPs Audrey Wise, Stan Thorne, Bob Cryer and Norman Atkinson, plus John Redford, Bert Smith and Campbell Malone. Fraser stressed that

The Flying Pickets

they would 'consider the next steps essential for gaining support to ensure that Brothers D Warren and E Tomlinson are not returned to prison' and the use of the 1875 Act. It was unanimously agreed that the SNCC 'be formed of present members' and those invited, but other names were 'to be considered by the Chairman and Secretary'. They were to seek a meeting with George Smith to discuss a meeting of union leaders and another with all Labour MPs when parliament reassembled. They would also write the first 'News Letter'. (It looked forward to a working Labour majority and 'a new era with a united trade union and labour movement' capable of creating a society which 'believes in justice not revenge'.) UCATT and the TGWU would be asked to contribute. The SNCC would meet in October.

On the 18th the Greater London Association of Trades Councils thanked the CDC for supporting a meeting. 'Our objective is to get as much activity as we can just about the time the appeals are heard.'

The CDC heard that money was yet to come in from the sale of *The Shrewsbury Three* and badges, but they had already broken even. Brian Williams was blacklisted and would receive an 'unemployment grant'. The £100 given to get the SNCC 'off the ground' was 'money well spent'. It would have its own treasurer and 'continue until new picketing laws are introduced'. Bill Jones 'gave a lengthy report on a conversation he had had with Bro Barlow'. The appeal was due on 24 October, but 'would most probably not be heard until after Christmas'. From now on the CDC officers would meet fortnightly and the full CDC monthly.

In the next few days the CDC acknowledged that Campbell Malone might find it difficult to be on the SNCC, but he could pass on information via Bert Smith. Malone was 'very disappointed to learn of the various disagreements which have occurred' and hoped that 'notwithstanding anything that may have been said that you will continue with the struggle until Des and Ricky are finally safe and the position of future pickets safeguarded'.

On 2 October the CDC heard that Malone thought that the sentences would be reduced or suspended at the appeal. The CDC would attend the London Trades Council demonstration and send a statement to the *Star* and the *Charter*. 10,000 copies of the next bulletin would be printed. *Bulletin No 18* could not 'stress enough' that 'pressure be stepped up'. Resolutions 'must be sent immediately from your Trade Union branches and Trades Councils demanding that the General Council of the TUC strictly adhere to the decisions reached at the TUC Congress'. Site and factory delegations were needed at the Court of Appeal lobby in London on 24 October.

The *Charter*'s front-page headline was 'Pickets Get TUC Support.' Barry Scragg thanked Congress delegates and indicated that the SNCC would 'play an important part in the final stages of the campaign'. Arthur Murray told his story and made a few choice remarks about lawyers, witnesses, judges and police:

No trade unionist should be made to fear the knock on the door in the middle of the night and to be taken away for interrogation just because he was engaged in official union activity. No trade unionist's wife and family should have to endure the nightmare of their husbands being involved in massive trials facing hundreds of charges.

'Every effort was now being made to keep Des Warren and Ricky Tomlinson from going back to jail.'

Dave Ayre was now Charter Area Secretary for Teesside. Crook UCATT received *Bulletin No 17* on the 9th—they were one behind.

On the 10th Labour won almost 1,000,000 votes more than the Tories, but had a three-seat majority. 29 CPers got 17,000 votes.

Days later Lord Chancellor Elwyn-Jones was 'almost literally wringing his hands' because Lord Widgery had told him about the Appeal Court's decisions. Roy Jenkins recalled:

'Dreadful news, dreadful news,' he began in his beautiful voice. He expressed great sympathy for me. 'Of course, for the sake of the rule of law you will have to uphold what they say, but it will be difficult, very difficult.' I think he was surprised at the alacrity with which I assured him I would do this. It was absolutely clear to me that, while there was room for doubt about the tactical wisdom of the Court of Appeal's handling of the matter, I could not go round the country fulminating about the rule of law and even contemplate taking a purely political decision to commute these sentences.

Civil servants dropped proposals to reform picketing law from Labour leftwinger Michael Foot's Employment Protection Bill.

On the 29th, at the Court of Appeal, defence counsel stressed that the judge 'invited the jury to assume there had been a conspiracy and go on from there to decide who had been a party to it'. Widgery commented: 'We are asked to say'—he didn't say by whom—'that the crisis is now past, but the great difficulty is that, if it is true, the deterrent effect of the original sentence has contributed to a period of relative peace.' The Appeal Court turned down the applications, refused leave to appeal to the Lords and sent Warren and Tomlinson back to prison.

You are on the line

On 28 October the CP Merseyside Organisation Committee had minuted: 'Personal Difficulties refusal to accept Parol[e]. Jumpy Meeting this Sunday Best to go and see them. Nat[ional] holiday— TUC Pardon. What ever Date. Meets 20th Nov[ember] IF Don't act—UCATT & T&G[WU] NAT. Defence C[ommi]ttee make Call.'

Next day 2,000 men from eleven Manchester sites went on strike in protest at the jailing of Warren and Tomlinson, called for an all-out strike and sent flying pickets to the docks. Demonstrations took place in Glasgow, London and Liverpool, where 1,000 lobbied the UCATT office, called for an all-out strike and stayed out.

On the 30th the *Star* urged: 'Let the Home Secretary now ask the Queen for a pardon.' George Smith assured Flint UCATT that he would call on the TUC to implement its Congress resolution 'fully'.

CDC *Bulletin No 19* noted that Lord Widgery had admitted that the sentences were 'intended as deterrents, and deterrents they had been', so quashing them would be 'undoing all the good work that had been produced'. 'This decision clearly illustrates the class nature of the judiciary and must surely dispel any doubts as to whether the trial was political or not.' The UCATT EC had called on regional councils 'to bring about full scale stoppages for a mass lobby of parliament on the 21st November'. The CDC urged the TUC to make it 'an official one day stoppage'. (The SNCC also wanted a strike and a mass lobby of the Labour Party Conference.)

Next day's CP *Weekly Letter* noted the 'initial wave of protest' and 'calls by the TUC and trade union leaders for the government to act to secure the release of the two men. But far stronger pressure is needed to compel Roy Jenkins to take action so that a free pardon is granted.' The CP Manchester Area Committee wanted 'resolutions, telegrams from TU Branches, Shop Stewards' committees, etc' to the TUC, UCATT, TGWU, Home Secretary and MPs for the two men's 'immediate release'. CP North Wales Area noted that Len Murray and Jack Jones had demanded that Jenkins release them. Industrial action was 'already widespread' and there would be a meeting in Flint on 7 November. (3,000 Liverpool men were on strike and 4,500 more came out next day.)

During October £790 was withdrawn from the Defence Fund's TSB account, leaving £5.64, and £2,000 from the Nationwide, leaving £525. In line with CP policy, the fund would not reopen.

On 1 November the TGWU's George Wright, now Secretary of the Wales TUC, told Jenkins that the trials and sentences were 'brought about by political intervention' and so it 'would be perfectly proper for the men to be freed by political intervention'.

On the 4th the LCDTU argued: 'Mass Action Can Free Them'. UCATT, the TGWU, union general secretaries, the TUC General Secretary, the Labour Party Secretary and 'numerous' MPs demanded the two men's release. Stewards' committees were sending 'resolutions and deputations' to union leaders, 'pressing for industrial action'. The LCDTU wanted meetings and lobbies of ECs, MPs, Constituency Labour Parties and UCATT's Head Office.

Next day the UCATT EC told branches that it was asking the TUC to ask Jenkins to meet a delegation and also to convene an emergency General Council 'to discuss future united action'. Should Jenkins 'fail to respond' the EC would organise an 'all-out lobby' of Parliament on the 21st. Their motion for the Labour Party Conference argued that the sentences were 'completely disproportionate' and demanded that Jenkins 'act immediately'.

On the 8th the SNCC wanted UCATT's strike on the 21st moved to the 28th, London demonstrations and a lobby of the Labour Party Conference. PM Harold Wilson would be asked to meet a delegation.

Campbell Malone had lodged an application for leave to appeal to the Lords against the two men's convictions. He told George Smith that 'the greater the outcry', the easier it would be to persuade the Court of Appeal that any point of law they established was of 'public importance'. Legal aid hadn't been granted. Would the Defence Fund pay £486 for two QCs? (It would.) The men weren't getting papers: 'Perhaps the Committee could look into this.'

On the 18th the *Star* reported that a Glasgow Trades Council, Scottish TUC, UCATT and TGWU meeting of the 'leaders of 900,000 Scottish trade unionists' called on the TUC to 'organise and lead a lobby of parliament to release the two Shrewsbury pickets'.

In England, the CP's North West leadership discussed 'developments on the Shrewsbury pickets campaign'. (No decisions were recorded.) The CP Merseyside meeting minuted: 'If TUC make call— make through Regional Committees ie Frasher, ? Tocher.'

Next day Jenkins indicated that the men might be paroled, but he was 'unable to offer any prospect of clemency' before May 1975.

The Flying Pickets

Harold Wilson pointed out that he had no right to interfere and the issue was 'sub judice'. The TUC called for a lobby of parliament.

The CDC minutes for the 20th are not publicly available.

Garry Davies was setting up a South West London Defence Committee on the basis of Labour councillors and branches, union branches and trades councils, and he understood that the CDC was calling for a TUC decision for the immediate release of the two men and for scrapping the 'conspiracy' laws. (Billy Regan wanted 'leaflets and public meetings (we can always fix you up with speakers)'. 'Keep pushing the local MPs'—'you are on the line.')

The SNCC minutes for the 25th are not publicly available. Soon after, the Defence Fund's TSB savings account was closed and £206 put into the cheque account. During November £620 had been withdrawn in cash.

On the 28th hundreds of north west trade unionists travelled on special trains to lobby the Labour Party Conference, where delegates resolved that the 'conspiracy' charge should be 'phased out'.

Jenkins told Barry Jones MP: 'I cannot usurp the functions of the courts and should recommend interference with sentences they pass only on the basis of considerations which the courts have not been able to take into account.' He could not comment because an appeal was pending. (Jones was asked why he didn't support the 24. He shrugged his shoulders and admitted that he could have done more.)

Tony Benn's edited *Diaries* first mention Shrewsbury on the 30th.

Casson's gave copies of the trial photographs and police and lumpers' statements to the CDC, who organised an exhibition. Tribunite MPs said that the TUC and union leaders would give only verbal support. George Smith told a CDC delegation that since Warren, Tomlinson and O'Shea had their own lawyers, the UCATT EC had 'abandoned the 24', but he promised to try to get a Parliamentary Inquiry. George Henderson at the TGWU saw the photographs and acknowledged that nobody was causing damage.

On 4 December the CDC heard that the Warren and Tomlinson had had an extra week's wages, because the appeals were taking longer than expected. If their wives wanted help it would be 'looked on favourably'. Bert Smith reported that UCATT had been 'inundated' with telegrams and phone calls from 'all sections of the labour movement' and had urged Len Murray to contact Jenkins immediately. Smith hoped they 'could start an esculation' before the EC met. The London Regional Committee had arranged a lobby and Eric Hughes had been asked to convene stewards' meetings. All regional committees would meet 'as soon as possible'. If the pickets weren't released after the TUC met Jenkins then 'we must stop out'. Barry Scragg said that the UCATT EC and the SNCC 'must put on the pressure' and 'things must be moving within a week'. It was 'unwise to produce a new bulletin until it was seen which way things were moving', but 'we have learned by past mistakes' and the campaign must get the 'full support' of the movement. The CDC would call for 'mass stoppages' on 5 December and lobbies of the UCATT EC and the TUC.

If the CDC met on the 18th the minutes aren't publicly available.

A draft discussion document for the CP North West District Congress noted that 'leadership of the national movement to free the "Shrewsbury 6" was centred on the North West and the Merseyside in particular'. The final version 'congratulated our building comrades on the energy and tenacity of the long campaign to release the Shrewsbury pickets'. The issues involved were 'wider than the building industry' and it was a challenge 'to all communists, to the left and to all active trade unionists'. 'For if we are not fighting for the changes and uniting the left forces—who is?' 'If the *Morning Star* is not leading the struggles daily—what paper is?

That's a defeat

In August Industrial Research & Information Services had published *The International Socialists*. It noted Roger Protz and Roger Rosewell's two-month suspension for applying for full-time jobs in the NUJ without EC permission and Andreas Nagliati's resignation as Industrial Organiser. The IS printshop employed thirty people, brought in £1,500,000's worth of business a year, subsidised *SW* and the rank and file papers and gave IS £40,000. The CP was making 'very little impact', so 'trade unionists and the trade union movement' should be very concerned about IS.

Steve Jefferys reported to IS's September Conference:

> Only in the building industry did the employers feel strong enough to launch an all-out attack on trade unionists through the Shrewsbury trial, the Broome case and the spread of the lump. But in almost every other industry where militancy has developed or strikes have taken place the police are much more in evidence than previously.

The Flying Pickets

Cambridge branch tabled the only resolution on Shrewsbury. 'Conference demands that the editorial board of *SW* puts greater emphasis on truthful and accurate reporting', because there had been an 'under-reporting of violence' in relation to one Shrewsbury trial.

Tony Cliff had completed *The Crisis: Social Contract or Socialism.* The world was 'drifting into the most serious economic crisis since the 1930s', national markets were increasingly dominated by a few huge concerns, the rate of exploitation had doubled in the past century, raw material prices were falling and the rate of profit on investment had halved in the past 25 years. After the fourfold oil price rise, the longest boom in history was coming to an end and market forces were producing a traditional worldwide capitalist crisis. The Labour government in Britain was fuelling inflation by cutting company taxes and making the public sector subsidise the private sector. Labour, Liberal and Tory leaders all agreed that wages had to be held down. Unemployment was over 5 percent, 3,000,000 pensioners lived in houses built before 1919 and one in five did not have an inside toilet and one in six had no fixed bath; yet the 1973 rate of house building was the lowest since 1947. Workers shouldn't accept a 'Social Contract' that cut their standard of living and undermined the welfare state. *'The best-organised workers must not hold back, for if they do the whole working class will be held back with them.'* Union leaders, for all their 'left' rhetoric, supported this rightward shift and sowed illusions in parliament. 'The majority of CP members in industry' were 'pure syndicalists'. 'Many party members are not even readers, let alone sellers,' of the *Star*. The CP's 'incapacity to mobilise its own members' was 'unbelievable'. Cliff wanted a 'revolutionary socialist workers' party'.

A Rank and File Conference Organising Committee leaflet announced a conference on 30 November:

1   Organise now for strike action to free the Two!
2   Build local action committees of trade union representatives to campaign for effective solidarity.
3   Force the trade union officials, particularly in TGWU and UCATT, officially to organise mass strikes.

'Clearly the struggle against wage restraint and against the Social Contract is part and parcel of the fight to defend the right to picket.' The conference would have an emergency session on Shrewsbury. Scots lorry drivers had won £40 for 40 hours in an unofficial strike using flying pickets: *'That's a victory'*. Tomlinson and Warren were in jail for picketing while on official strike—*'that's a defeat.'*

The next *SW* believed 'the Two' were 'singled out', 'not because they had committed a violent crime, but because the ruling class saw the effects of effective picketing during the 1972 miners' strike'.

Now, the very day after the Scottish lorry drivers won a victory through strong picketing, the ruling class puts the knife in.

In the middle of a strike wave the judges have sent three [*sic*] men back to jail to prove to the working class that their class will use *any* means to defend and maintain their system...

The Labour government let these men stay out of jail for five months pending the appeal to soften the trade unions into accepting the Social Contract...

The Labour government could repeal the Conspiracy Laws at any time, but they won't. They might have to use them themselves to see that the system isn't seriously challenged in the future...

It's action that will count.

The R&FOC Secretary, Roger Cox, added: 'The lead in the fight to free the two lads will come from the rank and file, and we've got to organise to make it successful.' Dave Adshead reported that 5,000 had marched in Birmingham against the lump and unemployment and in support of the unions' pay claim. Pete Carter had called for 'a determined fight against the lump and a campaign for a national strike in summer 1975'. Ken Barlow 'announced the return of flying pickets on lump sites'. Lumpers were carrying TGWU cards.

The UCATT Northern Regional Committee 'noted with serious concern the fact that these two brothers were again in prison' and wrote to the TUC. Branches should 'send a telegram of compassion seeking a "pardon"' to the Home Secretary.

On the 4th Jim Nichol—now IS National Secretary—told Mike Williams that IS members were 'disgusted but not surprised' by the Labour government's collusion in jailing the 2 and 'would like to know where moneys should be sent'. If collection sheets were available 'we would like at least 500 to start with'. (Williams replied that the CDC had 'not yet reopened our appeal for cash as we are hoping to pressurise' UCATT and the TGWU 'to release the money which they have collected in the name of the Shrewsbury 24'.)

SW reported that Liverpool strikers in support of the 2 had voted to go back on their stewards' recommendation and had been asked to support a parliamentary lobby. Building workers Jan Golab and Terry Horan pointed out that UCATT London Regional

Council had called an official strike, yet many officials refused to call sites out and it had taken until 1 November for the TGWU to organise an 'emergency' meeting. UCATT convenor Jeff Shaw stressed: 'We need a paper capable of publicising the truth in the labour movement.' *SW* wanted demonstrations, lobbies and resolutions, but 'much more of a political struggle' was needed. The R&FOC regretted that the *Star* was 'insulting militant workers' who 'happen to be members of IS' as 'ultra-left'. The organisation was 'pleased to have CP members, Labour Party members and trade union activists of no political affiliation at all. We all work together because of the urgent need for workers to unite in struggle.' *SW* noted that *Tribune* accepted R&FOC advertisements, but the *Star* refused them.

Crook UCATT urged the EC to implement the conference policy of 'direct action' to secure the 'immediate release' of the two pickets and read a circular about the R&FOC Conference. The next Crook UCATT meeting heard an EC statement and correspondence from the CDC. It resolved that 'should actions/lobbying take place', delegates should attend. No delegates were able and willing to attend the Constituency Labour Party General Council.

SW stressed that 'constitutional channels' should be used, but the government had 'the police/employer/judiciary lobby to satisfy'. Readers should go for strikes, 'probably' on the 28th. The next *SW* reported that an IS building workers' meeting had focused on the pay claim, UCATT-TGWU rivalry, the lump and a slump that was 'beginning to bite'. Union cards were being issued to sub-contractors in 'blocks', 'virtually ensuring the growth of the "organised lump".' The next *SW* argued: 'Shrewsbury: Lift that blackout!' Pickets at Thames TV in London included 'delegations' from the Joint Sites Committee, the TGWU International Branch, Moorfields Eye Hospital and a Portuguese workers' committee. (A photograph showed four people.) Manchester sites were coming out next day and there was to be a march and lobby in London. The R&FOC called for a picket of the Labour Party Conference. (Fifty turned up.) The appeal for delegates to the R&FOC Conference was met by 'a well-orchestrated smear campaign from the Communist Party and the right wing', who pointed out that 'many IS trade union militants play leading roles', but it was 'absurd to ignore the fact' that the National Rank & File Movement 'still falls far short of what is needed'.

Stewards at a Pochin site in Manchester tabled a motion for the R&FOC Conference that condemned the leadership for failing to build a mass campaign leading up to the October appeals, to make clear calls for an organised contingent at demonstrations and to mount a campaign after the Court of Appeal decision. It called on delegates to pledge themselves 'to organise an all-out strike to free the two and remove all anti picketing laws'.

A R&FOC motion called on the Labour government to repeal the 1875 Act and release Tomlinson and Warren, but acknowledged that it would do so only 'if subjected to mass pressure from the trade union movement'.

The R&FOC 'Free the Shrewsbury Two' leaflet offered responses to 'tough questions', set out the key contradictions in the prosecution case and stressed the political role of the judiciary. The 'pious resolutions' from the TUC, UCATT and the TGWU hadn't been acted on because the leaders hoped that the Labour government would parole the two men and 'ensure that the underlying issues can safely be forgotten'. The rank and file had 'to force our union officials to do their job':

1   Fight within all unions for commitment by union executives to official strike action, particularly UCATT and the TGWU.
2   Pressurise the TUC itself to instigate strike action.
3   Raise money for the imprisoned men's families.
4   Publicise the Shrewsbury case by meetings, film shows, distribution of relevant literature etc.
5   Establish local Shrewsbury Defence Committees of bona fide trade union representatives to further the campaign in the localities.

The Rank & File Movement was a 'network' 'fighting for such policies *within* the unions'. Yet its perspective was indistinguishable from those of the *Charter*.

On 30 November 468 delegates from 313 union bodies attended the R&FOC Conference. Over half were manual workers and 49 stewards' committees were represented. A majority adopted the R&FOC's perspective. Ken O'Shea spoke 'on behalf of my two jailed brothers', stressed the need for 'a good collection for the wives and children' and called UCATT and the TGWU 'a bloody disgrace'. 'I don't see the trade union movement getting them out unless it gets a stick of gelignite up its arse.'

On 3 December the Court of Appeal turned down the Warren and Tomlinson's applications and sent them back to prison.

The war for Jenkins' ear

The December *Charter* acknowledged that this was the 'end of the road' in terms of the legal process, so it was 'the total responsibility of the British trade union and labour movement to win their release as quickly as possible' and 'pressure must be immediately brought to bear on the TUC and labour movement to turn the many fine resolutions and words into decisions of action' if the two men weren't out by 1 January 1975. Jim French was now a Labour councillor in Darlington. He contributed 'SCREW THE SOCIAL CONTRACT'.

> Do we have a Social Contract or not? One cannot fail to be impressed by all the hot air that has been expelled by the leaders of the trade union movement of Britain, but one has got to ask the question, 'Will the employers honour it?'
> Well it depends on the employer. If you happen to work for Magnet Joinery... then you are out of luck.
> Magnet have just put on temporary lay-off all employees at the three factories. Their reason is over-production. They do, however, intend to carry on expanding! They won't feel the pinch of course.
> The Chairman of the company, whose salary in '72-73 was £64,168 or £1,234 per week, and the top directors, who earn over £10,000 per year plus dividends, are probably at this moment cancelling their extra winter holiday (my heart bleeds).
> Because of the state of our industry there was not a lot we could do. They had obviously done their homework for some months beforehand, but we will remember and if I am still there when the boom comes, I'll screw every pound out of them, Social Contract or no.

On 4 December the CDC decided that £600 would be kept in the Defence Fund to cover tax demands and pay for a leaflet. There would be a 'final grant' of £350 to Elsa Warren and Marlene Tomlinson and £240 to Brian Williams's wife. The rest would go to the SNCC. Eddie Loyden MP would be asked how much police operations at Mold and Shrewsbury had cost and the police report to the DPP. Pete Kavanagh had been paid £104 for Christmas cards and 'every effort would be made to distribute them before the weekend'. The 'Shrewsbury Independence Fund' cards had a *Star* photograph of Warren and Tomlinson and a caption: 'Happy Christmas—at Home or in Jail?' The South West London Defence Committee reportedly sold 11,000.

Barry Jones MP thought it 'unfair' of Flint UCATT 'to say that I had not done my bit for the pickets'. Home Office officials were 'sick' of his 'representations'. Jeff Douglas replied: 'I have never read of you asking any questions on the matter in the House, neither was the issue mentioned in your last election address. There have been numerous public meetings in and about our area, Eric Heffer spoke at one but I don't recall seeing you at any.'

Reg Prentice, the Minister of Education and one of Roy Jenkins's closest allies, complained that the Labour Party Conference had 'set a bad example'. The debates on Clay Cross and Shrewsbury were 'deplorable'. Some speakers tried to raise law-breakers to the status of working class heroes.

According to Tony Benn, Labour MPs had been told there could not be a Parliamentary Labour Party meeting on Shrewsbury, since it was 'sub judice'. Eric Heffer spoke at a PLP meeting on the 12th, 'not as a minister but as a member of UCATT'. 'These are good men and they shouldn't be in jail, and we must get them out before Christmas.' There was an 'overwhelming vote' to have a special meeting the following week. (It's not clear if it happened.)

Harold Wilson told the TUC that he 'could not express a personal or government view'. Roy Jenkins wouldn't recommend clemency without 'new facts' or 'overwhelming compassionate reasons'. 'I can't usurp the function of the courts.' Tories cheered. The TUC called a lobby of parliament on 14 January.

On the 23rd George Smith told UCATT branches and Regional Councils to 'put in hand co-ordinated arrangements' to 'see that the lobby is carried out successfully'. The SNCC told supporters: 'Wherever possible special trains to be run, and trade unions asked to finance them.' 'Colleagues in London to be requested to organise a procession and demonstration.' A call for a public inquiry would be considered. 'All trade unions and political organisations to be asked to forward resolutions to the Prime Minister.' London supporters could mount a vigil at Jenkins's office. 'Industrial action should take place' on 14 January, but the 'building trade union would have to give a lead'. The SNCC would meet six days after that.

On Christmas Eve Warren and Tomlinson refused to work and were put in separate cells. Like IRA prisoners, they refused to wear prison clothes, went 'on the blanket' and demanded political status. Warren was 'sick and tired of reading about resolutions'. The Home Office stopped all visits.

IS leader Duncan Hallas had supported Tony Cliff's perspective and now edited *International Socialism*. The December issue promised an 'important article' on the 1930s CP-led Busmen's Rank and File Movement, showing 'the causes of its progress and its ultimate decline'. In 'active preparation' was an article on the Charter by 'a group of IS building workers'.

SW noted that the 'war for Jenkins' ear' continued, yet he agreed with the chief police officers, the judiciary, the Confederation of British Industry and the press about 'upholding the rule of law'.

> Prentice and Jenkins have one way of maintaining the fiction of the rule of law, and they want to appease the employing class.
>
> [Michael] Foot, Benn and Co have another method of maintaining the same fiction and they want to appease the protests of organised labour.
>
> But there is one thing the Foots and Benns will never do. And that is publicly challenge the whole rotten fiction which enabled the Shrewsbury pickets to be tried and jailed.

The last *SW* of 1974 carried an R&FOC 'Advertisement': 'We Supply The Tools For Building A Movement to Free the Shrewsbury Two'—*Free the Shrewsbury Two*, an unnamed film, the Shrewsbury Dependants Fund and The Combine. A photograph showed 'more than 40 workers' protesting the media blackout on the jailed men at a picket of the BBC's London studios. A woman carried a placard: 'Royal Group Dockers Support the Shrewsbury Pickets'.

Dave Ayre recalls:

> Reuben Barker and I heard a member of the embryo Irish Civil Rights movement talk about how British troops crashed into his grandmother's house, causing her great stress and fear, and we read Eamonn McCann's *War and an Irish Town*. It all helped us to understand the oppression of the Catholic population in the North of Ireland and British imperialism. Our political horizons gained an international dimension. There weren't many leftwingers in the north east, but non-sectarian friendships developed and we had wide-ranging political arguments.

In December Crook UCATT heard about the SNCC plans. Dave Ayre and Bill Kerriss reported on the 'breakdown of Xmas release appeals', though there might be parliamentary lobbies and 'representations'. The branch voted for Jim French, who was their nominee for the post of Northern Regional Organiser for painters. On the 29th UCATT Northern Regional Committee 'learned with pleasure that Bro French had taken up his duties' and appointed him as a delegate to the Annual Meeting of the Northern Regional Council of the Labour Party.

During December the Defence Fund received £132 from Seal Sands AUEW and £36 from UCATT members at a Hindley Green site. Stewards at Fords Halewood voted £25 for the families, but Simon Fraser had 'advised us against making direct contact'. Pete Carter sent £10. Bill Jones paid in £50 for books and cards. Jeff Douglas asked Cinema Action about the 'bare minimum' needed to complete their film: 'In a week or two the fund will be exhausted.' (Mike Rosen sent the CDC a free copy of a film.)

Tony Cliff's *The Crisis* was published on 1 January 1975. A quarter of a century later Cliff recalled that the impact of the 20,000 copies was 'almost zero'. The timing of the book was 'terribly wrong', but he didn't admit responsibility for that. The 'collapse of militancy was not clear', but he had predicted it sooner than most.

CHAPTER 18

Would Jenkins free
his own father?

What do we do next?

In January 1975 Labour MP Joe Ashton's 'Free the Shrewsbury Pickets—a call to Roy Jenkins' appeared in the *TASS Journal*. It was a 'bitter irony' that an Oxford graduate and Tory Home Secretary pardoned a picketing miner convicted of 'conspiracy' in 1937, whereas a miner's son, Oxford graduate and Labour Home Secretary refused to do so now. Jenkins's Tory predecessor, Robert Carr, believed the longest sentences 'should have only been six months'.

On 3 January Bert Ramelson told Des Warren that Jenkins and his 'cronies' were 'digging their heels in and we must see the lobby as the launching pad of a broader and more militant movement exerting even greater pressure on the government until it becomes irresistible'. There would be 'considerable stoppages' in some cities, but he had 'no illusions' that the lobby would 'achieve your release'.

The CDC sent £114 to Marlene Tomlinson and Elsa Warren.

On the 8th the CDC heard that Jim Arnison wanted a quote from the two women. 'Concern was expressed' at the *Star* coverage of Warren and Tomlinson's form of protest. UCATT and the TGWU would pay for Midlands and North West trains for the parliamentary lobby. Three CDC members would go. The four pickets who had been jailed were invited.

On the 12th 'The Making of Two Union Martyrs' appeared in the *Sunday Times*. The Shrewsbury 6 and the Tolpuddle Martyrs were now being compared in *The Times* and not just *SW*. The speeches from the dock had been set to music. The Combine had travelled the country 'satirising the court proceedings' at 'various trades councils' and Arnison's 'well-researched tale' had been 'upstaged' by the National Film School students' film show at the National Film Theatre. The UCATT EC argued that 'creating heroes from the 1972 strike will not protect any future UCATT pickets' but that 'clarifying the law regarding the rights of pickets will'.

Next day the CDC heard that Harold Wilson did 'not feel able to meet a delegation' from the TUC General Council.

On the 14th there was a train from Scotland to London and two from the North West. The two trains from the Midlands were packed. Dave Rogers recalls that Banner Theatre had a close working relationship with Ken Barlow and CPers played 'a very positive coordinating role'. It was probably on this occasion that they performed a reworked version of a Broadside Theatre show about the pickets on the train, carriage by carriage!

On the march in London there were AUEW, TASS, Hackney Direct Labour, Post Office Workers', London Defence Committee and East London Defence Committee banners. A record number of constituents queued to question MPs, but Ken Barlow recalled people asking: 'What do we do next?'

Next day's *Star* attacked 'extremists' who had called for a mass demonstration from Euston. 3,000 marched from there. They and the 10,000 from Tower Hill met 'many hundreds' outside the Commons. Dai Francis criticised the 'very evasive and non-committal attitudes of many MPs' and called on the TUC to organise strikes. McKinsie Jones agreed. 45 Labour MPs signed an early day motion demanding the release of the pickets, Syd Bidwell, Chair of the Tribune Group, believed that Jenkins couldn't resist the pressure. Audrey Wise disagreed. 'This matter will be settled ultimately by the strength which is shown by working people.' The TUC met the Chair and Vice-Chair of the Parliamentary Labour Party and the Home Office minister, Alex Lyon. (Jenkins was on holiday in the USA.) Len Murray said that further action could not be 'ruled in or ruled out'. A 'spontaneous meeting' heard Alan Sapper of the TUC General Council and General Secretary of the ACTT insist that 'further progress' depended on mass action by the shop floor'.

Sapper—who had argued for a one-day strike in support of the Pentonville 5 in 1972 and had appeared on LCDTU platforms—had spoken to an 800-strong R&FOC meeting in Central Hall Westminster. Steve Jefferys later noted that Jim Hiles and Kevin Halpin of the LCDTU 'found themselves impotently trying to stop' other CPers 'entering the hall'. He saw the march from Euston and the meeting as the 'strongest challenge yet' to the CP.

Crook UCATT delegates had included Dave Ayre, Bill Kerriss and Reuben Barker. Reuben recalls: 'When we got back the bosses called me into the office. They were really upset. We said we'd been down there asking MPs for more building work in the NE. That was the best excuse we could think of.' They reported back to the branch and commended Ernest Armstrong, the Labour MP, for his hospitality and 'sympathy towards the trade union case'.

The CP *Weekly Letter* felt that it was 'not only the numbers' on the lobby which 'were impressive', but also 'the breadth of representation from the trade union movement in industries in all parts of Britain'. The 'decisive thing' now was to 'increase pressure on the government' by 'local demonstrations and industrial action all aimed at building up pressure on the General Council demanding it call a one-day strike'. The CP Manchester Area Committee noted: 'Branch discussions to take report from this Sunday's District Cttee.'

On the 17th Ramelson told Warren that '15,000' lobbied the Commons, but Jenkins was 'digging his heels in and it will require much bigger efforts to shift him'.

> There were also a few stoppages, but unfortunately mainly on building sites, though the Felixstowe seamen struck and joined the lobby as a body. There were also a few stoppages in engineering. We have to build on that until the whole industry is willing to stop if Jenkins does not listen to reason—he will then have to be confronted with the whole strength and power of the working class which, if it is used, is irresistible. I assure you we will do all we can to bring this about.

He was delighted about the TUC delegation and 'whole executive councils of unions' and MPs 'actually on the march'.

The *Daily Mail* wheeled out Clifford Growcott, who now claimed that 'a brick' hit him on the back of the leg at Brookside in 1972. 'I was beaten and kicked to the ground like a football. Then I was struck on the head with a brick.' He was 'too ill from his injuries to testify at the trial'. (His statement was very different.) His eye was now 'completely useless'. Stanley Rawson added: 'Three or four held me while another gave me a good hiding.' 'Seventy of them set on five of us, and half of them were drunk before they got to our site.' (He didn't say that he pointed a shotgun at them or that a lumper threatened to decapitate a picket with a shovel.)

On the 26th Len Murray stressed in the *Sunday Mirror* that the 'Two' weren't guilty of violence or intimidation, but were 'in prison for what they did'. 'Conspiracy' law was inappropriate for industrial disputes. TUC-affiliated unions and Trades Councils should 'step up the pressure' through deputations to MPs. (The General Council rejected the Scottish NUM's call for a one-day strike.)

On the 28th the *Birmingham Evening Mail* described 'scenes of violence' on 6 September 1972 as 'more in character with Nazi or Communist regimes than with the British way of life'. The editor refused to debate with Ken Barlow, who noted that the Kent NUM EC had called for a one-day strike, a print union and eleven 'important' Trades Councils had made a similar call to the TUC and Labour MPs were 'beginning to bombard the Home Secretary'.

Billy Regan's *The Shrewsbury Case: Some More Evidence for the Home Secretary* questioned the role of the police, the judiciary and the state and argued that the jailed pickets 'at the very least merit a public enquiry'. It was printed by Rye Express Ltd (TU) in London and published by the CDC and the South West London Defence Committee. On the 30th Regan asked Simon Fraser to send a copy to Len Murray with a request to 'meet a small delegation from our committee'. He also sent a copy to Roy Jenkins, whose Private Secretary replied that 'it may be possible'.

You're going to have to come off the protest

The February 1975 UCATT *Viewpoint* carried the slogans 'FREE THE TWO NOW' and 'NAME THE DAY!'

On the 3rd the CP North West District Secretariat noted:

> The campaign for the TUC call for a one day strike on the Shrewsbury Pickets is gaining momentum with an important Conference convened by the Liverpool Trades Council this Sunday, February 9th. The Liaison C[omm]ttee for Defence of Trade Unions has also convened a National Conference under the slogans '*Reject the Social Contract—Free the Shrewsbury Two*' on Saturday 22nd March.

(District membership had fallen by 1,111 in three months.) Next day CP Merseyside Area Committee noted 'full support required'.

On the 4th Warren was taken to Lincoln and Tomlinson was moved to Leicester, but both refused to wear prison clothes.

On the 9th, at the SNCC, Simon Fraser argued successfully for waiting to see what happened at the appeals, but for asking Len Murray to congratulate the TUC on the 'highly successful' lobby, sending a 'strong protest' to Wilson and Jenkins about transfers to closed prisons, naming the day for a 'one-day stoppage' and threatening 'a continuous stoppage until they are released'. If they weren't released by 1 March, 'steps would be taken to convene a national conference'. Midlands, Merseyside and Manchester supporters should send fifty delegates to lobby the TUC. UCATT Midland Region was 'compiling a booklet on the trials'. The SNCC wanted some. Barry Williams, President of Liverpool Trades Council and a leading CPer, was invited to join the SNCC.

Jenkins stopped Warren's visits until he wore prison clothes. Three Tribunite MPs grilled Warren about his criminal record.

The CDC met on the 12th. Six members were present. (Bob Williams had gone to Rhodesia.) Barry Scragg reported that he, Bill Jones, Andy Kelly, Arthur Murray and McKinsie Jones had met George Smith of UCATT, George Henderson of the TGWU and John Monks of the TUC. *The Shrewsbury Case* 'went a long way to enlightening them'. The CDC called for site delegations to lobby the TUC. 1,000 copies of the *Final Bulletin* argued that the men 'remain wrongfully imprisoned', but the campaign had 'undoubtedly been a great success, bringing to light the dangers in the use of the conspiracy laws against trade unionists'.

Next day Martin Flannery proposed to the Parliamentary Labour Party that the Shrewsbury issue should be debated in the Commons. Tony Benn noted that the Chairman, Cledwyn Hughes, claimed 'there was no time, it would divide the party, it would be unhelpful', but then 'horrified Jenkins by indicating that he intended putting the matter to the vote'. Jenkins said it would 'put the Government in difficulty, as it somehow was a cabinet decision'. (It was not.) He 'would be forced to present information that would be damaging, and he hoped to get the pickets out anyway'. (Jenkins recalled that he was not going to 'turn like a squirrel in a cage': 'I would have felt I had to resign had it gone wrong.') Benn abstained, Michael Foot voted against and the motion was defeated by 63 votes to 25.

Wigan Building Workers' Action Committee organised a march to London. St Helens Trades Council, Lancashire NUM, Merseyside docks stewards, Fords Halewood Transmissions and various union branches supported them, but CP stewards, union officials and Liverpool Trades Council were against. On 22 February 6,000 supporters walked with the marchers to Trafalgar Square.

Warren heard about the 'hostile opposition' from CDC CPers: 'Desi doesn't want this. He wants the TUC moving.' He did, but 'action would have to be forced on them'. Bert Ramelson told Warren: 'Oh, it's only a gang of students.'

On the 24th MPs Martin Flannery and Stan Thorne moved a Bill designed to prevent the use of 'conspiracy' law against trade unionists. Substantial numbers of Labour MPs abstained or were absent and the Bill was defeated by 166 to 143. (Warren was told that Benn was 'tied by the cabinet', but he wasn't impressed.)

The TUC General Council postponed a decision on the UCATT EC request for a one-day stoppage until after they met Jenkins. A large contingent from the Wigan Builders' Action Committee was outside Congress House as Len Murray strode past placards reading 'OUT WITH THE LABOUR TRAITORS' and 'CALL A GENERAL STRIKE'. One General Council member believed that 'the protest is virtually over', but the TGWU committed its 1,750,000 members to strike. Labour's majority was down to one.

On the 27th Barry Scragg told Flannery that 'a small delegation' would meet him and 'any of your colleagues who are concerned over the continued imprisonment of our two brothers'.

The UCATT *Midland Regional Bulletin* advertised a lobby of Leicester Prison. It also asked sites and factories to send telegrams and resolutions and to elect a delegate for the TUC Congress lobby.

Workers Against the Law

The February 1975 *International Socialism* advertised Laurie Flynn's *Workers Against the Law: The Truth About the Shrewsbury Trials*. It noted that after Warren and Tomlinson were sent back to jail there was 'scarcely a whimper from the Labour government or their co-partners in the Social Contract, the leaders of the TUC'. The CDC's eyes were 'fixed on the official machine'. They hadn't involved the London dockers who led the movement to free the Pentonville 5, or approached 'left wing leaders' in the NUM, or defied the judge's threat to imprison defendants if there were demonstrations. They hadn't used 'the working class or underground press' other than the *Star*, which 'confined itself to court reporting of the most conventional variety'. For 'sectarian reasons' the CDC tried to prevent the three who didn't get jail sentences at the first Shrewsbury trial from speaking in support of those who did. This was 'fully in accord with the policies and attitudes' of the CP. Flynn argued that resolutions for official action should be pushed, support for the families and powerful propaganda were needed and 'some of our energies' could be used to tackling the Labour Cabinet, even though they were 'slavishly devoted to capitalist law and order'. In addition, if 'the issues are clearly explained to rank and file workers' they would organise 'in a much more direct and determined manner than the purveyors of conference hall rhetoric'. It was vital to 'promote industrial action and achieve it if the campaign is to be successful', but 'hefty pressure will have to be brought to bear', breaking the media's 'conspiracy of silence' and 'building a genuine rank and file movement' that can tackle Shrewsbury and other issues. Otherwise, 'our masters' would 'shackle working class power and make workers pay the price of salvaging their crisis ridden system'.

Alistair Goulding, the TGWU convenor at McAlpine's Strand site, had an article in the February *International Socialism*. There were 500,000 lumpers, and the TGWU recruited craftsmen in competition with UCATT, which was nearing insolvency and 'unionising the lump' by 'check off' arrangements. The *Charter* was 'dependent on what the CP considers to be electorally expedient' and the line 'has increasingly demanded that militants wait on TUC decisions, or for election results', after a shaky start in 1974:

> The first Liverpool conference called for a series of lobbies and one-day strikes but the opportunity was lost. In early January, Birmingham shop stewards called a conference for the 21st, for which they prepared a resolution pledging themselves to open-ended strike action to lead the way.
>
> The CP undermined this initiative, and the second Liverpool Trades Council Conference was called for the 2nd Feb. In preparation, they slandered as splitters any group that didn't trust 'unity' under the direction of the CP. At Liverpool they foisted upon the broad left the weakest option open to them—more conferences, another day of action, and more pressure on the trade union bureaucracy. Their reasoning was that the builders were too weak to take the lead, and that the movement as a whole was unprepared. Yet the Birmingham builders had announced their readiness. Also, the miners' conflict was in full swing, and NUM delegates were at the conference with messages of solidarity.

The CDC campaign was 'solely oriented towards lobbying for official action' and its commitment to strikes was merely 'verbal'.

The IS National Committee voted narrowly in favour of abolishing itself and for a Central Committee of nine to run the organisation between annual conferences, with a purely advisory 'National Council', elected from 'districts' of groups of branches, which would take over branches' right to elect conference delegates. Full-time organisers would be delegates by right. This reorganisation would take place before the next conference, where a 'closed slate' system would be used for CC elections. Rival slates were permissible, but no slates could be amended. The 1974 perspective had 'overestimated the speed with which the economic crisis would drive workers to draw revolutionary political conclusions'.

In the March *International Socialism*, Steve Jefferys' 'The Challenge of the Rank and File' argued that the 'deepening crisis' wasn't 'strengthening the "left trend" in the labour movement' and workers weren't turning 'more and more to the left leaders in the trade unions and in parliament for socialist policies', as the CP argued. Moreover, 'as the crisis steadily worsens, the left reformist path will become an increasingly blind and occasionally bloody alley'. Workers 'must attempt to forge strong defensive rank and file organisations'. 'No socialist trade unionist today seriously argues for leaving it to the MPs to free the Shrewsbury pickets'. The 1973 LCDTU conference had proved that 'under no circumstances would it allow any democracy or calls for action that would embarrass the left trade union bureaucracy', so IS must 'nourish the fragile roots of rank and file organisation while erecting between and over them the patchwork umbrella of a national movement'.

Ian Birchall's 'History of the International Socialists' in the March and April *International Socialism* argued that the high level of activity required of IS before the February 1974 general election had meant that 'resources were strained almost to breaking point'. Labour's 'hairsbreadth victory' resulted in an industrial situation that was 'much more fragmentary than under the Tories', leading to problems for a small organisation that was 'more and more confronted with tasks that required a much bigger organisation'. There had been 'a sharp internal debate' about Cliff's 'political' perspective, but it had won a majority and less than half the outgoing National Committee had been re-elected. This 'inevitably meant the replacement of some people who had a record of long service'.

I never had any trouble with the Cabinet

The March 1975 *Viewpoint* urged the TUC to 'Call One-Day Strike'.

The SNCC met on 1 March. No minutes are publicly available, but they called for a conference on 19 April and a May Day strike.

On the 5th Jack Jones confirmed that the TGWU Research Department would study *The Shrewsbury Case*. The TGWU wrote to the TUC, calling for a one-day stoppage. The TUC's Finance and General Purposes Committee asked to meet Jenkins.

The exact chronology remains uncertain, but Tomlinson appears to indicate that by early March Bill Jones, Pete Carter and Alan Abrahams had told him: 'You're going to have to come off the protest.' He refused, but Abrahams insisted: 'Dezzie isn't well. He's not sleeping and the liquid cosh is messing up his head. His feet are bad, but they won't let him wear surgical shoes. He can barely walk.' Then he should come off. 'Yeah but he's too proud. He won't come out while you're still in here.' 'If you do the rest of your time, Dezzie won't last the distance.' Tomlinson still wouldn't agree, but 'Alan's voice softened to a whisper: "We're ordering you, Rick".'

On the 14th Barry Scragg, Arthur Murray and Mike Williams discussed the trial photographs with CPer Pete Kavanagh—now a TGWU official—and they also visited the *Star*.

It was Billy Regan—not John Carpenter—who brought Marlene Tomlinson to visit Ricky. The solicitor Campbell Malone had agreed with his decision to ask Jenkins to recommend clemency. Tomlinson told Warren: 'I think there's such a lot to be done by both you and I to help get this inquiry started into our case that for you to spend a day longer in gaol than is really necessary is a day wasted.' Warren called him 'spineless and a turncoat' and told Malone that he could not do the same. Bert Ramelson asked Ken Barlow to try to get Warren to call off the protest, but Barlow refused.

The LCDTU saw it as 'a critical time' for Labour and the unions. Its 'National Delegate Conference' in London would be on the 22nd.

The Wales Committee of the CP put 'Release the Shrewsbury Two' third behind the Common Market and the Social Contract:

* Intensify Campaign for direct action now.
* Put comrade in charge.
* All out for Feb 26th lobby.
* And widest delegation to March 22nd Conference with maximum calls for action.
* Mass sale of Midlands campaign pamphlet.
* Organise a mass picket of Government representative in Wales.

On the 19th Bill Jones told the CDC that the *Final Bulletin* gave 'the impression we had disbanded the campaign altogether', so he had drafted a statement to be sent to the *Star* and *Tribune*. BBC TV's *Panorama* had asked him for Llywarch and O'Shea's addresses, but he told them that it 'would be far better' to get information from the CDC. (Barry Scragg appeared and gave the fee to the Defence Fund, but Roger Bolton's programme evidently wasn't screened.) McKinsie Jones and Murray had 'managed the meeting very well' at Blackpool and Murray was to be a delegate to the LCDTU Conference. The TUC lobby would be 'well looked after by the London lads, but sites able to send delegates should do so'.

Next day Labour MP Anthony Kershaw told a UCATT branch that he did not support the jailed pickets. 'In my opinion they richly deserved what they got. You may not be aware that these two men assaulted their fellow workers with iron bars and chased them across building lots and generally behaved in an outrageous fashion.' The branch sent the letter to the CDC without the recipient's name and address.

On 22 March the WRP's *Workers' Press* quoted Campbell Malone: 'Some' CDC members believed that Warren 'should cooperate with his jailers in order to get out as soon as possible'.

On the 24th Jenkins told a TUC delegation that Tomlinson had complied with the rules and had been transferred to an open prison. Warren's refusal damaged his case for the Parole Board. A UCATT-sponsored MP would advise Warren to comply.

Bert Ramelson wrote to Warren:

> There comes a time... when consideration has to be given as to whether a particular form of action can any longer further the ultimate objective...
>
> 1) You are absolutely right in your conviction, which I share, that the success of the campaign will be determined not in parliament but by what happens outside parliament, and in particular how far we are successful in exerting pressure on the General Council to call for national industrial action.
>
> You are well aware that if it were possible it would put backbone into some of the vacillating MPs and we would then be in a position to combine both extra-parliamentary and parliamentary action.
>
> One of the problems of getting the General Council to act is the reluctance of rightwingers and the vacillation of some in the centre and even on the left...
>
> ... your non-cooperation makes it difficult for Jenkins to move from his intransigent position, and it is having a considerable effect on some of the members of the General Council who might otherwise take a more determined attitude for action. In a sense it is letting them off the hook.

2) What has made the position from your point of view even weaker is the fact that the united stand of you and Eric is now broken...

... the bulk of the movement who recognise your conviction as a vicious political action will understand that your acceptance of parole, if we cannot force your unconditional parole through industrial action, will continue to believe in your innocence and that you are a victim of the class struggle. Furthermore, once you are released, whether by pardon or parole, you would have the opportunity and we would do all we can to provide platforms to use that opportunity, of exposing the class nature of the trial.

It is my advice, therefore... that you would help to develop the official movement, which you realise is so important, by ending your individual protest.

He claimed that Elsa's view 'coincides with mine'.

Next day Jack Jones let the TGWU proposal for a one-day strike on 1 May 'lie on the table' at the TUC General Council, reportedly because it 'might affect the minds of the parole board in a counter-productive way'. The meeting urged the jailed pickets 'to cooperate with the prison authorities'.

Soon after, the *Star* claimed that Ramelson visited Warren and he had 'decided to comply with prison rules', but Warren was sure that it was Campbell Malone: 'someone seems to have been in one helluva hurry to convince someone else I had changed my mind'. It 'really stuck in my craw'.

The *Charter* reappeared after a four-month break. Its 'General Strike Call' noted that unemployment in the building industry was the worst since 1962, yet there was a housing shortage. With 20 percent inflation, the 1972 wage settlement was now hopelessly inadequate, so pressure had to be applied to union leaders. Delegates should be elected to the Liverpool Conference on 26 April.

The *Charter* reprinted an article from *The Miner* of 11 December 1926 about a campaign to release miners and the Monmouthshire Miners' Agent, who was a JP, county councillor and member of the police committee. (TUC leaders had called off the General Strike that May and left the miners to fight alone.) Miners 'should exert the strongest possible pressure through their organisations, local Labour Parties, local authorities, etc, etc, on the Government to secure the release of our unjustly convicted comrades'. The agent had been at a Pontypool pit where 'police were out in force to ensure that scabs were successful in breaking through the picket lines'. Reportedly, he 'mounted a coal truck' and 'shouted that the police had acted with terrible ferocity. He saw one old man, who had been sitting down peacefully, struck over the head by a policeman's truncheon. Eventually, police reinforcements were brought in and the crowd was dispersed'. The agent got nine months for 'riotous conduct' and two others were also jailed. 'Deputations went to the Home Office and eventually the Tory government bowed to the pressure.' The agent took a trip abroad, paid for by the Liberal *Daily News*. By 1929 Arthur Jenkins's family had a car and a maid. The *Charter* asked: 'Would Jenkins free his own father?'

Roy Jenkins believed that Warren and Tomlinson were 'rough thugs' who 'deserved their sentences', though 'there was a belief on the left that I should automatically release them on pietistic grounds'.

> I did not however regard either the external circumstances or their behaviour as being in any way comparable with my father's case. Nor, I think, at the end of the day did the TUC. I believe that the 'Shrewsbury Two' were claiming to be above the law at a time of great trade union power, whereas my father's claim was not to be below the law and not to be discriminated against because of a climate of repression at a time when the miners were sinking into weakness as they lost a battle against wage reductions.

As for 'sporadic small demonstrations' and the *Star*'s frequent headlines, he 'did not find any of this formidable, for I had settled my mind on the issue, and I never had any trouble with the Cabinet'.

On 17 April the Home Office told Arthur Murray that Jenkins could 'recommend interference with the decision of a court only if fresh evidence of substance is produced and that is not the situation here'. However the charges still on file would not be proceeded with.

The IS Opposition

On 9 March, 25 IS members including Jim Higgins, Roger Protz and John Palmer had met in Birmingham to work out a different perspective to Cliff's. Their draft was discussed by fifty members in London on the 22nd and by 8 April 100 members had agreed to 'The Platform of the IS Opposition', which appeared in the April Pre-Conference Discussion Documents. It acknowledged the 'lull in the class struggle' after Labour's election, the slowing tempo of recruitment and the fall in the paid sale of *SW* to 18,000; but there was 'a very large gap between a group of 3,000 and the revolutionary party' and 'the route to the mass party' was through the unions. *SW* should aim at the 'advanced section of militants'—above all manual workers—and not the 'inexperienced, traditionless but rebellious youth' that Cliff favoured. 'The situation where major disputes within the leadership of IS are kept from the membership has got to stop' and Cliff had to become 'a disciplined member of a collective'. The R&FOC Conference had been a qualified success and the rank and file papers had a circulation of 30,000, yet the R&FOC leadership was 'composed entirely of IS members' and had had 'no more effect than to disorient our own membership'.

The EC supported the R&FOC's 'major contribution in keeping alive the Shrewsbury campaign':

> Showings of the Shrewsbury film have been organised and
> national leaflets distributed. Notably some 30,000 copies of the
> R[&]FOC's one penny fact sheet has been sold. With the closing
> of the CP dominated N[orth] Wales Defence Committee the
> R[&]FOC emerged as the only body within the movement
> continuing to campaign with a Shrewsbury Dependants fund.

An R&FOC member had argued about the Shrewsbury issue on TV in December 1974, and the R&FOC organised the march from Euston and the 800-strong meeting in January 1975 and a demonstration outside Lincoln Prison. (Geoff Brown recalls going on a coach from Manchester to 'make a noise'. Around 100 had turned up, mainly from IS.) The LCDTU had been 'miraculously conjured up' in March, 'in response to disquiet within the CP at the limited successes' of the R&FOC, but rejected a joint campaign.

The April IS *Internal Bulletin* argued that there was a general drift to the right in the CP-dominated union Broad Lefts, while the TUC's token demonstration on Shrewsbury had 'cut the ground from under those right wing elements in the movement who argued that Tomlinson and Warren deserved to be in prison'. The TUC wanted to head off pressure for more decisive action. However, IS '*overestimated the speed with which the economic crisis would drive workers to draw revolutionary conclusions*'. Comrades should build factory branches and fractions and replace the ineffective LCDTU and, ultimately, the CP. No National Committee minutes were to be circulated, the national mailing was to be reduced and only one copy of district and branch minutes was to be kept.

Alistair Goulding noted in the April *International Socialism* that employers predicted '300,000 unemployed building workers this spring'. So far in 1975, 'only half as many new houses were started' as in 1973, and 'building activity' had 'steadily decreased' after government spending cuts. Big contractors were looking for smaller jobs and might drive out smaller firms, who were launching 'a concerted attack' on wages and conditions. Building workers needed a 'mounting consciousness of the contradictions within the Labour government' and to raise the demand for nationalisation without compensation, under workers' control. A Manchester site had been occupied after the management contravened 'first in, last out'. Birmingham stewards demanded that employers take their workforce to their next contracts and instituted overtime bans. 'Militant organisation is emerging outside the direct influence of the Charter.' 'Many' CPers and their 'periphery' were 'confused by the failure of the party's strategy to free the Shrewsbury pickets'. Unless the CP was challenged, 'the Charter will remain an exclusive platform' for 'rhetoric veiling reformist illusions'.

By 30 April the 'Platform of the IS Opposition' had received 137 signatures. A meeting was planned for 18 May, but they failed to put up a persuasive alternative at the Conference on the 31st and Cliff and his supporters won by default. The major organisational changes were accepted. The CC became the *SW* Editorial Board and Chris Harman was appointed as Editor, though Foot and Flynn stayed on as journalists.

Pie in the sky

Jim French isn't sure exactly when this happened, but he recalls:

> I didn't like the way that Darlington Council officers told us what to do and I left the Labour Party. I didn't know any IS members in Darlington and nobody asked me to join. Anyway, I agreed with the CP's programme, so I joined Charlie Lowther's branch. There were only eight or nine of us and most of the others were elderly. I got a little political education, but that party tradition was waning. The books I was given were light at first, but soon got heavier—Maurice Cornforth's *Dialectical Materialism*, for example—and I wasn't always able to follow them. But we discussed the Shrewsbury trials, sent money and tried to work out what was going on.

The Flying Pickets

The UCATT Regional Secretary said: 'Stop flying kites, French'; and told him to pick firms out of Yellow Pages and pay a visit.

Back in February the UCATT Northern Regional Committee had ordered 1,000 leaflets on the Shrewsbury issue and wrote to the EC.

> We deplore the non-committance by far too many MPs within the House of Commons with respect to amendments intended to remove harmful legislation in such as the Conspiracy Act in relation to normal trade union activity including picketting, and call upon the EC through the medium of the TUC to make it clear to Labour MPs and indeed other MPs, their repugnance of this sheer arrogance and misuse of parliamentary democracy by their abstention on such a grave issue relating to this question.

The Regional Committee supported the EC 'request to the TUC for a one-day national stoppage' and invited Elsa Warren 'to enlighten the delegates' about her 'personal experiences' at their conference. Crook UCATT heard from the Charter and the CDC and elected delegates for the Charter Conference. They were concerned about the 'lack of national activity' about Tomlinson and Warren.

On 26 April 300 delegates attended the Charter Conference. Billy Regan acknowledged the 'meetings, marches, rallies, lobbies of parliament and a number of approaches to the Home Secretary from the TUC, but time itself has confirmed that the only way to release the lads would be by the use of massive industrial action.' 'Many sites, branches and trades councils have urged the TUC to call an official stoppage on May 1st', but it preferred the Parole Board. Barry Scragg noted the Labour Party NEC call for 'immediate release' and the TUC's 'numerous meetings with Jenkins and Wilson', yet 'all they have achieved were empty promises of parole, in other words "pie in the sky".' Further talks would be 'a substitute for what is really needed'. He urged delegates 'to make sure the maximum pressure is put on the TUC' to 'activate in full the decision of last year's Congress'. The Conference Policy Statement argued that the TGWU and UCATT 'should now lead the troops into battle' and the TUC 'should call for industrial action'. The Charter 'has not appeared regularly enough' and steps had been taken to get 'a great increase in the number of issues', but it needed £400 'to keep going in these crazy days of inflation'. Arthur Murray, Elsa Warren and Marlene Tomlinson spoke. Over £500—including £110 from the Liverpool Teaching Hospital site and its CP branch—was raised, plus £200 in

IOUs. The Editorial Board, now 'under the direction' of Pete Carter, aimed to produce an issue every six weeks.

On the 28th Sunderland Trades Council told the CDC that they hoped to hold a joint public meeting with UCATT Northern Region in mid-May to help 'fight for the release of Bros Warren and Tomlinson', but had been 'given to understand that Mrs Warren will not be available owing to going on holiday'. Mike Williams suggested to Elsa Warren that she might like to reply and sent £7.50 for her and Marlene Tomlinson. UCATT Northern Regional Committee heard she was 'unable' to accept the invitation.

A May Day rally at the AUEW offices in Salford, dedicated to freeing the 'Two', defending the right to picket and building a 'special dependants' fund', was sponsored by South Manchester Hospital NUPE, the SLADE committee at the Phoenix Print Shop, four AUEW branches and stewards at a Manchester site, who went on strike for the day. Speakers included Ian Hayes, the site convenor, Bill Geddes from Hammersmith Hospital site (which been on strike in support of the jailed men), Bernard Panter of the AUEW Manchester District Committee and the London IS docker Michael Fenn.

Liverpool Teaching Hospital site struck in support.

On the 8th the Parole Board did not recommend release. Jenkins told MPs that he had no power to overrule the decision, but both men had complied with prison rules and there would be special reviews.

A CDC statement believed that Jenkins told the TUC: 'If you don't rock the boat the lads will have early parole', but it was 'surely time now that we did rock the boat, for every other way was doomed to failure before being tried'. They called for resolutions.

Dave Ayre reported to Crook UCATT on the Charter Conference. They read a Charter letter and expressed 'strong feeling' about the jailed pickets 'continuing solitary confinement'. Protest letters went to the Northern Regional Committee and the Home Office. Soon after, the branch heard of the Northern Regional Secretary's 'sympathies with branch proposals' on the Two. He would inform the EC. Bill Kerriss and Dave Ayre were unanimously re-elected as Branch President and Secretary, but 'considerable concern was registered' 'following reports on the effects of solitary confinement on the mental health of Bro Des Warren'. The matter would be raised at the Trades Council 'to broaden support and information'.

On the 18th the TUC General Council visited Jenkins. He recalled: 'Jack Jones took the lead, but most of the right wing leaders came too, although one or two of them a little sheepishly. I had the impression that the bulk of the deputation was not so much angry as amazed that I would not concede.' He told them that the Parole Board would hear Tomlinson's application before the end of June, but Warren's hearing would be in August.

On 28 May, Billy Regan wrote to Hugh Scanlon, General Secretary of the AUEW, who had seconded the UCATT TUC Congress motion: 'As you are aware after marches, lobbies and meetings with the Home Secretary, our brothers are today still behind bars, the promise of early parole being only an exercise to dampen down any positive action.' Regan urged 'the maximum pressure' on the TUC 'to implement the full resolution'. On the 30th the CDC ordered 1,000 leaflets headed 'Free them now'.

A month went by. Early in July the *Charter* noted that the TUC were 'afraid to call for action'. 'Full support' should be given to Nottingham Trades Council's demonstration outside the prison and to 'a major demonstration' at the TUC Congress. Tomlinson's 'Building Workers Stars' told readers to prepare for a shock, since the TUC 'may decide on some positive action'. (Warren wrote something, but Pete Carter later told him that he didn't receive it.)

Tomlinson got his release date and wrote to Warren:

As you know the parole carrot has been dangled in front of me, but I wouldn't accept it until I had a visit from Marlene, Billy and Peter Carter. Marlene had agreed to go along with me and stick it out until September but Peter Carter overruled and told me it was important that I get out on the 25th and prepare the foundation of a new attack on your behalf. So I leave on Friday.

He had obeyed a CP EC member. Warren didn't know what to think.

On the 9th the CDC agreed to publicise the TUC lobby in the *Star* and discussed 'finance' for Elsa Warren and Marlene Tomlinson. Barry Scragg 'reiterated the committee's past decision'.

Simon Fraser sent out agendas for the SNCC, which was 'approximately £100 in debt', due to the cancelled April conference. Could members 'raise funds to meet this liability and any further expenditure'? He 'would appreciate your attendance', so that definite action can be taken' to make it 'a meaningful organisation'.

A fortnight went by. On the 22nd Bert Ramelson told Warren about the 'deplorable flagging in the campaign', though the Parole Board would 'undoubtedly be influenced by the possible consequences at the September TUC if they refuse'.

The next *SW* carried a photograph of IS National Secretary Jim Nichol and CPer Pete Carter flanking Ricky and Marlene Tomlinson outside prison. Ricky was 'to campaign to get my mate Des out'. He began a 'whirlwind tour of the country', speaking with Paul Foot of IS.

CHAPTER 19

The key to my cell

Spineless maggots

By August 1975 the auditors had prepared a Defence Fund balance sheet, but Ken Barlow wanted to discuss the 'final disbursement' and the CDC 'may wish to re-phrase some of the descriptions'. The CDC asked Bill Jones to 'speed matters up'. 'Every effort would be made to fill at least one coach' to the TUC Congress lobby. (There are no more publicly available minutes for a year.)

After the demonstration outside Nottingham Prison, the screws harassed Warren. He went on hunger strike and was refused a family visit, but After Tom Litterick MP threatened to raise it in the Commons. The visit went ahead and Warren came off the strike. On 14 August he was sent to Lincoln Prison and put in the punishment 'Block'.

On 2 September the CDC and South West London Defence Committee invited TUC Congress delegates to see the trial photographs and asked for 'positive action now to free Des Warren'. Marie Patterson OBE didn't mention him in her Presidential Address. Mick McGahey, Scottish NUM EC member and a leading CPer, called for a general strike, but the EETPU's Tom Breakell denounced Warren and Tomlinson for 'gangsterism'. Tomlinson got to his feet in the public gallery and asked: 'What do you know about Dezzie Warren? Do you know how long he's been in prison? How long has he got to stay there? When are you going to get off your fat arses and do your job?' Patterson threatened Warren's supporters with the police and had them ejected. Some delegates joined them. A large majority called on the TUC to 'use the full strength of the trade union movement' to secure Warren's release.

According to Roy Jenkins, the TUC had been 'following rather than resisting a Communist and Trotskyist-inspired campaign', but after the 'thuggery' at Blackpool, there was 'a noticeable diminution in the fervour of the General Council's demands upon me'.

George Smith told Flint UCATT that the EC couldn't 'take uni-lateral steps', since the TUC was now 'the body responsible'.

The *Sunday Times* published an interview with Clifford Grow-cott, who now claimed that 'twenty to thirty men' had been 'pelting me with bricks' at Brookside in 1972. He was 'saved by the inter-vention of another group of pickets', but was warned that if he 'came back in the job I would not walk off again—both my legs would be broken'. (He mentioned one assailant in his statement and at the trial and none of those alleged threats.) He had 'lost the sight of his right eye' and got £1,000 from the Criminal Injuries Compensation Board. Lumpers earned '£15 a week over the union minimum' and he was on £80 (worth about £450 today).

The October *Charter*'s headline was '£1.50 Per Hour Now'. A short anonymous article, 'Des Still Inside', noted that screws were giving him 'a rough time'. 'We must continue to demand a one-day national strike.' A photograph showed Marlene and Ricky Tomlinson on his release in July, courtesy of the *Star*: 'One of Eric's first jobs' had been to visit the Commons to win MPs' support 'to continue the fight for the release of Des and to change the conspiracy laws. During the next few months he will be speaking at meetings all over Britain.' Anonymous Liverpool and Birmingham phone numbers were given for readers who wanted him to speak at their site, factory or branch. Alex Weir was now the Charter's Blackpool Area Secretary.

The November *Charter* noted that a Manchester Building Work-ers Forum's social evening raised £100 for the *Charter*. 250 turned up and Tomlinson was guest of honour. Police had stopped him as he drove there in Warren's car and sixty police with dogs raided the social. Warren's parole application had been turned down: 'however well-intentioned TUC visits to Wilson and Jenkins may be, they will not free this innocent victim of trade union bashing.' He was 'a polit-ical prisoner and trade union leaders must make a resolute call for industrial action'. Otherwise he was unlikely to be released before 6 September 1976. Pete Carter noted that George Smith had been re-elected by an overwhelming majority of the 3 percent of UCATT members who voted and had moved a motion at the TUC that sup-ported the government's £6 wage ceiling. Smith's weekly rise was £21.80. The lump was flourishing and 20 percent of building work-ers would soon be on the dole. Bolton, Sheffield and North Staffs Areas were no longer listed.

On 4 November Bert Ramelson told Warren that the TUC had 'not seen Wilson as they promised', but the PM wanted to discuss 'the whole question of conspiracy laws after the Law Commission report on the subject in January'. The TUC found this unsatisfactory, but 'unless we succeed in developing a much bigger head of pressure than we have been able to mount so far they are not likely to do much'. Ramelson would meet 'friendly MPs'. (Tom Litterick insisted that 'whatever can be done' in the Commons 'has been done'.)

The trial photographs were shown to a small group of Tribune MPs and to thirty more in December. South West London Defence Committee produced a Christmas card with the TUC Congress resolutions and the slogan, 'MAKE THESE WORDS DEEDS'.

The December *Charter*'s front-page headline was 'SUBBIES—the New Menace'! The campaign to free Warren had been 'maintained'. Tribunite MPs and 'various representatives of UCATT' had been to see him, but the problem was the 'half-hearted and indecisive' UCATT EC and the TUC. 700 copies of the *Charter* had been sold to Liverpool Corporation workers, but Bill Jones, Convenor of the Minor Works Department, saw 'room for improvement'. A 'finance and circulation manager' would 'chase up cash'. Eddie Nash appealed: 'Support Your Paper'.

Jenkins might change the 1875 Act when it was 'practicable'.

UCATT leaders wanted to visit Warren: 'Many of my comrades will say that I'm wrong not to meet them, that we must involve them in the campaign, but let's not forget the desperate, cowardly, self-interested role that these spineless maggots have played in the Shrewsbury issue.' He wouldn't 'play footsie with traitors'.

On the 28th Tomlinson wrote to Warren: 'It amazes me how people (some of your old pals) can argue against the call for action on your behalf. Rose Davis has done more on her own to draw attention to her husband's case than all the combined efforts of the North Wales Defence Committee.' (George Davis had been convicted of armed robbery in March 1975.)

The Defence Fund's Nationwide account was emptied of £640 and closed. December's income was £849, but £409 went on delegates' expenses, £133 for bulletins and postage, £117 to Elsa Warren, £107 for Corporation Tax and £54 to Marlene Tomlinson. £17 was for Warren's subscription to the *Star*.

I see you're on the hard stuff

In January 1976 the CP North West Area Committee agreed to take up the 'suggestion of a petition to Jenkins' and 'get names of possible sponsors', including MPs, stewards and convenors.

By February the UCATT North West Regional Secretary, Eric Hughes, had issued the Distress Fund balance sheet from 27 October 1973 to 29 December 1975. Income was £7,171. Garry Davies and Terry Renshaw had received £100, Brian Williams and Arthur Murray £620, McKinsie Jones £770 and Elsa Warren £4,663 (about £31,000 at today's values). The balance was £249. With EC approval, Hughes appealed for donations.

On the 8th Elsa Warren was admitted to hospital, suffering from nervous exhaustion. Four of the children were taken into care and she was given drugs and electro-shock therapy. On the 16th the screws told Des that her letter had been returned as 'excess mail'.

On the 18th, Hughes, James Callaghan (Labour MP for Middleton and Prestwich), John Carroll (Mayor of Rochdale) and the AUEW Manchester District Secretary, John Tocher, supported the North West Branch of Rochdale and District Labour Party's efforts for the Warren family. Belt and Braces Road Show's 'musical entertainment for all those sick with sacrifice', *England Expects*, was a 'despicably truthful analysis of Britain's economic crisis presented with brilliant clarity, wit, musicianship, and outstanding performing skill'. It 'undermines the very basis on which entertainment has always been so dextrously employed by our wiser and betters to keep us underfed, under-privileged, badly-housed, mystified, misinformed and completely happy'. It included a debate about strategy between a union militant and a revolutionary. There was self-doubt on both sides. 300 turned up at Langley Labour Club and Committee members saw it as 'nothing more than Communist propaganda', but Middleton North West Labour Party thanked Abe and Eric. Warren's family received £158.

On the 24th Warren was transferred to Leicester Prison and began suffering from 'nervous tension'. Dr Smith, who had been sent from the high security Gartree Prison, prescribed drugs and assured him that they weren't addictive. On 1 March Warren asked permission to phone Elsa. (Jenkins refused.) He petitioned. (Jenkins refused.) On the 5th Elsa discharged herself because the treatment made her feel worse. She and Dr Alistair Wilson, a veteran CPer, visited Warren and Wilson advised him to place himself in Dr Smith's care. On the 8th Warren petitioned to consult a solicitor to take proceedings against Jenkins. (Jenkins refused.) He was put in a cell with an epileptic. He was due for home leave on the 12th, but began a hunger strike. He was allowed home a few days later, but going back to Leicester was a heartbreaking experience for the family and he was put in a double cell. On the 18th he went for the prescription. A screw remarked: 'I see you're on the hard stuff.'

Warren recalled: 'I walked around very slowly, not speaking to anyone. I would fall asleep in my cell when I was not working. My mouth was dry all the time. I spoke as if I was drunk.' On 1 April he came off the 'liquid cosh', but had trouble moving his fingers, couldn't swing his right arm, limped on his right leg and found it difficult to turn his head. Both doctors and Elsa appealed for his release on compassionate grounds. Jenkins replied that with 'continued good behaviour' his application for restored remission would be considered in three months.

They need a deterrent just as much as the Tories

In April the *Charter* reappeared after a four-month break to advertise the Charter Conference. Union leaders were going along with Labour incomes policy at a time of massive price inflation and widespread 'respectable' lump. The *Charter* wanted May Day demonstrations, a national day of action on 26 May, lobbies of MPs and the TUC's Special Conference and 'action committees' to press for recalling the TUC Congress and the Labour Party Conference. George Smith had got short shrift from Jenkins about Warren's case. 'Nothing short of industrial action will bring about his release.'

On the 24th the Charter Conference attracted 256 delegates from 'most parts of the country' except Scotland. Chairman Alan Abrahams deplored the two-year wage settlement. Speakers pointed out that people needed houses, yet 300,000 building workers were unemployed and 800,000 out of 1,200,000 were not in a union. The fundamental problem remained the lump. Pete Carter stressed the need for a wider circulation of the *Charter*. (£300 had come in for seven issues that cost £1,500.) Elsa Warren got a standing ovation. £678 was collected, plus £165 in IOUs. Bill Jones introduced the 'Statement on Shrewsbury Pickets'. The Conference 'Policy Statement' noted that Jenkins had seized on the TGWU and UCATT's 'failure to give leadership'. Under new a new conspiracy law, Warren would have got three months in prison. 'This Conference calls for renewed activity by the TU movement for the immediate release of Des Warren' and 'further pressure' should be put on MPs (This appeared in the September *Charter*.)

In May, Warren was allowed a week's leave. He kept a scrap book. In the first five months of 1976 the number of strikers had declined by one-third and days 'lost' were down 46 percent. An estimated 500,000 lumpers cost the Inland Revenue £100,000,000 a

The key to my cell

year. Expensive new houses were sold quicker than they were built. Some London flats cost £500,000 (worth about £2,500,000 today).

The Warrens were guests of Blackpool Trades Council and Des Warren told his prison experiences to the Press Officer, Bernard Fawl, and Alex Weir. They included petty victimisation, provocation, harassment, false charges, lying, injustice and corruption amongst screws at Sudbury and Lincoln. A prison psychiatrist had told him that the Parole Board had discussed 'eight cases of a political nature' in 1974. Four were given parole and four were turned down. On 19 September 1975, Sir Lou Petch, Mr Justice Beaumont and 'Lady somebody or other' discussed the case of a man in the same prison as Warren. He had written to the Home Office, but his letter was confiscated and nothing came of an 'independent inquiry' by JPs. Warren praised a few Labour MPs, but the Labour Cabinet was carrying on 'the conspiracy that was perpetrated by the Tory government'. With the 'new pay deals and the restrictions on the working class, they need a deterrent just as much as the Tories'.

Early in June the *Star* reported that UCATT Conference delegates had told the EC to 'disregard any bodies setting a ceiling on wage increases'. The Labour government, with TUC support, was trying to impose a 4.5 percent pay ceiling in a period of uncontrolled price rises and cuts in social services. Delegates instructed UCATT's TUC delegates to support free collective bargaining, but George Smith refused to carry out the resolution. His threat to ballot the members on a different policy caused 'uproar'. He told reporters that the debate was 'a declaration of war by certain elements'. 'We are suffering from more than our share of outside interference'. (The ballot paper wrongly suggested that the resolution was against acceptance of the £6 increase due on the 28th.)

On the 25th the *Star* reported that considerable pressure had been applied to Jenkins by MPs Audrey Wise, Dennis Skinner, Tom Litterick and Norman Atkinson. Warren had served an unprecedented 71 percent of his sentence, but Robert Relf, who had been jailed for refusing to remove a signboard with 'For Sale—to a white family only', had been released. Jenkins announced that Warren's release date was 3 September. He was 'suffering from a slight paralysis of the right hand and leg and has been told by doctors that this has been brought on by nervous tension'.

The July NFBTE *National Builder* contained 'UCATT, Communist Influences and Industrial Relations'. It noted that, 'in spite of an appeal from Mr Len Murray', 'extremists' at the UCATT Conference 'defied the platform by 112 votes to 89'. Elsewhere, George Smith

The Flying Pickets

blamed 'left wing extremists and the Communist Party in particular'. They had tried to 'discredit' the EC 'until such time as they may try to possess the whole of the executive seats', yet they also had 'to struggle in order to maintain their so-called leadership of the left' and 'try to create policies that will offset the policies of the International Socialists' and 'the other twopenny halfpenny groups'.

On the 14th Smith claimed that an 'intense communist campaign had been launched to win control' of UCATT. The conference resolution was overturned by 2,700 votes in a 6.5 percent turnout.

On 5 August John D'Arcy analysed the UCATT EC in *Contract Journal*. Three of the eleven members were CPers, but two CPers and two 'moderates' had to stand for re-election in September. Two other 'moderates' had become officials and retirements were due, so the planned reduction to seven could be completed before 1981 and that hastened the possibility of a CP majority.

There was no *strategy*

Warren was unexpectedly released at midnight on 5 August. He told the *Star* that he owed 'a great debt of gratitude to the thousands of trade unionists', Labour MPs and 'especially' the CP and the *Star* 'for all the efforts put in on my behalf and the help given to my family'. TUC leaders had 'had the key to my cell in their pockets all the time'. He wanted 'to resume my place in the struggle'. The CP General Secretary, Gordon McLennan, added: 'Des is very proud of his membership of the Communist Party. We are very proud to have him in our ranks.' The *Star* added that Jenkins had got a £60,000 (£300,000) a year job at the European Economic Community.

On the 9th the *Star* stressed that the CP had been 'playing a leading role' in the fight for the pickets' freedom, but it was 'largely the rank and file of the trade union movement who fought for their release'. Ricky Tomlinson had 'worked ceaselessly for the freedom of Des'. The *Star* didn't mention Paul Foot or IS.

The August *Charter* headline was 'Rightwingers Pose Threat to UCATT Democracy'. The EC appeared 'anxious to collaborate with bosses in clearing out "militants".' 'Des Warren Freed at Last' noted that he was 'a victim of Tory trade union bashing'. Jenkins had 'refused to use his powers'. There was no list of area secretaries.

Warren wanted to 'expose the real conspiracy of Shrewsbury' in a pamphlet 'setting out all the facts', take 'legal action against the Home Office' and win a public inquiry. He had a brief meeting with

McLennan, but Garry Davies and Glasgow CPers told him that 'the campaign for our release had been blocked by certain well-known party members' and the leaders 'made no attempt to mobilise its industrial activists'. Those who acted did so on their own initiative. Ramelson wasn't enthusiastic about a pamphlet. The *Star*'s George Matthews said: 'You write it and we'll look at it.' One CP leader told him: 'You've done your bit. Sit back. With your reputation you should never have to pay for another pint in your life.'

Warren was blacklisted. He changed his name by deed poll, grew a beard, died his hair ginger and walked onto sites muffled up in an overcoat and scarf, but was always recognised. Ramelson had promised to 'provide a platform to expose this conspiracy', but it was 'Don't ring us; we'll ring you' and they rarely did. He read the CDC minutes. They 'never showed any sign of a discussion about the stage our fight was going through'—'there was no *strategy*'.

In September the TUC Congress backed UCATT's demand for a parliamentary inquiry. The Labour Cabinet ignored them.

On the 15th the CDC met for the last time. Barry Scragg acknowledged that the campaign for Warren's release 'had not been a 100 percent success'. Bill Jones blamed UCATT and TGWU officials. Over 1,900 Defence Fund receipts had gone out, including only 23 to the TGWU and 54 to UCATT branches, plus an unrecorded number to LCDTUs, Action Committees, *Charter* Groups and 'Other Political Groups', including IS, the IMG, Workers' Fight and the CP. Delegates and speakers received £3,329 and solicitors £2,686. Bulletins cost £2,017 and postage and phone bills £925. The Birmingham CP bookshop and Lawrence & Wishart were paid £793. Clerical assistance and stationery cost £634 and the 'Welcome Home' buffet-dance took £501. The *Star* got £221 and car maintenance cost £168. The SNCC received £100. Room rent at the Raven cost £64. £50 had gone to Liverpool Trades Council. Almost £21,000 out of £33,000 went to 'Members of the 24'. (63.5 percent, compared to a similar strike fund that paid 80 percent.) Those who had handed in cheques would be reimbursed. Ricky Tomlinson would get £25, Alf James, John Seaburg and Edward Williams £50, Des Warren £73, Terry Renshaw and Mike Pierce £100, McKinsie Jones £119, Brian Williams £420 and Arthur Murray £560. The 6 would get £500 more, except Warren, who would get £200, because he had already received £300. £15 was to go to the Charter.

The November *Charter* focussed on the 'Sell-Out' at the national wage negotiations. George Smith and Jack Jones were 'the two biggest cowboys in the game' for supporting Labour's incomes policy.

An anonymous article described the activities of Truemid, an organisation reportedly staffed by CIA union busters. Phil Beyer could prove that he was blacklisted for his union activities and employers ignored a tribunal order for his reinstatement. Jim Arnison's 'interview' with Warren contained few direct quotations. He recognised, 'more than ever, the importance of the struggle of the rank and file' to 'win the leadership to do the job they are there to do'. Yet 'many top leaders' in the TUC were 'completely isolated from the effects their policies have on the rank and file' and six men were 'deciding everything'. Workers 'need to establish ownership and control of our own trade unions'.

In November Cynthia Baldry died from a rare, incurable disease, aged 26. According to John Bloxam, Workers' Fight sent the *Star* an obituary notice as a paid advertisement, describing her as 'A Revolutionary Communist; initiator of the campaign to publicise the political conspiracy against the "Shrewsbury 24" and to rouse the labour movement in their defence; fighter for the rebirth of a mass communist women's movement.' The *Star* sent back a version that omitted 'Revolutionary Communist' and the references to her key role in starting the defence committee's propaganda campaign.

The right to work

In July 1975 Crook UCATT heard that Tomlinson had been paroled and that Warren's parole would be 'under review in September'. They asked the Northern Regional Committee and the EC to 'press for a pardon for these workers—due to the restriction of job availability for holders of criminal records'. In August the Regional Committee heard the EC's recommendation that they should 'use our efforts for the release of Bro Warren' and backed the idea in principle. In September, Dave Ayre was one of the TUC Congress delegates who walked out with Tomlinson and lobbied outside. In October, Crook branch agreed to 'await the TUC policy'. In December it confirmed Dave Ayre's nomination as a delegate to UCATT's General Council and the next National Delegate Conference. A collection for the *Charter* raised £1.70.

IS membership was going down. According to one account, there were 600 fewer members in September than eighteen months earlier. At the December Party Council the IS Opposition was required to dissolve or be expelled. Ian Birchall estimated that 'about 150 members left'. They included Jim Higgins, Roger Protz, John Palmer and

Granville Williams. According to Opposition members, hundreds more left. (Six years later Birchall felt that the factional struggle had been an 'unnecessary polarisation'.)

During 1975 official unemployment was 1,000,000 and was probably nearer 1,500,00. Strike days had gone down from 13,000,000 to 3,000,000 and many strikes were defensive.

In January 1976 Crook UCATT heard that their nominations for TUC Congress and Labour Party Conference delegates had been 'received later than the stipulated date and were consequently null and void'. They had been posted in good time. The branch was told not to give branch funds to the Charter, so they took collections instead. Delegates paid their own expenses and members paid for their own copies of the *Charter*. The branch affiliated to the IS-led Right to Work Campaign and Dave Ayre reported on UCATT members going on the Manchester to London march. Steve Hope proposed going for the support of the regional committee, other unions, trades councils and the Labour Party. (Their call for 'physical action and support' was defeated by eight votes to three at regional council.)

On 3 March *SW* reported that Colin Barnett (NUPE Divisional Organiser and TUC North West Region Chairman), Harry McShane and Ricky Tomlinson wished the Right to Work march every success as it set off from Manchester. Tomlinson recalled his father's death at 55 'for someone else's profits'. When he was a boy he saw families 'brought to their knees by unemployment'. 'Women with sticking plaster round their fingers where their wedding rings used to be. Making excuses to us children about how they'd hurt their fingers: how they'd put too much soda in the washing water.' Right to Work Campaign people had been arrested for picketing and charged with a 'breach of the peace'. 'Who is going to be arrested for breaching their peace of mind for throwing them on the dole?'

Crook UCATT heard about the march and Reuben Barker (who had been sacked from Lax's) noted 'the marked absence of reporting on this issue in the media'. Dave Ayre and Steve Hope reported on the police attack on the marchers and on the Albert Hall rally. The branch asked Eric Heffer MP to call for a public inquiry. (He did. He also supported the victims and the trade union inquiry.) The branch pledged itself 'to support all meaningful actions to fight unemployment' and asked the Trades Council to support the 'Day of Action' in London on 26 May. Steve Hope reported the Charter Conference concern about Warren and his family's 'plight'.

In summer the branch heard about a Durham Right to Work Campaign and the national organisation's plans for the TUC Special

The Flying Pickets

Congress. Dave reported on trade union and TUC leaders' 'overwhelming support' for the Social Contract. The branch raised the issue of free collective bargaining at the Trades Council, elected Dave as its delegate to the Right to Work Campaign National Council and was concerned about Barnet Trades Council's report on police violence on marchers. It sponsored the September march and lobby of TUC Congress, donated £5 and collected £3 to help three local unemployed youths to go on the march to the Labour Party Conference. It noted Truemid's 'campaigning against left wing infiltration' in UCATT in *Contract Journal* and *National Builder*.

In autumn the branch nominated Dave for the UCATT Regional Council and sent a delegate to the Right to Work Campaign Conference. Wear Valley District Council Direct Labour Department had asked for voluntary redundancies. (Dave recalls that they got about half to take the money. 'I suppose their idea was to get a secure job, but unemployment was rising as other workers also took the money.') Reuben Barker was nominated as delegate to the 1977 TUC Conference and Dave as delegate to the Labour Party Conference. Dave, Steve Hope and Bill Kerriss reported on a London demonstration against unemployment. The local MP, Ernest Armstrong, had been unable to meet them.

In January 1977 the branch sent £2 to a struggle in North Wales.

Custer's last stand

In 1976 Ricky Tomlinson and other members of the 24 and the CDC had worked at Pontins' Tower Beach holiday camp at Prestatyn, renovating 300 chalets. The 'cabin' was a gutted chalet with no heating, running water or washing facilities, and there were no bonuses, holiday stamps or travel allowances. They elected stewards and used contacts at Shotton, Flint, Holywell, Wrexham and Chester UCATT, Liverpool Teaching Hospital site and Ince Power Station site to build up 'Pontamb Site Fund'. Mike Williams was Treasurer.

In January 1977 the stewards called in the Liverpool UCATT official and CPer, Lou Armour, and organised the lumpers working for the subbies, Ambrose Ltd. They had no bonus scheme and a 'cabin' with no glass in the windows and no heating. They elected stewards and the Joint Shop Stewards Action Committee elected CPer Barry Scragg as convenor. Soon afterwards six men were suspended for refusing to use unsafe working methods on dodgy scaffolding. The Factory Inspector insisted on the scaffold being strengthened, but said nothing about the working methods. Scragg called a meeting of Ambrose employees, but site management sacked them all and then threatened the Pontins men with the sack if they came out in support. They came out. Days later 200 members of UCATT, EEPTU and GMWU—including foremen and those off sick—were sacked, allegedly because of low productivity. Yet they were earning £1 an hour bonus on the management's scheme. They went for their wages and they occupied both sites and put a picket on the gates. There was about £500 in the fund; but solicitors needed £400.

Pontins refused to attend a Regional Conciliation Panel because they were in the holiday industry, not the building industry, even though they owned all the building firms on site. Stewards explained to potential supporters that managers ignored Working Rules, the Contracts of Employment Act and the Employment Protection Act, and asked for donations to be sent to the Secretary, N Hewitt. Pontins refused to attend a second Regional Conciliation Panel that recommended reinstatement. Pontins issued writs against 75 workers to repossess the site. The occupation continued and the stewards issued 'Official Pontin Dispute: The Facts'. It explained that they wanted to protect jobs and conditions in an area with 20 percent unemployment. Cheques should be made out to 'Pontins Site Fund'. (The statement appeared word for word in a local paper.) A third Regional Conciliation Panel reinstated the men and negotiations began on bonus and conditions. Scragg reported in the March *Charter*.

Pontins managers set bonus rates, but when men began earning bonus the managers claimed that 46 men's productivity was too low and sacked them. The men put on a picket and the others refused to cross. After six weeks, Pontins secured High Court writs. The occupation ended, but deliveries were picketed with almost total success. Pontins hired a brewery lorry and paid someone to drive it through the picket. Early in April three carloads of pickets followed the lorry to report the driver to the brewery stewards. The lorry's windscreen was broken. Scragg was interviewed by police next day, but wasn't cautioned or charged. Pontins allowed work to restart, promised no more lay-offs, paid the men £100 a week and conceded a closed shop. The fund held almost £5,000. £24 went to the *Star*.

Late in June, in the last week before the contract was completed, five men were charged with breach of the peace and two with criminal damage. They would be at Mold Crown Court in October. 'Pontin's Pickets Defence Committee' included Tomlinson, Arthur Murray, Charlie Jones, Jeff Douglas and Mike Williams. The £660 in the fund was transferred to a 'Defence Fund'.

The Flying Pickets

The trial began in November. Scragg was accused of banging the lorry door and abusing the driver and a passenger. He and Williams were found guilty of using threatening and insulting words and behaviour. Fred Parkinson was guilty of damaging the windscreen. The trial had cost £40,000. The men were unemployed and couldn't pay fines, costs and damages, so the Defence Fund gave them £870. The Defence Committee issued a leaflet: It was 'acceptable for someone to drive at speed through a picket line endangering people's lives, but for pickets to call out—scabs, blackleg or try to find out where deliveries are picked up from, is threatening and insulting'. 'We have seen yet again how the law and the courts are used as a weapon of the ruling class against workers in struggle.'

Shrewsbury: Whose Conspiracy?

Frida Stewart was born in Cambridge in 1910, the daughter of the Dean of St John's College. She enjoyed a privileged childhood, but in the 1920s and early 1930s her musical studies took her to Italy and Germany and she witnessed the rise of fascism. In the mid-1930s she joined the CP, worked on artistic projects with the unemployed in Manchester and married a fellow CPer, Len Knight. In 1937 she went to Spain, drove an International Brigade ambulance, helped refugee children, visited front line trenches in Madrid and broadcast and reported on the war. After the fascists won she returned to Britain, raised funds for Basque refugee children and organised concerts and meetings all over the country. Then she went to France and organised a boat for 2,000 Spanish refugees to Mexico. She was working with refugees when the Germans invaded in 1940. Following months of internment she escaped to Britain with forged papers supplied by the Resistance and a letter from Charles de Gaulle hidden in a cigarette and worked with the Free French forces.

According to Jim Higgins, from 1945 Knight worked for a CP company trading with China. They recruited CPers as office staff, but did not allow them to form a cell or join a union. This led to 'no end of aggravation', because she was 'an extremely strong minded person with an acute sense of justice and fair play'. Like Higgins, Frida and Len Knight left the CP in 1956 and joined the Trotskyist SLL, but had very unhappy experiences, so they formed a small faction. Len was expelled for punching the London Organiser when he visited them in the small hours and Frida and Higgins were expelled for intervening noisily at a meeting. After the Czechoslovakian and Polish events of

1968-1970, CP leaders became slightly more critical of Russia. In 1974 Lawrence & Wishart published Frida's book on the French Resistance. *The Shrewsbury Three* had sold out quickly, yet it hadn't been reprinted.

The South West London Defence Committee had shown the trial photographs to Amnesty International and in July 1975 Amnesty had 'adopted' Warren as someone 'imprisoned, detained, restricted, or otherwise subjected to physical coercion or restriction by reason of his political, religious, or other conscientiously held beliefs'. In October, Shirley Summerskill, Jenkins's deputy at the Home Office, said that Warren was not an Amnesty 'prisoner of conscience'. In summer 1976 Amnesty's Director, David Simpson, claimed that Warren's case 'did not actually reach either adoption or investigation stages' and 'other contentious evidence' had 'cast a fair shadow of doubt'. The 'Borderline Committee' had 'eventually decide against adoption' on account of 'various pieces of evidence connected with the violence issue'. (Warren had been cleared of affray.) Knight drafted a 'Suggested Synopsis' for a book on the Shrewsbury pickets that would set out the 'lessons to be learned' for 'the general reader'. She was one of 25 people at a South West London Defence Committee meeting, where Howard Levenson of the NCCL and Jim Arnison argued that Tory Attorney General Sir Peter Rawlinson's prosecution of North Wales pickets was a political decision. Laurence Lustgarten argued in the *New Law Journal* that since Statute Law took precedence over Common Law, the maximum three-month sentences for 'conspiracy' under the former made the sentences and the Court of Appeal's confirmation of them unlawful. No lawyer challenged this interpretation. Knight told Campbell Malone that she had a 'fair amount of information' from UCATT members and Elsa Warren. Could she read the transcript of the first trial? He sent her documents relating to the 1972 strike and Peter Hetherington at the *Guardian* sent *Shropshire Star* cuttings. She asked Garry Davies for information and addresses. Tomlinson phoned Knight and 'seemed most willing to cooperate'. He had a prison diary, hoped she could use it and suggested that she came to North Wales to meet some pickets. In September he told the CDC about her project.

In autumn, Knight went to North Wales and met Gwynfor Roberts and Ken O'Shea, who had been out of work since March. Shirley Williams told her that it was 'no joke being a picket's wife' but she had enjoyed the CDC work. Mike would speak to her. McKinsie Jones gave her 'a rundown of his story'. Knight tried to get the address of the first trial's jury foreman, but the Lord Chancellor's

Department told her that this couldn't be done except in those cases 'where the interests of justice demand otherwise'. She sent a copy of the letter to Arthur Murray, who discussed it with the North Wales Charter. Murray, Tomlinson and Williams showed her round the Shrewsbury and Telford sites picketed in 1972 and Williams took photographs to challenge evidence given by key Crown witnesses.

By early 1977 Warren had drafted a pamphlet. Ramelson said it was libellous, yet a lawyer asked for no political changes. The party couldn't print it. Barry Docherty attacked CP leaders for not calling a national meeting when the sentences were handed out and the LCDTU for not co-ordinating action. In February Dave Jackson offered to help Knight. Warren paid her a visit. Afterwards, Elsa wrote on his behalf, because of his 'slight disability', and enclosed his 'Defence of the Shrewsbury 24'. In June, Warren's barrister, John Platts-Mills, told Knight that a public inquiry would be 'on the narrowest basis imaginable' and the European Commission would take too much time and effort. He loaned her the transcript of the first trial. Knight told Lawrence & Wishart that she had '19 more or less completed chapters', but the final one was 'not in a fit state to submit' and she would like 'expert help' from 'a political/trade union/legal angle'. She knew they had 'reservations', but were they interested? Skelley was 'approaching' UCATT.

The Liverpool building worker Peter Liversidge wrote to Joan Johnson, Robert Tressell's only grandchild. He, Garry Davis and Des Warren had been at the commemoration of Tressell's gravestone in Liverpool. *The Ragged Trousered Philanthropists* 'could have been written by the three of us because we feel that "our mate" was spot on' about the 'difficult time he had trying to make workmates look through the window of enli[gh]tenment'. They had 'been on the blacklist at sometimes for quite a long time'. '"Old Bob's" Book was what really started us on the road to Socialism.'

Warren recalled a Merseyside CPer and building workers' leader who 'made a great number of criticisms of the party, none of which can be dismissed as trivial'. He 'kept repeating: "What I can't understand is: Why?"' (Alan Abrahams was now a UCATT official.)

In October Knight told Lawrence & Wishart that she 'would not like to be thought partisan' and would 'very much like' George Smith to see it. She had noted IS's 'hard-hitting and useful pamphlet', *Pickets on Trial*, and the WRP's three-week march of over sixty building workers in support of Warren. John Llywarch 'must not be judged too hardly'. However, the Charter 'fell down badly' by not publishing the *Charter* during the strike.

Warren's *Shrewsbury: Whose Conspiracy? The Need for an Enquiry*, was published in Glasgow in December. He aimed 'not to castigate the movement of which I am proud to be a member, but rather to appeal to it' to 'learn from our mistakes, so that a similar dose of capitalist medicine is never repeated'. He asked why, with the support of the Labour Party NEC, Tribune MPs, the 'vast majority of industrial and white collar unions, several massive lobbies of parliament, culminating in support at two Labour Party conferences and two Trade Union Congresses (1974-75), did we remain in jail?' He believed that the trade union and labour movement had 'failed to educate the mass of workers' to understand 'the real and fundamentally restrictive nature of "democracy" capitalist style'. He had re-read Lenin's *State and Revolution*. 'Socialism requires the capitalist system, and its organ of dominance, the state, to be dismantled and replaced by the state of the working class.' He also paraphrased the early 20th century Italian Marxist, Antonio Gramsci:

> Like conspiracy law, capitalist democracy is a catch all, [and] it tries to persuade acceptance of class privilege, but coerces if that fails; it is able as required to absorb or confront, concede or contain, to penetrate working class organisation or to smash it; it is at one moment iron fisted and intransigent, the next friendly and flexible; its primary aim is to maintain capitalism at any price and by any method.

It was 'crucial' for the movement to *'unite now behind a demand for a full enquiry into the events surrounding the Shrewsbury frame-up'* and acknowledge that a Labour government had 'defended and sustained' it. Not uniting in an 'organised campaign effective enough to free these innocent men and put right the injustice done to them and their organisations, may well prove to be one of the biggest mistakes ever made by our movement'. Warren acknowledged the 'invaluable help of a small number of Communist Party activists'.

Tribunite MPs booked a Commons room for the launch and CPer Jack Henry helped to introduce it. The *Star* did not report the event.

Early in 1978 Warren talked with Glasgow CPers who didn't agree with the new CP programme and who were outraged that Jimmy Airlie, the CP Govan Shipyard convenor, had agreed to build ships that had been blacked on Tyneside.

Warren privately acknowledged that some CPers felt he was 'being used to further the political ends of a faction' in the CP, but he agreed with Barry Docherty, who had arranged for him and Alan

The Flying Pickets

Abrahams to visit Glasgow in 1973 to win support and had lost his job after leading a strike in support of the jailed pickets.

In March 1978 a doctor diagnosed Warren with Parkinsonism, but a London doctor disagreed though his 'nerves were in a bad way'. Knight put him in touch with a Liverpool specialist. In May the *Star* parodied Warren's conclusion: 'Law and democracy under capitalism are nothing but an empty sham.' In reply, he pointed out that 'to expect a system based on exploitation to be truly democratic would be illogical and naïve'. In July, Knight offered her book to Pluto Press and Croom Helm, but without success. In September, Ken Barlow noted that 'when the book is published we shall be pushing it for all we're worth'. Brian Williams, one of the 6, wanted a copy.

Late that year the *Star* refused an article by Arnison that detailed drugs abuse against Warren in prison. The story appeared in the *Sunday Times*. A specialist had confirmed that Warren suffered from 'Parkinsonism caused by therapy given in prison'. According to Warren, books by Arnison and Jim Tait (another *Star* journalist) didn't appear because they 'wouldn't be able to give a complete account of Shrewsbury without condemning the Communist Party'.

CHAPTER 20

They've been coming for us ever since

Solid, organised teamwork

In January 1977 IS became the Socialist Workers Party. The CP's Trotskyism Study Group noted the SWP claimed *SW* sales of 27,000, but the paid sale was around 20,000, while the claimed membership of 4,500 was 'about 3,000' and turnover was 50 percent. The departure of the last IS Opposition members, including 'a large group of industrial workers', had 'dealt a considerable blow' to the National Rank and File Movement and Right to Work Campaign, which had no 'significant support in the labour movement'.

In February Dave Ayre was elected to the UCATT Northern Regional Committee. (CPers Jack Spowart and Charlie Lowther were Regional Chairman and Regional Organiser for woodworkers.) In spring Dave and Bill Kerriss reported to Crook UCATT about the LCDTU conference against unemployment and the Social Contract and the branch unanimously supported its decisions. Dave, Bill, Steve Hope (Vice-Chairman) and Reuben Barker were elected as branch officers. £2 went off to Pontins, the *SW* appeal and the Right to Work Campaign (to help with John Deason's trial costs). Branch officers attended a second local LCDTU meeting against the Social Contract and the branch put a May Day greeting in *SW*. In summer the *Final Bulletin* from the Pontins dispute reported a successful conclusion. Dave and Steve 'outlined their experiences on the picket line' at Grunwick's. The officers went to a local LCDTU meeting and the branch sponsored the Right to Work Campaign march and would consider 'further support should any unemployed building worker be involved'. Dave, Steve and Bill reported 'concern at the attitude of the police' at Grunwick's in 'attempts to get scabs into the factory'. In autumn, Steve reported on the Right to Work Campaign march from Skelmersdale to the TUC Congress in Blackpool and noted the 'subjective reporting' in the media. Three branch members had attended the Right to Work Campaign and LCDTU lobby and Dave might attend a Rank and File Conference of construction workers in London in October. The branch sent two delegates to the Rank and File Conference in Manchester. £2 went to the Pontins Picket Defence Fund and £5 to Newcastle Trades Council's Grunwick Strike Defence Fund. Dave and Steve gave 'detailed and documented evidence of police brutality' at Grunwick, including Steve's beating. The branch supported the SWP-led Anti Nazi League and asked the Trades Council to support. Dave and Reuben were unanimously re-elected as branch officers and Dave was nominated as delegate for UCATT National Delegate Conference. Wear Valley Trades Council gave £5 to the FBU's bitter dispute with the Labour government.

In 1978 Wear Valley Trades Council and UCATT Northern Regional Council affiliated to the ANL. Crook branch sent delegates to the Carnivals, sent money after the Nazis damaged the London office, supported the TUC march against unemployment and plugged away at the Shrewsbury issue. Dave recalls:

> Armed with Laurie Flynn's fantastic *Pickets on Trial* we
> attended Joint Branch and Stewards Organisation meetings. In
> Newcastle, when George Smith was in attendance, I spoke
> about how UCATT's EC had declined to come out in support of
> the 24 because, as they claimed, the union's constitution didn't
> allow them to support members who broke criminal law. I
> could sense the discomfort on the platform. Smith leaned over
> to Jim Harper and asked who this 'character' was that was
> challenging the EC position. I was instructed to sit down and
> withdraw my statement, but the message was implanted. The
> same thing happened on Teesside. Slowly the message became
> more widespread.

Wear Valley TUC expressed concern to the local Labour MP.

UCATT Northern Regional Council read Warren's *Shrewsbury: Whose Conspiracy?* It debated his request for support for a public inquiry 'at length' and 'resolved to seek advice from Head Office' about buying copies, because the request came from 'a source unknown'. Crook branch bought ten after Dave Ayre gave them a summary and the Regional Committee bought 25. At the May Regional Council, after a lengthy debate, the issue wasn't 'progressed'—the pamphlet was out of print—but they sent a letter to Sir

George Smith who was seriously ill. (He died in November.) In June, Wear Valley TUC supported the Right To Work Campaign.

Jim French didn't read Warren's pamphlet:

> Wimpeys got the multi-million pound contract for a huge Caustic Chlorine plant at ICI Wilton. They employed about 400 men and half were building workers. I was young and keen and recruited all of them, so the TGWU missed out. I had three great stewards and I visited the site regularly. Wimpeys thought the men would do as they were told, and at first they brought flasks and bait, because there was no canteen; but after numerous battles we won a canteen for hot meals. One warm July day someone ran over a water pipe with a dumper and the toilets broke down. After three days there was a bit of a smell and since the toilets were right next to the canteen the lads were up in arms. We gave the company two days to fix the problem. A week went by and nothing happened, so the lads took no persuading to down tools. It went to a National Disputes Panel in London and we won.

The UCATT Northern Regional Committee felt the strike was 'to be criticised', but there was 'some substance in the complaint' and Wimpeys should make an ex gratia payment for lost pay. Wimpeys 'insisted that the lads wouldn't be paid, but a Disputes Panel made them do so'. 'It was a fine example of solid, organised teamwork.'

In 1979 Jim Harper retired—he got an OBE—and Charlie Lowther became Northern Regional Secretary. Jim French recalls:

> I thought that the stewards were the life blood of the union— right at the point of production: the meat in the sandwich, so to speak. The other regional organisers used to say: 'The trouble with you, Frenchie, is that you always think the lads are right.' I still do and I always tried to use my politics to guide me, though that wasn't always possible for reasons of self-preservation. I had no mates among the other regional organisers until Charlie became regional secretary—a dear comrade.

Dave Ayre's 'Instinctive Socialism' appeared in the Durham Strong Words Collective's *But the World Goes on the Same: Changing Times in Durham Pit Villages*. Crook UCATT supported the 'Defend Our Unions' campaign, agreed to site collections for the Right to Work Campaign and responded to strikers' appeals. Wear Valley

TUC supported the branch's call for a public inquiry into the murder of SWP member Blair Peach at an ANL demonstration and for the Special Patrol Group to be 'terminated'. (The SPG was a mobile serious crime squad and used baseball bats, crowbars and hammers.)

The stranglehold of reformism

Back in 1976 Pete Carter had been elected as UCATT convenor at Sandwell Direct Works in Birmingham. Just before the 1977 CP Congress Sid French led 700 members into the New Communist Party. A CP Commission examined inner-party democracy. In 1978 Mick Costello succeeded Bert Ramelson as National Industrial Organiser. The CP had only 26 factory branches.

In May 1978 the *Economist* published a Tory policy group report, drafted by Nicholas Ridley MP, which targeted the NUM. A future Tory government should build up coal stocks, especially at power stations, introduce coal and oil firing, plan to import coal, encourage hauliers to recruit non-union drivers, cut off strikers' social security benefits and build a large mobile police squad to deal with pickets.

In 1979 union membership peaked at 13,400,000, TUC affiliated membership peaked at almost 13,000,000 and the number of days 'lost' to strikes peaked at over 29,000,000. Yet the CP had lost 28 percent of its members in four years and now had 20,000. Proposals to democratise internal structures were defeated. The party split on the question of the 'Eurocommunist' *Marxism Today*, but the Soviet Union continued to buy 12,000 copies of the *Star*. Pete Carter became a full-time official. The Tories got in.

In January 1980 Des Warren reissued *Shrewsbury: Whose Conspiracy?* with an 'Introduction'. The trials were 'Act One'

> In the ruling class onslaught against trade union rights throughout the 1970s and now into the 1980s with Thatcher's Tory government giving huge pay rises to the judiciary, police, regular army and reservists, coinciding with proposals to outlaw secondary picketing, weaken the closed shop, cut social security to strikers' families, and other measures.

The lessons of Shrewsbury were being ignored, even though it 'shows how the leadership of our movement measures up to the heat of the class confrontation. Perhaps this is why Shrewsbury is such an embarrassment' to those 'who would like to forget all about it'. Some left wing leaders claimed it was a 'dead issue'. The TUC and UCATT had refused to allow his solicitor to see their files. 'Unfortunately, I also have to condemn the leadership of my own party, the Communist Party which I have belonged to for sixteen years.' 'Advocates of the "British Road to Socialism"'—the CP programme—'stick their heads in the sand' and 'do everything to ignore anything which is a contradiction' including Shrewsbury. The CP had advised him 'to cooperate with the prison regime, to wear prison uniform, etc, and submit applications for parole'. That would have meant 'recanting and accepting guilt from a political trial' and 'the establishment would have used it to slander our movement and to underpin the deterrent effect which the Tories hoped the sentences would have'. 'At no time did the party offer to help write, produce or distribute' his 1977 pamphlet and 'steps were taken to discourage party members from reading it', yet 5,000 copies weren't enough. The *Star* review of the decade gave half a sentence to Shrewsbury. The CP was in the 'stranglehold of reformism'.

Warren's pamphlet was printed by Astmoor Litho Ltd of Runcorn and published by New Park Publications Ltd, both owned by the WRP. In March, Warren resigned his CP membership. He met a Belfast woman who had been tortured for days and sexually assaulted and whose brother was on the blanket and another woman whose son had been murdered by paratroopers in Derry.

In May, Mike Williams told Eddie Nash that the 'Charter movement and the general movement' in North Wales was 'at a standstill and does not seem likely to be getting onto its feet for many years to come', so 'we are closing down'. Nash was grateful for a 'splendid donation' that 'helped to lift a weight off my shoulder'. The Charter was almost moribund.

In August, after talks with Sid French and the SWP, Warren joined the WRP, whose working class members had 'fought valiantly' for his release. He also issued a lengthy statement to counter 'various slanders' that the CP was 'trying to put around'.

Trade union density was almost 58 percent, but using the recession as a lever the Tories set about helping to 'modernise' British capitalism at the cost of millions of jobs, while introducing anti-union laws backed up by specially trained police.

In 1981 Pete Carter was one of the three national co-ordinators of the TUC-sponsored People's March for jobs from Liverpool to London. He argued that the CP leaders' 'complete omission' of 'the importance of the rank and file contribution' left those comrades with top union positions 'wide open to the criticism of a bureaucratic conception of left advance' and favoured 'new thinking'. The *Star* editor and his deputy lost their seats on the CP's EC.

In 1982 the WRP published Warren's book, *The Key to My Cell*, which he wrote with Chris Corrigan. He concluded that the CP did not want 'any national action independent of the trade union bureaucracy' over Shrewsbury and 'collapsed its campaign' in January 1974. There was 'no *strategy*. The CP didn't want any.'

Nick Warren recalled his father's 'usual line'. 'They misled the campaign and bent and buckled and kow-towed to right wing union leadership. They did everything to contain the movement and preserve their relationships with Labour rather than give a political organisational lead to the kind of mass action that would have got the job done.'

A bit of pointing

In 1980 Dave Ayre was elected as UCATT Northern Regional Vice-Chairman and was soon the subject of a formal complaint from Barney McIntyre, Russ King and Jim Graham (no relation) about an article that allegedly 'defamed full time officers and members of the Regional Committee'. The branch had asked him to write it, so he refused to apologise, but was given a 'severe reprimand'. At the National Delegate Conference he successfully moved a Crook UCATT motion that expressed 'total opposition to Labour Only Sub-Contracting', noted the 'failure of legislation to eradicate the "lump"' and called for an improvement in the basic rate, membership education, 'a concerted campaign of industrial action against companies operating "lump schemes"' and for 'steps to be taken by UCATT to provide / control labour to employers'.

In 1981 Crook UCATT delegates attended a Rank and File meeting and found London sites in a 'shocking state'. Subbies paid lumpers' union dues and 'helped to destroy grass roots organisation'. There were ten officials and two stewards. In the north east subbies cut corners on safety to undercut law-abiding firms' tenders and paid only £100 compensation for a death. Labour local authorities used unskilled youngsters to do work formerly done by union members and over 35,000 NE building workers were unemployed.

By 1982 Crook UCATT felt that the Wear Valley was one big Manpower Services Commission scheme and was outraged that Les Wood—UCATT General Secretary—told members to cross 'unofficial' health workers' picket lines. The differential between craftsmen and labourers' wages was £15 a week and 250,000 were unemployed across the country. The branch heard from Warren about his book and ordered ten copies. Gwen French was given a handbag and cheque for working on the branch banner, but she asked for the cheque to go to striking health workers and Jim French handed over a cheque from Darlington UCATT for the buffet. Dave Ayre and founder member Wilf Goodwin unveiled the banner. Its motto was 'Socialism Through Revolution'. In UCATT and at the TUC Congress Dave 'sought to widen' the Shrewsbury campaign. Jim French helped to organise the UCATT Broad Left and borrowed Dave's copy of *The Key to My Cell*. Crook branch voted for an inquiry into the jailings of Warren and Tomlinson, but Les Wood claimed that George Smith did 'everything' he could. The branch wrote to Warren, who told them about an upcoming conference. Dave recalls: 'Some of us attended WRP meetings and rallies and travelled to London demonstrations.' Dave also spoke at Building Workers' Group meetings from North Yorkshire to Edinburgh. (According to Brian Higgins, Tony Cliff ordered SWP members to stop publishing *The Building Worker* and disband the organisation, because its membership had shrunk and it was an obstacle to the party's development. Higgins was expelled, but a rump kept going.) Dave recalls that Warren's WRP membership and local contacts 'pulled us in that direction, though they didn't try to recruit us'. He was elected as regional delegate to the next TUC Congress and as a Trustee of the General Fund. Wear Valley TUC criticised the TUC's 'lack of support' for ASLEF and 'its subservience to government'.

From October 1982 to January 1983 UCATT Northern Region membership fell from 27,107 to 20,573. There were 91 UCATT Northern Region branches, compared to 200 twelve years earlier. Jim French organised the Northern Feeder for the TUC's People's March for Jobs. Dave Ayre was elected as Regional Chairman and Chairman of the Trustees. He and the Crook UCATT Chairman, Peter Hansom, went to the WRP's All Trade Union Alliance conference and were impressed with the number of young people who spoke about their experience of government schemes.

Dave had laid bricks for the CP bookshop in Westgate Road, Newcastle, and for Peter Jobe, the convenor at a large print works at Team Valley Estate in Gateshead that printed roubles for the USSR. He also laid bricks at the 'Days of Hope' bookshop in Westgate Road, which was run by Alan Milburn. (He later became Darlington's New Labour MP and a member of two Blair Cabinets.)

One SWP comrade, Geoff Hartnell, worked at Tursdale Mining Workshops. He later joined the WRP, but we remained friends, and he asked if I and a few mates could do 'a bit of pointing' at a disused Byker warehouse that they wanted to turn into a printshop. It was huge and the work took up most of our weekends for some time, but I met Dave Temple—Norman's nephew—a pit electrician, a great bloke and a really sound working class intellectual.

The Great Strike

In January 1984 Crook UCATT members went to the picket of the *Stockport Messenger* printshop in Warrington and they wanted to know why the EC wouldn't support Warren's campaign.

The Tories decided to take on the NUM, implemented the Ridley plan and provoked the NUM into a defensive struggle. On 2 April, Wear Valley TUC took a collection for the NUM strike fund and offered to 'assist with picketing'. Crook UCATT members raised £22 and sent £5 a fortnight to the NUM. They supported the Trades Council's collection of provisions on Crook Market Place, observed police 'abuses' of pickets—whilst they turned a blind eye to untaxed, scab-driven lorries being driven into them—and sent an emergency motion to UCATT Conference calling for a 50p levy on members and 'widening support to mass action'. Delegates to Wear Valley TUC 'reported at length' on 'picketing abuses and violence' by police. Street collections and Crook and Bishop Auckland stalls raised £130 a week, plus food—'Agreed that whole of funds be donated to Miners Hardship Fund.' By summer Crook UCATT was part of a Miners' Support Group and organising to give Nottinghamshire strikers' families a holiday. A striker addressed the branch. Wear Valley TUC heard reports on Families Support Groups and police numbers on picket lines. Nottinghamshire strikers' wives reported a 'Northern Ireland like situation' and 'police harassment'. A permanent stall was to be maintained in Crook Market Place and by August there was a stall at Willington. £50 came in from Tursdale Workshops and £60 from the local Labour Group. Strikers reported on DHSS attempts to 'increase hardship'. In autumn, Crook UCATT heard how strikers were disadvantaged by the Electricity Board and refused to send their collections to UCATT Head Office. 38 families needed £15 a week and the branch had raised over £1,000 out of a local total of £4,000, while Labour-controlled

Durham County Council was issuing licences for private open-cast sites. Wear Valley TUC raised £169 from each of two benefit concerts, £88 from a *Building Worker* conference and £30 to £35 a week from the Crook stall. By November there was enough money to 'sustain families' and by December £3,000 plus 7,000 francs had been collected in Wear Valley's twin town, Ivry sur Seine. Thousands came from the twin town in Germany. Dave Ayre and Peter Hansom reported to Crook UCATT on the WRP celebration, where £3,000 was collected.

Early in 1985 an Ivry sur Seine deputation met some strikers and invited them and their families to their CP stronghold. Some of the lads helped in the SKF strike. In March, after the NUM strike was defeated, the remaining money went to miners sacked for 'misconduct' and a collection was taken for the victims of a mining disaster in France. Crook UCATT concluded that the Tory government would 'spare no effort to break organised labour'. Wear Valley TUC heard a report on the closing stages of the strike and criticised the TUC for a lack of leadership. They would continue to support sacked miners and called on the TUC to win an amnesty for those in prison. In May plans were made to send strikers' children for a holiday at Ivry sur Seine.

The local labour MP, Ernest Armstrong, announced that he would stand down. His daughter Hilary, the Constituency Secretary, confirmed that Crook UCATT's 421 members couldn't send a delegate to the candidate selection meeting or make a nomination, because their previous year's affiliation fee had not been paid. (It had been sent to Durham by mistake.) Dave Ayre recalls that branch officers visited her home and found her in a secret meeting. She said: 'Take no notice of these... They're Trots.' The branch's candidate was removed from the short-list and the matter wasn't resolved until after Hilary was selected. (She was elected MP in 1987. By 2007 she had been a spokesperson and minister for eighteen years.) Crook UCATT supported Dave for Secretary, Regional Council, General Council and the TUC Congress.

In 1986 Crook UCATT voted unanimously for Jim French as the next Regional Secretary and challenged some branches' votes. Edward Ablett won, but Lowther began an inquiry. Ablett got the job, but in highly controversial circumstances. Crook branch heard about stewards at a Laing's site in London who got rid of subbies, only to be sacked and blacklisted. The EC failed to make the dispute official or back the victimised men or support those who were sued for damages. Sub-contracting was increasing in the Northern Region and young workers on government schemes were made to work on Bishop Auckland golf course while balls were flying through the air. The branch heard speakers from the dispute over union recognition with Murdoch's papers at Wapping, where brutal police tactics were in evidence against mass pickets.

On many important questions we have nothing specific to offer

Back in 1983, after a seven-year legal battle, Des Warren got £3,000 from the Home Office. The principle of liability was established, but his condition deteriorated. Crook UCATT sent a letter of support.

In 1983 the CP Congress sacked the *Star*'s editor and deputy, but they refused to go. The People's Press Printing Society owned the paper. In 1984 the number of days 'lost' to strikes peaked at over 27,000,000, but the CP was so split that it was unable to offer strong leadership in the NUM strike. In March 1985 Pete Carter pointed to the NUM's failure to condemn violence, seek support from bishops and churches and hold a 'national demonstration'. He also criticised the use of mass picketing as 'the *only* way forward', since this was why some left wing union leaders failed to deliver solidarity. The Eurocommunist CP leaders got a majority at the Congress and began a purge. *Marxism Today* published an attack on shop stewards. The CP's Industrial Organiser, Mick Costello, replied angrily in the *Star* and was sacked. His replacement was Pete Carter. (In the next three years 3,000 left or, like Gill, Ramelson and Costello, were expelled.)

In 1985 union membership was down to 10,700,000 and TUC affiliated membership was under 10,000,000.

In March 1986 Carter argued that a 'limited trade union consciousness' was not enough. The policies of the CP, the Campaign Group of Labour MPs and the Militant Tendency had led to a 'major setback for the movement' in the NUM strike and in Liverpool City Council. The 'strike weapon' was necessary, but 'not in itself sufficient'. The NUM failed to win 'broad political support'.

On many important questions we have nothing specific to offer. The party has not always been kept informed about our industrial strategy. Important decisions have been taken by a few, which not only served to undermine our base in industry, but weakened the party as a whole.

We have not over a period been successful in the development of a cadre policy. There has been, and still is, a weakness in the relationship of our trade union comrades and their local party branches.

Labour MP (and ex-CPer) Eric Heffer called this 'a repudiation of the previous 60 years of Communist Party strategy'. The *Star* denounced it as 'meandering' by someone who hadn't 'the status within the movement to be taken seriously'.

The WRP had split in 1985. In August 1986 Des Warren's 'A Message to the TUC' appeared in *Workers' Press* (formerly *Newsline*). The 'scale of the state's attack on picketing in 1973' was 'not yet fully realised'. 'One of the major lessons' was how the state 'learned to create an atmosphere of violence, by provocation, as we have witnessed in the recent miners' strike'. If union leaders 'had not retreated at decisive times' there 'would not have been further whole-sale criminalising of pickets in the miners' strike'. The CP had 'unable to carry out a real campaign, even for its own members', back in 1974. The 'campaign of words, with workers reduced to a protest force, got all the trade union leaders off the hook' and 'guaranteed every opportunist leader that he could make radical speeches without having to put his money where his mouth was'. Jenkins had now left the Labour Party for the Social Democratic Party, 'but can any trade union member stand up honestly and say that the present leaders would act any differently?' It was ten years since his release. 'They've been coming for us ever since.'

The Des Warren Trust Fund

By 1986 Warren's Parkinson's was worsening and Dave Temple suggested a trust. Dave Ayre recalls: 'There was no chance of UCATT being involved, nationally, so I wrote to Tomlinson.' He had been blacklisted and had worked as a club compère, entertainer, agent and actor. Warren refused to speak to him for a decade, but in 1986 he asked to see him. When he arrived Warren was on the floor with his arms permanently bent and his chin locked against his chest.

In 1987 Crook UCATT agreed to help set up a trust. Dave Temple arranged for Dave Ayre to meet the NUM's lawyers:

Early in 1988 Reuben Barker and I visited Des in Chester to give his carer, Pat, a bit of respite. It brought the severity of his illness home to us. He suddenly started shaking a thin mattress and indicated that it had to be laid on the floor. Then he fell backwards on it until his medication kicked in. We were exhausted, what with the long train journey to Chester and the stress of seeing Des like that; but when we woke up on the Sunday he was up and about and as lively as a cricket. He asked: 'Who's looking after who?' The flat faced a solid brick building and Des said: 'I've counted every bloody brick in that wall and I think I know each one personally.' We took him for a walk along the nearby canal. He was finding it difficult, so Reuben and I took an arm apiece and encouraged his leg mobility. Yet he never lost his sense of humour and those walks will say in our affectionate memories forever.

Reuben was deeply moved. He successfully proposed that Warren's picture should appear on the new Trades Council banner and in spring he reported to Crook UCATT on a second visit. Warren's health wasn't good and Pat came for two hours on weekdays but not at weekends. Peter Heathfield, National Secretary of the NUM, and Tony Benn MP might become trustees. Reuben and Dave visited Warren again to give his elderly mother a break. Crook UCATT agreed to make a donation and hold regular collections.

By summer Durham Mechanics' Union had circulated 500 collection sheets for the Des Warren Trust Fund. Peter Heathfield, Billy Etherington (MP for Sunderland, Secretary of Durham Miners Mechanics' Union and Vice-President of the North East NUM), John Cummings (MP for Easington) and, at Dave Temple's suggestion, Dave Ayre were trustees. Donations were to go to the Miners' Hall in Durham. Durham Mechanics' donated £1,500 and paid for 2,000 copies of the appeal. Wear Valley Trades Council donated £5. In September, *The Durham Miner* carried an article on the trust. Warren needed full-time attention that 'cannot be provided by the resources-starved health service'. Etherington was quoted: 'We consider that Des is a victim of a vicious war against trade unionism and must not be forgotten.' Donations should go via the Durham Mechanics' Durham office. £1,000 a week came in. The Trust paid for Warren to spend a fortnight in a special care home and employ a carer, and he paid a brief visit to Crook. Dave Ayre took overall responsibility for secretarial and administrative duties, but Geoff Hartnell carried some of them out. By October standing orders contributed £90 a month. Money came from individuals, UCATT and other union branches and trades councils, but not UCATT Northern Region or the EC.

In 1988 Jim Arnison reissued *The Shrewsbury Three* with a new Introduction in which he reflected on 1974-1979: 'Unfortunately, as with all previous Labour governments, this one continued along the path of class collaboration and ended its days in serious conflict with the trade unions and other key sections of the labour movement,' while the Charter 'subordinated consistent rank and file work to the job of getting leftwingers into the trade union bureaucracy'.

It was hard to find a job in the Wear Valley. Reuben recalls:

> Once the Witton Park ironworkers came out and won the highest pay award in the industry, but then the management took the jobs to Teesside and closed the works. It had all been pulled down by 1984 and then the pits began to dwindle. I worked on government schemes; but later I worked for Quinroys at Spennymoor, Johnson and Sons and Shepherd Construction in Darlington, at Kilhope and Catterick.

Jimmy Graham had returned to building work.

> Local authority workers got to know about the Shrewsbury trials and the jailing of Warren, Tomlinson and others, and we supported them in principle. In 1975 I worked for British Rail Engineering, joined the National Union of Railwaymen and stayed there until the works closed down in 1984. I went back into the building trade on sites in Durham, and in 1987, at Catterick Garrison, I got a job with Shepherd Construction and met Reuben and Dave. They told me about being pickets during the strike and we became very good friends. I wanted to go to Bishop Auckland Branch, but couldn't find when and where it met.

In 1989 he joined Crook Branch.

By April 1989 the Trust income had dried up. There was £2,000 in the kitty, yet the UCATT Northern Regional Council hadn't responded to letters. (Barney McIntyre claimed that UCATT could not support a member with a criminal record.) Pat hadn't had a holiday for over a year. Dave Temple printed hundreds of letters free of charge and Dave Ayre addressed the envelopes and mailed them; but the Northern Regional Council and the EC still refused to support the Trust. Crook UCATT asked the NUM to raise the issue at the Northern Regional TUC. It also appealed to UCATT General Council, but the General Secretary, Albert Williams, and his Assistant, Jimmy Hardman, tried to sideline the appeal. (Williams was later suspended and several officials left the union.) Money began coming in, but Dave Ayre was concerned at some unions' failure to give support. Warren's health improved while he lived at Wolsingham and efforts were made to provide extra care. Warren and Pat married. Dave recalls:

> We did what we could to improve their quality of life and a closer, more personal relationship developed. Dave Temple, Geoff Hartnell, Peter Hansom, Reuben Barker and I were regular visitors. Des and Pat were found a council house at Murton in County Durham, but he wasn't getting the correct care, so they decided to go back to Chester.

The Trust eventually raised around £12,000.
Dave Ayre retired in 1996, but remains a trustee.

> I read that Cuban doctors were at the forefront of pioneering treatment of Parkinson's and raised it with a good friend and comrade of mine, Denis Doody, the UCATT convenor for the Wakefield local authority. We decided that Des could well benefit and Denis arranged for us to visit the Cuban Embassy in London, where we presented a profile of Des's case. Of course, we consulted with Des and Pat at every stage and his consultant gave us his cautious blessing, but we were bitterly disappointed to see Des's condition deteriorating to such a point that though we had the money, his doctor advised us that his health was too fragile to make the long-haul trip, even with the care we planned. After lengthy discussions with Des and Pat it was decided that rather than risk further deterioration and even premature death, the trust should improve his quality of life and give Pat respite, because her health was in jeopardy. Her devotion to Des was profound. She was a member of a Pentecostal Church and prayer sustained her. Des told me, with some reticence, that she was deeply religious. I replied: 'Who are we to deny any person any source of strength?'

From 1999 Warren had a special wheelchair. Dave recalls:

> It was paid for mainly by the trust, but with assistance from the British Legion, and Dave Temple arranged holidays for Des and Pat in a cottage in Weardale, not far from where I live. Des wanted to go to the Durham Miners' Gala. Crook UCATT has a tradition of holding a social and political evening on the

Friday before, with a buffet and speakers, so we decided to dedicate that year's social to Shrewsbury. Des and Pat were keen to 'go for it', but only the County Hotel in Durham could accommodate his needs, so the trust paid an extravagant price. It was well worth it. We invited Ricky and Rita Tomlinson and it was a phenomenal occasion.

The struggle continues

Reuben Barker retired in 1999 after being Crook UCATT Treasurer and active in the Trades Council for nearly thirty years.

My father and mother both retired at 65 on a pension of £4.10s a week. One week somebody stole it from them. Hunger is a sharp thorn, whether it was my parents' or that of the one who stole from them. I've always argued for shorter hours and better wages and I'm a big believer in bringing down the retirement age and a good pension. I voted Labour all my life but never joined the party. Retiring early was the best thing I ever did. Old miners told me that if it hadn't been for the 1926 strike they'd have been dead, because the fresh air and the garden produce helped them back to good health. I well remember when politicians talked about new technology cutting working hours by half. One day Balfour Beatty workers were renewing water pipes in a trench at my gate, working a ten-hour day, seven days a week. They couldn't accept the coffee and biscuits I offered. They weren't allowed to stop, even though the weather was bad, and they had no cabins or drying cabinets.

Reuben became Chairman of Durham UCATT retired members.

Jim French retired in 2002. He does a bit of woodturning and is Darlington UCATT Treasurer, co-ordinator of the Retired Members' Association and on the National Pensioners Convention's EC.

Was it all worth it? There's an old saying, "What goes around comes around". So I never give up hope. When I was starting out socialism was just round the corner. Now I know it will take a lot more struggle and hardship before people stand up for a socialist society. When does the struggle end? When you're in the box!

The Flying Pickets

He gets the *Star* each day to keep himself 'abreast of what's going on in the world and at home'. Gwen still 'keeps him right' and he goes cycling with his lifelong comrade, Dave Ayre.

In 2001 Des Warren's former barrister, John Platts-Mills, noted in his memoirs that the police didn't bring a case against the North Wales pickets in 1972 because any violence was 'spontaneous and sporadic' and they couldn't identify 'wrong-doers'. The Shrewsbury trials were the only case he knew where the government ordered a prosecution 'in defiance of the advice of senior police and prosecution authorities'. (In 2001 Barry Jones MP became a Lord.)

In 2003 Ricky Tomlinson wrote: 'Many union bosses have become part of the establishment' and 'unions are like corporations, always looking for takeover targets or mergers. The leadership act more like CEOs than shop stewards. They build fancy offices, have chauffer-driven cars and forget about the rank and file.' 'New Labour should stop masquerading as a party for workers.'

Dave Harker, the author of *Tressell*, deputised for Reg Johnson, Robert Tressell's grandson-in-law, and presented Des Warren, Ricky Tomlinson and Arthur Murray with the Construction Safety Campaign's Robert Tressell Award. A few days later Glyn Davies was the compère at Shotton Labour Club. Three of the 32 had died, but Warren, Tomlinson, McKinsie Jones, O'Shea, Renshaw and Murray were there. Davies read out Jim Arnison's letter: 'the movement failed to act sufficiently strongly against this pernicious attack on our rights', but the publication of the police report to the DPP would have led to the 'total collapse' of the first trial. He was scathing about 'this New Labour Gang under Tony BLIAR'.

The trust supported Des right up to his death from pneumonia in April 2004, aged 66. Dave Harker, Reuben Barker and Jimmy Graham were at the funeral, along with many union delegations. Jimmy was moved by Tomlinson's speech about how he and Warren suffered. 'After what the establishment got up to, I wouldn't put anything past them.' Reuben recalls giving Pat a great big hug and he and Jimmy went round with a Book of Remembrance. Everybody signed, including the bar staff. Sadly, Pat died a few weeks later.

Jimmy was now Crook UCATT Treasurer.

I owe much of what I know about unions to Reuben and Dave. They taught me that workers have to support other workers, whatever their struggle may be. In recent times I've been on picket lines with them at the Magnet Joinery strike in Darlington, London, and elsewhere. The 1972 strike and what happened at Shrewsbury is still the 'big one' for building workers. I'm working harder than ever in my union work. We need unions more than ever, and we need to make younger people aware of the history of working class struggle.

Jimmy retired in 2005 after an accident at work. He is Secretary of Wear Valley Trades Council and a Trustee of the Des Warren Trust Fund.

Dave Ayre still loves the Durham Miners' Gala and organises the Crook UCATT social and political event the evening before:

Speakers have included Arthur Scargill, George Brumwell, then a UCATT EC member, Dennis Doody from Wakefield, Lol Irwin, the retired UCATT Midland Regional Secretary, Bob Crow of the RMT, Tony O'Brien, National Secretary of the Construction Safety Campaign, John Flanagan of the Merseyside Asbestos Victim Support Group and Spencer Wood, Matthew Cartledge and Steve Cottingham of O H Parsons and Partners. In 2006 Steve and Geoff Bottoms spoke about the Miami Five campaign they spearhead. The Trust still exists. We'd like to offer our most profound thanks to all those who responded and especially to those who still do. Our aim is to contribute to the campaign to clear the names of all the North Wales 32. The campaign continues.

The struggle continues.

A working conclusion

We've done our best to tell these interweaving stories dispassionately, so that readers can draw their own conclusions; but here are ours.

We believe that Marx was correct to argue that socialists—and especially revolutionary socialists—have a duty to *doubt everything* and then *say what* is to the working class, however painful, though it's obviously very important that we carry out those duties in that order and the test can only come through practice.

Early in 1972 the miners fatally damaged the Tory government and that summer the dockers smashed the Industrial Relations Act. At that point members of the unofficial and mainly Communist-led Building Workers' Charter were leading a strike and in September they claimed credit for the victory on pay, though the official union negotiators failed to end the lump. Nevertheless, it was a serious defeat for the big contractors, so they put together a dodgy dossier and persuaded Tory ministers to criminalise effective mass picketing. In November the police focused on North Wales, a weakly unionised area, yet they found so little evidence that they had to drop the charges. However, the big contractors and the Tory government persisted and early in 1973 the police used what would now be illegal methods to extract new statements from unwilling pickets. They also 'lost' many lumpers' statements and took new ones and then a few policemen backed up the lumpers' outrageous claims. Arrests began in February. Most charges related to picketing at Shrewsbury and Telford New Town on 6 September 1972, yet police had been present almost from the first and had made no arrests or cautions all that day.

As soon as UCATT and TGWU leaders heard their solicitor's advice about the 'affray', 'illegal assembly' and 'conspiracy to intimidate' charges and the likely costs, they abandoned their members completely. The 32 pickets were on their own, but a group of North Wales Charter members formed a defence committee and Charter members working for contractors at BSC Shotton, including some of the 32, welcomed the help of a tiny Trotskyist group,

Workers' Fight, to publicise the pickets' case. In spring several pickets were found not guilty or given small fines at local magistrates' courts and Mold Crown Court, yet 24 of them were still to be tried at Shrewsbury. All were blacklisted, most had economic dependants, some had mortgages and the trial could be months away and very long, so the money-raising campaign had to be developed. After the committal hearings in June, Communist Party Charter members intervened decisively.

The CP had little electoral support and it was increasingly hard to see why any socialist should join a small reformist party that had no chance of getting into office when there was a much larger and partly left wing Labour Party that was much better placed. Consequently, the CP and its weekday paper, the *Morning Star*, were in long-term decline. On the other hand, some industrial comrades had considerable economic clout in certain areas, including Merseyside. Since the later 1960s CP militants had been encouraged to lead struggles, get elected to full-time union positions and influence other left wing officials and Labour MPs to try to 'steer' the state leftwards and win reforms on behalf of the working class without the need for a revolution. In 1970 some of these rank and file CPers built the Building Workers' Charter movement and became strike leaders in 1972, but many supported divisive 'company agreements' and argued for accepting a settlement that failed to end the lump. Other CPers were unhappy about that, but took the party line in public, and several eventually became full-time union officials.

By late summer 1973 the North Wales Defence Committee included at least one local CPer and two leading CPers from Merseyside and had become the Charter Defence Committee. The CPers rapidly marginalised Workers' Fight and gradually worked in more comrades until they had a majority. All but one CDC speaker was a CPer, and several were not CDC members or even from North Wales. (In October the only non-CP speaker went to Ruskin College Oxford. He helped to build two defence committees and spoke at others, but when he returned to North Wales he found that his place on the CDC had recently been filled.)

In October six of the 'Shrewsbury 24' were selected for the first Shrewsbury Crown Court trial. The Tory-appointed Crown lawyers proceeded only on the judge-made common law charges—under which any picket found guilty would be liable to an unlimited jail sentence. Late in December, after a majority of jurors was somehow led to believe that guilty verdicts would result in fines, the Tory-appointed judge imposed three suspended and three unsuspended jail sentences. The Court of Appeal later quashed the 'affray' convictions but acknowledged the 'deterrent' character of the other sentences and effectively agreed that the 'Shrewsbury 3' were political prisoners.

How did the big contractors, the Tories, the police and the judiciary get away with such unsafe verdicts and savage sentences?

The CP-led CDC had badly underestimated the Tories' determination to make an example of the North Wales flying pickets by any means necessary and later acknowledged that they had conducted an 'all out for money' campaign up to late December. Crucially, they had no Plan B. What the Shrewsbury jailings required were immediate political strikes like those that freed the Pentonville 5, but there was no national lead and no attempt to bring militants together over Christmas to discuss strategy and tactics. The CP Industrial Organiser left it to his comrades on the CDC.

Building workers' lives aren't like those of miners and dockers. Contracts last two years or so, at most, and then union activists have to start afresh in whatever jobs they can find—unless they're blacklisted. Across the country, individual CPers and other socialists led scattered strikes in protest at the December jailings, and there were also some strikes in factories, but the CPers on the CDC were determined to maintain political control and asked all the strikers to go back, even though some of the strike leaders (including fellow CPers) were promptly sacked. The CDC's cobbled-together Plan B—a 'lobby of various conferences'—started far too late, was obsessed with the official movement, had serious illusions in left-reformist union officials and MPs and generally followed the Popular Front strategy that had had such disastrous consequences for the Spanish Revolution in the 1930s. Moreover, the CDC stayed 'stuck in North Wales'—as Des Warren put it—and remained tightly controlled and inward looking, mainly because the CP had a rival on the left.

The Trotskyist International Socialists had a very useful political analysis, a successful weekly *Socialist Worker* and a growing network of working class activists, but IS had insufficient comrades on enough sites to challenge the CP. In addition, from June 1973 IS members were engaged in a nasty factional struggle that was, at best, premature and was allowed to continue for eighteen months. (A history of IS's development into the SWP is long overdue and hopefully will form the core of Ian Birchall's biography of Tony Cliff. A Truth and Reconciliation Commission might also help.) The faction fight consumed valuable energy and resources at a point when IS was already overstretched by trying to fill the growing political gap that the CP was vacating on the left. IS leaders organised too late around the Shrewsbury issue and badly underestimated the CP's determination to marginalise them. IS leaders on Merseyside were completely ineffective and other north west leaders were scarcely any better, though individual members did what they could. In September 1973 SW journalist Laurie Flynn's *Pickets on Trial* made an important contribution, because it provided a clear political analysis and suggested a plan of action, yet it wasn't given operational priority until after the first three pickets were in jail.

Early in 1974 the three pickets not jailed at the first Shrewsbury trial supported IS's efforts, not those of the CDC, so the CP used underhand methods to 'rein them in' or 'outlaw' them in order to marginalise IS. In February three more pickets were jailed at the second Shrewsbury trial. By then the *Morning Star* journalist, Jim Arnison, had completed *The Shrewsbury Three*, but it focused on only two of the first three jailed pickets, so the CDC asked him to write about the other members of the 'Shrewsbury 6'. From then on—if not before—the CP tried to shift all the political responsibility for the Shrewsbury defeat onto the UCATT and TGWU leaders, the TUC General Council and the Labour Party. Given how cowardly and useless these organisations had been, and the disgusting methods used by their mainly right wing leaders, this wasn't very hard to do. Yet many socialists and trade unionists had serious illusions about the 1945-1951 Labour governments. They had forgotten that Britain had been bankrupted by the war, that the Cabinet accepted the economic and political conditions for receiving Marshall Aid from the USA and so broke strikes with troops, failed to socialise the 'nationalised' industries, committed Britain to NATO and spent obscene amounts of money on US nuclear weapons.

In spring 1974 Labour came into office as a minority government on the back of the largest wave of industrial militancy since 1926, but at the end of the longest boom in capitalism's history and the beginning of what turned out to be the first global recession since the war. Many Labour voters believed that the right wing dominated Cabinet really would make the rich's 'pips squeak' and they also had huge illusions about the likelihood of real reforms in favour of working people, including freeing the jailed pickets. The UCATT and TGWU leaders and the TUC General Council hoped that the Labour Cabinet would get them off the hook, yet most ministers, MPs and union officials had long accepted the 'impossibility' of socialism and the 'inevitability' of capitalism. In reality, a handful of left wing MPs saw their role as promoting laws that marginally improved the lot of

The Flying Pickets

workers under capitalism, while left wing union officials policed the rank and file so as to carry out orderly collective bargaining and get a few crumbs from the employers' tables. Consequently, the right wing Home Secretary, Roy Jenkins, easily resisted the CP-led lobbying campaign and 'never had any trouble' from the Cabinet that included 'leftwingers' like Michael Foot and Tony Benn

The 1974-1979 Labour government effectively generalised the Tories' criminalising of effective mass picketing and legitimised individualist 'monetarist' economics among many right wing Labour voters. This rightward shift helped to demoralise left wing voters and paved the way for Labour's defeat and the Tories' victory in 1979. The same pro-capitalist ideas proved vital in the Tories' assault on the miners in 1984-1985 and remain powerful today, when almost all MPs and union leaders are unblushingly wedded to capitalism.

As Thatcher, Blair and Brown have taught us, political reforms can be taken away, so those of us who seriously want to build a fairer world need to join trade unions, become active, read the unofficial labour movement and socialist press, listen to a wide range of views in branches and at conferences, be in awe of nobody and test all potentially useful ideas in practice. However, we also need to be clear that trade union activity alone was not, is not and will not be an adequate response to political attacks by Conservatives, Liberal Democrats or New Labour. In order to begin to make irreversible social changes in the interests of working people we need to understand the connections between economics and politics and link rank and file union activity to the building of a fully democratic socialist party with an internationalist perspective that includes as many serious reformists and revolutionaries as possible.

Getting justice for the North Wales 32 and seeing off all the anti-union laws are acid tests for today's labour movement. Our view is clear. *No justice, no peace.*

Bibliography

Archives

Birmingham City Archives. The Paul Mackney Papers, MS 1591 (IS papers).

Denbighshire Record Office, Ruthin. DRO DD/DM/1281/30-32, *Chester Chronicle*.

Durham County Record Office, Durham. D/X 1075/12 (Crook AUBTW/UCATT branch and UCATT Northern Regional Committee and Council minutes. Crook Trades Council minutes and related documents).

Greater Manchester Record Office, Manchester. G/COM (Communist Party papers).

Liverpool Record Office. M/329/COM (CP papers), *Liverpool Daily Post* (North Wales edition).

Modern Records Centre, University of Warwick. The Frida Knight Papers, MSS 430. Correspondence, documents and cuttings (with Dave Harker's *A Draft List of Part of the Frida Knight Papers*).

National Museum of Labour History, Manchester. CP/CENT/PERS, CP/CENT/ORG (CP papers).

The Robert Tressell Family Papers. See Dave Harker and Reg Johnson, *A Working Bibliography*, www.unionhistory.info

Working Class Movement Library, Salford. North Wales 32 Collection (with Dave Harker's Catalogue), *Building Workers' Charter*; *International Socialism*, *Morning Star*, *Socialist Worker*, *Weekly Notes*.

Publications
(London, unless otherwise indicated)

Anon, 'Shrewsbury', *International Socialism* (IS) 62 (September 1973), p8.

Arnison, Jim, *The Shrewsbury Three* (Lawrence & Wishart, 1974; reprinted Liverpool: Jim Arnison, 1988).

Arnison, Jim, *Decades* (Salford: Jim Arnison, 1991).

Arnison, Jim, and Edmund and Ruth Frow, *The New Paths Are Begun* (Manchester: Manchester Trades Council, 1993).

Austrin, Terry, 'The "Lump" in the UK Construction Industry', in Theo Nichols, ed, *Capital and Labour* (Fontana, 1980), pp302-315.

Beckett, Francis, *The Enemy Within* (John Murray, 1995).

Benn, Tony, *Office Without Power* (Arrow, 1990).

Benn, Tony, *Against the Tide* (Hutchinson, 1990).

Birchall, Ian, 'The British Communist Party 1945-64', *IS* 50, January-February 1972, pp24-34.

Birchall, Ian, 'History of the International Socialists, *IS* 76, March 1975, pp16-24, and IS 77, April 1975, pp22-28.

Birchall, Ian, 'The Premature Burial', *Socialist Register* 1979, pp26-50.

Birchall, Ian, *The Smallest Mass Party in the World* (SWP, 1981).

Birchall, Ian, review of Jim Higgins' *More Years for the Locust*, *Revolutionary History*, Volume 7, Number 1 (1998), pp200-203.

Bloxam, John, 'Cynthia Baldry, 1949-1975', www.workersliberty.org

Callaghan, John, *Cold War, Crisis and Conflict* (Lawrence & Wishart, 2003).

Callinicos, Alex, and Mike Simons (1985), *The Great Strike* (Socialist Worker).

Carter, Pete, 'The Building Industry Experience', in Eric Hobsbawm, ed, *The Forward March of Labour Halted?* (New Left Books, 1981), pp27-32.

Carter, Pete, 'Striking the Right Note', *Marxism Today*, March 1985, pp28-31.

Carter, Pete, *Trade Unions: The New Reality* (CPGB, 1986).

Cliff, Tony, *The Crisis: Social Contract or Socialism* (Pluto, 1975).

Cliff, Tony, *A World to Win* (Bookmarks, 2000).

Cliff, Tony, and Donny Gluckstein, *The Labour Party* (Bookmarks, 1996).

Communist Party, *Trotskyist Organisations in Britain* (CPGB, ND [1977]).

Corrigan, Chris, 'Des Warren', *The Independent*, 28 April 2004.

Darlington, Ralph, and Dave Lyddon, *Glorious Summer* (Bookmarks, 2001).

Durham Strong Words Collective, *But the World Goes on the Same* (Whitley Bay: Strong Words, 1979).

Eaden, James, and David Renton, *The Communist Party of Britain since 1920* (Basingstoke: Palgrave, 2002).

[Flynn, Laurie], *Pickets on Trial* (IS, ND [1973]).

Flynn, Laurie, *Workers Against the Law* (Socialist Worker, ND [1975]).

Foot, Paul, 'The Seamen's Struggle', in Robin Blackburn and Alexander Coburn, eds, *The Incompatibles* (Harmondsworth: Penguin, 1967), pp169-210.

Foot, Paul, *The Anti Cameron Report* (Langley: Rank and File, 1967).

Goodman, David, 'The Reform of Trade Union Law' (Workers' Educational Association, October 1974).

Goulding, Alistair, 'The Building Industry. Background to a Rank and File Movement', *IS* 75, February 1975, pp22-28, and 'The Building Industry in 1975', IS 77, April 1975, pp29-30.

Hain, Peter, *Political Trials in Britain* (Allen Lane, 1984).

Harman, Chris, 'Communist Party in Decline', *IS* 63, October 1973, pp19-28.

Heffer, Eric, *The Class Struggle in Parliament* (Gollancz, 1973).

Heffer, Eric, *Never a Yes Man* (Verso, 1991).

Higgins, Jim, *More Years for the Locust* (International Socialist Group, 1997).

Higgins, Jim, *Speak One More Time* (Socialist Platform, 2004).

Hilton, William, *Foes to Tyranny* (AUBTW, 1963).

Industrial Research & Information Services, *The International Socialists* (IRIS, 1974).

Jefferys, Steve, 'The Challenge of the Rank and File', *IS* 76, March 1975, pp7-15.

Jenkins, Roy, *A Life at the Centre* (Pan, 1992).

Keep, John, *Trade Unions and Socialist Politics* (Verso, 1988).

McGuffin, John (1974), *The Guineapigs* (Harmondsworth: Penguin).

McIlroy, John, and Campbell, Alan, 'Organising the Militants: the Liaison Committee for the Defence of Trade Unions, 1966-1979', *British Journal of Industrial Relations* Vol 37, No 1, March 1999, pp1-31.

Maguire, Kevin, 'Des Warren', *Guardian*, 1 May 2004.

Marxists Internet Archive, www.marxists.org

Milton, Nan, *John Maclean* (Pluto, 1973).

National Federation of Building Trade Employers, *Violence & Intimidation* (NFBTE, 1973).

Platts-Mills, John, *Muck, Silk and Socialism* (Paper Publishing, 2002).

Reid, Betty, 'Trotskyism in Britain Today', *Marxism Today*, September 1964, pp274-283.

Reid, Betty, *Ultra Leftism in Britain* (Communist Party, 1969).

Shaw, Martin, 'The Making of a Party? The International Socialists 1965-1976', *Socialist Register* 1978, pp100-145.

Smith, George, *UCATT and the Shrewsbury Trials* (UCATT, ND [1974]).

Stevenson, Graham, www.graham. thewebtailor.co.uk/archives

Thompson, Willie, *The Good Old Cause* (Pluto, 1992).

Tomlinson, Ricky, *Ricky* (Time Warner, 2003).

Townshend, Jules, 'The LCDTU', *IS* 56, March 1973, pp7-8.

Townshend, Jules, 'Communist Party in Decline: 1964 to 1970', *IS* 62, Mid-September 1973, pp18-27.

Warren, Des, *Shrewsbury: Whose Conspiracy?* (Glasgow: Des Warren, 1977).

Warren, Des, *Shrewsbury: Whose conspiracy?* (New Park, 1980; reprinted Liverpool: Justice for Pickets Campaign, 2007.)

Warren, Des, *The Key To My Cell* (New Park, 1982; reprinted Liverpool: Living History Library, ND [2007]).

Warren, Des, 'They've Been Coming For Us Ever Since!', *Workers' Press*, August 1986, p3.

Warren, Nick, *Thirty Years in a Turtleneck Sweater* (Ebury, 2005).

Widgery, Dave, *The Left in Britain* (Harmondsworth: Penguin, 1976).

Wood, Leslie, *A Union To Build* (Lawrence & Wishart, 1979).

Index

The Flying Pickets

Index

971 531 276

Oliva - Avenida Pollença.
la fonda.
la font del Gall